TAKEN INTO
CUSTODY

TAKEN INTO
CUSTODY
The War Against Fathers, Marriage, and the Family

Stephen Baskerville

CUMBERLAND HOUSE
NASHVILLE, TENNESSEE

Taken Into Custody
Published by Cumberland House Publishing, Inc.
431 Harding Industrial Drive
Nashville, TN 37211-3160

Cover design: James Duncan Creative
Text design: John Mitchell

Library of Congress Cataloging-in-Publication Data

Baskerville, Stephen, 1957-
Taken into custody : the war against fathers, marriage, and the family / Stephen Baskerville.
p. cm.
ISBN-13: 978-1-58182-594-7 (hardcover : alk. paper)
ISBN-10: 1-58182-594-3 (hardcover : alk. paper)
1. Divorced fathers. 2. Fathers. 3. Domestic relations courts. I. Title.

HQ756.B385 2007
306.89'2—dc22

2007013973

Printed in the United States of America

2 3 4 5 6 7 8—13 12 11 10 09 08 07

For
Olivia and Charlotte

CONTENTS

ACKNOWLEDGMENTS

Scholars often develop the illusion that we labor in isolation. Long hours in dusty archives and disagreements with colleagues tend to reinforce this illusion. In this instance, I have never been more conscious that what I have produced is largely a community effort. Without the information—letters, stories, documents, clippings, studies, books, e-mail messages, and telephone calls—collected and sent to me by hundreds, perhaps thousands of people, this book would not exist. It is not possible to name all these people, and many would prefer I not do so. Many existed in the most anguished circumstances at the time they communicated, having lost children or relatives, and some were hours or minutes away from arrest. It is enough to state here that these men and women are heroes and victims of what will someday be revealed as the most repressive governmental regime ever erected within the United States.

Those I have called upon repeatedly for information, expertise, assistance, support, and more include (but are not limited to) Jed Abraham, Ed Bartlett, Don Bieniewicz, Paul Brundage, Paul Clements, Charles Corry, Richard Doyle, Bruce Eden, Richard Farr, Warren Farrell, Roger Gay, Tom Golden, Stanley Green, Ron Grignol, Don Hubin, Lindsay Jackel, Ron Jagannathan, Barry Koplen, Ed Kruk, Mike LaSalle, Jeffery Leving, David Levy, Melanie Michael, Stuart Miller, Paul Mozen, Molly Olson, Judy Parejko, Paul Robinson, Mark Rogers, Glenn Sacks, Jim Semerad, Walter Schneider, Al Sinsheimer, Jane Spies, Murray Steinberg, Dean Tong, Ed Truncellito, Jim Untershine, David Usher, Richard Weiss, Bill Wood, Cathy Young, and the staff of the Men's Health Network. Special honor is also due to some heroic individuals whose short lives were almost certainly made shorter by their years of resistance to the divorce regime: Michael Ellis, Louise Malenfant, Robert Seidenberg, Wilbur Streett, and doubtless many others. I would like to give special thanks to David and Ileana Roberts and my colleagues at the American Coalition for Fathers and Children: Michael McCormick, John Maguire, and Stephen Walker.

Research for this book was assisted by a Charlotte and Walter Kohler Fellowship at the Howard Center for Family, Religion, and Society in the summer of 2004 and by a fellowship funded by the Earhart Foundation, also at the Howard Center, during the academic year 2005-06. A grant from the Achelis and Bodman Foundations at the Howard Center in 2007 assisted in the preparation of the final manuscript. I am grateful for the assistance and encouragement of Allan Carlson, Bryce Christensen, Joseph Dolan, and Larry Jacobs. I am also grateful to those who have provided opportunities to speak about these issues to various organizations and gatherings, published my work, given me feedback, and otherwise provided support: Ted Baehr, Joseph D'Agostino, Patrick Fagan, Richard Falknor, Joseph Farah, Peter Ferrara, Deal Hudson, David Kupelian, Wendy McElroy, Michael McManus, William J. Murray, Grover Norquist, Michael Peroutka, Paul Craig Roberts, Phyllis Schlafly, Michael Schwartz, Jon Utley, Paul Weyrich, and Don Wildmon. What I did with this mountain of help is of course my responsibility alone.

Last but far from least is my gratitude to my daughters Charlotte and Olivia, who provided the inspiration, patience, and love without which this book never would have been started, let alone finished.

INTRODUCTION
The Crisis of Fatherhood and Marriage

There's no way to rule innocent men. The only power any government has is the power to crack down on criminals. Well, when there aren't enough criminals, one makes them. One declares so many things to be a crime that it becomes impossible for men to live without breaking laws.

— Ayn Rand, *Atlas Shrugged*

The decline of the American family has reached critical and truly dangerous proportions. A few years ago, advocates of "family values" could be dismissed as puritanical Cassandras, agitated about pornography, popular culture, secularization, abortion, and homosexuality. No longer. The breakdown of the family now touches virtually every American. It is not only the major source of social instability in the Western world but seriously threatens civic freedom and constitutional government.

Since the 1960s, we have been warned about a growing crisis of single-parent homes and fatherless children.[1] Initially, this concerned mostly low-income communities in the inner cities. Four decades later, it has expanded to the affluent. The erosion of marriage, out-of-wedlock births, divorce, and fatherless children are now mainstream problems that threaten the general society. Some 24 million American children or about 34 percent live in households without their fathers. For African-American children the figure is 66 percent. Nearly 2.5 million children join the ranks of the fatherless each year.[2]

No successful human society has ever been based on the mother-child dyad or on any other structure than the married, two-parent family.[3] So much has been written in recent years about the destructive effects on both children and society of fatherlessness that it hardly needs to be labored. Virtually every major social pathology of our time: violent crime, drug and alcohol abuse, truancy and scholastic failure, unwed pregnancy, suicide, and other psychological disorders—all these correlate more strongly to fatherlessness than to any other single factor.[4] According to the National Fatherhood Initiative, "Children who live absent their biological fathers are, on average, at least two to three times more likely to be poor, to use drugs, to experience educational, health, emotional, and behavioral problems, to be victims of child abuse, and to engage in criminal behavior than those who live with their married, biological (or adoptive) parents."[5]

The overwhelming majority of prisoners, juvenile detention inmates, high school dropouts, pregnant teenagers, adolescent murderers, and rapists all come from fatherless homes. Children from affluent but separated families are much more likely to get into trouble than children from poor but intact ones, and white children from separated families are at higher risk than black children in intact families. The connection between single parent households and crime erases the relationship between race and crime and between low income and crime.[6] It is hardly an exaggeration to say that fatherless children are tearing down our civilization.

Predictably, politicians have responded by devising new social programs, beginning in the 1990s. Declaring that "the single biggest social problem in our society may be the growing absence of fathers from their children's homes, because it contributes to so many other social problems," President Bill Clinton ordered a Presidential Fatherhood Initiative called "Strengthening the Role of Fathers in Families." Vice President Al Gore declared more accusatorily that "absent fathers are behind most social woes" and chaired a Federal Staff Conference on Fatherhood, which issued a report called "Nurturing Fatherhood." Congress established bipartisan Task Forces on Fatherhood Promotion, issued resolutions on fatherhood, and debated bills like "Fathers Count," which committed millions of dollars "to reconnect fathers to their families." Both the governors' and mayors' conferences have also created fatherhood task forces. "Over the past four decades," President George W. Bush has stated, "fatherlessness has emerged as one of our greatest social problems."[7] At his request, Congress recently committed $100 million annually to promote "healthy marriage" and "responsible fatherhood."

Policymakers have been encouraged by scholars and professional advocates for fatherhood and marriage. David Blankenhorn, the influential author of *Fatherless America*, calls the crisis of fatherless children "the most harmful demographic trend of this generation." David Popenoe, in *Life Without Father*, issues a similar wake-up call. Nonprofit organizations, like the National Fatherhood Initiative, National Center for Fathering, and numerous local groups founded during the 1990s, many with federal money, aim to "restore" and "promote" fatherhood and "good fathering." The exceptions prove the rule. When a journal of the American Psychological Association published a cover story belittling the importance of fathers, it was barraged with criticism.[8]

During the present decade, the political emphasis has shifted to marriage, but the basic issue remains the same. The principal social function of marriage has always been to establish paternity and create fatherhood.[9] Groups like the Alliance for Marriage and the Institute for Marriage and Public Policy proclaim that marriage is no longer a purely private matter but a valid and urgent topic for public debate. "Marriage is more than a private emotional relationship," declares one team of scholars and advocates. "It is also a social good."[10]

FATHERS ABANDONING CHILDREN?

Yet amid the enthusiasm for wedding bells and for "Dad, God, and apple pie," some fundamental questions are not being asked. These concern not only social forces and cultural changes that have been eroding family integrity and parental authority for decades, but more immediately the growing intervention of government into private life. Ignoring these questions can render the most well-intentioned measures ineffective and even counterproductive. How precisely the government can "promote" marriage or something as personal as a parent's relationship with his own children is a problem few are stopping to explain. What precisely does a government agency do when it attempts to "promote" and "encourage" marriage and "good fathering" and "responsible fatherhood"?

Connected to this question is an even more basic one: Why has this problem arisen in the first place? We hear about the erosion of marriage and millions of children growing up without fathers, but we are not told why. It is said that fathers are "disappearing from the lives of children,"[11] but people do not simply "disappear." It is difficult to see how we can mobilize to address a problem when we do not understand why it exists. There seem to be some things the marriage and fatherhood promoters are not telling us.

The conventional wisdom, put forth by politicians, civil servants, journalists, and scholars, is simple: Fathers are abandoning their children. Clinton claimed the fathers pursued by his administration "have chosen to abandon their children."[12] "Some fathers are forced away by circumstances beyond their control," President Bush acknowledges. "But many times when a couple with children splits up, the father moves away or simply drifts away." Blankenhorn is more categorical: "Never before in this country have so many children been voluntarily abandoned by their fathers," he declares. "Today, the principal cause of fatherlessness is paternal choice . . . the rising rate of paternal abandonment."[13] Popenoe writes that fathers "choose to relinquish" the responsibilities of fatherhood: "Left culturally unregulated, men's sexual behavior can be promiscuous, their paternity casual, their commitment to families weak."[14] Perhaps, but no evidence is presented for any of these statements.

The claim is echoed by commentators on both the left and right. "Conservative preachers and liberal feminists are united in their disdain for philandering men who abandon their children," notes journalist John Tierney.[15] The news media and scholars from across the spectrum faithfully parrot the government line that family breakdown can be laid at the door of fathers. "Marital unions dissolve under emotional or financial strain," writes one liberal scholar. "Husbands abandon wives and children with no looking back." "Millions of men walk out on their children," says another leftist researcher, ". . . or, for whatever reason, lack contact with their children."[16]

Conservatives likewise believe that "growing numbers of older men are leaving their wives and children to marry young women."[17] The assertion is held to be so self-evident that no proof is required (though neither is any voice permitted to contradict it). In his eloquent work on "the end of courtship," Leon Kass ironically blames feminism for "male liberation—from domestication, from civility, from responsible self-command" plus "an excuse for shirking the duties of fatherhood."[18] Kass notes that the vilification of fathers is bipartisan: "Contemporary liberals and conservatives alike are trying to figure out how to get men 'to commit' to marriage, or to keep their marital vows, or to stay home with the children, but their own androgynous view of humankind prevents them from seeing how hard it has always been to make a monogamous husband and devoted father out of the human male." Kass stereotypes this nameless male with every cliché in the book:

> To make naturally polygamous men accept the conventional institution of monogamous marriage has been the work of centuries of Western civilization, with social sanctions, backed by religious teachings and authority. . . .

As these mores and sanctions disappear, courtship gives way to seduction and possession, and men become again the sexually, familially, and civically [sic] irresponsible creatures they are naturally always in danger of being. . . . Executives walk out on their families and take up with trophy wives. . . . Low-status males, utterly uncivilized by marriage, return to the fighting gangs, taking young women as prizes for their prowess. Rebarbarization is just around the corner.[19]

It may be indeed, but some basic facts are being ignored here. And commentators like Kass seem unaware that words like his are used in courtrooms throughout America—also without presenting any evidence—to incarcerate citizens without trial.

Given the ubiquity of this assumption, it is not surprising that a more disturbing side to the nation's discovery of fatherhood also enjoys bipartisan support. "On the left and on the right, the new phrase to conjure with is 'child support,' observes Bryce Christensen. "The deadbeat dad now holds a place of singular dishonor as a selfish fugitive condemned by liberals and conservatives alike."[20] While Ronald Reagan seems to have coined the term, it was Bill Clinton who took the issue on the campaign trail in 1992. "We will find you!" he intoned. "We will make you pay!"[21] In the 2000 election, Al Gore called for incarcerating more fathers, and his rival in the primaries, Bill Bradley, conveyed a similar message. "Politicians seeking election or re-election routinely support child-support enforcement, and there is little public debate about the issue," notes another scholar. "It is a widely accepted, popular issue among Republican and Democratic voters and politicians, and . . . child-support enforcement legislation is easily proposed and passed in Congress."[22]

As if to illustrate the point, Barack Obama took up the theme campaigning in 2007, as did British Conservative Party Leader David Cameron. "We have too many children in poverty in this country," Obama told a civil rights gathering. "And don't tell me it doesn't have a little to do with the fact that we got too many daddies not acting like daddies." A federal judge opines that fathers deserve "a kick in the pants."[23] A state government announces measures to hunt them down like "dogs."[24]

An unchallenged monopoly of opinion is always unhealthy, especially when it is used to rationalize expanding government power and summary punishments. Unanimity silences dissent, and when both ends of the spectrum or both major parties agree, no opposition remains to check the abuse of power. Columnist Charles Krauthammer could have had fatherhood policy in mind when he observed, "It is an iron law of Washington that when everybody agrees on something, it must necessarily be wrong."[25]

In fact, no evidence is presented for any of these sweeping statements on paternal abandonment. No government or academic study has ever demonstrated, in fact no scientific evidence has ever been adduced to show that large numbers of fathers are voluntarily abandoning their children. While individual examples can always be found of any reprehensible behavior, there is simply nothing to indicate that the epidemic of fatherless children is caused primarily by fathers deserting their families. In fact, when pressed, no reputable scholar seriously argues that it is the cause. And as we shall see, clear and overwhelming evidence exists that it is not.[26]

All these policymakers and commentators are either failing or refusing to recognize some basic facts about who is walking away from whom and the role of the state in allowing, encouraging, and even forcing them to do so. The assumption that government has a legitimate role in ameliorating the family crisis glides much too quickly over the more fundamental question of whether government has had a role in creating it. For what we are seeing here is almost certainly an optical illusion. What we are led to believe is an epidemic of irresponsible fathers is more likely a massive abuse of government power.

RUPTURING FAMILY BONDS

Contrary to assumptions of well-meaning people, the forces destroying the family today are not limited to culture and values and personal irresponsibility, and they are not being effectively addressed by preaching at people to be better spouses, parents, sons, and daughters. Certainly these factors play a part, but limiting our focus to personal imperfections has left us dangerously vulnerable to misinformation, inaction, and despair. When the eminent political scientist James Q. Wilson weighed in recently on family dissolution, it was only to throw up his hands: "If you believe, as I do, in the power of culture, you will realize that there is very little one can do."[27] Like many, Wilson is reduced to advocating counseling and "education."

In reality, the principal assault on the family today comes directly from government. This threat began with the vast machinery that has grown up around the welfare "state," but it has moved far beyond that. How welfare has discouraged family formation among the poor, driven fathers from homes, and subsidized single motherhood is now widely known. The expansion of these problems to the middle class, mostly through divorce, is also reaching general awareness. But a more startling and insidious development has been almost completely ignored, even by critics of welfare.

What began as a seemingly benign system of public assistance has, in the ensuing decades, not only expanded but quietly metamorphosed into nothing less than a miniature penal apparatus, replete with its own tribunals, prosecutors, police, and jails: juvenile and "family" courts, "matrimonial" lawyers, child-support enforcement agents, child protective services, domestic violence machinery, and more. The objects of this peculiar governmental underworld are not criminals but ordinary parents and children—law-abiding citizens who find themselves forced into quasi-criminal and even criminal proceedings, often through literally "no fault" of their own, by a Kafkaesque system of mock justice that operates by its own rules, separate from the constitutional order, largely in secret, and with almost no oversight or accountability. While parents generally and children are ensnared in this apparatus, its first targets are fathers.

The growth of this machinery has been accompanied by a huge propaganda campaign that has served to justify punitive measures against citizens who are not convicted of any crime. "Is there a species on the planet more unjustly maligned than fathers?" writes columnist Naomi Lakritz. "Fathers are abusers, bullies, deadbeats, child molesters, and all-around sexist clods who have a lot of gall wanting a relationship with their children once the initial moment of conception is over."[28]

The campaign against fathers by government, the media, and feminists has been so overwhelming—including what television journalist Bernard Goldberg describes as "a million stories at the networks on deadbeat dads"[29]—that only recently have a few individuals dared to question the conventional wisdom. "In recent years, fathers have been the subject of a tidal wave of critical thinking and punitive action," observe authors Sylvia Ann Hewlett and Cornel West. "If the past few decades have seen a systematic war against parents, the battles waged against fathers have been particularly ugly and fierce."[30]

It is not my purpose here to debunk negative stereotypes of fathers.[31] That task has already been accomplished in a number of important works, both scientific and cultural. "Virtually every aspect of what I call the 'bad divorced dad' image has turned out to be a *myth*, an inaccurate and damaging stereotype," writes social scientist Sanford Braver. "Not only is this myth seriously inaccurate, it has led to harmful and dangerous social policies."[32]

What Braver diplomatically terms a "myth" may be more of a hoax—an intentional falsehood perpetrated by interested parties with a tangible stake in weakening fatherhood and assuming its functions. For the recent attention to fatherhood by government and the media has not emerged in isolation. It has accompanied concrete policies that, in diametric contrast to the rhetoric of the politicians, have the effect and possibly the purpose of rupturing the bond connecting fathers with their children and replacing it with the power of the state.

The argument of this book is that governments throughout the United States and other democracies are engaged, by accident or design, in a massive campaign against fathers and fatherhood, and that this campaign lies at the root of the larger crisis that is undermining parents generally, threatening the institution of marriage, destroying the family, and ruining the lives of children. It will suggest that even well-intentioned fatherhood and marriage campaigns could exacerbate the problem by further infusing the power of the state machinery into private family life. Weakening fatherhood and parenthood creates a vacuum of power which the state can fill.

In addressing the consequences of public policy, what may be more important than refuting cultural stereotypes is simply to confront the central truth about the cause of fatherless children. "Women are lone parents in 84 percent of cases not because men abandon their children," writes columnist John Waters, "but because . . . the fathers have been constructively banished, with the collusion of the state, which encourages women to abuse the grotesque power we have conferred on them."[33] This is what Braver calls the "dirty secret" of modern family policy. It is the seminal falsehood from which a brood of misbegotten government policies has been hatched. The British government "treats all absent fathers as feckless, even though some may be the blameless victims of destructive behavior by women," observes Melanie Phillips, one of the few journalists to face this truth squarely:

> Most divorces . . . are initiated by women. Many divorced fathers have their homes and children taken away from them and are all but destroyed. They are then clobbered by the Child Support Agency, which treats them as if they are the guilty party. . . . Even if a father shares childcare equally with his ex-wife, he will have to pay the mother for the child's upkeep. . . . Even if she's gone off with a man earning £100,000 a year, scooping up the family home and the children en route, her ex-husband will have to pay her—thus supporting behavior he may even believe is damaging his children. . . . He may be deprived of all contact with his children by courts which stack the cards against him. . . . It is not uncommon . . . for women to make entirely spurious charges of violence against their ex-husbands just to prevent them from

having access to their children. . . . Courts are overwhelmingly disposed to believe them, even when there isn't a shred of evidence. . . . Most physical abuse of children is perpetrated by women.[34]

All this is usually dismissed, when it is recognized at all, as the product of "prejudice" or "gender bias." Such jargon does not begin to explain what is taking place. What we confront here is a bureaucratic machine of a kind that has never before been seen in the United States or the other English-speaking democracies.

The implications reach far beyond fathers and even beyond the family itself, for forcibly severing the intimate bond between parents and their children threatens the liberties of all of us. "The right to one's own children . . . is perhaps the most basic individual right," writes Susan Shell, "so basic we hardly think of it." By establishing a private sphere of life from which the state is excluded, family bonds also serve as the foundation of a free society. "No known society treats the question of who may properly call a child his or her own as simply . . . a matter to be decided entirely politically as one might distribute land or wealth," Shell continues.

"No known government, however brutal or tyrannical, has ever denied, in fact or principle, the fundamental claim of parents to their children. . . . A government that distributed children randomly . . . could not be other than tyrannical. . . . A government that paid no regard to the claims of biological parenthood would be unacceptable to all but the most fanatical of egalitarian or communitarian zealots."[35]

As a statement of society's moral consensus, Shell's points are unexceptionable. Yet they also provide an unintended commentary on the ignorance that pervades today's debates over marriage, children, and the family. For current law and practice have rendered Shell's words both prescient as principles and factually false. What she says "no known government" has ever done is precisely what most of the Western democracies have been doing for almost four decades. It is creating precisely the tyranny she predicts.

This book is about our unwillingness to confront the most destructive and dangerous injustice in our society today: the systematic seizure of children by government officials and the criminalization of their parents. A parent today who has committed no legal infraction can have his (or sometimes her) parenthood and relationship with his children criminalized entirely through the actions of others in ways that are completely beyond his control. It focuses largely on fathers and on divorce, because these are the ones most commonly involved. But because the father is, as Margaret Mead once pointed out, the weakest link in the family chain, the threat to fathers is the first step in a larger assault on parents generally and the family as an institution.[36] The state-sponsored destruction of fathers and fatherhood is connected to a larger trend of government agencies assuming control over children from parents of either or both genders in what has been characterized as "the assault on parenthood" or "the war against parents."[37]

Few people to whom it has not happened realize how easily and how frequently children are taken from their parents with no grounds or allegations of wrongdoing. "People who have not personally gone through divorce and custody 'wars' may believe that it would never happen to them or their children," writes Anna Keller. "They believe that their own relationships with their children are inviolable; that their importance to their children or their value as loving parents could never be publicly or legally challenged; they believe that they would never be refused information about their children by their children's school or doctors, or drive by their children's house and be forbidden to see them or find that they don't know where and with whom their children are."[38]

Fewer still realize how easily and swiftly the parents are then turned into criminals. The separation of children from their parents for reasons that have nothing to do with the children's wishes, safety, health, or welfare is now routine. Though the number of mechanisms by which this can happen is growing, the most common is involuntary divorce. As family law now operates in America and elsewhere, one parent can have the other summoned to court and, without presenting any evidence of legal wrongdoing, request that he be stripped of all rights over his children and effectively ejected from the family, and in almost every case the judge will oblige without asking any questions.[39] Government officials acting on their own can do much the same to both parents.

"In our time, political speech and writing are largely the defense of the indefensible," wrote George Orwell. "Thus political language has to consist largely of euphemism." Nowhere is Orwell's observation more valid today than in the politics of the family. The very words *divorce* and *separation*, now so common, carry connotations that are very different from the present reality, and the vast literature on divorce that continues to pour forth from the presses, both popular and scholarly, is full of highly misleading information. Modern divorce involves government officials evicting people from their homes, seizing their property, and taking away their children. Divorce today means the invasion and destruction of private life by the state.

Introduction

To understand what is at work here, it is necessary to examine and discard some legal jargon that serves more to obfuscate than to illuminate. Foremost is the term "custody," which I have adopted in my title. Common sense notions of young children needing their mother—along with the mistaken belief that fathers are behind the dissolution of most marriages—lead many people to accept the overwhelming bias toward mothers in custody decisions. But it is important to understand that "custody" is not the right to parent one's children; it is the power to prevent someone else from parenting his children and to marshal the penal apparatus—courts, police, and jails—to ensure he stays away from them.

Custody is only partly about children, in other words; custody also confers power on grownups. The double entendre in my title points to the fact that custody now includes the power to bring the penal system into the home to punish family members—not for legally recognized offenses but for ordinary family differences. Throughout this country and abroad, large numbers of fathers and some mothers are being criminalized and incarcerated for what begins as nothing more than a spouse's hurt feelings or a private grievance. What we call winning "custody" means the power to turn family members into outlaws.

For centuries our social order has been based on the principle that authority over children resides with their parents, unless the parents have done something to forfeit it. Yet that power has now been transferred to state officials such as family court judges and their clients in the bar associations, psychotherapy professions, and social work bureaucracies. "Our society has chosen to leave all such family-role decisions to the free choice of the people until one of the parties decides to end the marital relationship and files that request with the government," writes Wayne Anderson. "At that moment the government assumes control of family decisions and ends the free choice of the divorcing parents."[40] This government takeover of the family was traditionally justified when both parents agreed to divorce or when one violated the terms of the marriage contract and incurred the legal consequences for doing so. What is new is that the government now assumes this control over the family and an innocent parent not by the mutual agreement of both parents but at the mere request of one.

Euphemisms have rendered it difficult for even well-informed people to grasp what is taking place. The commonplace of divorce has left us too ready to abdicate our most fundamental rights and responsibilities over our private lives without realizing the full implications. We are told a marriage has "broken

21

down" or the parents "can't agree." Therefore government officials "must" step in and assume control of the children.

But this begs critical questions. As we will see, the state and its agents are not neutral parties. They have a very tangible interest in declaring such an impasse. It creates a major extension of state power. Through divorce, the modern state achieves one of its most coveted and dangerous ambitions: to control the private lives of its citizens.

From the outside, it may not appear at first that the state has invaded and occupied the family. After all, it has been invited in by one party. But it is an invasion nonetheless. For through "no-fault" divorce, one parent can now declare unilaterally that the marriage has "broken down" and invite the state in to take control and remove the other parent without that parent having committed any legal transgression. What the government then offers to the parent who invites it in is the promise that her invitation will be rewarded; the state will establish her as a puppet government, a satrap of the state within the family. This requires that not the faithless but the faithful parent be punished.

Never before has it been considered the legitimate role of state officials to conduct inquisitions into private lives and issue opinions concerning the state of people's marriages. Until now, the role of the state and judicial system has been to determine if someone has violated the law or a legally binding contract and to apportion penalties accordingly. The issue for public inquiry and debate then is not the marital difficulties of individuals but under what circumstances the state should be permitted to insert the deadly force it commands into private households.

What we are describing here is the divorce industry, a massive and largely hidden governmental and quasi-governmental machine consisting of judges, lawyers, psychologists and psychiatrists, social workers, child protective services, child-support enforcement agents, mediators, counselors, and feminist groups, plus an extensive host of economic interests, such as divorce planners, forensic accountants, real estate appraisers, and many others. These officials and professionals invariably profess to be motivated by concern for the "best interest" of other people's children. Yet their services are activated only with the dissolution of families and the removal of parents. Whatever pieties they may proclaim therefore, the hard reality is that they have a concrete interest in encouraging family break-up, and virtually all their power and earnings derive from the harm that divorce inflicts on children. "Fights over control of the children," reports one former divorce insider, "are where most of the billable hours in family court are consumed."[41]

Harsh as it may sound, it cannot be denied that these officials are united by one overriding interest: having children separated from their parents. Without the power to remove children from their parents—and most often their fathers—this industry cannot thrive, and these officials will have no business. And so it must declare that the parents are criminals and that the fathers have "abandoned" their children, even when this is plainly not true. Put simply, the first principle of the divorce industry, the basic premise without which it has no reason to exist, is the removal of the father from the family. Once this is accomplished, the state is free to assume control over mothers and children as well.

The linchpin of the divorce machinery is the family court, a relatively new institution that has arisen over the past four decades. Most people expect courts to serve as a remedy for injustices against citizens and the exploitation of their children. More often they are accomplices in the act. Far from punishing child abduction, the courts reward it. In effect, they take part in it. This is how divorce attorneys and judges generate business. The rapacity of the legal industry is now the stuff of popular legend. Yet it is usually assumed that while divorce lawyers profit from family breakdown, they do not actually cause it. It is no longer tenable to accept this.

Family courts are the lowest in status in the judicial hierarchy and little more than branches of an extensive bureaucratic *apparat*. Yet they possess some of the most sweeping powers. Many operate behind closed doors and leave no record of their proceedings, virtually free of oversight or accountability. Supreme Court Justice Abe Fortas once described them as "kangaroo" courts, and many others have done the same since.[42] In the name of family law they can and do freely violate major articles of the Bill of Rights and other provisions of the Constitution and international human rights conventions. Their first function is to remove children from parents who have done nothing legally wrong.

Some see the abuses of family court as part of a larger destruction of the family, individual rights, and the entire sphere of private life by the modern state in general and the judiciary in particular. What is happening in family courts will be recognized by many as but one example of the larger violation of fundamental constitutional rights by the very tribunals that should be their foremost guardians. "The legal system . . . is increasingly run for the enrichment of lawyers and not for the public," writes columnist Robert Samuelson. "Lawyers have fostered a system that works ponderously, intensifies conflict, and creates uncertainty." Samuelson was writing with reference to civil law, and in no area of the law is his observation more valid—or more destructive—than in the law governing families and children, where the most effective method of creating business is to favor the litigious. "At all levels of American society . . . the idea that American courtrooms strive toward justice is no longer taken seriously," observes the *Wall Street Journal*. "The courts are greatly feared for their ability to ruin, but they aren't much respected anymore by the American people." Walter Olson, author of *The Litigation Explosion*, writes that "lawyers have more power to ruin your life in America than they do in any other advanced country. . . . Lawyers . . . are so widely disliked in this country because they are so very widely, and correctly, feared for the power without responsibility they wield."[43]

Yet none of these critics mentions that they can also take away your children, nor that those who do—the practitioners of family law—have the lowest reputation of all, even among other legal professionals. Courts that are supposed to provide citizens with justice now instill them with fear. "Most of the people I work with are afraid of the legal system," says one divorce lawyer.[44]

On the larger political stage, the judiciary has become the object of enormous criticism for its "activism" and usurpation of democratic decision-making involving a host of high-profile issues, including abortion, affirmative action, school prayer, and education generally, and more recently marriage and the family. Yet while these issues are unquestionably important, these same critics ignore a center of judicial activism that exerts a far more direct impact on the lives of tens of millions of Americans. It seems strange that, with so much attention focused on the abuses of judicial power, virtually no attention is given to what we will see is the most powerful and least accountable sector of the judiciary, the family courts.[45]

Family law today is the largest and fastest-growing sector of the civil judiciary, accounting for at least 35 percent of all civil litigation. It is estimated that, as a percentage of state cases filed between 1984 and 1995, family cases grew by 70 percent.[46] As we will see, much of this growth is self-generating.

Family law today represents the most massive civil rights abuses and the most intrusive perversion of government power in our time. Not since the internment of Japanese-Americans during World War II have we seen mass incarcerations without trial, without charge, and without counsel, and what is happening today is on a much larger scale. Not since segregation have we seen the highest levels of government complying with the violation of the civil rights of vast numbers of American citizens. Never before have the president and vice president of the United States, along with cabinet figures and members of

Congress from both parties, used their office as a platform to publicly demonize millions of private citizens who have no opportunity to reply in their own defense. And never before has the "health" secretary commanded a gendarmerie of almost 60,000 plainclothes agents, some of them armed, whose sole purpose is to oversee the family lives of citizens.

'CULTURE OF SECRECY'

Whenever possible I have relied on existing scholarly research. As will be seen however, family law lies shrouded in secrecy, largely impervious to the eyes of researchers. Rather than relying on personal "interviews," therefore, I have tended to supplement the scholarship with journalistic accounts, on the principle that they are at least more authoritative than the mere word of interested parties. There are naturally some problems with this. One is that journalists have no freer access to the workings of this legal underworld than scholars, and few try to gain it. Maureen Freely is more forthright than most reporters about the things she does not know and cannot seem to find out. Family courts "operate in secret," she notes:

> Alas, the culture of secrecy also protects the entire system from proper public scrutiny. . . . Even insiders are foggy about the details. . . . There are no case studies or data on outcomes. . . . We do not even know how often courts make decisions in favor of resident parents, how often they decide to make an order allowing for shared parenting, or how often they decide that non-resident parents should not be allowed to have any contact with their children whatsoever. What we do know is that there has in recent years been a proliferation of groups speaking for the thousands of non-resident parents who believe the courts have denied them the right to see their children without cause.[47]

Reporters purport to be objective, though all have their biases, and seldom are they biased in favor of those who have been designated as "batterers," "pedophiles," and "deadbeat dads." More serious though is that even when they attempt to be fair to fathers, as some are doing, they seldom probe deep enough to uncover what I will argue to be the decisive question in understanding the fatherhood crisis and the criminalization of parents: who legally ended the marriage.

Some will immediately object: Can this possibly be determined? In the age of no-fault divorce isn't it old-fashioned or overly judgmental to worry about who ends a marriage? No one is perfect, and there are two sides to every story. What business is it of ours or the government who did what? Does it matter if the father (or mother) has done something legally wrong? As one fathers' rights activist writes, "It's nobody's bloody business, particularly the government's, whose fault your divorce was!"[48]

Yes, it does matter. In a free society, public tribunals exist to dispense justice against violators of the law or legal agreements. When they stop dispensing justice they begin to dispense injustice; there is really no tenable middle ground. Courts are part of our government, supported with our taxes, and when they are called to intervene in the private lives of citizens to remove people from their homes and take away their children we have a right and an obligation to know why. The judicial function inherently involves punishment, and, when no objective standards exist for determining fault or responsibility then fault becomes subjective and can be placed wherever the government wishes to place it. This is why the "fault" that was ostensibly thrown out the front door of divorce proceedings has re-entered through the back. "According to therapeutic precepts, the fault for marital breakup must be shared, even when one spouse unilaterally seeks a divorce," observes Barbara Whitehead, author of *The Divorce Culture*. "Many husbands and wives who did not seek or want divorce were stunned to learn . . . that they were equally 'at fault' in the dissolution of their marriages."[49]

This abdication by the courts and other public institutions has led directly to voyeurism and invasions of personal privacy, both by the courts themselves and by the media, far more intrusive than fixing responsibility for the violation of a legal contract. To take one example: "Frank . . . was married with two young sons," begins one newspaper article. "In 1987, his marriage broke down. He lost his children, his house, his furniture . . . " and so forth.[50] Yet legally speaking, a marriage does not simply "break down" by itself. As John Campion points out with respect to comparable legal agreements, "No one would ever say 'the mortgage broke down.'"[51] Someone (and it is usually *one*) consciously acted to legally end it by filing official papers and in so doing to enlist the government as an instrument to separate Frank from his children. While the newspaper quaintly describes Frank as having "lost" his children and property (as if perhaps he had misplaced them), the precise fact is that government officials forcibly confiscated them and will arrest and incarcerate Frank if he attempts unauthorized interaction with them.

This newspaper is doing precisely the opposite of what journalism should be doing. A newspaper that apparently considers acts of legal wrongdoing

Introduction

beyond its scope of inquiry has no compunction about issuing a gratuitous comment about the personal life of a private individual ("his marriage broke down") about which it cannot possibly know anything firsthand and which in any case is none of the newspaper's or its readers' business. At the same time, it is refusing to question the governmental authority that has invaded Frank's private life by seizing his children and property. Like the nameless governmental authorities that have perpetrated this action, the newspaper is violating Frank's privacy and then refusing to say why under the guise of respecting the very privacy it is violating. The crucial fact of public interest is not Frank's marriage as such but that the government assumed control over a man's private life. The next important question is, did any evidence exist of legal wrongdoing, either criminal or civil, by Frank to justify this state intervention. If our government is involved, we have a right and need to know why.

This newspaper account is relatively sympathetic to the plight of divorced fathers, and I am being harsh to make a point. When journalism abdicates its role as the watchdog of government and instead takes on the function of soap opera, venturing into personal lives and opening them to public view, this erodes the distinction between public and private and with it the boundary of state action.[52] Many journalistic accounts today are far more intrusive. But regardless of who benefits from the spin in any given "he said/she said" account, prying into private lives weakens not only journalistic standards but citizens' privacy. Once our voyeuristic libido has been satisfied, we can all throw up our hands at how complicated the affair invariably is, declare that it is for the courts to sort out, and walk away with no consequences to ourselves.

Unfortunately, this has been the trend of not only journalism but of scholarship. The family crisis has never been seriously examined by scholars concerned with state power. Instead they have been the almost exclusive domain of therapeutic disciplines like psychiatry, psychology, sociology, and social work, which have produced mountains of literature, almost all of which misses the point as clearly as this newspaper article. As Dickens once said of lawyers, scholars have a prodigious capacity to create work for themselves, which they accomplish largely by devising controversies which have no possible resolution. Thus the proliferation of ever-more-esoteric studies that approach family issues from every possible angle except the central one. Consider these titles from Princeton University's Bendheim-Thoman Center for Research on Child Wellbeing: "The Impact of Definitional Changes on the Prevalence and Outcomes of Cohabitation," "The Hispanic Paradox and Breastfeeding: Does

Acculturation Matter?" "Documenting the Prevalence and Correlates of Multi-Partnered Fertility in the United States," "Diversity Among Unmarried Parents: Human Capital, Attitudes, and Relationship Quality."[53] All these government-funded studies are geared to influencing *how* government officials should exercise control over families rather than *whether* or *why* they should at all.

An example of the current academic approach to divorce and fatherhood is provided by the influential scholar Elaine Sorensen of the Urban Institute in her article "Can Non-Custodial Fathers Pay More Child Support?"[54] Framed in this way, the question strongly invites an affirmative answer. But the question also contains certain unquestionable assumptions. To answer her own question Sorensen invokes all the trappings of her trade. She presents a barrage of statistics, all suitably qualified with the appropriate cautions. And her answers are nuanced; at times one might conclude that some fathers indeed cannot pay more. Like our newspaper reporter, Sorensen appears detached and non-judgmental. Among scholars in this field she is in fact considered relatively moderate toward fathers, in contrast to many who are openly hostile. Still, the undefended assumption is that if they can pay more they should be made to.

Left unasked are much more fundamental questions: What have the fathers done to incur a child-support obligation in the first place? What wrongdoing are they guilty of that they may not care and provide for their children as they see fit? If they do pay more will the money benefit or even reach their children? What adults have an interest in having them pay more and who will benefit? These questions are simply never asked in the scholarly literature, because they would undermine the edifice at its foundations.

Scholars, of all people, should be raising questions others are not asking and provoking us to think from fresh angles. Family research is funded largely by the federal government, however, and questions that embarrass the government do not lead to research grants, promotions, or influence within policy-making circles.[55]

The breakdown of fatherhood, marriage, and family, in other words, has never been systematically examined as a political phenomenon. For better or worse, this book is the first attempt to do so.

Chapter 1

JUDICIAL KIDNAPPING

There can be no doubt that behind all the actions of this court of justice, that is to say in my case, behind my arrest and today's interrogation, there is a great organization at work. An organization which not only employs corrupt warders, oafish inspectors, and examining magistrates . . . but also has at its disposal a judicial hierarchy of high, indeed of the highest rank, with an indispensable and numerous retinue of servants, clerks, police, and other assistants, perhaps even hangmen, I do not shrink from that word. And the significance of this great organization, gentlemen? It consists in this, that innocent persons are accused of guilt, and senseless proceedings are put in motion against them.

— Franz Kafka, *The Trial*

The one great principle of the English law is to make business for itself. . . . Viewed by this light it becomes a coherent scheme and not the monstrous maze the laity are apt to think it. Let them but once clearly perceive that its grand principle is to make business for itself at their expense, and surely they will cease to grumble.

— Charles Dickens, *Bleak House*

N o one realizes it can happen until it happens to him. A man comes home one day to find his house empty. On the table is a note from his wife saying she has taken the children to live with her sister or parents or boyfriend, or to a "battered women's shelter."

Soon after comes a knock on the door. He is summoned to appear under an "emergency" motion to a family court within a few hours. In a hearing that

29

lasts a few minutes his children are legally removed from his care and protection, his right to make decisions about them is abrogated, and he is ordered to stay away from them most or all of the time. He is also ordered to begin making child-support payments, an order is entered to garnish his wages, and his name is placed on a federal government data base for monitoring "delinquents." If he tries to see his children outside the authorized time, or fails to make the payments, he can be arrested. Without being permitted to speak he is then told the hearing is over. No members of his family, the public, or the press have been permitted to be present, and no record will remain of what was said.[56]

This scene, with variations, is acted out in America hundreds, perhaps thousands of times every day. The man may be accused of domestic violence or child sexual abuse, in which case there may be no hearing at all or he is not notified of it, but the police will simply come to his door and order him to leave his home within hours, or even minutes, even if no evidence has been presented against him. Without being formally charged, he will not be allowed to see his children at all or perhaps only with a supervisor present or at a visitation center where he and his children will be observed and for which he will pay an hourly fee. The man may also be ordered to pay alimony and the fees of lawyers he has not hired and threatened with arrest if he refuses or is unable. The mother may take the children hundreds or thousands of miles away where he either cannot see them at all or he must quit his job and leave his home to do so. Or perhaps he is the one that leaves with the children, and she finds the note.

Whatever the complications, the court will act now and ask questions later: He is stripped of "custody," refused access to his children, and ordered to pay. His protests that he has done nothing wrong will be of no avail, and his requests to know the allegations against him will be met with silence. He will be assured that the order is "temporary" and that eventually there will be a "trial," at which he will be the "defendant." He will be required to hire a lawyer and submit to humiliating questions about the most intimate matters of his private life. If he refuses to hire a lawyer he will be ordered to pay his spouse's lawyer. Either way, he will pay $50,000-$150,000, and possibly much more, to see his children. If he refuses to answer questions or to pay he can be jailed without trial and without a lawyer and lose access to his children altogether. If he objects, he can be ordered to undergo a psychiatric evaluation. The state seizes his children with no burden of proof to justify why. The burden of proof is on the father to demonstrate why they should be returned.

When he goes to "trial" the most private corners of his and his children's lives will be scrutinized with an intensity that attorney Jed Abraham characterizes as an "interrogation."[57] Armed with inside information supplied by his most intimate and trusted confidante, the court will probe the deepest recesses of not only his life but his mind and soul. He will be asked if he loves his children, how much does he love them, does he kiss them, where does he kiss them, what does he say to them, what does he do with them, what does he feed them, how does he bathe them, where does he take them, why does he take them there, why doesn't he take them here, why did he buy this, why didn't he buy that. Nothing is too private for the eyes and ears of the court.

And no answer is correct. If he works long hours, he is a careerist who neglects his children. If he cares for his children, he is failing to earn as much income for them as he might. If he disciplines his children, he is controlling or even abusive. If he does not, he is neglectful. If he does not bathe them, he is neglecting them. If he does, he may be molesting them. If he fails to express sufficient love for them, he is uncaring. If he does, he is indulgent. Child-rearing decisions about which reasonable people might disagree become grounds to separate him from his children. From here on the court will decide what is correct child-rearing, and the court will micromanage the children's lives and family relationships according to whatever child-rearing philosophy it chooses. All his imperfections and private details will be thoroughly explored and discussed at upwards of $400-$500 an hour, and the ordeal lasts as long as the lawyers and judge wish to drive up the fees. This is what gives to these "kangaroo courts" the "Kafkaesque" quality about which virtually every father remarks.

In the custody trial the father will be labeled the "defendant," and it does have the quality of a prosecution. Yet because he is unlikely to be charged with any infraction (much like Joseph K. in Kafka's novel), or at least nothing for which evidence will be presented, he will find it impossible to defend himself. If abuse allegations are made, he is not likely to be formally charged but will simply be kept from his children. "The authorities will act quickly to 'protect' your children from you," warns Abraham. "They'll curtail your visitation during their investigation; you'll be restricted to being with your children only in the presence of a supervisor, and you'll be ordered to pay the supervisor's fees."[58] Ironically, the one thing that cannot be debated in the court is legal guilt or innocence—such as violating the marital contract or leveling false accusations. For to admit the most rudimentary notions of justice would be to undermine the logic of the proceeding.

Whatever the outcome of the trial, for the rest of his children's childhood they and he will live under constant surveillance and control from the court. He will be told when he can see his children, what he can do with them, and where he can take them. He may have no access to their school or medical records and no voice in any decisions regarding their health or education. He will be told what religious services he may (or must) attend with them and what subjects he may discuss with them in private. He will be told how much he must pay, and the money will be deducted automatically from his paycheck. He can be ordered to work certain hours and at certain jobs, the earnings from which will be confiscated. The days and hours he is authorized to see his children may bear no relation to when he must work at his job, but if he wants them changed he will have to go to court, and pay. If he loses his job or is hospitalized he will be declared a felon and jailed for failure to pay child support. His home can be entered by officials of the court. His visits with his children can be monitored by officials and restricted to a "supervised visitation center," for which he will pay and where he and his children will be watched and overheard throughout their time together. His financial records will be demanded and examined by the court and his bank account will be raided. Anything he says to his wife can be used against him in court. His children can be compelled to act as informers against him. He can be ordered to sell his house and turn the proceeds over to attorneys he has not hired.[59]

As for his children, they effectively have become wards of the court. They can be placed in day care or other institutions without their father's consent, and the father can be ordered to pay for it—in addition to his regular child support. If they react adversely to the destruction of their home or object to the separation from their father, they can be put on psychotropic drugs, committed to a psychiatric hospital, placed in foster care, turned over to the custody of social workers, or incarcerated in a juvenile detention facility—all without the knowledge or consent of their father. "You'll watch them from afar as they grow up with the kinds of psycho-social problems that children who live with their fathers rarely have," writes Abraham. "You'll watch from afar, and you won't be able to do anything about it."[60]

In the jargon of family law, faithfully parroted by the media and academia, this father has "lost custody," a simple and harmless enough sounding formulation of events, so common as to be mundane. But this jargon disguises far-reaching implications. In plain English, this father's unauthorized association with his own children is now a crime. Proceeding from this, his failure to conform his private life to an assortment of court directives controlling his movements, finances, and personal habits—directives that apply to no one but him and that prohibit what anyone else may lawfully do—is from this point grounds for arrest.

Is all this an unavoidable investigation and regulation of a family "breakdown" when decisions "must" be made between "warring parents" in a "custody battle," as the government and the media invariably phrase it? Or is it the invasion of private family life by a state machinery that is out of control? As we shall see, the answer would seem to hinge on one question: whether the father concerned has given either consent or grounds for a divorce. If he has, then a case might be made for such an inquisition (though perhaps not for the invasive and reckless abandon with which it will be conducted). But if not, this would appear to fulfill the direst prophecies of those who have warned that we are constructing yet another bureaucratic dictatorship of the kind which the last century saw too many. And this time we are using children.

But what is beyond dispute is that all this can and does happen to fathers and the children of fathers who are not accused of any legal wrongdoing and who never agreed to any separation or divorce.[61] It also happens to mothers. Professor Donald Hubin explains in the more scholarly language of the law journals:

> The procedures for "awarding" custody *pendente lite* do not require evidence, or even an assertion, that the person whose parental rights are abridged has abused, or is likely to abuse, his or her parental rights. They do not require evidence that the retention by both parties of their parental rights would be harmful to the children or even contrary to their best interest. . . . The procedures lead to the direct and substantial denial of parental rights without any requirement of evidence that a state interest is involved . . . virtually without any of the standard due process protections.[62]

Parents summoned to these courts have entered a nightmare world where children are abducted and exploited and even abused by government order, where parents are forced to stay away from their children, prevented by the police from protecting them, incarcerated without charge or trial, and driven into bankruptcy and poverty, and where the Bill of Rights may as well not exist.

As we will see, the astonishing but incontrovertible fact is that with the exception of convicted criminals, no group in our society today has fewer rights than fathers.[63] Even accused criminals have the right to due process of law, to know the charges against them, to face their accusers, to a lawyer, to a trial, and to expect knowingly false accusations to be punished. A father can be deprived of his children, his home, his savings, his future earnings, his privacy, and his freedom without any of these constitutional protections. Once a man has a child, he forfeits his most important constitutional rights.[64] And mothers are not immune.

How is this possible in a country with the most open and free system of government in the world? And why does no one seem to know about it? Surely one must have to do something wrong for this to happen. He must have been at least accused of violence, or infidelity, or substance abuse, or—something?

These questions are what a rapidly increasing number of parents suddenly find themselves asking. As the answers finally dawn on them, they try to explain to incredulous friends and family members that they have not done anything that is legally actionable in a court of law, yet they were summoned to one. Everyone assumes "he must have done something."

"In the beginning, insiders dismissed [the stories], assuming them to be made up by disgruntled fathers who must have done something unspeakable, or else why would their children's mothers have taken such extreme action?" writes Maureen Freely. "Because if things were as bad as these people say, wouldn't we know about it already?"[65] It seems the very magnitude of the injustice may be the most formidable barrier to the acceptance that it is taking place. "It is remarkable that such a grossly unjust system has not been noticed," writes Melanie Phillips. "One explanation is that no one knows what happens . . . until it happens to them—and even then they can't believe it. Any objections are dismissed as implausible."[66]

The media generally report this with a series a clichés and euphemisms— "divorce," "custody battle," "fatherlessness," "deadbeat dads," "domestic violence," "child abuse," and "parental kidnapping"—while ignoring the underlying legal framework that connects all these phenomena.[67] We hear about the high rate of "divorce," but we are seldom told that the vast majority of divorces with children are the actions of one parent acting alone. We hear of ugly "custody battles" involving "warring parents," with no hint that most begin as unilateral child snatchings that are planned with the assistance of court officials and rewarded by the courts. We witness the official witch hunt against "deadbeat dads," with seldom a word to the effect that few of these men have ever been convicted of anything or that most were divorced over their objections and without grounds and therefore did nothing to incur "obli-gations" which are often patently impossible to pay. We are besieged with daily reports of "male violence" with little indication that female violence is equally common. We hear harrowing tales of child abuse but not the fact that it is overwhelmingly committed by single mothers and their boyfriends once the father has been forcibly removed and is no longer able to protect his children. We have been told that more than 2,000 child kidnappings occur in America every day and that they are overwhelmingly by a parent,[68] but there is no indication that most are instigated following family court orders. We hear about fathers who "abandon" their children, but not that virtually every one of these fathers is under a court order to stay away.

In short, the media will go to any lengths to avoid admitting that we are in a massive epidemic of government-sponsored child stealing. So pervasive is the demonization of fathers today that fathers themselves share in it even after they have become its victims. "It is typical for a man to believe . . . the media myth of the Evil Male," writes Robert Seidenberg. "While he knows that he is a great father himself, he thinks everyone else is a deadbeat dad."[69]

AUTOMATIC MOTHER CUSTODY

Contrary to popular perception and what limited media attention it does attract, the problem is much deeper than simply bias against fathers in custody decisions. Such bias certainly exists.[70] This is despite statutes and constitutional rulings prohibiting gender discrimination in family courts.[71] No official figures are available on the gender division in custody awards, though it would be a simple statistic to compile, because judicial interests lobby to prevent such records from being kept.[72] Yet despite formal legal equality between parents, it is generally agreed that some 85 percent to 90 percent of custody awards go to mothers.[73] "Although patterns may vary from state to state," concludes one scholarly survey, "it appears that, over all, mothers obtain sole physical custody ten times more often than fathers."[74] One scholarly analysis of a feminist-dominated study published by the Massachusetts Supreme Court reached these conclusions:

- Mothers get primary residential custody 93.4 percent of the time in divorces.
- Fathers get primary residential custody 2.5 percent of the time.
- Fathers get joint physical custody 4 percent of the time.
- Fathers get primary or joint physical custody less than 7 percent of the time.[75]

One peer-reviewed study found a clear preference among judges in four states for maternal custody.[76] An office of the Virginia General Assembly reports that 96 percent of custodial parents are mothers and 4 percent are fathers.[77] In Arlington, Virginia, over an eighteen-month period maternal custody was awarded in 100 percent of decisions.[78]

Perhaps most telling is the testimony of litigants themselves. "Not a single father thought that the system favored them in the slightest, and three-fourths thought it favored mothers," Sanford Braver found. "And mothers tended to agree that the system was slanted in their favor."[79]

This imbalance is often attributed to simple, old-fashioned prejudice. Though formal legal equality between the genders inhibits judges from expressing their biases openly, occasionally some still do. "I ain't never seen a calf following a bull," declares a Georgia superior court judge. "They always follow the cow. So I always give custody to the mamas."[80] "Children should be with their mother," declares another judge, enunciating a principle with which many may be inclined to agree, until they learn that the father had won custody after his violent and unstable wife allowed the five-year-old girl to contract a sexually transmitted disease. This judge overturned the decision, and the court began garnishing $1,700 each month of his $2,800 net income for child support.[81] "We see bizarre cases where abusive and violent mothers are given child custody to 'save their motherhood,'" writes attorney Peter Jensen. "One sees fathers kept from the bedsides of dying children because their presence might upset the mother."[82]

As these cases indicate, bias against fathers goes well beyond the rationale of, "all else being equal," children belong with their mothers. Automatic mother custody applies largely regardless of the mother's behavior or legal culpability. "Washing their hands of judgments about conduct . . . the courts assume that all children should normally live with their mothers, regardless of how the women have behaved," observes Phillips. "Yet if a mother has gone off to live with another man, does that not indicate a measure of irresponsibility or instability, not least because by breaking up the family . . . she is acting against their best interests?" Phillips writes that "hostility towards men pervades the whole system and deprives many blameless fathers of contact with their children."[83]

Though judges are not supposed to favor mothers, they often seem to go out of their way to express their dislike of fathers. A superior court judge in California was "admonished" but not reprimanded for sending an e-mail message saying he intended to "screw" a father. "I say screw [the father] and let's cut [the attorney] off without a hearing," the e-mail stated.[84] Fathers almost universally report being insulted and harangued with the *obiter dicta* of judges as if they were naughty boys or juvenile delinquents. A rare instance of a judge speaking on the record was provided by Richard Hunter, former chief judge of the King's County Family Court and then a member of the New York State Commission on Child Support:

> You have never seen a bigger pain in the ass than the father who wants to get involved; he can be repulsive. He wants to meet the kid after school at three o'clock, take the kid out to dinner during the week, have the kid on his own birthday, talk to the kid on the phone every evening, go to every open school night, take the kid away for a whole weekend so they can be alone together. This type of father is pathological.[85]

Gender bias alone cannot account for this degree of animosity. Most people can probably understand and tolerate some discrimination against fathers when divorces are agreed by mutual consent. What is happening in family courts today is very different. It is one thing to recognize that young children need their mother; it is another altogether to say they need her to have the power to arbitrarily keep away their father. Yet current judicial practice allows her to do precisely that. In fact she can have a half-dozen previous divorces, she can desert the marital home, she can abscond with the children, she can commit adultery, she can level false charges, she can assault the father, she can even abuse the children, and none of these (except possibly the last) can be even introduced as evidence in a custody hearing. For a father the simple fact of his being a father will be used to keep him away from his children six days out of seven, deprive him of any decision-making role, and dissolve his marriage over his objections.[86]

For many of us, the key factor in our acceptance of mother custody is the perception that fathers are initiating or at least acquiescing in the dissolution of marriages. Yet among researchers and family counselors this assumption has long been known to be false. In "the largest federally funded study ever on issues confronting divorced fathers," Sanford Braver has shown that at least two-thirds of divorces are initiated by women, whether measured by official filings or surveys of couples. Moreover, few of these divorces involve grounds, such as desertion, adultery, or violence. Most often the reasons given are "growing apart" or "not feeling loved or appreciated."[87]

Other studies have reached similar conclusions. The Australian Institute of Family Studies found women were "more than three times as likely as men to initiate separation," mostly for reasons such as "communications problems" and "drifting apart."[88] And the decisive factor that is not generally appreciated is possession of the children. The proportion of divorces initiated by women ranged around 60 percent for most of the twentieth century and climbed to more than 70 percent in the late 1960s when no-fault divorce was introduced, according to law professor Margaret Brinig and economist Douglas Allen. "Women file for divorce more often than men," their report states. "Not only do they *file* more often, but some evidence suggests they are more likely to *instigate* separation, despite a deep attachment to their children and the evidence that many divorces harm children." And the bottom line is indeed the children: After analyzing twenty-one wide-ranging variables, the Brinig-Allen study concludes that the parent who anticipates gaining custody of the children is the one most likely to file for divorce. "We have found that who gets the children is by far the most important component in deciding who files for divorce."[89] If the parent who initiates the divorce without legal grounds can expect sole custody, it would appear that what we call "divorce" has in effect become a kind of legalized parental kidnapping.

As for the callous brute whose sexual urges drive him to ignore his children, a survey commissioned by the AARP found that not only do 66 percent of women report that they asked for the divorce, men are over 50 percent more likely than women to avoid divorce because of its impact on the children. "Fifty-eight percent of men delayed their divorce because of concerns about their children," says the AARP. "Far fewer women had this worry." More than 50 percent fewer in fact: 37 percent. "Not believing in divorce" was the next most important reason men cited. "The idea of an older man leaving his wife for a younger woman is ingrained in the American psyche— and that has created a misconception about divorce," said *AARP* magazine Editor Steve Slon. "But . . . as this survey makes abundantly clear, women are more than willing to chart a new life for themselves if they're in an unfulfilling marriage."[90]

These are cautious, scholarly estimates. Others (some with ironic axes to grind) put the proportion much higher. Shere Hite, the feminist popular researcher on female sexuality, found "91 percent of women who have divorced say they made the decision to divorce, not their husbands." David Chambers, a divorce attorney who openly expresses extreme hostility to fathers, insists that "the wife is the moving party in divorce actions seven times out of eight."[91] Author Robert Seidenberg reports that "all the domestic relations lawyers I spoke with concurred that *in disputes involving child custody*, women initiate divorce *'almost all the time.'*"[92]

It is difficult to overestimate the importance of this fact. All the hardships, indignities, and prosecutions fathers now endure might be understandable if, as is still popularly believed, it was they who were walking out on their families, giving legitimate grounds for divorce, or even agreeing to it. Understandably, Braver observes, "this belief appears to fuel much of the vindictiveness of gender-based divorce debates, since the logical conclusion is that society should find a way to punish divorced men for their escapades . . . by imposing various sanctions."[93] Even those who do not reflexively blame the father for the divorce nevertheless assume that divorced parents by definition bring their troubles upon themselves. As a nationally syndicated newspaper columnist remarked to me when I tried to convey the magnitude of the ordeal, "People who get divorced are asking for it."

Almost four decades after the institutionalization of unilateral divorce nationwide, it is surprising how ubiquitous this assumption remains—and the consequent tendency to blame forcibly divorced and legally innocent parents for actions that are entirely beyond their control—even among people who write about these issues for a living. "So what, you might say. That's the price of divorce," writes Canadian columnist Heather Bird, perceptively. "When you decide you don't want to be married to the other parent any longer, you automatically forfeit the right to see your children every day."[94] In preparation for an article, the sympathetic editor of a influential news magazine warned me with the following words: "I'm sure that many of my readers would have a very strong bias against divorced fathers, simply because they were divorced. (I confess that I had the same prejudice when I was first confronted with this issue.) . . . They will say, in effect, 'Well, you wouldn't have had these problems if you'd just stayed married!'"[95]

Contrary to the simplistic rhetoric of some parents' rights groups, most people seem to consider this is a reasonable assumption. People who voluntary renege on their marital vows without recognized legal grounds arguably do give the state an interest in seeing to the well-being of their children. Most people agree that children are entitled to the security of knowing their parents are committed to giving them a stable home until they reach some legally recognized age of emancipation. Parents who refuse to give that commitment are leaving their children in a state of limbo, and those who renounce it are violating a legal contract and, arguably, providing the state with a plausible "compelling interest" to intervene. This, indeed, was the legal assumption before the creation of family courts and unilateral divorce.

It is this well-intentioned, commonsense understanding that is exploited by the divorce industry and that impels those who call for repeated crackdowns on supposedly dissolute fathers. "I believe children should not have to suffer twice for the decisions of their parents to divorce," Senator Mike DeWine stated on the floor of the U.S. Senate; "once when they decide to divorce, and again when one of the parents evades the financial responsibility to care for them."[96]

But from the unchallenged scientific evidence, the vast majority of fathers and some mothers make no such decision. It is they who are being abandoned—or perhaps more precisely expelled—by a divorce that is over their objections and over which they have no say. The regime engineered by the divorce industry is based on a legal anomaly whereby parents can be forcibly divorced and then blamed for the divorce that is beyond their control.

How much is this happening? We do not have firm figures. We do know, as Brinig and Allen indicate, that changes in divorce law were followed by an explosion in the divorce rate. The explosion continues, with well over a million divorces each year in the United States. Some estimates now predict two-thirds of marriages will end in divorce[97] (in addition to over one-third of all American children now born out of wedlock).[98] Of these about 80 percent are unilateral, though the figure may be even higher when children are involved.[99] Children are involved in about three-fifths of divorces, which, allowing for childless divorces, still means more than a million children annually are separated from one parent at the sole instigation of the other.[100] These figures would indicate that, by a cautious estimate, at least 700,000 parents are involuntarily divorced every year and control of their children is taken over by the state. For all we can be certain, all 16 million parents now being pursued as quasi-criminals by armed enforcement agents of the federal government have been involuntarily separated from their children through no legal fault or agreement of their own.

This realization changes the dynamic fundamentally. One might indeed argue a "compelling state interest" in providing for abandoned children, and we can all sympathize with the "get tough" approach against parents who abandon their children.[101] There is no state interest—other than augmenting its own power—in using the law enforcement machinery to forcibly separate children from their parents.

More is at work here than couples deciding to part ways. Under "no-fault" laws, divorce has become a means not simply of ending a marriage but of seizing monopoly control of the children, who become potent political weapons conferring leverage backed by penal sanctions. Divorce today is less likely to be a reasoned, mutual decision than a power grab by one parent, assisted by lawyers, judges, and other officials. By extending the reach of the state over the children and the forcibly divorced parent, unilateral divorce has turned children into weapons of not only parental but governmental power.

These findings on divorced fathers are echoed in research on unmarried, often poorer and younger fathers who are often presumed to be less responsible. Without divorce papers to document who is instigating the break-up of these families, it is more difficult to authenticate their experience. Moreover, by not committing to contractual marriage in the first place, these fathers arguably have given the state a plausible pretext to intervene to protect the welfare of their children, for the reasons already mentioned and because a claim is more often made on their behalf on government assistance. Nevertheless, there is reason to believe that the separation of these fathers from their children is just as likely to be involuntary. A study of low income fathers in the north of England found that "the most common reason given by the fathers for not having more contact with their children was the mothers' reluctance to let them":

> Most of the men were proud to be seen as competent carers and displayed a knowledge of child-care issues. Caring for their children, changing nappies, or feeding them was not seen as a woman's job. Several felt that they were better carers than the mothers were.[102]

An American study of young, low-income, and unmarried fathers presents a picture that, while far from ideal, does not show them abandoning their children: 63 percent had only one child; 82 percent had children by only one mother; 50 percent had been in a serious relationship with the mother at the time of pregnancy; only 3 percent knew the mother of their child "only a little"; 75 percent visited their child in the hospital; 70 percent saw their children at least once a week; 50 percent took their child to the doctor and large percentages reported bathing, feeding, dressing, and playing with their children; and 85 percent provided informal child support in the form of cash or purchased goods such as diapers, clothing, and toys.[103]

Another research team concluded that "unmarried fathers are by no means indifferent to their children. In the first place, about 83 percent of mothers (and 91 percent of fathers) said that the father contributed financially during the pregnancy, and similar percentages reported that he contributed in other ways (for example, by providing transportation)." The authors add:

> Half of all mothers were living with the father of their child when the child was born; another 33 percent were romantically involved, though not cohabiting. Nine percent were "just friends," and only 8 percent had little or no contact with the father. Just 1 percent reported the father as unknown.[104]

Many fathers' groups and the small but growing media attention they have attracted tend to focus on the proportion of cases where mothers are granted custody in preference to fathers. Yet the larger question would seem to be why mothers are routinely given sole custody in the vast majority of cases where the father has done nothing legally wrong and never agreed to the separation in the first place. In other words, why is it so easy to steal a man's children? When most people become aware of this reality they are generally outraged, and their tolerance for the bias toward mothers evaporates. Especially given the growing awareness over the past decade of the importance of fathers in the healthy upbringing of children, the need of children for their mothers does not justify arbitrarily depriving them of their fathers or the fathers of both their children and virtually all their significant constitutional rights.[105] And once again, the genders can be reversed, so that children are deprived of their mothers.

Neither is old-fashioned gender bias an adequate explanation for why it is happening. More important is political corruption in the family law system. Though the courts promiscuously invoke both traditional stereotypes about motherhood and modern ideas of women's rights, it is really a question of money and power, specifically that of the lucrative divorce industry, which offers parents—usually but not necessarily mothers—a tempting package of financial and emotional incentives to file for divorce. As one lawyer reportedly told a client who asked him to stop a divorce, "There's too many people making too much money in the divorce business."[106]

Family courts in other words, far from providing a remedy to parental child-snatching, are almost certainly part of the problem. So willing are family courts to reward this practice that some parents describe the courts themselves as a legal "child-kidnapping and extortion racket." From the perspective of the father whose children have been taken, a "gang of four"—the mother, two lawyers, and a judge—has colluded to kidnap his children and hold them for ransom. "Rather than hold my wife accountable for kidnapping my daughter," one father told a public hearing in Alexandria, Virginia, in 1995, "the system was eager to reward her for it."[107]

Some may dismiss the term "kidnapping" as hyperbole. But in the right, politically acceptable circumstances, its validity is readily attested without challenge. Striking an outraged pose because German family courts, as she puts it, "condone kidnapping" of American children, *Washington Post* columnist Sally Quinn describes "chilling" practices that in fact are no different from what American courts routinely do to American parents on a much more massive scale. "Germans who marry and divorce Americans take their children back to Germany," she notes. The rest of the story is equally accurate as a depiction of practices throughout the United States:

> Then, in a scenario worthy of Kafka, the American parent is deprived of any custody or visitation rights. After several years, the children don't know or remember their other parent. The courts then decree that the children don't want to see that parent and would be traumatized by any visit. The courts also bill the American parents for child support. If these parents refuse to pay, and still try to see their children any way they can (say, from a parked car across the street from the house), they are thrown in jail for nonpayment.[108]

In fact not only is the legal machinery an accomplice; in some ways it is the principal instigator. A mother who consults a divorce attorney will be advised that her best strategy for gaining custody is simply to take the children and their effects and leave without warning. If she has no place to go, she will be told that by accusing the father of sexual or physical abuse she can obtain a restraining order immediately forcing him out of the family home. She will also learn that not only can she not be punished for either of these actions, they cannot even be used against her in a custody decision. In fact they work so strongly in her favor that failure to apprise a female client of these options may constitute legal malpractice.

Far from being punished for child-snatching and false accusations then, the mother is almost certain to be generously rewarded. "No matter how faithless," writes Bryce Christensen, "a wife who files for divorce can count on the state as an ally."[109] Mothers who abduct children and keep them from their fathers, with or without abuse charges, are routinely given immediate "temporary" custody. In fact, this is almost never temporary. Once she has custody it cannot be changed without a lengthy (and for the lawyers lucrative) court battle. The

43

sooner and the longer she can establish herself as the sole caretaker the more difficult and costly it is to dislodge her. The more she cuts the children off from the father, alienates them from the father, levels false charges, delays the proceedings, and obstructs his efforts to see his children, the more she makes the path of least resistance (and highest earnings) to leave her with sole custody.[110] In short, the more belligerence she displays and the more litigation she creates, the more grateful the courts will be for the business she creates.

As for the father, any restraint he shows throughout this ordeal is likely to cost him dearly, as most discover too late. On the other hand, reciprocal belligerence and aggressive litigation on his part may carry enough hope of reward to keep him interested. Revealingly, the latest wisdom counsels nervous fathers that the game is so rigged that their best chance is not to wait for their day in court but to imitate the techniques of mothers: If you think she is planning to snatch, snatch first. Then conceal, obstruct, delay, and so forth. "If you do not take action," writes Seidenberg, *"your wife will."*[111] Thus we have the nightmare scenario of a race to the trigger, to adopt the terms of nuclear deterrence replete with the preemptive strike. Whoever snatches first survives.

Far from merely exploiting family breakdown after the fact then, domestic relations law has turned the American family into a game of "prisoners' dilemma," in which only the most trusting marriage can survive and the emergence of the slightest marital discord renders *not* absconding with the children perilous and even irrational. Willingly or not, all parents are now prisoners in this game.

That this is indeed the dynamic behind the divorce epidemic is further confirmed as the logic is taken to its macabre conclusions. Not only are mothers enticed into filing for divorce with financial and emotional incentives; in some cases, they are being forced into it with threats and actions against their children. Mothers now report being told by social service agencies that they must divorce their husbands or lose their children, even in instances where neither parent is charged with any wrongdoing.[112] In short, state officials now possess the power to break up families by imposing divorce on happily married parents.

WHAT IS GOING ON HERE?

How did all this come about? A combination of cultural, legal, and political factors is largely responsible. The advent of "no-fault" divorce in the early 1970s, often blamed for leaving wives vulnerable to abandonment, has left fathers with no protection against the confiscation of their children. "No-fault" is a misnomer (taken from car insurance), for the new laws did not stop at removing the requirement that grounds be cited for a divorce, so as to allow for divorce by "mutual consent," as they were misleadingly promoted at the time; they also created involuntary or what Maggie Gallagher calls "unilateral" divorce. This means that either spouse may end the marriage at any time without any agreement or fault by the other. "No-fault divorce gave judges, at the request of one-half of the couple, the right to decide when a marriage had irretrievably broken down," writes Gallagher. "Today, while it still takes two to marry, it takes only one to divorce." Moreover, the spouse that divorces or violates the marriage contract through adultery or desertion incurs no liability for the costs or consequences, creating a unique and unprecedented legal anomaly. "In all other areas of contract law those who break a contract are expected to compensate their partner or partners," writes Robert Whelan, "but under a system of 'no fault' divorce, this essential element of contract law is abrogated. Divorce comes to be regarded as one of those things that just happens."[113]

As many critics point out, no legal system can operate on such principles. "What if American law refused to enforce business contracts and indeed systematically favored the party that wished to withdraw, on the grounds that "fault" was messy and irrelevant and exposed judges and attorneys to unpleasant acrimony," asks Gallagher, ". . . so that when disputes arose, thieves and owners would be left to work things out among themselves, because after all, one cannot legislate morality?"[114] Columnist Melanie Phillips also notes this peculiar legal principle. "In every other area of law, it aims to make people who have done wrong accept the consequences of their actions," she notes. "Imagine saying of a neighbour who tears down the next door's fence that he shouldn't be held responsible and made to pay for the destruction because it would make it more difficult for the two of them to live next door to each other afterwards."[115]

In fact the legal implications go much further, because the courts do not remain neutral but actively take the side of the wrongdoers and punish their victims. Attorney Steven Varnis points out that "the law generally supports the spouse seeking the divorce, even if that spouse was the wrongdoer, by granting divorces with little regard for a spouse who may not desire it."[116] More than three decades after its advent, selective reporting by the media means that few people who have not experienced it directly understand the full implications of "no-fault" divorce. "I never knew what no-fault divorce really meant," said one woman after her first visit to a lawyer. "Never, in my wildest dreams did I imagine that one person could force another person into a divorce."[117]

These laws, enacted throughout the Western world, can in retrospect be seen as one of the boldest social experiments in modern history. The result effectively ended marriage as a legal contract. Today it is not possible to form a binding agreement to create a family. Regardless of the terms by which it is created, government officials can, at the request of one spouse, simply dissolve a marriage—and the private household it creates—over the objection of the other. Gallagher aptly titled her 1996 book *The Abolition of Marriage*.

What is striking about these laws, as Gallagher and others have pointed out, is that they were passed while no one was looking, largely for the benefit of divorce practitioners, including "lawyers, judges, psychiatrists, marriage counselors, academics, and goo-goo-eyed reformers."[118] No popular clamor to dispense with restrictions on divorce preceded their passage; no public outrage at any perceived injustice provided the impetus; no public debate was ever held on their merits in the national media. "The divorce laws . . . were reformed by unrepresentative groups with very particular agendas of their own and which were *not* in step with public opinion," writes Phillips. "All the evidence suggests that public attitudes were gradually dragged along behind laws that were generally understood at the time to mean something very different from what they subsequently came to represent."[119]

Attorney Ed Truncellito filed suit against the State Bar of Texas in August 2000, alleging the legislative history of no-fault divorce law in Texas makes clear that "the law was meant for 'uncontested-only' cases." He insists that "the state bar knew all along that the no-fault law was being misapplied, but they covered it up for financial gain."[120] Truncellito claims that "no one is married" because the laws created "unilateral divorce on demand." Though feminist groups were involved,[121] the changes were passed largely by and for the legal business, which has benefited in terms of both power and profit. Relieved of the burden of dispensing justice, the courts were set free to generate business for their officials and political clients by assuming control over the children of parents who had been forced into divorce litigation.

Dickens's observation "the one great principle of the . . . law is to make business for itself" could hardly be more strikingly validated.[122] Family courts, in the words of one legal authority, "interpret their 'social responsibility' to mean accommodating and streamlining adult choices to end marriages."[123] Nothing in the law requires a judge to honor the divorcing parent's initial request to strip the other parent of his children. A judge could "just say no" and rule that, *prima facie*, neither the father nor the children has committed any infraction that justifies being forcibly separated, even temporarily, that they have a fundamental human and constitutional right not to be separated, and that neither the mother nor the court has any grounds to separate them. Yet such rulings are virtually unheard of. One need not be cynical to recognize that judges who refused to reward divorce and child snatching would be rendering themselves largely redundant and denying earnings to a huge entourage of lawyers, custody evaluators, psychologists and psychiatrists, attorneys *ad litem*, mediators, counselors, child-support enforcement agents, social workers, and other hangers-on of the court. And all these officials have a strong say in the appointment and promotion of judges.

Family court judges sit at the bottom of the judicial hierarchy, typically paid upwards of $100,000 a year.[124] Like any salaries, theirs are based on the demand, and increased business naturally means increased compensation. "Judges and staff . . . should be given every consideration for salary and the other 'perks' or other emoluments of their high office," one judge urges. "With the improved status of judges and family court systems comes their proper position in judicial budgets as worthy of appropriate funding." It is now a cliché that courts are "overburdened and under-resourced."[125] Yet it should be recognized that it is in their interest to be overburdened, and they do what they can to overburden themselves. Family court judges and lawyers are not always held in high esteem, even by other legal practitioners. Yet the remedy is apparently not to re-evaluate the work to which they dedicate themselves but to increase their remuneration. This will result in "improved services" and more customers. The judge openly suggests that his colleagues' aim should be to increase their volume of work:

> With improved services more persons will come before the court seeking their availability. . . . As the court does a better job more persons will be attracted to it as a method of dispute resolution. . . . The better the family court system functions the higher . . . the volume of the persons served.[126]

By these principles, public tribunals are not an unfortunate but necessary response by the government to a social problem arising spontaneously from beyond its control. They are a business, part of an economy where supply creates its own demand, and a quality product will attract more paying customers. "Doing a better job" here means attracting more divorcing mothers with windfall divorce settlements. The more satisfied the customers, as the judge says, the more will be attracted, and business will boom as the divorce rate escalates ever higher.

47

As with most state courts, family court judges are usually appointed and promoted by commissions dominated by bar associations, to which they become effectively answerable.[127] Judges therefore have a strong incentive to channel money to the lawyers. The main source of the money is fathers. Having seized legal control of his children, the judge then presides over a feeding frenzy in which everything the father has and can earn in the future is doled out to political clients of the court.

The most obvious example is attorney's fees. It is not unusual for a father earning $35,000 a year to amass $150,000 in fees when trying to recover his children, according to William Dawes, a Washington attorney.[128] This is seldom the case for mothers. One affluent promoter of divorce to mothers boasts that her divorce cost "only" $11,000, a relative bargain.[129] For fathers this would be unusual. Not contesting custody is not necessarily any protection, since judges have various methods to ensure that a father's property and earnings are confiscated for lawyers. Fathers who represent themselves report being branded as "arrogant" and punished with adverse rulings. They are typically interrupted and insulted by judges so often they are unable to speak at all.

If this fails, less subtle forms of pressure are available. Parents who do not hire lawyers are also ordered, on pain of incarceration, to pay the fees of lawyers they have not hired. In a kind of judicial shakedown, judges regularly order involuntary litigants to pay the fees of attorneys, psychotherapists, and other court officials they have not hired and jail them for failing to comply.[130] What are invariably described as "reasonable attorney's fees" are not determined by the market forces of supply and demand but are set with the backing of the penal apparatus, with the police and jails acting as the attorneys' private collection agency. There is thus effectively no limit to what can be charged. Rates run as high as $2,000 an hour, as in the case of one father who, according to court documents, was ordered to pay a lawyer he had not hired $1,000 for a thirty-minute hearing.

Massachusetts Judge Arline Rotman ordered one father to pay $10,000 to an attorney with whom Rotman had a long-standing friendship and who had given a speech praising Rotman in Boston's Mechanics Hall. "I had seen winking back and forth during the hearings," the father said. "I'm in the midst of testifying about the children, and I saw this wink and nod between the two, and the judge cut me right off."[131]

Yet collusion between judges and lawyers need not be so personal or visible. Though obviously punitive, the terms of this award are much less severe than some. Ken Gallahan of Alexandria, Virginia, who was earning about

$35,000 yearly and was never charged with any wrongdoing, was summarily jailed by Judge Leslie Alden in January 2000 for failure to pay $2,200 to a psychotherapist he did not hire, and released only when his mother paid the fees, according to court documents. In October, he was ordered jailed without trial for twelve months for failing to pay $15,000 to a lawyer he had not hired for a divorce to which he had neither agreed nor given grounds.[132] In the same jurisdiction, Tahir Khilji, earning $10,000 a year in Pakistan, faces jail for his inability to pay $20,000, fully two years of his salary, to a lawyer he also did not hire for a divorce he did not request.

Such thievery has become so rampant that even the *New York Times* has reported on how easily "the divorce court leads to a jail cell." The *Times* describes how Marvin Singer was jailed without trial for failing to pay an attorney he did not hire $100,000—only half of what the court claimed he "owes." "These soon to be ex-husbands—and it is almost always husbands—are tossed in jail not for abusing wives or children but for contempt, which is legalese for not doing what the judge ordered." The *Times* reports matter-of-factly how a divorce lawyer deems it a "scandal" that such orders are sometimes not willingly obeyed. "If I pay that," Singer is quoted as saying, the judge "can order me to pay another $100,000, and send me to jail again if I don't."[133]

What is taking place here should be made very clear: Citizens who are completely innocent of any legal wrongdoing and simply minding their own business—not seeking any litigation and neither convicted nor accused of any legal infraction, criminal or civil—are ordered into court and told to write checks to officials of the court or they will be summarily arrested and jailed. Judges also order citizens to sell their houses and other property and turn the proceeds over to lawyers and other cronies they never hired. Summoning legally unimpeachable citizens to court and forcing them to empty their bank accounts to people they have not hired for services they have neither requested nor received on threat of physical punishment is what most people would call a protection racket. Were any other public officials to use their position of public trust to coerce money out of private citizens, they would likely face indictment. Yet family court judges do this as a matter of routine. This is by far the clearest example I have ever encountered in my professional research of what we political scientists term a "kleptocracy," or government by thieves.[134]

Given this power of divorce officials to simply take whatever they want from parents who are forced into divorce litigation against their will, it is not surprising that other interests are getting their noses in the trough. In Britain,

"Wives too poor to divorce their husbands are to be offered bank loans to finance court proceedings." *The Independent* later reveals that these "poor" women are actually too affluent to qualify for legal aid; their husbands have substantial earnings, and the banks are counting on a share of the spoils. "Aimed at housewives whose only wealth is tied up in the family home," the article continues, "the brains behind the scheme were encouraged by last year's House of Lords ruling by which a husband was ordered to pay his sixty-six-year-old wife £1.5 million in their divorce settlement." Couched as the altruistic generosity of caring bankers chivalrously riding to the rescue of "poor" women in unspecified "tragic cases of injustice," these robber barons will simply loot forcibly divorced fathers (and the inheritance of their children). Bankers Leopold Joseph and Sons "will recoup its investment from the final settlement." The scheme is expected to "pave the way for an American-style 'equal share' settlements which would dramatically increase payments to wives."[135]

WHY NOT SNATCH BABIES FROM GROCERY STORES?

Similar relationships connect judges with other patronage clients whose role is ostensibly to help determine custody and "the best interest of the child." To understand how this works, it is necessary to remember that under "no-fault" divorce the guilt or innocence of a parent in ending a marriage has no bearing on custody, even when it is clear who ended it; neither does the continued willingness of one parent to hold the marriage together. The notion that a parent who has abrogated or violated a marital contract he or she freely entered might by that fact alone be a less fit parent, or that a parent who tries to hold the family together for the children's benefit might by that fact be a more responsible parent—none of this is allowed to enter decisions on custody. Put more simply, the centuries-old principle that a parent has a simple right to be left alone with his or her children so long as no evidence of wrongdoing is presented against him or her is no longer recognized. Instead what we witness is the macabre spectacle of a judge taking it upon himself to determine "the best interest of the child" on whom he is forcibly inflicting a divorce and whose family he is using the power of his public office and the full force of the state to destroy.

This innocuous-sounding phrase is a masterpiece of legal obfuscation, all the more cynical for its professed compassion. Who could possibly be opposed to "the best interest of the child"? Not only is the phrase vague, it provides a pretext for several radical legal innovations. Fathers' groups complain it is a ruse for judges to award automatic mother custody, regardless of her behavior or legal guilt. "When someone mentions the best interests of the child," writes columnist Al Knight, "it is code for the best interests of the mother."[136] "What is in the best interests of your children is this," prominent publisher and television personality Judith Regan publicly instructs a private citizen from the pages of *Newsweek* magazine (a citizen who has done nothing to make himself or his family public figures and who has no similar platform from which to reply). "You should act according to the best interest of your wife."[137] Courts have indeed held simply that "what is good for the custodial parent is good for the child."[138] No explanation is given for how it can be in the best interest of children to arbitrarily order one of their parents to stay away from them six days out of seven, and perhaps altogether. For all the posturing it permits, the best interest standard "is powerless to preempt divorce in the first place," attorney Steven Varnis points out, "which would be in the child's best interest in the majority of cases."[139]

Yet there is an even more telling case against the "best interest of the child" standard. It transfers from parents to the state the power to determine what this best interest is, over the objections of parents who have done nothing to forfeit the right to decide for themselves what is best for their children. It gives state officials virtually absolute control over children to dispose of as they please, and its perils are not limited to fathers. "Such a criterion is dangerous because it renders the claims of all parents to their natural children tenuous," writes Robyn Blumner of the American Civil Liberties Union. "Children could be given over to any set of new parents who offer a more advantaged upbringing." Blumner is writing about adoption challenges, but the principle is the same—with precisely the consequences she predicts already being realized—for fathers in divorce cases.[140] The Supreme Court of Illinois has likewise held with respect to adoptions:

> If the best interests of the child are to be the determining factor, persons seeking babies to adopt might profitably frequent grocery stores and snatch babies when the parent is looking the other way. Then, if custody proceedings can be delayed long enough, they can assert that they have a nicer home, a superior education, a better job, or whatever, and the best interests of the child are with the baby snatchers.[141]

"The law, thankfully, is otherwise," the court concludes. Not for fathers it is not. The court has succinctly described precisely the custody principles of divorce court.[142]

Many accept this practice on the assumption that a judge must decide
what is best for a child when the parents "cannot agree." But allowing one
parent to surrender both parents' decision-making rights over the children to
government officials because of "disagreement"—without any infraction by
the other (who may disagree only about losing his or her children)—is a dangerous principle and invites collusion between the divorcing parent and state
officials. Judges and civil servants are far from disinterested parties. When we
equip judges and other government officials with the power to make decisions
about the best interest of other people's children, it may well become the best
interest of the judges and officials. "I represent your kids, but I don't want to,"
Judge Robert Page confesses. "Because I don't love your children. I don't even
know them. It is a legal fiction that the law's best interest is your children."[143]

The "best interest" standard is also a money-maker for the legal industry.
"It provides what might be called hair-trigger litigability," writes Walter
Olson, author of *The Litigation Explosion*. "Everything comes to be relevant
and nothing, as the lawyers say, dispositive. Does your ex swear? Smoke?
Gamble? . . . Perhaps none of these peccadillos significantly endangers a child,
but all can have some effect and you never know what will tip the balance. So
it can't hurt to bring them all up."[144] The courts having dispensed with all
objective standards for determining guilt or innocence, fault becomes a subjective free-for-all, cynically couched in terms of what officials claim is good
for children they do not know and about whom, as Page acknowledges, they
do not care.

The "best interest" also transforms judges from dispensers of justice into
dispensers of patronage in appointing any number of "experts" or cronies for
lucrative employment as "custody evaluators."[145] In pursuit of the nebulous
"best interest," the judge may dispense entirely with questions of justice in
favor of whatever quasi-scientific child development theories are currently
popular among the court's favored experts. "As society has become more complex and the presentation of cases involves greater use of social sciences,"
writes Page, ". . . family courts utilize experts in many fields, both court-
appointed and privately retained, to advise on issues requiring specialized
knowledge."[146] In practice this means that principles of justice and even the
constitutional rights of parents are excised from the proceeding in favor of
social science theory colored by political ideology. "Family lawyers . . . maintain that justice has no place in their courts," writes Melanie Phillips. "Family
court judges thus preside with equanimity over injustice, having turned themselves into a division of the therapy and social work industries."[147] And the

more children brought before the courts by divorcing parents expecting favorable verdicts from the experts, the more employment is created for the experts.

Foremost among these experts are psychologists and psychiatrists, who are ubiquitous in family court proceedings and who have achieved unprecedented power in the legal system.[148] Yet it is not clear that these experts serve any purpose other than to provide judges with a rationale for what they are already disposed to do: remove children from their fathers. Perhaps the most succinct indication of the politicization of psychotherapy through divorce is from the highly influential Freudian book, *Beyond the Best Interests of the Child*, where Joseph Goldstein, Anna Freud, and Albert Solnit opine that "the non-custodial parent should have no legally enforceable right to visit the child, and the custodial parent should have the right to decide whether it is desirable for the child to have such visits."[149] This is not a clinical opinion; it is a political one. It says nothing about the mental health of children or anyone else. It pertains solely to the use of coercive government power to criminalize a social relationship: contact between parents and their children.

Psychologist Sanford Braver calls such expert advice "little more than guesswork." "There is absolutely no credible evidence that these [methods] are valid predictors of which spouse will make the best primary parent," Braver writes. "In fact, there is no evidence that there *is* a scientifically valid way for a custody evaluator to choose the best primary parent." Braver diplomatically attributes the obvious one-sidedness of evaluators' recommendations to "gender bias," but pecuniary interest among his colleagues in the psychotherapy professions is probably a sounder explanation. He reveals as much when he quotes a professional custody evaluator to the effect that "almost all" his business would be lost were there a simple presumption of joint custody.[150]

"What a bonanza those [divorce] courts are for my ilk," writes Harvard child psychiatrist Robert Coles. "We are the ones who get the patients, who are appointed mediators, who decide when the children should visit which parent."[151] These officials rarely testify in open court, so they are not subject to cross-examination, and they may be covered by judicial immunity, so they are not accountable for their testimony.[152]

Once again documentation is scarce. Most media accounts are credulously sympathetic to the courts and psychotherapists. An admiring 2,000-word essay in the *Washington Post* extols forensic psychologist Stanton Samenow. The article openly sneers at parents' "proclaimed 'love' for their kids." Yet the professional psychologist's love for other people's children is accepted without question: "Samenow . . . saw that the children were pawns [of their parents], their lives being ripped apart. They needed help, and his heart went out to them." Samenow's heart may be encouraged by the fact that judges force involuntarily divorced parents to hire him at a rate of $225 an hour, whereupon he proceeds to probe the deepest recesses of their personal lives and conducts "aggressive" interrogations of themselves and their children. Samenow, whose expertise is criminal law, is depicted as a "psycho-detective, delving into every detail" of the families' private lives. He compares parents unfavorably with "criminals and juvenile delinquents":

> He interviewed parents and children at length, administering psychological tests. He talked with relatives, friends, neighbors, teachers, clergy, doctors, babysitters, bosses, and other psychologists who had treated the parents. He made home visits, sometimes hiring helpers who spent weekends observing a family at home over half a year. His goal was to learn the elusive "truth," sorting out charges and countercharges, in effect psychoanalyzing the parents, getting to know them so well that he could recommend exact details for realistic custody arrangements.

Like Hercule Poirot or Sherlock Holmes, his "persistence usually paid off" in unmasking the malefactors: legally unimpeachable parents whose children he is taking away and whom he compares to violent criminals in his book, *Inside the Criminal Mind*. "People could keep up a good front for a time," he says, "but eventually revealed their true natures as family events unfolded." *Post* reporter Phil McCombs himself gets into the spirit of issuing gratuitous public commentaries on other people's personal lives. "I believed that Lois had some legitimate, although exaggerated, concerns about her husband," whom she accused of being a sexual pervert and child molester, he opines ludicrously. "The challenge for her was to bear in mind that, whatever Frank's flaws, he remained the children's father, and they adored him." The *Post*'s conception of balanced reporting is to allow that insinuations of criminal pedophilia leveled without evidence might be "exaggerated." No evidence is provided that "Frank" has committed any legal infraction to warrant these off-the-cuff opinions in a major newspaper that he might be raping his own children.[153]

More probing investigations have uncovered practices more consistent with Braver's view and the experience of countless parents. Dave Brown of the *Ottawa Citizen* has produced a series of accounts of "how the psychology field generates business for itself" in family court by launching investigations of parents who are under no suspicion of unfitness or wrongdoing.[154] "Every client, parent or child, in juvenile court appears to have a court-ordered therapist," concludes one of the few official investigations, by a San Diego grand jury. "The court employs therapists from an approved list. . . . The jury is not convinced that all of these children and parents need therapists."[155]

Extended investigations by the *National Post* and the *New York Daily News* also found questionable practices by government-appointed psychotherapists. To begin with, the courts have never determined precisely who is a qualified expert or by what criteria parents and children are to be evaluated. "Assessors are not required by law to have any specialized training, pass any exams, or follow any particular rules," Donna Laframboise of the *National Post* found in her serial report on Canadian and American courts. "No one evaluates them independently to ensure that they are competent and unbiased, or keeps track of how well families whose lives have been rearranged according to their dictates have fared afterward."[156] The *Daily News* likewise found that "there are no standards . . . for how much time the experts should spend with family members, how their meetings should be conducted, or what tests should be applied."

By some informed assessments the typical practitioner is incompetent. "Your average psychiatrist and psychologist are not adequately trained to do forensic evaluations on children," according to Stephen Herman, who says he has rendered custody evaluations for seventeen years. "People with no prior experience are now starting to do this work, holding themselves out as experts."[157] Scholars agree. According to noted psychologists Ralph Underwager and Hollida Wakefield, courts often approve as experts "persons with only undergraduate degrees or less, one or two weekend seminars or workshops, and maybe a four-hour in-service training program."[158]

The other unknown is the criteria by which parents and children are evaluated and what renders a parent who, until the divorce, was not even suspected of unfitness suddenly liable to a government parenting assessment. "If you put 10 psychiatrists or psychologists in a room, you'll get 10 different opinions," attorney Joel Mayer is quoted as saying in the *Daily News*. It is not difficult to see how pressure arises to find or manufacture problems.

Two expert opinions presented to an Acting Supreme Court Justice in New York illustrate the arbitrary nature of the testimony. The first expert diagnosed a father as having a "dysthymic disorder" marked by chronic low-level depression and a "mixed personality disorder," that included "obsessive-compulsive behavior, rigidity, grandiose thinking, and passive-aggressive traits." The second, a forensic psychiatrist, diagnosed the same father as having a "schizotypal personality disorder." Again, these diagnoses are not the reason for the custody dispute, and no one initially alleges that the father is abnormal or unfit; the divorce is initiated first, and then the psychological evaluations are invoked to justify removing his children. Hofstra University law professor Andrew Shepard asks: "What made all these people all of a sudden lunatics and unfit to parent?"

In such circumstances, the result is inevitably determined less by science and more by politics. "Word is out as to who is biased in which direction. Everybody knows," attorney William Herman tells the *Daily News*. "There are lawyers who believe that any degree of preparation for dealing with the psychiatric forensics is legitimate, including pre-testing—a pre-interview by another professional who gives tips on how to conduct a winning interview."

Even aside from their qualifications and methods, the larger question is why these "experts" are necessary in the first place, since in most cases there is no question about the fitness. Further, a parent need not agree to this invasion of his and his children's privacy to be left with the bill. Stephen Herman, associate clinical professor of psychiatry at Mount Sinai Medical Center, provides one explanation for their popularity. "A lot of psychiatrists, psychologists, and social workers are very nervous about being able to make a living," he explains. "More and more mental health professionals want to do forensic work because they can dodge managed care and sometimes get big bucks." And the bucks are big indeed, as one more group of superfluous officials accepts the open invitation to rack up fees at the expense of parents who want no part of them. "I know of cases where absolutely outrageously high fees have been charged," Herman tells the *Daily News*. Laframboise likewise found that parents were stuck with bills of up to $25,000.

The tyranny of the mental health division of the divorce industry and the results-based nature of their "science" is illustrated in a Toronto case in which the court's mental health consultant recommended using the children as a form of psychotherapy for the mother. Should custody be awarded to the father, theorized Dr. Michael Elterman, the mother "will interpret this to be a rejection of her as a parent and . . . may out of hurt, withdraw from being an active parent to the children." Elterman theorized that giving the mother sole custody "will bolster and sufficiently make secure her role with the children that she will be magnanimous in her facilitating the contact between the children and their father."

The father naturally was outraged. "What he decided was that my former wife's ego is so insecure that the children should be employed as tools to stabilize her," he told the *National Post*. "And because I love them so much, I would figure out some way—even though I didn't have custody—to protect them from the worst damage that she could do." This kind of bizarre, contorted reasoning is not unusual among experts who are wheeled on stage to provide a rationale for what they know a judge wants to hear and what will result in a steady stream of fees for all concerned.

A second psychologist described the mother as "suffused with anger and resentment. . . . This emotional state of rage within her . . . is a key to [the mother's] personality and is a dysfunctional state." Thus the children should "not be placed at risk in an emotionally unstable environment such as would appear to be the case with sole custody to their mother." This psychologist expressed dismay that Elterman would suggest that "the best interests of the children are served by placing them in a position of caretaker to a parent." Yet Justice Ian Meiklem ruled that denying the mother custody would risk "profound harm to the children's relationship with their mother" and was therefore not in their best interest. "If there is a tendency now for [the seven-year-old] to take it upon herself to comfort her mother," wrote the judge, "this tendency would assume greatly enlarged proportions if she perceived her mother as 'losing' custody."

Laframboise's investigation depicted Elterman as running a "custody report mill": "It took Dr. Elterman approximately eight working days to complete his assessment, yet his CV appeared to indicate that he was conducting in excess of 200 of them a year."

The college's professional standards committee declared that a custody assessment should take at least twenty-five hours to prepare. "By simple calculation, Dr. Elterman's statements would suggest completion of over 250 custody evaluations in one year, about one evaluation per day, an implausible achievement," said the committee.

Nevertheless, it concluded unanimously that he had violated no ethical standards and that the father's complaint should be dismissed. The father's request for a transcript of the committee's deliberations was denied on the grounds that it might expose Elterman to civil liability, betraying the ethics panel's concern to protect its own members more than the public.

Larger questions are at issue here than just whether such fathers are receiving unfair treatment; nor is the point that fathers are always the victims and mothers the perpetrators. As with most journalistic accounts, we do not and cannot know all the facts in this case; it is easy for journalists to omit key facts and subtly slant a story against a parent, as fathers in particular well know. Yet despite the possible variations in the he said/she said aspect, this case is consistent with a larger pattern regardless of whether the father or mother is the aggrieved party.

To play devil's advocate, we may consider the possibility that in this case the usual roles were reversed and the reason the mother was "suffused with anger and resentment" was because the father (a lawyer) and the courts were trying to take away her child without any grounds, in which case one might conclude she had good reason for her anger and resentment. Perhaps her husband was divorcing her without cause or had cheated on her, in which case it was he who betrayed her and their child, and she has a legitimate grievance.

Yet if this is the case, the point is the same. For what is clear from this account—and what is so universal that it is never disputed, even by those who defend the existing practice—is that these are not the criteria on which this or any other case is being decided. Rather, the court, like all such courts, abdicated its responsibility to administer justice to the innocent party and instead took refuge behind "experts" who base their judgment on highly uncertain, debatable, esoteric, and in this case apparently quite contorted social-scientific theories about what is best for someone else's child. The Soviet-style insult added to the injury is that the innocent parent (of whichever gender) would then become a candidate to generate additional fees for the therapists by being ordered into an "anger management" class.

In a second case investigated by Laframboise, the Complaints Committee of the Ontario Board of Examiners in Psychology acknowledged that custody evaluators included false accusations of spousal and child abuse and of an extramarital affair in their report on one father but concluded the errors were trivial. The father disagreed that justifications for taking away his children were trivial. "That report cost me seven years out of my children's lives," he says. " I had virtually no contact with three of my four children. I missed all their graduations, the chance to go to football games with them. My parents weren't allowed to see their grandkids." Says another father: "There are children that are being destroyed by this process, and it's for money."

JUDICIAL DECEIT?

The cronyism is so pervasive and receives so little scrutiny that complacency seems to be leading to clear illegalities. In May 1999, *Insight* magazine uncovered a private "slush fund" operated by Los Angeles family court judges and paid into by attorneys and other "court-appointed professionals." These included "monitors" who received lucrative appointments to watch fathers accused of child or spousal abuse while they were visiting their children. This involves more than payments resulting in certain individuals receiving preference; it raises the question of whether parents and children are being forced to endure (and pay for) the ordeal of having their visits monitored because the parent needed watching or because the watchers have paid the judges.

What is involved here was not simply individual lawyers bribing individual judges to favor particular cases, but a system of institutional bribery. Aside from the nonpayment of taxes and the use of the public building to house and fund a private organization, the far more serious matter is the destruction of families by creating work for those employed in destroying them. "The bar associations made donations to the judges' association," and "a great deal of money moved to the . . . accounts from direct payments by attorneys and other court personnel." Apparently the arrangement has been an open secret for years, yet oversight law-enforcement officials took no action, possibly because they were part of the system.

"Parents with business before the superior court say they feel caught in a web of judicial deceit that borders on an organized racket," writes *Insight*. "But for years their requests for the investigation fell on deaf ears, as elected officials and law-enforcement agencies did nothing." Family courts are inextricably intertwined with other branches of government, including prosecutors and law-enforcement agencies. It is hardly surprising that these failed to investigate and prosecute those who, in patronage terms, are effectively their superiors. "A dozen county, state, and federal agencies have had the opportunity to do something. . . . All failed to act." One policeman who began to investigate was ordered to shred his documents.

"I felt violated, almost numb, when I learned that the judges were making money through the child custody system," said one father. "The judges have too much power, and nobody is monitoring these guys." *Insight* describes how "court personnel are making a living by decimating the bank accounts of the litigants," who can be "subjected to psychiatric evaluations or face losing their child." "Litigants are forced to pay thousands of dollars for the services demanded by the court, not including the fees each side already is paying attorneys," the magazine reports, though this practice is not limited to Los Angeles and is not even considered illegal. "But the child-custody cash register doesn't stop ringing. The system continues to rake in money for its swarm of support personnel long after custody has been awarded." *Insight* does not mention that in most cases one litigant—the one most likely to be hit with the coerced fees—probably never asked for the divorce in the first place.[159]

These judges, lawyers, and others are unlikely ever to see the inside of a jail cell. It is highly likely that parents have been sent to jail because of their racket. It is even more likely that parents have been bankrupted by the fees of lawyers and "monitors" who have paid into the judges' fund and had their relationship with their children ruined by court-imposed separation and a regime of monitored visits. One father is said to have spent $100,000 on attorneys' fees, but in family law there is nothing extraordinary about that sum.

Similar corruption in the family courts has been the subject of investigations in Marin County, California, where parents lodged a recall petition against family court judges who were also being investigated by the FBI. The Marin judges were accused of channeling "alimony and child-support funds to attorneys who were their 'cronies' and otherwise showed 'gross favoritism' to 'certain litigants and lawyers.'" Consistent with what we have found elsewhere, the Marin judges are alleged to have approved "fee-gouging by experts and court appointees."[160]

Yet overt racketeering is only the tip of the iceberg, since the real scandal is not what is illegal but what is legal. Many quasi-legal methods exist for lawyers and psychotherapists to compensate judges for forcing citizens to hire them. Even journalists who investigate the courts have trouble grasping this distinction between the corruption of a necessary system that addresses a real problem and what is by its nature a predatory machine that itself creates the problem. *Insight* asserts that the "cozy financial connection between judges, attorneys, and some court-appointed professionals" is likely to be destroying the lives and children of litigants by influencing "the outcome of their cases." But this understates the matter: For parents and children sucked into the divorce machine against their will, it is creating their cases in the first place.

PATRONAGE, GRAFT, AND KICKBACKS

The largesse dispensed by the multibillion-dollar divorce industry is not limited to the judiciary but is spreading and corrupting other branches of government as well. Another small indication of what is almost certainly a larger practice surfaced in April 1999 when four current or former Arkansas lawmakers, including the most powerful member of the Arkansas Senate, were named in a racketeering indictment by the U.S. attorney on charges of receiving kickbacks and arranging government contracts for personal benefit, almost all connected with divorce, child custody, and child-support enforcement. One scheme was to provide legal counsel to children, known as an attorney *ad litem*.[161]

Anyone familiar with the custody business will recognize what is taking place here. The very notion of yet another lawyer in a custody battle, this time ostensibly representing the children against both their parents, is as exploitative as it sounds. In reality, this attorney is simply one more client in the judge's patronage, and parents who are horrified at the thought of having their children interrogated by a lawyer can be forced to pay the bill as part of a divorce proceeding of which they wanted no part.[162] Attorneys *ad litem* are notorious for cronyism and tend, like psychotherapists, to provide judges with a rationale for what they are disposed to do anyway. A two-year investigation into court appointments in New York state by a special inspector general found that "cronyism, politics, and nepotism" were rampant in appointments of attorneys *ad litem* and other officials.[163]

Dallas television station WFAA News 8 seems to have found a fairly typical example when it reported that lawyer Kip Allison charged two parents $65,000 for sixty-four days' work as an attorney *ad litem*. Allison admitted to spending only two of the 310 billed hours talking with the children who were ostensibly his clients. The children say it was even less. "I met him once, and we talked for like fifteen or twenty minutes," one child is quoted as saying. "The second time he didn't talk to me or Daniel. . . . He talked to my stepsister, Jessica." Reporter Valeri Williams relates, "Many family court lawyers and judges were willing to talk with us about big problems in the system with *ad litems*, but very few were willing to speak on the record for fear of retaliation in future cases."

Apparently Allison in turn hired still another attorney at $125-$150 an hour. He also arranged to collect some of his fee by taking half of the monthly child-support payment. The investigation further found that Allison and one parent's attorney "were among the top ten contributors to Judge [Craig] Fowler's 1998 campaign, and that Allison was on the campaign's steering committee."[164]

Such superfluous officials are an open invitation for precisely the kind of graft and kickbacks detailed in the Arkansas indictment. John Brummett of the *Arkansas Democrat-Gazette* writes that "no child was served by that $3 million scam to set up a program ostensibly providing legal representation to children in custody cases, but actually providing a gravy train to selected legislators and pals who were rushing around to set up corporations and send big checks to each other." As the Dallas investigation and many parents have found, attorneys *ad litem* perform few duties other than consulting with other attorneys, so there is seldom any tangible measure of whether any work is actually being performed. In fact, the wonder is that the U.S. attorney felt able to quantify the scam.

State Senator Nick Wilson says the payments he received were "no different from what is done by other attorneys in Arkansas." He may have a point, since it is clear he did virtually nothing: "It included referring other attorneys and doing administrative work regarding the program." It is an indication of the complacency of those involved that they allowed themselves such sloppiness, when a few concocted documents would probably have protected them. "Anything that I had anything to do with made money for the state," Wilson insisted. He may have a point here too, since it is ultimately the state and its operatives that benefit from this looting of parents; the children in whose name the plunder is exacted have little to do with it.[165]

The Arkansas case helps explain a less obvious part of the system: why legislators protect ethically questionable practices by judges and lawyers. Legislators are themselves often lawyers of course (and a striking number appear to be divorce lawyers),[166] but it is not always clear how they themselves profit. The courts too were not out of the loop, having approved the scheme. According to Brummett, the attorney *ad litem* program "not only sailed through the legislature without extended comment or eligibility restriction," as is usual with anything advertised for children, "but got its insider contracts expeditiously approved at the Arkansas Supreme Court, where the members are supposed to uphold our highest ideals of justice and propriety."[167]

It is worth noting that the senators were indicted not for receiving contracts by their own firms, which is apparently considered legal, but for personal kickbacks, mail fraud, and money-laundering. Here again the real scandal is not what is illegal; it is what is legal. "Legal or not, a sitting state legislator ought to choose not to profit from state contracts," writes Brummett. "Legal or not . . . sitting legislators shouldn't be receiving those regional child-support enforcement contracts." Given that judges and attorneys have close relationships with legislators in every state in America, one wonders where else children are serving as the pretext for public officials to line their pockets.

Even good programs can of course become the material for graft. The largesse flowing from involuntary divorce, however, is an open invitation for all connected with it to help themselves from the pockets of forcibly divorced parents. One lawyer involved in the Arkansas *ad litem* scheme said he was looking for a "cash cow": "He wanted a program that, when he relocated, would provide him with steady income for little work."[168]

What happened in Arkansas, like the slush fund in Los Angeles, is not likely an aberration or perversion of an otherwise benign process of government. The fundamental, underlying fact that is never pointed out in media reports or addressed by investigators or politicians, no matter how outraged a posture they adopt, is that none of these scandals could have occurred if governments had not empowered themselves to impose divorce upon unwilling and innocent parents and use it as a pretext to seize control of their children.

'WALKING BUNDLE OF CASH'

Those who witness the divorce industry firsthand testify to its destructiveness. "A custody fight is a form of child abuse," says Andrew Shepard of Hofstra University Law School. "We have a divorce system that encourages fighting, bitterness, children being caught in the middle."[169] Yet even these criticisms are in danger of becoming clichés that understate the seriousness. In fact, the naiveté of journalists, scholars, and even parents' groups constitute a formidable barrier to reform of a system that is driven not by imperfections or inefficiencies but by money and power and extremist ideology. "These systems have become very efficient little cash machines," a lawyer tells *Michigan Lawyers Weekly*, "generating profits rather than working for the best interests of children and their families."[170]

The obfuscating effect of the clichés is illustrated by columnist Heather Bird, who writes sympathetically about a perfectly fit and blameless father locked in an utterly unnecessary battle with his dead wife's sister over custody of his daughter. Like many observers, Bird is perplexed by the inanity of it all: "What followed was a probing series of assessments by social workers who examined all aspects of the extended family dynamics. They found he was a fit father but, by the time the case finally made it to court, the little girl was almost five and there was a body of thought that she had bonded so strongly with the aunt, it would be wrong to remove her."

For an explanation, Bird turns to the very officials who are staging the ordeal and profiting from it: "A psychiatrist with a specialty in family law once explained to me that there is an inherent bias in the system because of the place the concept of 'mother' holds in our culture. . . . Rejecting someone else's right to mother feels uncomfortably close to rejecting one's own mother, even on a subconscious level."

Yet behind the psychobabble the straightforward reality is obvious: The child is a walking bundle of cash. The aunt, who had no claim on the child from the start, is seeking custody because she can collect windfall child support from the father. The social workers, psychotherapists, judge, and lawyers are letting her do it because the dispute generates income for them.[171]

Those who grasp the full dimensions invariably demand that such a cynical and exploitative system simply be destroyed, root and branch. "The system of adversarial attorneys, advocacy agencies, and judges constitutes an industry that deserves to be outlawed for crimes against humanity," declares columnist Kathleen Parker. "The divorce industry has to be dismantled, burned, and buried like the monster it is."[172] Unfortunately, so many people now have a stake in the divorce industry that proposals for meaningful reform are few. Those that arise are not likely to be effective, and some are likely to make matters worse.

As the horrors of the divorce litigation become too conspicuous to ignore, proposals have been advanced for less adversarial alternatives, such as counseling and mediation. Some states are passing laws requiring divorcing couples to use "mediation" before they go to court. This sounds benign, but there is little reason to assume it will make any substantial difference. "Conciliation, understood as attempted reconciliation of spouses, appears to be less and less a feature of divorce proceedings," writes scholar Helen Alvare, who notes that it is "being replaced today by the use of mediation not to save a marriage, but to make the terms of its dissolution more amicable."[173] Mediator Judy Parejko is even more harsh. "Mediation was pitched to the public as a service that would reduce the costs of litigation," she writes. "It sounded really good. But such well-intentioned messages served to cover up that no-fault was inherently *forced* divorce."[174]

Mediation takes place, as lawyers say, "within the shadow of the law," meaning no rational party concedes anything in mediation that they know they will win in court.[175] "A mother can simply refuse to give any consideration to the children's right to know both parents, perhaps allowing the father only fortnightly contact, as she knows this is the most likely outcome in any family court situation, should the mediation break down," writes Bruce Young of the School of Behavior Sciences at the James Cook University of North Queensland in Australia. "There is no benefit or incentive to the mother at all in conducting mediation sessions with any earnest, nor is there any emphasis placed on the well-being of the children."[176] Author Robert Seidenberg reaches a similar conclusion. "With the playing field slanted overwhelmingly in favor of the mother," he says, mediation is probably "a waste of time and money."[177]

In some ways mediation is simply another means for the same officials to generate profits, since, as Alvare notes, "the ranks of mediators are filled with lawyers, mental health professionals, and social workers." Some believe that mediation, far from providing an alternative to litigation, is a mechanism for avoiding due process of law, since it "takes place without rules of evidence, without recording, and without any judicial oversight."[178] One divorce mediator, who says her court-affiliated work was terminated by a judge and who was locked out of her office for trying to repair marriages, writes of her colleagues something similar to what we have seen among attorneys: "They were in the business of mediation, charging a hefty fee for their settlement-work, and without a steady flow of customers, their business would dry up."[179]

Further, when mediation is mandated by law, it is only likely to add one more level of patronage to be dispensed by the judge for the enrichment of favored judicial courtiers. "Mandatory mediation" can be imposed on parents who never sought a divorce in the first place and whose only aim is to get their children back. Says Alvare, "Parties may be required to attend mediation *before going to court with such requests*."[180] The emphasized words reveal the true intent: not that the court will deny a divorce to the belligerent, divorcing parent until that parent mediates, but that the court will hold the children of the resisting, non-divorcing parent until that parent capitulates.

Some jurisdictions are also mandating waiting periods and parent "education" classes for divorcing couples, ostensibly designed to impress upon them the harm done to the children by animosity. In Colorado, the Children of Divorce Protection Act would "require parents with children under the age of sixteen who are considering divorce to go through a year's waiting period and six hours of education focused on the effects of the divorce on the children." Yet even this modest measure is opposed by the state's divorce industry: the Colorado Bar Association, Colorado Domestic Violence Coalition, and the Colorado chapter of the Academy of Matrimonial Lawyers.[181]

"Forty-three states have authorized courts to require divorcing spouses to attend parent education classes," according to the *New York Daily News*. "The programs offer instruction in how to behave during a divorce and afterward, for the benefit of the children."[182] Again, such palliatives create the appearance that legislators and judges are acting to address the problem. They are based on the questionable assumption that involuntary divorce is being imposed on the children and one parent by well-meaning people who need only be "educated" to behave in a civilized manner as they destroy the children's home. "We start with the premise that parents all love their children and don't want to do anything to harm them," says Elizabeth Hickey, founder and director of a course in Utah.[183] This is hardly an infallible assumption, given that the parents concerned would not be there in the first place if at least one were not knowingly placing his or her desire for a divorce ahead of the needs of the children for a family.

Ironically (but not accidentally), the effect of such programs is to shift blame onto the parent who does not want the divorce. "The fact that one parent didn't want the divorce—or that one of them had broken the promises they'd made when they were married—these were issues I was supposed to ignore in my role as a *neutral* mediator," writes Parejko.[184] This tinkering will change little because it does not address the central power imbalance in unilateral divorce and endemic to the system of removing children from their parents. More than this, however, compulsory mediation and "education" programs are also geared to perpetuating the notion that the divorce epidemic is created by "warring parents" whose equally guilty and immature behavior testifies to the need for a detached judiciary to assume parental authority and disinterested "experts" who alone can be counted on to know and act according to what is best for other people's children.

"The goal is simple," the *Daily News* reports credulously. "Defang parents before they get to court. Teach them how to behave; maybe even shame them into acting their age." Here the judges and their hangers-on adopt the pose of sage wisdom and professional detachment, peering down at the unseemly cockfight that in reality they themselves have staged and forced upon at least one of the parents. "Judges, lawyers, and mental health experts lecture parents, lead them in role-playing and show videos that portray how children react to divorce when they are used as pawns by parents." The *Daily News* does not tell us how children react to divorce when they are used as pawns by judges, lawyers, and mental health experts.

Such measures may be worse than useless. Conducted by the very people who have a stake in encouraging divorce, these programs again merely add clients to the patronage machine and further transfer control of children to operatives of the state. Revealingly, in Canada it is the bar associations that are pushing for such classes, so parents who are forcibly divorced can also be forcibly re-educated into acquiescing in the injustice that has been imposed upon them before they have a hope of seeing their children. The Canadian Bar Association urges the federal government "to require parents to take mandatory parental education before they are permitted to *pursue court proceedings involving their children.*"

At first glance, this sounds like the state is requiring parents to take the classes before it will permit the divorce, but a closer look at the careful wording reveals that the intent is precisely the opposite. It allows the state to seize your children, and if you want to get them back you must first be "educated" by government instructors. The normally skeptical *National Post* describes this as "sweeping divorce reforms." In reality, it allows the state to further substitute its authority over children for that of their parents. "We want to pull away from the idea that parents have rights in relation to their children," says Jennifer Cooper, chairwoman of the CBA's family law section, which represents 2,200 divorce lawyers.[185]

A similar measure in Virginia is similarly described in the awkward wording of the *Washington Post*, which reports that parent education classes are "mandatory for anyone, married or not, *who goes to court over custody, visitation, or child support.*" Again, the fine print reveals how the measure, far from checking divorce, will insert additional layers of officialdom between parents and their children and intimidate parents who resist. "Even lawyers are rooting for the classes," the *Post* says. This is not surprising, since it places a government imprimatur on forced divorce. One should be suspicious of any "reform" that catches on like wildfire. In just four years, from 1994 to 1998, writes Helen Alvare, the number of U.S. counties with this kind of curriculum tripled from 541 to 1,516.[186] "This basically says: Divorce isn't the death of a family. It's the reorganization of a family," says Andrew Shepard. But an innocent parent will have no say in how his family and private life are reorganized.[187]

The principle that citizens can be coercively re-"educated" into accepting government action they regard as unjust or immoral has a Maoist quality. Noting that "mobs of unhappy dads who haven't seen their children for months or years" are beginning to picket the homes of family court judges, the *Guardian* newspaper recommends that what the protesters need is "education": "The system first needs to educate parents and provide a range of services, such as mediation and parenting classes."[188] Is the curriculum of this education likely to include information on the inherently harmful emotional and social consequences we know result for children from divorce? Or is it more likely to be an indoctrination in "good divorce"?[189]

In the experience of mediator Judy Parejko, such classes "stayed away from presenting any of the dismal facts about how divorce increased certain risks for children. . . . No one ever addressed the simple fact that—in most cases—having both parents stay living together was what most every child would want."[190] No one pretends that parents who disagree with divorce in principle and refuse to attend such classes or object to the curriculum are thereby denied a divorce and left in peace with their children while the divorcing parent departs alone. Instead, resisting parents become open to charges of being "uncooperative," "angry," or "in denial," whereupon they may be ordered into more "education," such as anger management classes, until they acquiesce. They will also likely be refused access to their children until their education is complete.

One therapist airs her views in a major research publication that legally innocent parents should be forced into government psychotherapy. "I have experiences with many clients who are violently angry but who do not meet the definition of a domestic batterer," she reports. In other words, they are law-abiding citizens who are predictably upset that the government has taken away their children. "I would like to see a collaborative or subsidized program with a requirement that such people go through it."[191]

Parent re-education programs are an invitation to an even more invasive dictatorship of the psychotherapists and ring eerily of the coerced psychotherapy and psychiatric prisons used against political dissidents in the Soviet Union. "Divorce is a great destroyer that is eating the heart out of society as well as savaging children's lives," writes British scholar Patricia Morgan. "Its depredations will not be reversed given ever so many mediators or conciliators."[192]

INHERENTLY PREDATORY

The distinction between a government operation that is necessary but flawed and one whose very purpose is inherently predatory and destructive is seldom recognized by would-be reformers, journalists, and scholars who examine the proliferating divorce machinery. Yet it becomes critical when evaluating possible remedies. Courts have their own systems for self-policing, of course, but these are predictably ineffective when the problem proceeds not from individual judges but from a system that is out of control. "If I complain to the presiding judge about Judge A, the good-old-boy network is going to kick in, and it's going to hurt my client," reports one lawyer. "Family court judges have tremendous latitude in making decisions, more so in some ways than in the other courts."[193]

A potentially more fruitful avenue for reform is public investigations of the courts, which can at least have the merit of shining light on government wrongdoing. Yet the few investigations that have been conducted have been dominated by legal practitioners. Consequently, they have asked very limited and even self-serving questions, and the answers they supply could well worsen the problem. Investigations do highlight the inescapable fact that family courts are by all accounts the most unsatisfactory sector of the judiciary and the one that generates by far the highest volume of complaints. A subcommittee of the Nevada Legislature found that "more complaints are filed against family practitioners than practitioners of any other area of law, and, nationwide, more complaints against family court judges are heard by judicial ethics committees."[194] Yet the courts' shortcomings are then invariably ascribed to operations that are "poor" and "inefficient."

Formulated thus, such a finding can easily be interpreted to mean that the courts are "overburdened" or "understaffed" and that the solution can be found in a further increase in funding. An investigation by the Australian Law Reform Commission found that "family court procedures are so riddled with inefficiencies, and its cases so poorly handled, that people are being denied justice." This sounds harsh, but worded in this way it is entirely consistent with the courts' own view that the solution for the problems they create is more money, more courts, and higher salaries. The Reform Commission's report points out the family court itself has long argued that it "is under-resourced for the tasks that it performs" and contains "an insufficient numbers of judges" [sic]. The Law Council concurs that "more judges are needed in the family court."[195]

Likewise in Britain, a report to the lord chancellor written largely by lawyers and judges details how children are routinely denied contact with non-custodial parents on an enormous scale and for extended periods by custodial parents. The authors' indignation might be put in perspective by recalling that the custodial parents are only able to do this because they have the backing of the courts and police, who are the ones that forcibly banished the non-custodial parents in the first place and who will summarily jail any non-custodial parent who tries to make unauthorized contact with his children.

No suggestion is offered anywhere in the report that the most obvious and straightforward solution might simply be not to separate the children from their parents to begin with. Instead the authors recommend a large increase in both the budget and the powers allocated to the very family court apparatus that is doing the separating.[196] The head of the social workers' union describes that apparatus as "a complete shambles" but likewise proposes to increase the size of the shambles with "more resources."[197]

More recently, British judges and some American politicians have responded with measures whose effect (and perhaps aim) is to further extend judicial power. In a well-publicized case, a British mother was jailed for three months for refusing to give her child's father access to their four-year-old son. "It is believed to be one of the longest sentences given to a mother in a British dispute over child access," notes the *Daily Telegraph*. "Jailing mothers . . . is rare and, when it does take place, the sentences are usually only for a matter of days."[198]

The case illustrates how family courts, which are often rightly accused of intentionally inciting discord between couples, have learned to fan the flames of gender war on the political level as well. Feminists portrayed the mother as a martyr. Fathers' groups claim this was precisely the intention of the sentence, which they also pointed out was minor compared to the ten months meted out to fathers like Mark Harris merely for saying hello to his child on a London street. One American legislator, Steve McMillan, wants to introduce such sanctions in Alabama, saying, "I've gotten so many complaints through the years about the custodial parent being uncooperative with the non-custodial parent.[199]

But the larger question is why courts are granting mothers this absolute power in the first place and then, when fathers complain, jailing them for exercising it. Would it not be simpler (and involve less judicial intervention all around) not to give them monopoly control over the children to begin with? In a further exercise of judicial micromanagement, the British child was given to the mothers' parents, rather than to the father, while she served her sentence.

One of the few public investigations of family courts in the United States was commissioned by the Nevada Legislature in response to numerous complaints and to an investigative series in the *Las Vegas Sun* (see below). Yet from the minutes of the investigation, it is clear that the proceedings were dominated throughout by judicial officials and a few social workers. The scope of the inquiry was limited to the question of "what may be done to help the family courts become more effective and efficient" and how to meet "the need for additional judges and personnel." In other words, the legal industry managed to steer the investigation away from questions of injustice and constitutional protections into the question of how to process more divorces more rapidly and remove more children from their parents.

The fact that the courts were labeled as "inefficient" and that the inquiry focused only on "delays" and large "caseloads" merely vindicates Dickens's principle that the aim of a bureaucratic judiciary is to expand its operations by pulling more citizens into its grip. The commission avoided questions such as why government officials were intervening in citizens' private lives or by what authority judges and other government officials are permitted to separate children from parents who have committed no legal infraction.

Only when litigants began to testify in the final stages of the investigation did the commission begin hearing about substantive issues of justice and injustice, constitutional principle, and due process of law. What is striking about the public grievances is how they involved fundamental questions of justice and due process that most of us in a free society take for granted. One father suggested the courts should "permit litigants to give testimony prior to rulings." A woman urged that officials "should not have the authority to seal court records" and that the practice of clerks "tampering or manipulating court case files" may have an adverse impact on cases. She also urged that "judges should not be given absolute authority to incarcerate family court litigants" without trial. She thought "litigants must be given an opportunity to face and respond to their accusers in court." She and another mother believed that knowingly false accusations of domestic violence and other crimes should be punished.

A father submitted a report alleging that the family court operated entirely outside the bounds of the Constitution. He thought that "denying litigants the right to an evidentiary hearing" was not entirely proper and that "litigants must be able to hear evidence and cross-examine witnesses." He pointed out that litigants had no access to court documents, such as "evidence and testimony collected," nor did they have "the opportunity to respond to allegations and the right to confront their accusers." Numerous parents spoke angrily of "corruption" in the courts and of not being permitted to see their children for years.[200]

Yet none of the judicial officials who dominated the proceedings even acknowledged any of these grievances, either to deny their accuracy, to offer to look into them, to voice concern that such serious allegations could contain some truth, or to correct them if verified. Neither did the legislators. Almost ten years after the investigation, none of the reforms pertaining to basic due process proposed by the litigants has even been debated, let alone implemented. As if to illustrate the consequences, Nevada's family courts became the focus of national attention in June 2006 when a family court judge was shot, allegedly by a litigant.

A more penetrating investigation of the family court system in Butler County, Ohio, was conducted by County Commissioner Michael Fox, who released a scathing report in May 2003. "The Domestic Relations and Juvenile Courts of Butler County foster a culture of secrecy, fear and judicial abuse that violates the most fundamental and sacred rights guaranteed by our nation's Constitution—the rights of due process of the laws," he wrote. Fox asserted that litigants "are routinely excluded from court proceedings and deliberations, told to wait outside the hearing room in a hallway while their lives, personal property, children and homes are divided up by strangers." None of the points in Fox's complaint appears to be unique to Butler County:

> The world of juvenile and domestic relations is a secret world where the courts treat public scrutiny with open contempt and hostility. The pretense for this secrecy is to protect families from embarrassing disclosures about their personal and private lives. The real function, however, is to protect the court from public scrutiny and oversight.
>
> . . . The outrage is muted by an incestuous network of insiders who are spared the crucible of public scrutiny by a system that operates behind locked doors, disciplined by a real fear of being punished if the members ever break ranks and rail against the injustice they see daily.[201]

In response to the report, the county's Republican Party held a private meeting and told Fox to back off or risk losing the party's endorsement when he came up for re-election, "Mike Fox's political future was threatened over this disagreement with the domestic relations court," said a Republican insider.[202]

Inquiries by journalists are hardly more probing than those of legislatures and suffer from the absence of records in what amount to secret courts. One newspaper reported in its weeklong investigative series into family courts in 1997 that "[i]nadequate court records prevented the *Las Vegas Sun* from thoroughly investigating allegations of judicial gender bias and poor case management."[203] As this wording indicates, the newspaper (like the Nevada Legislature) was more concerned with inefficiency than corruption.

An investigation of British family courts reported in a lengthy three-part series in the *Observer* newspaper in July 2000 was similarly scathing—but also similarly circumscribed—in the harsh language it used to indict the courts for injustice and inefficiency in what it clearly wanted to convey was a serious scandal. Yet when it came to details, the newspaper only pointed out that "budget constraints mean the [court] staff get only three to five days extra training a year." In the final installment of the series, the newspaper quotes a judge who writes in to say that the injustices can be rectified with more money and more judges. "Although the word 'resources' did not figure in the articles, it does in fact go a long way to explain the problem," contends the ostensibly outraged judge, "because the necessary number of judges and courtrooms are not being resourced/funded by central government."[204]

The question not being asked here is why it should be assumed that more funding, more judges, and more courts will have any result other than more divorces, more sole custody awards, and more fatherless children.

Two potential reforms that are gaining in popularity (and vehemently opposed by divorce officials) are a roll-back of no-fault divorce laws and a presumption of joint custody or "shared parenting" in cases of divorce and unwed childbirth. Both are under consideration by state and national legislatures. Both contain promise, though the danger is that the formality will be legislated while the substance is ignored, since courts can find ways to circumvent measures that limit their power. In any case, the merits of these proposals will be assessed more effectively after we have considered the operations of the divorce regime in more detail.[205]

In the meantime, one method is already available to curb the power of the divorce regime. It would be both safe and effective and does not involve pretentious social science, sophisticated social engineering, or voluminous policy papers. It requires few experts and hardly any studies or statistics. It does not require complicated changes in family policy. And it demands no additional spending. It is simple and old-fashioned—though not, given entrenched interests, necessarily easy. It is why our courts exist and what every public official at every level of government is formally sworn to do: enforce the Constitution.

Unfortunately, as we will see in the next chapter, the courts and their friends are now doing precisely the opposite.

Chapter 2

DIVORCE AND THE CONSTITUTION

Parents have the natural right to be with their own children, unless they are guilty of some egregious act. . . . Stealing children from their own parents has historically been considered one of the most inhuman acts of tyrannical dictators. . . . Slave owners sold the children of their own slaves to other men. Today we are appalled by knowledge of such inhumanity.

— Bai Macfarlane[206]

There is no crueler tyranny than that which is perpetrated under the shield of law and in the name of justice.

— Montesquieu

A dvocates of unilateral divorce often portray it as a "liberating experience" and claim it is a "citizen's right" and even a "civil liberty."[207] Yet when children are involved, it is no exaggeration to say that the regime of involuntary divorce has become the most authoritarian institution in our society today.

Contrary to general assumption, divorce today involves much more than spouses simply deciding to part ways. While divorce is often considered a "private" matter and therefore immune from the scrutiny of scholars, journalists, and the public, it raises fundamental questions about the government's role in private life. Far more than marriage, divorce by its nature requires active government intervention. Marriage creates a private household, which may or may not necessitate signing some legal documents. Divorce dissolves a private household, usually against the wishes of one spouse. It inevitably involves the state—including police and prisons—to enforce the divorce and the post-marriage order. Otherwise, one spouse might continue to claim the protections and pre-rogatives of private life: the right to live in the common home, to possess the common property, or—most vexing of all—to parent the common children.

Few people stopped to consider the implications of laws that shifted the breakup of private households from a voluntary to an involuntary process. If marriage is not a wholly private affair, involuntary divorce by its nature requires constant supervision over private life by state officials. Unilateral divorce, by its very nature, inescapably involves government agents evicting people from their homes, confiscating their property, and separating them from their children. Far from being a private matter, it inherently denies not only the inviolability of marriage but the very concept of a private sphere of life.

Proceeding from this, no-fault divorce introduced novel concepts into the legal system, such as the principle that one could be decreed guilty of violating an agreement that one had, in fact, not violated. "According to therapeutic precepts, the fault for marital breakup must be shared, even when one spouse unilaterally seeks a divorce," observes author Barbara Whitehead. "Many husbands and wives who did not seek or want divorce were stunned to learn . . . that they were equally 'at fault' in the dissolution of their marriages."[208]

The "fault" that was ostensibly thrown out the front door of divorce pro-ceedings re-entered through the back, but now without precise definition. The judiciary was expanded from its traditional role of punishing crime or tort to punishing personal imperfections and private differences: suddenly, one could be summoned to court without having committed any legal infraction; the ver-dict was pre-determined before any evidence was examined; and one could be found "guilty" of things that were not illegal. "Lawmakers eliminated a useful inquiry process and replaced it with an automatic outcome," writes Judy Pare-jko, author of *Stolen Vows*. "No other court process is so devoid of recourse for a defendant. When one spouse files for divorce, his/her spouse is automatically found 'guilty' of irreconcilable differences and is not allowed a defense."[209]

The "automatic outcome" quickly expanded into what effectively became a presumption of guilt against the forcibly divorced spouse ("defendant"). The very involvement of the judiciary, with its handmaid, the penal apparatus—machinery ordinarily reserved for punishing criminal or civil wrongdoing—indicates how marriage dissolution blurs distinctions our justice system was previously at pains to delineate carefully: private versus public, civil versus criminal, therapy versus justice, sin versus crime. When government stopped enforcing the marriage contract it began enforcing the divorce decree. The result was not the removal of the state from family life but an explosion of extensive and intrusive governmental instruments whose sole purpose is intervention in families. Once again, the leverage comes through children.

A CRIME TO BE A PARENT?

The right of parents to raise and care for their children without interference by the state has long been recognized by the Supreme Court and other federal courts as among the most fundamental rights of American citizens. Numerous judicial decisions have held that parenthood is an "essential" right, that "undeniably warrants deference, and, absent a powerful countervailing interest, protection." Parenthood "cannot be denied without violating those fundamental principles of liberty and justice which lie at the base of all our civil and political institutions."[210] Parental rights have been characterized by the courts as "sacred" and "inherent, natural right[s], for the protection of which, just as much as for the protection of the rights of the individual to life, liberty, and the pursuit of happiness, our government is formed."[211]

A substantial body of federal case law recognizes parenting as a "liberty interest," a basic constitutional right protected under the Fourteenth Amendment: "The liberty interest and the integrity of the family encompass an interest in retaining custody of one's children, and thus a state may not interfere with a parent's custodial right absent due process protections." A federal court has held that "the parent-child relationship is a liberty interest protected by the due process clause of the Fourteenth Amendment." Likewise, a parent's "right to the care, custody, management and companionship of [his or her] minor children" is an interest "far more precious than . . . property rights." Justice Thurgood Marshall wrote in another case, "We have recognized on numerous occasions that the relationship between parent and child is constitutionally protected," and "a (once) married father who is separated or divorced from a mother and is no longer living with his child" could not be treated differently from a father who is married and still living with his child.

As recently as 2000, the Supreme Court has reiterated that "parental rights are absolute": "The liberty interest at issue . . . the interest of parents in the care, custody, and control of their children—is perhaps the oldest of the fundamental liberty interests recognized by this Court. . . . [I]t cannot now be doubted that the Due Process Clause of the Fourteenth Amendment protects the fundamental right of parents to make decisions concerning the care, custody, and control of their children."[212]

I labor this point somewhat because the current practice of family courts is to act as if such precedents simply do not exist. One might expect these apparently unequivocal constitutional principles would be clear and strong enough to protect the rights of parents and their children not to be arbitrarily separated. Yet they are simply ignored in cases of involuntary divorce. It is not difficult to see why. The age-old principle stipulating, in the words of Supreme Court Justice Byron White, a "realm of family life which the state cannot enter"[213] is a direct threat to the *raison d'etre* of family courts, whose very existence is predicated on the principle that no realm of life is too private for the intervention of the government.

Before the divorce revolution and the rise of family courts, legal authority over children had long been recognized to reside with their parents. "For centuries it has been a canon of law that parents speak for their minor children," wrote Justice Potter Stewart. "So deeply embedded in our traditions is this principle of the law the Constitution itself may compel a state to respect it."[214] We have already seen that family courts have transferred from parents to themselves the authority to determine what is best for children, to the point where they routinely rule that the "best interest" of children lies in removing them from parents who have done nothing wrong and appointing lawyers to speak for children against their parents. Here too the new courts can be seen to be directly antithetical to ancient traditions and precedents of common law, for the very existence of family court proceeds from the principle that "the child's best interest is perceived as being independent of the parents, and a court review is held to be necessary to protect the child's interests."[215]

The implications extend far beyond family law. A very fundamental shift has taken place here in the power of government over private life, without the slightest opposition or even notice. If parents do not have ultimate control over their children (absent some legally recognized transgression by which they forfeit it), they effectively have no private lives, and government becomes total. Parents who resist the government's assumption of control over their children—not necessarily by open defiance but simply by exercising the ordinary acts of parenthood—become criminals, and those acts of parenthood, such as being with your children and making decisions about them, become criminal acts. Parenthood itself is criminalized.

While parents generally are the principal impediments to the expanding power of the courts, and while mothers also fall afoul of family court judges, it is the father whose presence constitutes an intact family and against whom the enmity of the judges is largely directed. In fact, it is no exaggeration to say that the existence of family courts, and virtually every issue they adjudicate—divorce, custody, child abuse, child-support enforcement, even adoption and juvenile crime—depend upon one overriding principle: remove the father. So long as fathers remain with their families, family courts have little reason to exist, since the problems they handle seldom arise in intact families. The power to remove the father is the cardinal power of family court.

This comes out, somewhat inadvertently, in a three-part investigative series in the *Observer* newspaper depicting behavior typical of family court judges. "The reasons given in reports as to why a father's access should be restricted or denied often seem arbitrary, to put it mildly," the newspaper comments. Any rationalization is clearly adequate; just get the father out:

> One applicant had cancer which . . . "could be upsetting" for his child. A man might be said to "lack sensitivity" or be "over-enthusiastic" or even "father-centered"—for which tendency one man was denied all contact with his child. In one case, it was noted disapprovingly that a father had told his son he preferred Scrabble to Monopoly and thought hyacinths smelled sweeter than roses. This was seen as "taking the lead in contact"—a form of emotional abuse, according to the reporting officer. One father wore a black shirt, which "could be intimidating." Another stood accused of "losing his temper with customs officials in a French airport" . . . and was therefore said to have an "unfortunate disposition." One report could find no reason why a child should not see more of his father but went on to conclude: "Nonetheless, the mother must be concerned about something." The father's contact was limited to two hours every six weeks.[216]

DOES THE CONSTITUTION APPLY?

For all the outpouring of concern about the family and judicial power in recent years, it is strange that so little attention is ever focused on the institution where the two meet: family courts. This is especially strange when one considers that the crisis of the family has coincided with a marked erosion of public respect for the legal profession and a widespread belief that the judiciary has assumed powers it was never intended to have.[217] Family courts are without question the arm of the state that routinely reaches farthest into the private lives of individuals and families. The very idea of a "family" court—whose rulings are enforced by plainclothes officials who amount to family police—should alert us to danger. Yet far from scrutinizing these tribunals, we give them virtually unchecked power. Shrouded in secrecy and leaving no record of their proceedings, they are accountable to virtually no one.[218] "The family court is the most powerful branch of the judiciary," according to Robert Page, presiding judge of the Family Part of the Superior Court of New Jersey. By their own assessment, writes Page, "the power of family court judges is almost unlimited."[219]

Predictably, with unlimited power, these courts are out of control. The eminent Roscoe Pound once observed that "the powers of the Star Chamber were a trifle in comparison with those of our juvenile court and courts of domestic relations."[220] The lowest and least prestigious sector of Alexander Hamilton's "least dangerous branch" of government, family courts routinely separate children from parents who have done nothing wrong, ignore due process of law, and even silence political dissent.

"Michigan courts do not provide a fair, or impartial, tribunal for any domestic relations litigant," says one attorney. "Instead, they customarily and regularly deprive litigants of due process of law."[221] As Pound indicates, these courts now occupy a place in our political system reminiscent of the dreaded "prerogative" courts of High Commission and Star Chamber in seventeenth-century England or the notorious chancery court in the nineteenth century. Malcolm X once described family court as "modern slavery," and Supreme Court Justice Abe Fortas characterized them with the term "kangaroo court."[222]

Though the system for adjudicating family law is different in each jurisdiction, the essential pattern is similar. Family courts describe themselves as courts of "equity" (or more pretentiously, "chancery") rather than "law." Strikingly, they do not consider themselves necessarily bound by due process of law, including the Bill of Rights; nor are the rules of evidence as stringent as in criminal courts. As one father reports being told by the chief investigator for the administrator of the courts in New Jersey, investigating a complaint of judicial wrongdoing: "The provisions of the U.S. Constitution do not apply in domestic relations cases since they are determined in a court of equity rather than a court of law."[223]

The Eleventh Amendment to the Constitution has been interpreted by judges to render themselves immune from lawsuits,[224] and they are protected from federal oversight by the "domestic relations exception," a blanket refusal by federal courts to review any case involving family law, even when it includes violations of fundamental constitutional rights.[225] As we have seen, family courts are accountable only to review boards dominated by bar associations.[226]

Divorce and the Constitution

Family courts usually operate behind closed doors and generally do not record their proceedings. Ostensibly the secrecy is to protect the family privacy of litigants, though more often it has precisely the opposite effect: The secrecy provides a cloak not to protect privacy but to invade it with impunity. "Is it possible," asks columnist Al Knight with reference to legislation that would automatically seal all family court records, "that the district court judges, divorce lawyers, special advocates and guardians *ad litem*, and a cadre of social workers might simply like less public attention paid to their activities?"[227]

The courts having successfully asserted the power to remove children from legally innocent parents, other violations of basic constitutional rights and civil liberties flow logically—and almost inexorably, much as one lie necessitates another. The entire divorce regime is nothing less than a massive assault on every major principle of the U.S. Constitution. One can run point by point down the Bill of Rights and other articles, and there is hardly one that is not routinely violated by family courts.

First Amendment guarantees of freedom of expression and religion have long been understood to include parents' relationships with their children. Yet family court judges routinely control what parents may say and do with their children, including what religious worship they may or must attend and what they may discuss in private, as well as what they may say about their legal case in public.

A 1997 ruling of the Massachusetts Supreme Court prohibiting a father from taking his children to Christian services received some media attention but no opposition from either churches or civil libertarians.[228] In Arlington, Virginia, a judge's 1997 injunction prohibiting a father from taking his son to Bar Mitzvah was reversed only after a protest in front of the county courthouse. The father's attorney, Charles Janus, called the order "a violation of the First Amendment right to freedom of religion" and due process.[229] In Arkansas, a father is ordered to take his child to the church of the mother's choice during his visitation time.[230] A vegetarian father in Arlington shows a court order preventing him from discussing "diet" with his children. A Missouri father cannot take his son to political meetings. An Arizona father is "restrained and enjoined from discussing with [his sixteen-year-old daughter] his claims that the attorneys involved in the case, and any judge that has been involved in the case, have acted improperly or in an illegal manner," reads one court order. "They are not to be discussed."

These are not isolated incidents. "The best interests test leaves courts free to make custody decisions based on parents' speech, and to issue orders restricting their speech," writes law professor Eugene Volokh. "This willingness of courts to disfavor a broad range of parental ideologies—. . . atheist or fundamentalist, racist or pro-polygamist, pro-homosexual or anti-homosexual—should lead us to take a hard look at the doctrine that allows such results."[231] Volokh documents how routine practices and rulings issued in family courts throughout America stand in direct violation of First Amendment protections and control intimate details of citizens' private lives: "Courts have . . . ordered parents to reveal their homosexuality to their children, or to conceal it. They have ordered parents not to swear in front of their children, and to install Internet filters. They have also considered, as a factor in the custody decision, parents' swearing, exposing their children to R-rated movies, a gun-themed magazine, unfiltered Internet access, photos of men in women's clothing, music with vulgar sexual content, and pornography."

All this is justified under the "best interests of the child" standard, which "leaves family court judges ample room to consider a parent's ideology":

> One parent, for instance, was ordered to "make sure that there is nothing in the religious upbringing or teaching that the minor child is exposed to that can be considered homophobic," because the other parent was homosexual. Parents have had their rights reduced based, in part, on their having told their children that the other parent was destined for damnation, or otherwise criticizing the other parent's religion. A court could likewise restrict a father's teaching his children that women must be subservient to men, since such speech might undermine the mother's authority.

Under the guise of protecting children from their own parents, the courts use the children as hostages to control the political expression of adults. "Many parents who know that certain speech might make a difference in their custody battles are likely to be deterred by this risk," writes Volokh. "Risk-averse parents may be deterred even by small risks, especially when the harm (loss of custody) is so grave."

Parents' attempts to educate their children in their own beliefs and instill in them religious or civic values are prohibited by family court judges. "Courts have restricted a parent's religious speech when such speech was seen as inconsistent with the religious education that the custodial parent was providing. The cases generally rest on the theory . . . that the children will be made confused and unhappy by the contradictory teachings, and will be less likely to take their parents' authority seriously," writes Volokh. "In one case . . . a court ordered 'that each party will impress upon the children the need for religious tolerance and not permit any third party to attempt to teach them otherwise.'"

So forced divorce allows officials the power to prohibit parents from confusing their children. Courts also prohibit parents from telling children of court orders restricting what they can tell them, "on the theory that such discussions are likely to remind the children about tension between the parents, or are likely to be accompanied by explicit or implied criticism of the other parent."

Once again, lest it be argued that parents necessarily surrender certain freedoms when they decide to divorce, parents who have not agreed to a divorce or who vigorously oppose it can still be stripped of these protections. "Child custody speech restrictions may be imposed on a parent even when the family's unity was abrogated by the other parent," Volokh observes. "The law here doesn't distinguish the leaving parent from the one who gets left." In other words, a law-abiding citizen minding his own business loses his First Amendment protections the moment his spouse files for divorce, without legal grounds, and turns the children over to government control.

Further, even divorce may not be necessary for the government to monitor and prohibit parental expression. "The law almost never restricts parental speech in intact families," Volokh notes. "You are free to teach your child racism, Communism, or the propriety of adultery or promiscuity. Judges won't decide whether your teachings confuse the child, cause him nightmares, or risk molding him into an immoral person. Judges won't enjoin the speech, or transfer custody to other people whose teachings will be more in the child's best interest." Yet this realm may also be threatened. "It's not clear that ideological restrictions limited to child custody disputes will stay limited," Volokh adds. "The government sometimes wants to interfere with parents' teaching their children even when there is no dispute between parents. . . . Many of the arguments supporting child custody speech restrictions . . . would also apply to restrictions imposed on intact families."[232]

Family law also criminalizes public speech and freedom of the press. In many jurisdictions it is a crime to criticize family court judges or otherwise discuss family law cases publicly. Parents like Alice Tulanowksi of New Brunswick, New Jersey, are placed under gag rules preventing them from publicly disclosing how government officials have taken control of their families and private lives. Yet officials themselves, and even private organizations such as the New Jersey Chapter of the Association of Family and Conciliation Courts, are "free to discuss the intimate details of Alice's case" in public meetings.[233]

Stanley Rains of Victoria, Texas, was cut off from his daughter for more than two years and gagged "from speaking, writing, or publishing his opinions" about the case, according to court documents. The order covers private conversations and correspondence, including contacts with mental health professionals and his minister. Issued April 21, 2001, with no evidentiary hearing and no official request, the order followed an article Rains published describing the harrowing conditions in supervised visitation centers.[234] He was also prohibited from distributing campaign literature critical the courts and of a political candidate who was a divorce lawyer, six days before the election. The order further precluded Rains from taking photographs of death threats written on the car of his eighty-year-old mother. "The tremendous power a judge assumes with office does not include the right to be free of criticism," his attorney, David Sibley, stated in a motion.[235]

Likewise, Kevin Thompson of Methuen, Massachusetts, received an order in March 2006 from family court Judge Mary Manzi prohibiting distribution of his book, *Exposing the Corruption in the Massachusetts Family Courts*. The court also impounded the records of Thompson's custody case, including its own order.[236] Manzi herself is sharply criticized in the book but did not recuse herself from the proceeding. The standard justification for secret courts is the one Manzi extended to censorship: "privacy interests of the parties' minor child." Yet Thompson's son had already been forcibly separated from his father, and his life was under the total supervision of state officials, so it is difficult to see what "privacy" the child had left. Thompson insisted that the true reason for the secrecy and censorship was not to protect family privacy but to invade it with impunity. "The only interests that are protected," he says, "are the interests of the racketeers and hypocrites who invade 'family privacy' by removing loving fathers from the lives of their children against their will and without just cause to fill their pockets."

As we have seen, many have trouble believing the harrowing tales of human rights abuses now taking place in American family courts and wonder why, if they are true, we do not hear more about it. One explanation is that such censorship is successful.

In Australia, it is a crime for a party to a family law case to speak publicly in any way concerning family courts, even if his own case is not mentioned, and fathers there have been arrested for doing so. Under Section 121 of the Australian Family Law Act, it is an offense to publish or disseminate any information which may identify or tend to identify any party to the proceedings in the family court. Yet here too the one exemption is the family court itself, which may publish cases, complete with names, on the Internet "in the interests of the legal profession."[237]

When an Australian father published a poem to his son on the Internet he had to do so anonymously, even though there was no reference to his or any other legal case. A group in Sydney planning a peaceful protest on the steps of the Family Court in 1998 (according to a source that cannot be identified precisely because of this rule) were told that "if any people who had any involvement with family court were identified in the group shots, the media and that person would be prosecuted to the fullest extent" of the law. The protesters wore black hooded masks.

In an admission of the role courts themselves play in child kidnappings, parents and the federal police who are involved in locating missing children must apply to the court for permission to publish the fact that their children are missing. When British father Len Miskulin launched a hunger strike in December 2000 in protest being cut off from his children, his ordeal was described in the *Daily Mail* newspaper. The British family courts responded by issuing a gag order against the press and public prohibiting the "dissemination" of any information about Miskulin or the strike. The order was issued "*ex parte*," meaning no one representing Miskulin or the media was informed of the hearing or present at it. Judge H. H. J. Tyrer also issued a "penal notice" criminalizing violations and included mention of news already published by the *Daily Mail*.[238]

The Australia Family Court, ostensibly an impartial and apolitical tribunal that dispenses equal justice to all parties, also publishes attacks on fathers' groups, which it describes as "a concerted lobby of disaffected individuals whose relationship breakdown had become an obsession."[239] Chief Justice Alastair Nicholson, who has served as president of the U.S.-based Association of Family and Conciliation Courts, also engages in polemic, telling a conference that fathers' groups constitute a "sinister element" that "have an agenda to change the law to the disadvantage of women."[240] Nicholson actively engages in public feuds with lawmakers over legislation to reform the family court.[241]

Australian family courts have closed Internet sites operated by parents' groups.[242] Likewise in Britain, "The Lord Chancellor . . . has shut down a Web site because it was being used to criticise judges," reports the *Independent*. "The case has serious implications for freedom of expression."[243] Also in Britain, the attorney general "is asking the High Court to jail a businessman who has accused senior judges of corruption, perjury, and mafia-like behaviour." He is charged with "scandalising the court," an arcane form of contempt that has not been prosecuted in Britain since 1931. Geoffrey Scriven "has accused judges up to the highest levels of covering up alleged legal misconduct in his divorce case. He faces an indefinite prison sentence if found guilty."[244] "Scandalising the court" is also considered an "old, rarely used" form of contempt in Australia, where it has similarly been resurrected to prosecute fathers for picketing outside family court.[245]

Resurrecting archaic laws to prosecute their critics is becoming popular among judges. While citizens cannot sue judges they accuse of violating their rights, apparently judges can now use the criminal justice system to punish citizens who criticize them. In New Brunswick, a citizen "faces a prison term for criticizing a judge." In January 2002, Stephen Osbourne was charged in Saint John with defamatory libel, a rarely used section of the Canadian criminal code, for criticizing a family court judge "by exhibiting placards with defamatory writings" in front of a government building. His attorney, Brian Munro, points out that the charges are in direct violation of the right to free expression, guaranteed in the Canadian Charter of Rights and Freedoms. The Law Reform Commission of Canada had considered removing the statute from the code in 1986, but in 1998 the Supreme Court of Canada upheld a conviction under it, also in a family court case involving "placards in front of a courthouse."[246]

In the United States, fathers who criticize family courts report that their children are used as weapons to silence their dissent. This by its nature is difficult to prove, but attorneys regularly advise their clients not to join fathers' rights groups, speak to the press, or otherwise express public criticism of judges. "I'm a police officer in D.C., but I live in Maryland," writes one correspondent who cannot be identified. "I was advised by my attorney NOT to join fathers' rights groups as the judges deem them too militant, so I've never had formal contact with any of them."

This man's fear is justified by the judges' own words. In a paper funded by the U.S. Justice Department, the National Council of Juvenile and Family Court Judges, an association of ostensibly impartial judges who sit on actual cases, attacks fathers' groups for their "patriarchal values" and for advocating "the rights of fathers instead of their responsibilities." While the paper stops short of explicitly stating that all fathers are wife beaters and child abusers, it claims that their constitutional rights are "at odds with the safety needs of the rest of the family." The supposedly politically neutral judges further ask, "How can we learn to counter the sound bites of fathers' rights groups?"[247]

Parents who publish works critical of the courts find their writings introduced as evidence against them in the same courts they have criticized. The former husband of singer Wynonna Judd was arrested and jailed for talking to reporters about his divorce."[248] In the protest at the Arlington, Virginia, courthouse in 1997 sheriff's deputies photographed the demonstrators. On Fathers' Day 1998, a father in California was planning to protest the fact that he had not seen his son in more than two years by staging a "mock hanging" of a father's effigy outside his home. Five squad cars and eight officers from the Los Angeles Police Department surrounded his residence, apprehended him, and took him into custody for a "psychiatric evaluation."[249] Scott Huminski, of Bennington, Vermont, was forcibly evicted from the Rutland County courthouse grounds for posting a sign on his truck critical of a family court judge.[250]

American judges are also closing Internet sites. A California judge shut down the Web site of a group called the Committee to Expose Dishonest and Incompetent Attorneys and Judges. Judge Francisco Firmat of Orange County, California, Superior Court ordered that the Web site, Amoralethics.com, be "disassociated [sic] and disconnected from all Internet search engines, indexes, and providers."[251] Texas Attorney General Greg Abbott formally asked a federal court to punish Charles Edward Lincoln, who holds a Ph.D. in political anthropology from Harvard University and is a University of Chicago Law School graduate, for criticizing the state's family courts. Abbott termed Lincoln's criticism, which consisted of filing some legal papers, as "bloodless terrorism."[252]

Intimidating parents for peaceful political activity is another method for discouraging dissent. In Alabama, "Employees at two Montgomery County courthouses are being told to be on the lookout for a man who made threats against a family court judge on the radio, authorities say." But the "threats" were described as "subtle, innuendo-type," and the only example was calling a judge a "crook."[253] Another activist "found himself under investigation" and police pounding on his door at 11:20 p.m. after he circulated a news story about the shooting of a judge."[254]

Ordering parents into forced labor is another effective method of stopping their mouths. According to court transcripts, John Murtari of Syracuse, New York, was jailed in July 2000 and told by the judge to work overtime hours rather than criticizing the courts. "If you put all the efforts you had in reforming the system, if you directed those specifically in paying child support, your life and Domenic's would be much better," the judge told Murtari. But the judge's concern for Domenic was by his own admission a facade, for apparently the harm to Domenic's life from the loss of earnings (not to mention the forced absence of his father) did not prevent him from jailing Dominic's father for six months. "Your continuing incarceration may be a detriment to Domenic. But that's not the question," the judge added. "The question is not best interests of the child at this point."[255]

Despite the constitutional guarantee of a right to petition the government for redress of grievances, a father is "restrained and enjoined from having any communication or contact with the Honorable Joseph L. Battle, circuit judge of Madison County, Alabama, . . . or members of his staff." A Virginia judge in 1999 directed a court official to monitor and report to the court on a father's published political writings critical of family courts, and his private correspondence.

A stark demonstration of how the confiscation of property can be used to curtail free speech and criminalize opposition was provided in Georgia. Following his congressional testimony critical of the state's family courts, Jim Wagner of the Georgia Council for Children's Rights was stripped of custody of his two children and ordered to pay $6,000 in fees to attorneys he had not hired. When he could not pay within fifteen days, he was arrested and jailed. "Instead of administering justice and applying the law, the court is attempting to punish Wagner for exposing the court's gender bias and misconduct to a congressional committee," said Sonny Burmeister, then president of the GCCR.[256]

The Fourth Amendment protects the "right of the people to be secure in their persons, houses, papers, and effects against unreasonable searches and seizures." Yet as we have seen, parents suspected of no legal wrongdoing and who have given no grounds or agreement for divorce are routinely ordered without warrants to surrender not only their children but personal diaries, notebooks, correspondence, financial records, and other documents. Those unwilling or unable to produce the demanded documents can be fined, ordered to pay attorneys' fees, and summarily incarcerated. We have also seen that fathers are regularly interrogated behind closed doors about intimate family matters most parents would not normally discuss with strangers, such as conversations with their children and spouse, and they can be jailed for failing to answer.[257]

On December 3, 1999, Peter Dougherty was placed in solitary confinement by "Judicial Commissioner" (not judge) Sylvia Shapiro-Pritchard of the Marin County, California, Superior Court for refusing to answer questions about his private life and for questioning the commissioner's credentials. "Ms. Shapiro-Pritchard became very angry, shouting at Peter: 'Shut up! Shut up! Shut up!'" according to one account, and then ordered the bailiff to incarcerate him.[258] In shades of Soviet psychiatry, citizens who refuse to submit to this inquisition—and even those who do not—can be ordered to undergo a "mental evaluation."

Fathers against whom no evidence of wrongdoing is presented are now routinely ordered to submit to "plethysmographs," where an electronic sheath is placed over the penis while the father is forced to watch pornographic films involving children.[259] Parents' homes are routinely entered by government agents to determine fitness, even when it has never been questioned. If the strains of losing their children or undergoing this legal nightmare are too great, parents are wise to conceal any contact with therapists, family counselors, or physicians, since these otherwise privileged consultations and records can be demanded, examined, and used to separate them from their children. Parents swept into this litigation are terrified to discuss anything with their children or spouses (or anyone) for fear that what they say will be used against them in court. This of course is likely the intent.

"Uncontrolled search and seizure is one of the first and most effective weapons in the arsenal of every arbitrary government," wrote Supreme Court Justice Robert Jackson, shortly after serving at the Nuremberg trials in 1949. "Among deprivations of rights, none is so effective in cowing a population, crushing the spirit of the individual and putting terror in every heart." Family courts routinely use children as informers against their parents, to monitor compliance with court orders and to report on how they otherwise conduct their private lives.[260] The vegetarian father mentioned above reports his children are used to verify his compliance with court-ordered dietary prohibitions and prohibited conversations.

Family courts also routinely use children to control the personal behavior of their parents. Ohio Judge William Chinnock gratuitously ordered the divorcing parents of one girl not to smoke or allow anyone else to smoke in her presence, though she was healthy and neither parent had requested the ban. Ironically but characteristically, Chinnock refused to comment on the authority by which he could use a child to control her parents' personal behavior, citing "privacy rules of juvenile court."[261]

According to the *New York Law Journal*, a non-custodial mother risks losing visitation with her son because she smokes, though the boy is healthy. Talk show host Dennis Prager called this "an unprecedented ruling" and "one of many candidates for Scariest Ruling of the Year."[262] In fact, it is unusual only in that it involves a mother; fathers routinely receive similar orders and worse. A father in Tennessee was threatened with jail for giving his son an unauthorized haircut[263] and, according to court documents, had his weekend visitation reduced when a judge decided that basketball was a more important Sunday activity than church.

Though the courts claim that the secrecy in which they operate is necessary to protect family privacy, the personal information they coerce from parents is readily available to anyone. Thus the secrecy would seem to be protecting family privacy less than judges. Butler County Commissioner Michael Cox has described inconsistencies in the secrecy rules governing his county's family courts and how easily private information coerced from involuntary litigants is readily available to anyone who seeks it. Cox writes:

> Every document filed in a domestic relations case must contain some of the most private information about a person's life. . . . The public can go to the Clerk's office or Web site and get a person's Social Security number, dates of birth, unlisted telephone number, and a host of other personal information, but cannot get the name of the judge assigned to the case. . . . The Clerk of Courts is required to make an individual's most private information fully available to the public, but is prohibited from publishing the identity of the judge assigned to the case. How does excluding the name of the judge assigned to the case promote due process or the public interest?
>
> Juvenile Court . . . blocks all public access to any document. All of the Juvenile Court records are sealed, and even parties to the cases have to clear formidable hurdles to get access to court records—access is time-consuming and costly and as a practical matter is virtually nonexistent.[264]

In at least one instance elsewhere, Cox's fears have been realized, as private information is used to intimidate or blackmail citizens who criticize the courts. Liz Richards, who heads a group called Family Court Reform of Annandale, Virginia, circulates electronic mail messages threatening to publicize information that she obtains through government files on the private lives of politically active parents. "I have vital information from his personal case file," she writes of one father. "I got copies of documents from his case file. . . . Unfortunately for you and ————, I know too much about ————."

She then details what she claims is information about his personal finances and private family life, including the contents of his bank account and what pastimes he undertakes with his children. This information entails no violation of the law by the father but was available to Richards only because it was demanded from him by a family court under threat of incarceration. Richards publicly solicits additional information on individuals' private lives "to give to the Virginia officials." "I want further documented evidence of malicious and dishonest conduct, to be passed on to Governor Gilmore and [Social Services Secretary] Claude Allen and others."[265]

The Fifth Amendment guarantee that "No person shall . . . be deprived of life, liberty, or property, without due process of law" does not prevent family courts from jailing parents on civil contempt for weeks, months, or even years without trial. In December 2003, in response to a letter from the American Civil Liberties Union, a Montgomery County, Pennsylvania, judge freed some one hundred prisoners who had been incarcerated without due process for allegedly failing to pay child support. The fathers were sentenced with no notice given of their hearings and no opportunity to obtain legal representation. ACLU lawyer Malia Brink says courts across Pennsylvania routinely jail such men for civil contempt without proper notice or in time for them to get lawyers. Fathers relate that hearings typically lasted between thirty seconds and two minutes, during which they are sentenced to months in jail or prison. Lawrence County was apparently jailing fathers with no hearings at all.

Nothing indicates that Pennsylvania is unusual. After a decade of hysteria over "deadbeat dads," one hundred such prisoners in each of the America's 3,000 counties is by no means unlikely. Though the men were released, it is not the end of their ordeal. The incarceration cost many their jobs and thus their ability to pay future child support. As a result, most will be returned to the penal system, from which they are unlikely ever to escape. Rendered permanently insolvent by the incarceration, they are farmed out to trash companies and similar concerns, where they work fourteen- to sixteen-hour days. Most of their earnings are confiscated for child support, the costs of their incarceration, and mandatory drug testing.[266] The practice is strikingly reminiscent of the Soviet forced-labor system, described by Carl Friedrich and Zbigniew Brzezinski in their classic study of totalitarianism:

> Not infrequently the secret police hired out its prisoners to local agencies for the purpose of carrying out some local project. . . . Elaborate contracts were drawn up . . . specifying all the details and setting the rates at which the secret police is to be paid. At the conclusion of their task, the prisoners, or more correctly the slaves, were returned to the custody of the secret police.[267]

The courts are also not above summarily jailing children who fail to cooperate with the criminalization of their parents. "Three young siblings, whose only crime was their apparent reluctance to testify against their father, were jailed for twelve days in Los Angeles County's overcrowded Central Juvenile Hall and brought to court in handcuffs and leg chains." The children had been kept "in the company of serious juvenile offenders." [268] Seventeen-year-old Jillian Shapiro was wrestled to the floor and handcuffed by two male police detectives when she refused to leave her father's apartment in Pennsylvania.[269]

Despite the constitutional prohibition on double jeopardy, the U.S. Justice Department reports that "some states, such as Utah, treat a domestic violence protective order violation either as a misdemeanor or as criminal contempt and a separate domestic violence offense," thus turning one alleged offense into two. Courts in California, Kentucky, Minnesota, New Mexico, and Texas have held that finding a defendant guilty of criminal contempt does not preclude, on grounds of double jeopardy, a subsequent prosecution.[270] Forced confessions, not permitted anywhere else in the law but now routinely employed in cases of alleged domestic violence, contravene the prohibition on self-incrimination, though despite official documentation of the practice, I have not been able to locate any case where courts have reviewed the practice.[271]

The Sixth Amendment stipulates, "In all criminal prosecutions, the accused shall enjoy the right to a speedy and public trial, by an impartial jury of the state and district wherein the crime shall have been committed . . . and to be informed of the nature and cause of the accusation, to be confronted with the witnesses against him . . . and to have the assistance of counsel for his defense." Yet a custody trial will most likely be held behind closed doors and with no record of what is said, free of scrutiny by press and public. Delays of months and years are common, as the parent with "temporary" custody may try to stall while establishing a *status quo* that the courts are reluctant to change.

Since the advent of no-fault divorce, involuntarily divorced parents can no longer demand a jury trial, with the result, in the words of attorney Wayne Anderson, that "the courts can now find the facts in a particular case to be whatever they wish them to be." "This is true, even though the jury trial is one of the few things that makes our system of justice superior to the judge-made decisions in places like Russia," writes Anderson. "As a lawyer, I am at a loss to explain how court decisions without a jury trial are any more fair here than they are in totalitarian states." Anderson notes that fathers regularly demanded jury trials in the days before they were prohibited, knowing they had a better chance of getting custody before a jury than before a judge.[272] While divorce and custody trials are technically not "criminal prosecutions," they often amount to the same thing, being the first stage in the criminalization and incarceration of fathers.

In child-support cases—which may indeed be criminal prosecutions—fathers are regularly jailed for extended periods without trial, without charge, and without a lawyer. A father jailed for "civil contempt" in a child-support case need not receive due process of law and may legally be presumed guilty until proven innocent. "The burden of proof may be shifted to the defendant in some circumstances," according to a handbook for local officials published by the National Conference of State Legislatures. The NCSL advocates these methods and urges its members to utilize them, so its interpretation is likely to be accurate.[273]

The father can also be charged with criminal contempt for which, according to the Sixth Amendment, he must be duly tried, but with fathers this is not always the case. "The lines between civil and criminal contempt are often blurred in failure-to-pay-child-support cases, particularly *if the court does not explicitly clarify the charge* facing the [allegedly?] delinquent parent," continues the NCSL, whose choice of words reflects a presumption of guilt. So, like Kafka's character, Joseph K., the father may not even know the charge against which he must defend himself. Further, according to NCSL "not all child-support contempt proceedings classified as criminal are entitled to a jury trial,"[274] and "even indigent obligors are not necessarily entitled to a lawyer."[275] In short, a father who has lost his children through literally "no fault" of his own must prove his innocence against an accusation that may not even be clearly defined, without counsel, and without a jury of his peers.

As we will see, accusations of spousal abuse and child abuse made without any evidence are presumed true and are used to separate fathers from children for extended periods and even for life, until proved otherwise. Accusations shown to be knowingly false (often made anonymously) are almost never punished and are not admissible in custody decisions.[276] As with child support, "the mere allegation of domestic abuse . . . may shift the burden of proof to the defendant."[277]

Such denials of due process and railroading of parents into jail and prison are often dismissed as the sour grapes of losing custody litigants. Yet they are increasingly being exposed and documented. For years fathers have claimed that courts alter official hearing transcripts and recordings and otherwise falsify or fabricate evidence against them; when permitted, some litigants go so far as to hire their own court reporters from neighboring jurisdictions. In one case, the "wife's lawyer worked some kind of backroom deal with the court reporter" to omit passages from the record in a case that was receiving publicity.[278]

Attorney Eugene Wrona of Allentown, Pennsylvania, claims to know from firsthand experience that at least three Pennsylvania judges knowingly condoned or participated in the fabrication of evidence by altering hearing tapes and transcripts. His repeated requests for copies of audio tapes immediately following hearings were denied, and he was only given copies or permission to make copies months later. Wrona found "dozens of changes" in the official record from what took place in the courtroom. When appealing one decision, Wrona discovered that the transcript "didn't bear any relation to what went on in the hearing." "This is criminal misconduct," Wrona says, "and these people belong in jail." Wrona is a semi-retired attorney who derives other income, "so I can be honest." He says attorneys in other Pennsylvania jurisdictions privately report similar practices. "If they want to keep their practice alive," however, they remain silent.[279]

Such practices are difficult to prove, but Zed McLarnon, an audio-visual expert with twenty years forensic experience working for insurance companies, proved that "tape recordings of his court hearings have been tampered with," according to the *Massachusetts News*. The newspaper investigated and obtained "photographic evidence that hearing tapes could have been edited at Middlesex Probate Court," as McLarnon and his attorney claim.[280] As a result of the tampering, McLarnon's son was kept from his father for six years without an evidentiary hearing ever taking place. The boy developed behavioral problems and was eventually turned over to the custody of social workers by the mother and her new husband, who worked for the state agency.

When McLarnon complained about the altering and other irregularities he was assessed $3,500 for the fees of attorneys he had not hired and jailed without trial by the same judges whose tapes were allegedly doctored. He was later assessed a further $16,400 for attorneys, and the court moved to seize his house and car. His attorney, Gregory Hession, charges that the court also "removed documents from his case file, falsified the case docket, refused to docket motions and hearings in the public record, and withheld the public case file for nine months."

McLarnon also alleges that in July 1996 he was dragged from his car, beaten by men who appeared from their shoes and car to be plainclothes police, and told to stay away from the courts if he ever wanted to see his son again. A report from the Malden Hospital Emergency Room confirms he was assaulted and cut. "McLarnon's case illustrates a critical new trend in the law," writes Hession, "which is little noticed until one is ensnared by it, that the state itself has become the main impediment to justice." The judiciary, Hession believes, "has been hijacked and subverted by people with a radically unconstitutional agenda." He adds:

> What is at stake in McLarnon's case is the rule of law and the Constitution.
> . . . His case pits the old constitutional system of justice against the new
> Orwellian system, which has no protection for certain categories of unfa-
> vored perpetrators of "crimes" against the state, such as parents . . . who do
> not get equal protection before the law. . . . It is a system skewed by political
> agendas, not truth . . . where government has assumed a role never allowed
> or contemplated under our . . . Bill of Rights—intruding into family auton-
> omy, paternal authority, child raising, and even minor family conflicts.[281]

Both Wrona and Hession say they contacted state and federal officials about the tampering, including the FBI, U.S. attorney, state attorneys general, and local district attorneys, but received no response. Wrona recounts that when he tried to file criminal charges with the local district attorney, he was physically escorted from the office by sheriff's deputies.

Tampering with official records appears not to be limited to courts but may now reach to the highest levels of government. Fathers' representatives claim testimony they submitted to the Ways and Means Committee of the U.S. House of Representatives in response to public solicitations in June 2001 and on other occasions either was not entered into the official record or was altered. Ironically, fathers' groups are never among the "invited witnesses" who alone testify orally to congressional committees—even when the legislation is explicitly directed to "fatherhood." Yet there is reason to believe they constitute the overwhelming bulk of written testimony, which is required by law to be entered into the public record.

Also contrary to the Sixth Amendment and centuries of common-law tradition, courts allow fathers to be prosecuted in jurisdictions not only other than where their alleged crime took place but where they have never set foot. The Massachusetts Supreme Court has ruled that a father "can be sent to Oregon to face criminal nonsupport charges—even though he has never been in that state and did not know his ex-wife and children moved there."[282]

In many cases the father is not even brought before a judge for a formal charge but instead is accused in an "expedited judicial process" before a black-robed lawyer known as a "judge surrogate" (or a variety of other names). This official wields substantial judicial powers that, according to a U.S. House publication, allow him or her to "take testimony and establish a record, evaluate and make initial decisions, enter default orders if the non-custodial parent does not respond to 'notice' or other State 'service of process' in a timely manner, accept voluntary acknowledgment of support liability, and approve stipulated agreements to pay support".[283]

Yet because they are not called "judges," their appointments are not confirmed by the legislature, so they are not accountable to citizens or their representatives. Unlike true judges, they are also free to lobby for or against the same legislation they adjudicate from their surrogate "bench," an obvious breach of the separation of powers. In effect, they are political activists in robes, and what is supposed to be impartial, apolitical justice becomes the hijacking of the judiciary to implement a political agenda disguised as justice. One litigant, forced to appear before a "marital master" in New Hampshire who had been denied a real judgeship, writes that during the master's tenure she simultaneously worked "as a radical feminist lobbying on proposed legislation" dealing with custody and child support.[284]

The Eighth Amendment's prohibition of "cruel and unusual punishment" does not stop family courts from summarily depriving parents of professional licenses, drivers' licenses, and passports that bear no connection with their alleged offense. Parents who are alleged (but again, neither formally charged nor proven) to be delinquent in child-support payments also have their cars booted[285] and their names published in the newspapers.[286] Two months after Louisiana created an Internet site "to embarrass deadbeat parents" by displaying their names, the state reported that it had collected nothing. Apparently unconcerned about the McCarthyite overtones, director of enforcement Gordon Hood insisted that the project was nevertheless valuable because it established a "list" that in itself constitutes proof of guilt. "Everybody might say he's a good guy," Hood suggests, "but I can say he's not. He's on the list."[287]

The Ninth Amendment's recognition of "certain rights" not explicitly enumerated has served as the basis for a constitutionally protected right of privacy, including the right of parenthood which is also held by an extensive body of federal and state case law to be protected by the Fourteenth Amendment. As we saw earlier, the case law proceeding from this amendment is simply ignored by divorce courts.

The Tenth Amendment, which reserves matters such as family law to the states, is also routinely ignored. Child-support enforcement has been federalized in the Office of Child Support Enforcement and legislation such as the

Deadbeat Parents Punishment Act and Child Support Recovery Act. Domestic violence law has also been federalized by the Violence Against Women Acts, enacted in 1994, 2000, and 2005, which dispense federal funds to states and localities. Yet no constitutional authority has ever been demonstrated for federalizing these functions, and no corresponding federal protections are enforced for the rights of those prosecuted.

Congress generally assumes jurisdiction over local affairs such as law enforcement through the interstate commerce clause, yet precisely how child-support collection and domestic violence can be classified as interstate commerce has never been demonstrated.[288] Congress originally claimed jurisdiction over child-support collection as a way of recovering federal welfare costs when it created the OCSE in 1975, but the extension of federal jurisdiction over non-welfare cases (now some 83 percent of all child-support cases and growing) was never explained or justified. "The federal government has no constitutional authority to be involved in the collection of child support," Congressman Ron Paul has pointed out, "much less invade the privacy of every citizen in order to ferret out a few wrongdoers."[289]

Fathers are also routinely ordered into employment, the wages from which are then confiscated. According to a California ruling overturning a century of precedent, this is no longer contrary to the Thirteenth Amendment prohibition on slavery and involuntary servitude.[290] Before the campaign against fathers began, courts consistently recognized that "Congress has put it beyond debate that no indebtedness warrants a suspension of the right to be free from compulsory service. This congressional policy means that no state can make the quitting of work any component of a crime, or make criminal sanctions available for holding unwilling persons to labor."[291] Yet states now routinely do precisely this. In April 1998, a *custodial* father in Illinois who stayed at home to care for his three children and who received no child support from the mother was arrested under "a little known state law that makes it a felony for a man to be 'deliberately unemployed.'" "Men in Illinois have become the target of a witch hunt," the Reuters news agency quotes his attorney as saying. "Men are hounded if they owe child support and mom is on welfare. Now Mom is the 'deadbeat parent,' and the man is hounded because he is on welfare."[292]

Judge Alex Kozinski of the Ninth Circuit U.S. Court of Appeals, writing for a unanimous panel in March 1999, argues that "not all forced employment is constitutionally prohibited." Kozinski points out that sailors who desert ship, soldiers drafted who refuse to serve, and unspecified "others" have been imprisoned, and had their sentences upheld, for refusing to work. "We conclude that child-support awards fall within that narrow class of obligation that may be enforced by means of imprisonment without violating the constitutional prohibition against slavery," Kozinski writes. In a related case, Kozinski gratuitously opines that "deadbeats . . . deserve a kick in the pants," which he apparently does not regard as contrary to the Eighth Amendment prohibition of unusual punishment.[293]

The demands of military discipline in time of war have often been invoked by governments to justify suspending the constitutional rights of civilians in peacetime. In resorting to this analogy, Kozinski not only ignores the Thirteenth Amendment and Bill of Rights but also misunderstands an ancient and fundamental principle of the common law. Military service (a civic responsibility and not a form of employment) has long been recognized as being governed by a standard wholly different from the liberty guaranteed to citizens in the course of their daily lives, and one from which even military personnel themselves are not exempt. Military discipline has long been understood to require physically coercive authority over the persons of soldiers that extends even to death, which cannot used to justify similar measures against civilians—or their property—in peacetime without destroying all liberty. No less an authority than John Locke invoked precisely this distinction between the strictures of military discipline and the sanctity of property rights when discussing "arbitrary" power in his *Second Treatise on Civil Government*:

> Neither the sergeant, that could command a soldier to march up to the mouth of a cannon, or stand in a breach, where he is almost sure to perish, can command that soldier to give him one penny of his money; nor the general, that can condemn him to death for deserting his post, or for not obeying the most desperate orders, can yet, with all his absolute power of life and death, dispose of one farthing of that soldier's estate, or seize one jot of his goods.[294]

To allow otherwise would be, in Locke's term, to "enslave" us—precisely the kind of slavery against which the Thirteenth Amendment is directed and which has now been reintroduced into family law through coerced child support.[295]

The regime of involuntary divorce, forcible removal of children, coerced child support, and knowingly false accusations is now warping our entire legal system, undermining and overturning principles of common law that have protected individual rights for centuries. The presumption of innocence has been inverted, as we have seen. The "defendant" in a custody "trial" must at his own expense amass evidence to prove, not that he has committed no infraction, but that he has been a positively "good" father—even if he has not been accused of being a bad one. (In other words, attorneys and judges demand and debate evidence that has no relevance to any point at issue, one suspects in order to drive up fees.) If he wants to see his children, he must also amass evidence *against* his spouse, whether he wishes to or not, much in the spirit of a cockfight.

Unilateral and forced divorce laws which permitted one partner to abrogate the marriage agreement without incurring any consequences clearly contravene the contract clause of the Constitution, which states that no state shall pass any law "impairing the obligation of contracts." Because these laws were applied to marriages that had been contracted under different laws and terms, they also constituted *ex post facto* laws, likewise prohibited by the Constitution. Also clearly *ex post facto*, the Child Support Recovery Act of 1992 imposed criminal penalties on child-support arrearages accrued before the passage of the act, when they were not criminal.[296]

The constitutional guarantee of a writ of *habeas corpus* is another clause that is all but ignored, since fathers incarcerated by family courts are seldom charged with any crime. The notorious Elizabeth Morgan case was only the most famous instance where a parent was held in civil contempt for two years and was publicized only because it involved a mother. Likewise in Rhode Island, a non-custodial mother who, according to the Associated Press, "does not believe women should pay child support" was released after two and a half years in prison for refusing to pay $48 a week in child support after intervention by the ACLU.[297] Much more common instances of fathers languishing in jail for failure to pay sums many times this amount receive neither publicity nor the assistance of the ACLU. Courts can and do summon fathers so frequently that they lose their jobs and then incarcerate them for failure to pay child support; the incarceration itself naturally has a similar effect.

The divorce regime is at the vanguard of a trend toward enacting bills of attainder or legislative declarations of guilt, which are explicitly prohibited by the Constitution. The titles of divorce-related laws indicates how the targets of legislation have become not deeds but persons: the Deadbeat Parents Punishment Act, the Violence Against Women Act, the Elizabeth Morgan Act, and in Illinois, the "Sexually Dangerous Persons Act." These measures eliminate the presumption of innocence because they punish not crimes but persons who are presumed (without trial or conviction) to have committed crimes.

The ominously titled Deadbeat Parents Punishment Act imposed punitive measures on millions of citizens who had been neither tried for nor convicted of any crime. The Violence Against Women Act applies its provisions to "abusers" and "battered women" (unqualified by "alleged"), imputing criminal culpability to groups rather than to duly convicted individuals. The bill reads like a virtual declaration of guilt against anyone accused of domestic violence, with such terms thrown about as if they refer to specific, proven convictions.

In December 2003, a federal appeals court struck down the infamous Elizabeth Morgan Act, whereby Congress legislatively separated father and child and "branded," in the words of the court, as "a criminal child abuser" a father against whom no evidence was ever presented in a court or elsewhere. "Congress violated the constitutional prohibition against bills of attainder by singling out plaintiff for legislative punishment," the court said. Though a textbook bill of attainder, it took six years for the court to act, during which time the damage was done, and the daughter grew up permanently estranged from her father. The very fact that a bill of attainder was used at all indicates a truly extreme politicization of criminal justice. Bills of attainder are rare, draconian measures used for one purpose: to convict political enemies who cannot be convicted with evidence.[298]

The child-support system also overturns the centuries-old common-law principle that a father could not be forced to pay for the stealing of his own children. "The duty of a father (now spouse) to support his children is based largely upon his right to their custody and control," runs one ruling typical of the age-old legal consensus, which most lay people today seem to assume still operates. "A father has the right at common law to maintain his children in his own home, and he cannot be compelled against his will to do so elsewhere, unless he has refused or failed to provide for them where he lives, and the statutes providing for the punishment of a father (now spouse) for the failure to support his children, were not intended to change the common law."[299]

As recently as 1965, the Oregon Supreme Court held that "a husband whose wife left him without cause was not required to support his children living with her, absent a court or proof that denying them support during the period the mother refused to return to the father would harm the children."[300]

Family courts in the United States and other democracies also routinely ignore and violate international human rights conventions to which their governments are signatories. Under the U.S. Constitution, such treaties are considered the "supreme law of the land." "Men and women of full age, without any limitation due to race, nationality or religion, have the right to marry and to found a family," states Article 16 of the Universal Declaration of Human Rights signed by the United States and almost every other nation in 1948. "They are entitled to equal rights as to marriage, during marriage, and its dissolution." The Declaration further states that "The family is the natural and fundamental group unit of society and is entitled to protection by society and the State."

Article 23 of the International Covenant on Civil and Political Rights, which came into force in 1976, similarly states, "The family is the natural and fundamental group unit of society and is entitled to protection by society and the State" and requires that "States Parties to the present Covenant shall take appropriate steps to ensure equality of rights and responsibilities of spouses as to marriage, during marriage, and at its dissolution."

SEPARATION OF POWERS

It is always tempting to dismiss such violations as aberrations, the result of excess by a few overzealous officials, since civil and human rights are violated by every government, even in democracies. Yet considered in the light of constitutional principle, the destruction of ancient protections is clearly systemic within the nation's family courts and endemic to a governmental regime whose very existence is predicated and dependent on the power to remove children from their parents. Far from simple violations of particular constitutional clauses, these practices and powers are undermining constitutional government in its most fundamental principles. The power to take children from their parents for no reason is arbitrary government at its most intrusive, since it invades and obliterates all of private life. Yet we have created a governmental machinery that exists for no other purpose.

While occasional violations of individual rights are to be expected in the most free and open society, what becomes truly dangerous is when the mechanisms for correcting such violations are compromised. Courts are often zealous in defending constitutional rights that have been violated by the other branches of government; it is not clear who is left to defend rights violated by the courts.

But what may be most insidious—because it undermines the material foundation of constitutional government—is when systematic means are mobilized to finance unconstitutional government operations. Like any system of unaccountable government, the divorce regime can only be sustained so long as it can be paid for. This is the effect of the system of child support, coerced on pain of incarceration from parents whose children have been seized by the courts through literally "no fault" of their own.

There is nothing more American in the history of political thought than the principle—which lies behind the American Revolution, the Constitution, and the separation of powers—that the right of property and the power to withhold revenue constitute the people's principal leverage against their government and therefore the ultimate safeguard of their freedom. Without this guarantee, other constitutional protections are mere scraps of paper. The revolutionary slogan "No taxation without representation!" was not simply a tax revolt by disgruntled property holders; it was a recognition of the political (even more than the economic) power of revenue. A similar slogan in the earlier English Revolution illustrates the principle perhaps more clearly: "No supply before redress of grievances!"

Historically, parliaments were called when kings needed money, and they soon learned to use finance as leverage and declare, "We will pay our dues provided the government responds to our wishes." This is why the "power of the purse" is lodged with the people's representatives in Congress, and the reason for the otherwise quaint clause in the Constitution requiring that revenue bills originate in the more democratic House of Representatives. "This power of the purse may . . . be regarded as the most complete and effectual weapon with which any constitution can arm the immediate representatives of the people," wrote James Madison, "that powerful instrument by which we behold . . . the people . . . reducing . . . all the overgrown prerogatives of the other branches of government."[301]

Delegating to courts the power to summarily extract revenue not only violates the separation of powers; it deprives the father of the only guarantee of his other rights, including the right to his children, which is the power of his paycheck. The fact that states sometimes use child-support money to balance their budgets, rather than sending it to the supposed beneficiaries, further confirms that coerced child support amounts to a system (and a highly regressive one) of extra-parliamentary taxation.[302]

From this perspective, allegations about fathers not paying child support, hiding savings with relatives, and so forth are not only one-sided; they may well indicate precisely the opposite of a father "abandoning" his children. They are the entirely predictable behavior of a father trying to recover his children, provide for them himself, and perhaps even hold his family together. Yet the swarm of officials who have a stake in seizing control of his family and property have little difficulty depicting such a father as "abandoning" or refusing to "support" his children.

'A VERITABLE GULAG'

To break this resistance, governments are erecting the most authoritarian machinery ever seen in America. "The advocates of ever-more-aggressive measures for collecting child support," writes Bryce Christensen, "have moved us a dangerous step closer to a police state and have violated the rights of innocent and often impoverished fathers."[303] Author and attorney Jed Abraham describes the child-support apparatus as "a veritable gulag, complete with sophisticated surveillance and compliance capabilities such as computer-based tracing, license revocation, asset confiscation, and incarceration. The face of this regime is decidedly Orwellian."[304]

Operatives of the divorce machinery indeed assume a vast array of intrusive powers over parents whose only offense is to have displeased their spouses, as well as over the general population who are not involved at all. A program growing out of the federal Deadbeat Parents Punishment Act allows agents of the inspector general's office of the Department of Health and Human Services to carry guns and issue arrest warrants, in open disregard for due process of law.[305] Sweeping powers have now been enacted allowing these non-uniformed, bureaucratic police acting without court orders to invade the privacy and seize the property of citizens involved against their will in divorce proceedings. A compilation by the National Conference of State Legislatures, which supports these powers, includes the following:[306]

- Administrative subpoenas to obtain financial or other information.
- Authority to order a change in the child-support payee.
- Authority to order income withholding.
- Authority to increase monthly payments for arrearages.
- Power to require parties to paternity or support proceedings to file with the state registry and update location and identity.

Laws conferring these judicial powers on executive branch officials are enacted under federal pressure. "The 1996 [welfare] reforms require states to adopt laws that give the CSE [child-support enforcement] agency authority to initiate a series of expedited procedures without the necessity of obtaining an order from any other administrative agency or judicial tribunal."[307] In virtually every state, child-support agents possess powers to gather information on private citizens beyond that of other government officials. According to NCSL, the information to which these agents have access includes:

- Vital statistics records
- Records concerning real and titled personal property
- Records of occupational and professional licenses and ownership of businesses
- Employment security records
- Records of agencies administering public assistance
- Records of the motor vehicles department
- Records of the corrections department
- Information contained in public utilities and cable television records
- Information held by financial institutions

These powers might be justifiable as means to assist the relatively modest number of truly abandoned children (which is invariably how they are presented in government literature). It is not clear that they are equally valid as methods of financing the forced separation of millions of children from their parents.

Hunting alleged deadbeats now rationalizes a series of intrusive government practices, including data-collection orders by the government to monitor information about all private citizens. In addition to automatic wage garnishing from all child-support obligors even before they become "delinquent," federal law now compels every employer in the nation to furnish personal information on all new employees to the federal government to build a federal database for enforcing child-support orders. The National Directory of New Hires requires employers to supply name, Social Security number, pay report, and other information on every newly hired employee to child-support enforcement authorities within twenty days, regardless of whether the employee is in arrears or even under a child-support order at all. The directory is an "electronic and centralized system" that matches all employees with parents listed in the Federal Case Registry.[308]

"Never before have federal officials had the legal authority and technological ability to locate so many Americans found [sic] to be delinquent parents—or such potential to keep tabs on Americans accused of nothing," observes the *Washington Post*, which describes the system as "an electronic dragnet."[309]

Fathers' groups are not alone in voicing alarm. "Just like in totalitarian societies, government bureaucrats will soon have the power to deny you a job, and the ability to monitor your income, assets, and debts," comments Libertarian Party Chairman Steve Dasbach. "Federal bureaucrats will have the ability to track every American from job to job, deny jobs to people who fall behind in child-support payments, and even share information with other government agencies." Though groups like the Libertarian Party did not previously question the reality of "deadbeat dads," their criticism might legitimately be directed at the entire child custody and child-support system. "This law turns the presumption of innocence on its head and forces every American to prove their innocence to politicians, bureaucrats, and computers."[310]

The directory effectively annexes the personnel offices of private companies as administrative agents of the government, forcing employers "to moonlight as unpaid police," in the words of *Forbes* magazine. In October 2003, General Motors, under pressure from Michigan's child-support office, withheld the bonuses of thousands of employees under child-support orders, even though about two-thirds of the employees were current in their payments.[311] Even officials invoke Orwellian imagery. "This is real Big Brother stuff," comments Emma Chacon, director of the Office of Recovery Services, which manages the registry in Utah.[312]

At least one state government has voiced dissent over the measure, including skepticism over the very reality of the alleged "deadbeats." "Under the guise of cracking down on so-called deadbeat dads, the Congress has required the states to carry out a massive and intrusive federal regulatory scheme by which personal data on all state citizens" is collected, the Kansas attorney general's office charged in a federal suit challenging the mandate's constitutionality.[313] Echoing terms used by fathers to describe coerced child support, one Kansas legislator called the federal directives "extortion," and colleagues in neighboring Nebraska described them as "a form of blackmail."[314] Employers who fail to devote company resources to register their employees can themselves be fined and arrested.

Government surveillance can be justified by the hunt for deadbeats where similar measures proposed in the name of other causes have failed due to citizen resistance. A proposal in 1998 to require banks to track customer transactions for signs of criminal activity prompted an outpouring of protest and forced regulators to scrap the plan, called "Know Your Customer." The action had been promoted as a method of tracking drug money. Yet measures too intrusive for use against drug lords are acceptable against fathers. No similar outcry has met the Financial Institution Data Match Program, which matches the records of parents with those of banks and other financial institutions, enabling the state to "freeze and seize" their accounts.[315] Under federal law, the institutions must disclose the names, Social Security numbers, and account details of alleged delinquents they turn up.

Taylor Burke, vice president of Burke and Herbert Bank and Trust Company in Alexandria, Virginia, does not believe banks should be asked to act as government agents. "We're all good citizens. But it doesn't mean we spy on our neighbors," he says. "It's really scary."[316]

Again, the "delinquents" are not the only ones targeted. "Foreshadowing an ominous national system, some California banks have begun sharing data on all of their customers as part of an effort to snare deadbeat dads," reports the *Privacy Times*. "Since the program is federally mandated, it is likely that this unprecedented data sharing is occurring in other states as well."[317] It is.

Officials nationwide are expanding the collection of Social Security numbers, again ostensibly to find deadbeats.[318] In December 2003, Michigan's secretary of state announced that drivers must divulge their Social Security numbers to facilitate child-support collection.[319] "Congress ordered the officials to obtain the nine-digit numbers when issuing licenses—such as drivers', doctors', and outdoorsmen's—in order to revoke the licenses of delinquents," the *Washington Post* reports.

"This is going to be nothing more than a huge invasion of privacy," said James Dean of Oshkosh, Wisconsin, who was unable to get a fishing license because he refused to provide his Social Security number. In Alaska, the regulation "has forced the state to collect Social Security numbers from people buying Alaska hunting and fishing licenses [and] has merchants grumbling and some customers seeing red." "We've had some real unhappy campers because of it," said Darrell Henry at Sentry Hardware in Fairbanks. "Why not have grocery stores collect our Social Security numbers?" one customer commented. "Or nice policemen asking passersby for their numbers? Or require that bowling alleys, bars, pool halls, sports stadiums, etc. collect Social Security numbers—just to track down deadbeat dads, of course. Heck to make it easier, let's just tattoo the dang things on our foreheads."[320]

Federally driven efforts are now under way to turn community organizations such as youth groups and churches into informers. The federal Office of Child Support Enforcement has entered into "cooperative agreements" with the YMCA of America and the United Methodist Church "to link the 2,200 YMCAs in the United States with the child-support offices in their communities."[321] Under the guise of promoting marriage, the Bush administration has begun dispersing grants to faith-based groups to enlist their cooperation in child-support enforcement.[322] The United Way solicits on behalf of the Texas attorney's general office for children as young as fourteen to serve as enforcement agents.[323]

Coupled with new information-gathering methods to tell the government what citizens are doing come new forms of secrecy to disguise from citizens what their government is doing. "Officials have not publicized their ability to obtain financial information because they do not want to alert delinquents to the ability of enforcement workers to seize or freeze financial assets," says Michael Kharfen of HHS. "We're setting aside some of the courtesies in order to accomplish what we're trying to do." So the end apparently justifies the means. These "courtesies" are citizens' constitutional protections. Kharfen describes the network as an "unprecedented, vast amount of information that is updated constantly."[324]

The line between the guilty and the innocent becomes so blurred as to become meaningless because government agents track parents who are behind on their payments, those whose orders are paid up, and those who are not under any orders at all. As with mandatory wage garnishing and the mandatory registration of all citizens under child-support orders (even those whose payments are current), the presumption of guilt against fathers was revealed by one agent who bragged to the *Washington Post* that "we don't give them an opportunity to become deadbeats." Lucia Edmundson of the San Diego district attorney's office advocates casting "a child-support net so wide that a few bystanders get caught" and insists that the falsely accused "still have to prove" their innocence.[325]

The assumption that not only are all parents under child-support orders already semi-criminals but that all citizens are potential criminals against whom preemptive enforcement measures must be initiated now in anticipation of their future criminality is chillingly expressed by the NCSL. "Some people have argued that the state should only collect the names of child-support obligors, not the general population," they suggest, "but this argument ignores the primary reason for collecting the numbers separate from awarding a support order: At one point or another, many people will either be obligated to pay or eligible to receive child support."[326]

WHEN CONTROL REPLACES JUSTICE

Identifying these "delinquents" whose crimes ostensibly justify this information gathering is itself highly problematic, as we will see in the next chapter. Even privacy advocates often do not question the existence of "real" deadbeat dads. But from the standpoint of constitutional protections one has to wonder. Governments invariably invoke an urgent public "necessity" whenever they violate citizens' rights, and when they invoke children, it is especially intimidating to question their motives. "I have problems with the Big Brother concept myself," Connie White, the "system-development manager" for the Virginia Division of Child Support Enforcement, told the *Washington Post*. "But the need for people to support their children far outweighs their need for privacy."

Yet the conflict between constitutional government and sound public policy is usually a false one. When we look beneath the surface, we usually find some more fundamental problem. While it is comforting to see all this as "excess" and to believe that "the end justifies the means," what is often overlooked is that the state may not be interested in the ends it professes so much as the means themselves, and that the supreme ambition of every government is to control the private lives of its citizens.

In her book *The Haunted Land*, Tina Rosenberg describes methods used by the secret police in the former Eastern Bloc to intimidate dissidents and gather information on citizens. What is striking from her account and others is how unconcerned officials were with the political opinions of those they monitored. "Practically no information in the Stasi files discussed East Germans' political ideas," she writes. What does emerge plainly is the state operatives' concern with the personal and family lives of their subjects. "The biggest surprise was the banality of the files," she quotes the head of a citizens' committee. "A lot of information about family, personal problems."

Yet this is surprising and banal only when one accepts official ideology too literally. It is not so unexpected when one considers that it is this sphere of life that the modern state has aimed to control. Doubtless many people sincerely believed communist ideology, at least early on, just as many today seem sincere in their solicitude for other people's children. But there comes a point when the ideology obfuscates more than it illuminates and when control replaces justice. In both the old bureaucratic dictatorships and the new authoritarianism emerging in the West, the family—and above all children—are both the objects the state aims to control and are its most effective tools for controlling everyone else.

"The Stasi recruited children as young as six," Rosenberg quotes a dissident as saying. "They would find a child in an unstable family and fill in the gaps in his relationships." Time and again family problems, and especially children, created the opening for the state to enter. "One informer . . . was pregnant and her marriage was disintegrating, and her Stasi handlers served as 'substitute fathers' for the child." Others spoke of Stasi agents as "father figures." The Stasi convinced the headmistress of one dissident couple's son to turn their child against them. Likewise, a mother who examined her file discovered that her Stasi handler "wrote it was obvious I loved my son, and as a result the Stasi developed a package of measures to take him away, trying to prove I was neglecting him."

In Czechoslovakia, "taking children as hostage for their parents' crimes was common practice." It is legendary that children whose parents participated in the Prague Spring reform movement in 1968 were subsequently excluded from the universities. Children provided an effective means of silencing dissent whenever authorities could force a choice between one's politics and one's children. One Czech dissident, whose daughter's college applications were rejected and whose son was turned down by the Prague School of Economics even though he had the fifth-highest qualifications of any applicant, reflects on the cost of his political activities by saying, "My only irresponsibility was to my family."[327]

Facile parallels with totalitarian dictatorships drawn by westerners who never experienced those terrors are a much-abused form of social criticism. Yet in this case, survivors of those dictatorships readily perceive the similarity. Bogumila and Jerzy Koss compare New York's family courts to the bureaucratic tyrannies they knew in Poland. "As children we lived through Nazi horror, then through Communist occupation," they write, "and now, in the United States, the 'Land of the Free,' we are persecuted by judicial tyranny."[328]

But in contrast to Nazi and Stalinist regimes, which used children as one weapon among many, today in the Western democracies children and families have become the central object of government policy, and parents rather than dissidents have become the targets. After experiencing American family law, Romanian dissident Mihai Muset gained a new perspective on totalitarian justice under communist dictator Nicolae Ceausescu, by whose regime he had been arrested for a protest. "I was sentenced to two months in prison," he recalled, "but at least I got to appear in court and talk to the judge. That's more than I got in family court."[329]

Chapter 3

DEADBEAT DADS OR PLUNDERED POPS?

Thieves for their robbery have authority
When judges steal themselves.

— *Measure for Measure*, II, 2

A parent whose children are taken away by a family court is only at the beginning of his troubles. The next step comes as he is summoned to court and ordered to pay as much as two-thirds or even more of his income as "child support" to whomever has been given custody. His wages will immediately be garnished and his name will be entered on a federal register of "delinquents." This is even before he has had a chance to become one, though it is also likely that the order will be backdated, so he will already be delinquent as he steps out of the courtroom. If the ordered amount is high enough and the backdating far enough, he will be an instant felon and subject to immediate arrest.

It is difficult to believe such a thing can happen in a country with the Bill of Rights. Yet according to figures from the federal government it is now happening to millions of fathers. The pursuit of these fathers by armed federal agents has now reached the dimensions of a national witch hunt, by far the most extensive this country has ever seen. "District Attorney investigators Al Duran and Phyl Peltier loaded their automatic handguns and strapped on their bulletproof vests at daybreak," a California newspaper reports. "One, a former San Jose policeman-turned-homicide-detective, and the other, a former San

Diego SWAT-team-officer-turned-sex-crimes-investigator, were preparing for the worst." The agents were going after not violent criminals or drug kingpins but fathers.[330]

In a short time, "child support" has gone from a minor matter affecting a few people on the margins of society to enter the national vocabulary as a sacred political cow. "On the left and on the right, the new phrase to conjure with is 'child support,'" writes scholar Bryce Christensen, who notes it is seen as "the best rhetoric in the world" by politicians: "a rhetoric unifying political figures" from both parties.[331]

Yet the new politics of child support is plagued by the same fundamental contradictions as child custody. Like custody, it is awarded ostensibly without reference to "fault," and yet disobedience brings swift and severe punishments. Contrary to popular belief (and centuries of common-law precedent), child support today has nothing to do with fathers abandoning their children, reneging on their marital vows, or even agreeing to a divorce. It is automatically assessed on all non-custodial parents, even those divorced over their objections and who lose their children through no legal fault or agreement of their own. It is an entitlement, in other words, for all divorcing mothers and one coerced not from taxpayers (though they pay too) but directly from involuntarily divorced spouses. A legally unimpeachable parent minding his own business can lose not only his children but his property and earnings and can be incarcerated without trial through "no fault" of his own.

Like custody, in other words, child support has nothing to do with justice. On the other hand, it is a punitive measure, enforced with police, courts, and incarceration, plus (as was seen in the previous chapter) a growing panoply of unusual punishments. It is Western society's most advanced measure yet to institutionalize the Marxist principle, "from each according to his ability, to each according to her need."[332]

In short, child support is no longer primarily a method for requiring men to take responsibility for the offspring they have sired and then abandoned, as most people are led to believe. Overwhelmingly it is now a regime whereby "a father is forced to finance the filching of his own children."[333]

Parents who allegedly fail to pay—"deadbeat dads"—are now the subjects of a national demonology, officially designated villains whose guilt is assumed unquestioningly by politicians, press, and public alike. Not since the collapse of the Weimar Republic have the top leaders of a major western democracy used their public office to verbally attack millions of their own citizens. A decade ago, George Gilder warned of the bipartisan bandwagon being marshaled to punish private citizens who have been publicly pronounced guilty without trial:

> The president wants to take away their driver's licenses and occupational accreditations. Texas Governor George W. Bush wants to lift their hunting licenses as well. Moving to create a generation of American boat people, Senator Bill Bradley is leading a group of senators seeking to seize their passports. Congressman Henry Hyde wants to expand the powers of the IRS to confiscate their assets. Running for president, Lamar Alexander wants to give them "jail time," presumably so they won't vote. Also running for president, Alan Keyes suggests caning, recommending "a trip to Singapore to learn how to administer a civil beating." Governor William Weld in Massachusetts wants to subpoena their DNA, put liens on their houses, and hound them through the bureaucracies of 50 states.[334]

Since then, most of these measures have been enacted into law (the exception, for now, is caning), and the hunt continues unabated, with politicians and other officials redoubling their quest for the elusive deadbeat.

The campaign escalated dramatically during the Clinton years. In 1998, President Clinton signed the Deadbeat Parents Punishment Act, which enjoyed overwhelming bipartisan support. The same year, Health and Human Services Secretary Donna Shalala announced the Federal Case Registry, a massive system of government surveillance which aimed to include 16 million to 19 million citizens, whether or not they were behind in their payments.[335] "Combined with the National Directory of New Hires," Shalala said, "HHS now has the strongest child-support enforcement resource in the history of the program." The following year, Clinton announced yet another "new child-support crackdown." "This effort will include new investigative teams in five regions of the country to identify, analyze, and investigate [parents] for criminal prosecution, and an eightfold increase in legal support personnel to help prosecute these [parents]."[336]

The rhetoric has abated under the Bush administration, but the measures continue. In July 2002, under a Clinton-era program called Project Save Our Children, HHS Secretary Tommy Thompson announced a "nationwide sweep" led by agents from his department and the U.S. Marshals Service of parents he says disobeyed government orders. The roundup was "reminiscent of the old West," in the words of the *Christian Science Monitor*. "Most Wanted lists go up, and posses of federal agents fan out across the nation in hot pursuit." In

Utica, New York, the raids included agents from the Violent Felonies Warrants Unit.

"More notable than any one arrest," reported the *New York Times*, "is the message that the Bush administration is sending about its decision to pursue a more aggressive approach by using federal criminal prosecution." Government billboards in Maryland announce, "We're Looking for You, Child Support Violators." Governments do not warn bank robbers or drug dealers that they are being targeted. The principle that the criminal justice system exists less to bring individual lawbreakers to justice than to "send a message" and spread fear among a target population of otherwise law-abiding citizens is, so far, unique to this offense.[337]

The December 1998 issue of *Government Executive*, a trade journal that describes itself as "government's business magazine" representing public and private bureaucracies, ran a cover story that blared out, "Where's Dad? HHS is leading a forceful change to make deadbeat parents pay up." The article detailed an "aggressive new enforcement approach" but nowhere made any allowance for the fact that none of these men had ever been convicted of anything. Strikingly, the article never addressed its own question, the most likely answer being that Dad is being kept away by the government. The mainstream media report the government line with similar credulity. Prestigious newspapers like the *Washington Post* cast aside their critical detachment and become cheerleaders for armed government agents:

> Scores of deadbeat dads and a few deadbeat moms were hauled off in handcuffs this week for ignoring court orders to pay child support. . . . Almost 70 percent of the 32,318 District parents under orders to pay child support are deadbeats. . . . Complaints and excuses were the order of the day. . . . As Gregory Wright, age 32, was shackled to the growing crowd in the back of a sheriff's transport vehicle, he spouted several excuses at once: "I was unemployed; it was coming out of my unemployment. I just got a job . . ."

"We're ratcheting up the pressure on these deadbeats," Westchester County Executive Andrew Spano tells the *New York Post*, which allows its pages to be used to publicly "shame" citizens who have been convicted of no crime by publishing their photographs.[338] Were these citizens wanted for murder, they would be described as "suspects," but the government and media have already convicted them.

The vast expansion of federal police power during the 1990s seems to have had little success. A July 17, 1997, headline in the *New York Times* reported: "Child-Support Collection Net Usually Fails." The federal Office of Child Support Enforcement and its state affiliates now maintain an army of some 60,000 enforcement agents (thirteen times that of the Drug Enforcement Administration, which has about 4,600 agents worldwide),[339] with which it wages a losing battle against fathers who more often than not are either unemployed, impoverished, imprisoned, disabled, or dead.[340] This does not include agents from the HHS Office of the Inspector General, which operates ten multiagency, multijurisdictional task forces serving all fifty states, the District of Columbia and Puerto Rico.[341]

States are also building mammoth, federally funded enforcement bureaucracies, such as the high-tech system in California. An investigation by the *Los Angeles Times* found that the system was so riddled with waste, fraud, and mismanagement as to be virtually useless. Father-hunting zealots nevertheless remain indefatigable. Then-OCSE Chief Donald Deering proposed doubling the number of enforcement agents.[342]

What may be most striking about this police mobilization is that the initiative has come entirely from government officials. No public outcry ever preceded these measures, nor did any public perception of such a problem even exist until government officials began saying it did. The public never demanded that government take action, nor has any public discussion of this alleged problem ever been held in the national or local media. No government or academic study ever documented a nonpayment problem. Journalists did undertake a media blitz of stories on alleged nonpayment during the 1990s, but this began after, not before, the government campaign, which journalists never questioned. The initiative has been taken throughout by government officials and quasi-governmental interest groups, whose power has greatly expanded as a result.

Needless to say, the voices of pursued parents are seldom heard amid the chorus of condemnation. The bipartisan certainty of their guilt is sufficient to set aside their right to trial and declare them public enemies by general acclaim. Yet there is reason to believe that this problem is largely an optical illusion and that what is being portrayed as irresponsible fathers is in reality a massive abuse of government power.

In recent years, a few cracks have appeared in the monolith. Economist William Comanor writes that "child-support obligations"—the only form of "obligation" or "debt" that most of the debtors have done nothing to incur—"are now treated far more harshly than any other form of debt." Attorney Ron

Henry characterizes the system as "an obvious sham," a "disaster," and "the most onerous form of debt collection practiced in the United States."[343] "The overwhelming majority of so-called 'deadbeat dads' are just judicially created," says another attorney. "Why all this talk about so-called 'deadbeat dads'? Because there is a lot of money to be made through that myth."[344]

When one begins to examine the objective data and the research of independent scholars, it turns out that the problem is mostly a creation of government officials. In fact, the myth of the deadbeat dad has already been discredited conclusively by Sanford Braver and other scholars. We have already seen that Braver is one of many social scientists who have found that few married fathers voluntary abandon their children.[345] Beyond this, Braver has also shown that little scientific basis exists for claims that large numbers of fathers are not paying child support. Braver found that government claims of nonpayment were derived not from any compiled database or hard figures but entirely from surveys of custodial parents. In other words, the Census Bureau simply asked mothers what they were receiving. No corroborative data were produced because none exist. Moreover, the government relies on these surveys of mothers, and these alone, in setting enforcement policy against fathers, and no effort is made to balance them with surveys of non-custodial parents.[346] Yet Braver found that fathers overwhelmingly do pay court-ordered child support when they are employed, often at enormous personal sacrifice.[347]

Astronomical figures on alleged (or "estimated") arrearages cited by officials—now $34 billion to $100 billion and constantly rising[348]—are devised by interested parties such as government agencies and private collection companies based on hypothetical formulas of what would be owed under circumstances that do not exist. They are simply numbers on paper and bear no relation to whether the separation of the children from their father was just, whether the father did anything to incur the "obligation," whether the amount "owed" is reasonable or even possible for him to pay, and whether it bears any relation to the needs or costs of the children.

Unemployment (itself often caused directly by divorce court action, as we shall see) has consistently been found to be "the single most important factor relating to nonpayment," and contrary to another public misconception, Braver details the acute financial hardships many involuntarily divorced fathers endure.[349] Contrary to highly publicized but inaccurate figures on the cost of divorce to women, peer-reviewed economic research concluded that "it is the non-custodial parent, usually the father, who suffers the most [from divorce]. In every case and for every income, according to our analyses, the payer of child support is never able to cover household expenditures if paying child support at guideline levels." The study adds, realistically, "These simulations may actually under-represent the circumstances of non-custodial parents because they do not include expenditures for their children beyond child support."[350]

The picture that emerges is one of fathers who, far from abandoning their children, make enormous sacrifices to support children who have been taken from them through no legal wrongdoing on their part and who make heroic efforts to remain in contact with them, often against overwhelming obstacles.

Other social scientists have found that as much as 95 percent of fathers having no employment problems for the previous five years pay their ordered child support regularly, and that 81 percent paid in full and on time.[351] Columnist Kathleen Parker concluded that "the 'deadbeat dad' is an egregious exaggeration, a caricature of a few desperate men who for various reasons—sometimes pretty good ones—fail to hand over their paycheck, assuming they have one." Deborah Simmons of the *Washington Times* observes that "there is scant evidence that crackdowns . . . serve any purpose other than to increase the bank accounts of those special-interest groups pushing enforcement."[352]

Braver's research undermined every justification for the multibillion-dollar criminal enforcement machinery, as well as government programs to "promote responsible fatherhood." If Braver is to be believed—and no scholar or official has ever challenged, let alone refuted, his research—the government is engaged in a massive witch hunt against innocent citizens, and no justification exists for the huge army of enforcement agents and panoply of criminal punishments. Yet almost a decade after Braver's book, no enforcement agency, public or private, has even acknowledged the accusation that they are whipping up public hysteria against a non-existent problem, let alone have they begun to adjust their policies. As Braver himself observes, "The far-flung federal bureaucracy involved with the child-support enforcement machinery would naturally feel threatened if the conviction became widespread that there might not really be a sizable problem with divorced fathers' child-support compliance, after all."[353]

STATE REVENUE VIA CHILD SUPPORT

A look at the government machinery reveals that it was created not *in response to* claims of widespread nonpayment but *before* them, and that it was less a response to "deadbeat dads" than a mechanism to create them.

Like the new divorce laws (and shortly after their enactment), the child-support regulations and criminal enforcement machinery were created while few were paying attention.

Under pressure from bar associations and feminist groups, President Gerald Ford signed legislation creating the Office of Child Support Enforcement in 1975, warning at the time that it constituted an unwarranted federal intrusion into families and the role of states. Contrary to professions of concern "for the children," the principal purpose was never to provide for abandoned or impoverished children but to recoup welfare costs for the government. In fact, no study ever has been undertaken by the Department of Health and Human Services, Congress, or any branch of government to explain the reason for the agency's existence.[354]

Almost immediately the program began to expand exponentially, increasing tenfold from 1978 to 1998.[355] This massive growth of law-enforcement machinery and reach was federally driven. In 1984, the Child Support Enforcement amendment to the Social Security Act required states to adopt child-support guidelines. The legislation was promoted by OCSE itself and by private collection companies—again, less to help children than to save the government money under the theory that it would help get single-mother families off welfare by making fathers pay more. "No statistical data available then (or since) indicated that such legislation would have the desired effect," writes Robert Seidenberg. Most low-income single-mother families do not have valid child-support orders, so the higher child-support guidelines could not help them. Because most unpaid child support is due to unemployment, and because "most non-custodial parents of AFDC [welfare] children do not earn enough to pay as much child support as their children are already receiving in AFDC benefits," according to researchers Irwin Garfinkel and Sara McLanahan, higher child-support guidelines could not help these children.[356]

Then, with no explanation or justification (or constitutional authority), guidelines and criminal enforcement machinery conceived and created to address the minority of children in poverty were extended, under pressure from OCSE and other interests, to *all* child-support orders, even the majority not receiving welfare, by the Family Support Act of 1988. This vastly enlarged the program and transformed a welfare provision into an entitlement for the affluent. Today welfare cases, consisting mostly of unmarried parents, account for only 17 percent of all child-support cases, and the proportion is shrinking. The remaining 83 percent of non-welfare cases consist largely of previously married fathers who are usually divorced involuntarily and who generally can be

118

counted on to pay. With wage withholding, "the number of dollars passing through the government collection system exploded,"[357] mostly from non-welfare cases for which the system was never designed, which currently account for 92 percent of the money collected.[358]

The 1988 law also made the guidelines presumptive and, for all practical purposes, compulsory. By one estimate the new guidelines more than doubled the size of awards.[359] Yet at that point it was already well known among policymakers and scholars that, with the exception of the relatively small number of poor and unemployed fathers, no serious problem of nonpayment existed. Not only was Braver presenting the results of his research, but a federal pilot study commissioned four years earlier by OCSE itself was published with similar findings. Originally a full-scale government-sponsored study was planned to follow up the pilot, but this was quashed by OCSE when the pilot's findings threatened the justification for the agency's existence by demonstrating that nonpayment of child support was not a serious problem. The Congressional Research Service also concluded at about the same time that no serious problem existed.[360]

Promoted as a program that would reduce government spending, federal child-support enforcement has incurred a continuously increasing deficit. "The overall financial impact of the child-support program on taxpayers is negative," the House Ways and Means Committee reports. Taxpayers lost $2.7 billion in 2002.[361]

This money does not vanish. It ends up in the pockets and coffers of state officials, for whom it constitutes a lucrative source of revenue and income. "Most States make a profit on their child-support program," according to Ways and Means, which notes that "States are free to spend this profit in any manner the State sees fit."[362] In other words, federal taxpayers (who were supposed to save money) subsidize state government operations through child support. This also transforms family courts from impartial tribunals into revenue-generating engines for state government.

In addition to penalties and interest, states profit through federal incentive payments based on the amount collected, as well as receiving 66 percent of operating costs and 90 percent of computer costs.[363] (When two states collaborate, both states qualify for the incentive payment as if each state had collected 100 percent of the money.) Federal outlays of almost $3.5 billion in 2002 allowed Ohio to collect $228 million and California to collect over $640 million.[364] "There is a $200 million per year profit motive driving this system" in Michigan alone, attorney Michael Tindall points out. "It dances at the string of federal money."[365]

To collect these funds states must channel payments through their criminal enforcement machinery, further criminalizing involuntarily divorced parents and allowing the government to claim its perennial crackdowns are increasing collections despite the program operating at an increasing loss. In January 2000, HHS Secretary Donna Shalala announced that "the federal and state child-support enforcement program broke new records in nationwide collections in fiscal year 1999, reaching $15.5 billion, nearly doubling the amount collected in 1992."[366] Yet these figures are not what they appear.

In simple accounting terms, the General Accounting Office, which accepts at face value all the official HHS assumptions and data for what is "legally owed but unpaid," found that as a percentage of what it claims is owed, collections actually decreased during this period. "In fiscal year 1996, collections represented 21 percent of the total amount due but dropped to 17 percent of the total due in fiscal year 2000," writes GAO. "As a result, the amount owed at the end of the period is greater than the amount owed at the beginning of the period."[367]

Yet there is a more fundamental and much more consequential sense in which HHS's claims of success are smoke and mirrors.

The ambiguity is "collections." When we hear of collections through enforcement agencies we assume it involves arrearages or targets those who do not otherwise pay and whose compliance must be "enforced." Yet in 1992 child support was still largely being paid directly from one parent to the other, without accounting by the state. Criminal enforcement methods were limited mostly to the low-income welfare cases for which it was originally created. Increasingly since then, however, all child-support payments—including current ones—have been routed through criminal enforcement programs by automatic wage withholding and other coercive measures which presume criminality.[368]

Low-income welfare-related cases (where collection is difficult) have remained steady since 1994, while non-welfare cases (where compliance is high) continue to increase.[369] The "increase" in collections was achieved not by collecting the alleged arrearages built up by poor fathers already in the criminal collection system but by bringing more employed middle-class fathers, who faithfully pay, into it.[370] And again, this accounting mechanism has the added effect of further institutionalizing their status as semi-criminals.

What was originally created as a welfare provision has been opened up to affluent clients with no means test or other eligibility requirement. Federal auditors have pointed out that the program was diverted from its original purpose of serving a welfare constituency to become a collection agency for the affluent, with "about 45 percent reported incomes exceeding 200 percent of the poverty level and 27 percent reported incomes exceeding 300 percent": "The rate at which child-support services are being subsidized appear inappropriate for a population that Congress may not have originally envisioned serving."[371] Federal taxpayers now provide some 100 public services—including wage-withholding, caseworkers, help desk workers, county attorneys, monthly invoicing, tracking debits and credits, asset seizure, free court costs, and a plethora of collection and enforcement services—not for public welfare cases but for what are supposed to be private civil divorce cases, where private remedies are available.[372]

One enforcement agency director openly acknowledged that the Clinton administration was twisting what had originally been a welfare-designed system to an entitlement serving the wealthy in order to encourage profiteering by state governments. Testifying before Congress, Leslie Frye, chief of California's Office of Child Support, charged that the administration moved "far beyond the congressional intent" in developing an incentive system that "in fact encourages states to recruit middle-class families, never dependent on public assistance and never likely to be so, into their programs in order to maximize federal child-support incentives." Concerned that California could lose out under the new formula, Frye lays out the incentive structure with startling candor:

> [T]he proposal also changes the way collections are counted for incentive purposes in a manner that is contrary to the principles underlying the PRWORA [welfare reform] and that will lead to financial pressures on states to expand their Child Support Enforcement Programs to encompass all cases in the state, including those families who have never had to interact with government in order to pay or receive child support. Indeed, those states which already have near-universal government programs for child support will receive huge windfalls of incentives under the proposal, while states which historically concentrated on poor and near-poor families will lose federal incentive revenue, compared to the current system.

In other words, the administration was stretching congressional intent (and already meager constitutional authority) to allow profiteering by state governments. The changes pressured states to expand their programs. "By recruiting 'never welfare' families into the IV-D program, we too could benefit from earning incentives on collections for middle class families, which generally are easier to make and higher than collections for poor families," Frye points out. "From a public policy point of view, however, we think this is wrong. We believe that Congress did not contemplate, in the PRWORA, creating a universal Child Support Enforcement Program."[373]

It is difficult not to conclude that the policy changes had nothing to do with improving the efficiency of collections, since collection could not and did not improve. Indeed, as Frye points out, states that worked to improve their welfare collections could not possibly gain and would probably lose in the competition with states that simply increased the size of their collections by bringing in more middle-class payers:

> Mixing the issue of removing the limit on 'never welfare' collections with the performance-based incentive system skews the results so that some states, notably those with near-universal child-support programs, would receive more incentives for poorer performance, while states with greater proportions of welfare or former welfare families in their caseloads may not ever be able to earn incentives at the current rate, no matter how well they perform.

The purpose of the changes, as Frye suggests, is simply to expand the size of the federal machinery.

The federal funding also supplies an added incentive to make guidelines as onerous as possible and to squeeze every dollar from every parent available (as well as to turn as many parents as possible into payers by providing financial incentives for mothers to divorce). "From 1989 to 1998," writes Georgia Assistant District Attorney William Akins, "the federal government provided welfare and collection incentive funds to the states based on the gross amount of the total child-support payments recovered from non-custodial parents, thus creating a corresponding incentive to establish support obligations as high as possible without regard to appropriateness of amount."[374] Thus the impossible burdens that plunder and criminalize otherwise law-abiding parents and the heavy-handed criminal enforcement measures that turn plainly innocent people into "deadbeat dads."

These facts have never been confronted or acknowledged by government officials who continue to demonize fathers. "We want to send the strongest possible message that parents cannot walk away from their children," says HHS.[375] Yet no evidence indicates these fathers are walking away from their children. When I confronted David Gray Ross, Clinton-era Office of Child Support Enforcement commissioner, about this at a conference in 1999 and asked what justification existed for using coercive enforcement methods against citizens who clearly had not abandoned their children or even agreed to part with them, he simply refused to answer the question. When I asked again after the session, he replied that the parents pursued by his office had evidently displeased their spouses, and that was justification enough for federal criminal prosecution. Ross then walked away, refusing to discuss the matter further.[376]

Perhaps most destructive is that this federal funding is subsidizing middle-class divorce and fatherless children. "While the new measures resulted in virtually no measurable improvement in the lives of impoverished single-mother families," Seidenberg points out, "it did create a windfall of income for middle-class and upper-middle-class divorced women."[377] Misleadingly promoted as a measure to help poor children whose mostly young and unmarried fathers had allegedly abandoned them, the new laws ended up as a means to plunder middle-aged and middle-class fathers who had done no such thing and whose children were taken from them through literally "no fault" or agreement of their own.

Empirical evidence indicates that this is precisely the effect. Economist Robert Willis calculates that child-support levels vastly exceeding the cost of raising children creates "an incentive for divorce by the custodial mother." His analysis indicates that only between one-fifth and one-third of child-support payments are actually used for the children; the rest is profit for the custodial parent. "We believe that this recent entitlement," write two other scholars, ". . . has led to the destruction of families by creating financial incentives to divorce [and] the prevention of families by creating financial incentives not to marry upon conceiving of a child."[378]

Another economic study also concluded that child support serves as "an unintended economic incentive for middle-class women to seek divorce." "As long as the middle-income father works at a level comparable to that before [during?] the marriage," write Kimberly Folse and Hugo Varela-Alvarez, who based their study on child support at an atypically low percentage of fathers' income (17 percent), "divorce can be attractive, or at least economically rewarding for her." This simply extends well-established findings that increased welfare payments result in increased divorce.[379]

In this case, however, a dimension of law enforcement is added, which becomes effectively a system of federal divorce enforcement. "Enforcement . . . is the critical variable in the choice dilemma because it represents a greater surety in the assessment of the probability of attaining rewards," write Folse and Varela-Alvarez. "Strong enforcement, while it is an agreed upon societal goal to protect children, may, in fact, lead to class-based micro-level decisions that lead to the unintended consequence of increasing the likelihood of divorce."[380] In other words, a mother can simply escape the uncertainties, vicissitudes, and compromises inherent to life shared with a working husband by divorcing, whereupon she acquires the police as a private collection agency who will force him, at gunpoint if necessary, to pay her the family income that she then controls alone.

At a time when governments are ostensibly trying to strengthen marriage, Bryce Christensen points out "the linkage between aggressive child-support policies and the erosion of wedlock." "Because the politicians who have framed such [child-support] policies have done nothing to reinforce the social ideal of keeping children in intact families," he explains, "they have—however unintentionally—actually reduced the likelihood that a growing number of children will enjoy the tremendous economic, social, and psychological benefits which the realization of that ideal can bring."[381]

While these writers diplomatically suggest that these effects are unintentional, this is not necessarily the case. No-fault divorce released women legally from their marital vows but gave them no means to finance their new liberation; alimony was too obvious an inconsistency for women who were ostensibly free and financially independent. Children provided the leverage. The effect of unilateral divorce combined with the new child-support laws has been to underwrite forced divorce, rendering it a very lucrative enterprise not only for mothers but for other interests such as state governments, whose fiscal solvency depends on the creation of fatherless children. "By allowing a faithless wife to keep her children *and* a sizable portion of her former spouse's income," writes Christensen, "current child-support laws have combined with no-fault jurisprudence to convert wedlock into snare for many guiltless men."[382]

CHILD-SUPPORT PROFITEERING

Like all law enforcement, child-support enforcement formally falls within the domain of the executive branch civil service. Yet the linchpin of the system is once again the family court. The bureaucratic nature of the family judiciary and its close links with the executive are revealed in Judge Robert Page's characterization of his court as a "social service delivery system," which "requires and provides necessary services either directly or by way of referral to outside

124

agencies."[383] These "outside" agencies are often "located physically within the court."[384]

Revolving doors and other channels connect family courts with executive branch enforcement bureaucracies. Judge Ross began his career as a family court judge before moving on to higher courts and a stint in a state legislature. The OCSE informs us that "he was honored as 'Judge of the Year of America' by the National Reciprocal Family Support Enforcement Association in 1983 and as 'Family Court Judge of the Nation' by the National Child Support Enforcement Association in 1989. In 1990, he was named as co-winner of the Golden Heart Award by ACES (Association for Children for Enforcement of Support)."[385]

The very fact that pressure groups are bestowing honors upon supposedly apolitical judges (and the fact that a federal government Internet page would boast about awards given to its employees by those with a financial stake in litigation) indicates their interest in family court decisions, primarily the one removing children from their fathers that sets the process in motion and then the punitive child-support award that necessitates their services. The NCSEA Web site lists its members as "line/managerial/executive child-support staff, state and local agencies, judges, court masters, hearing officers, government and private attorneys, social workers, advocates, corporations that partner with government to provide child-support services, and private collection firms."[386] In other words, it includes officials from at least two branches of government plus the private sector, all of whom have a financial interest in having as many children as possible separated from their fathers.

The child-support branch of the divorce machinery further blurs the separation of powers in the enactment of guidelines that determine child-support levels, because those who enforce and apply the guidelines also help enact them. According to the National Conference of State Legislatures, about half the states use child-support guidelines that are devised by branches of government other than the legislative.[387] In these states the courts and the executive branch enforcement agencies are making the rules they interpret and enforce (and in all states they seem to have a central role). In eighteen states the guidelines are devised by the courts. In nine they are created by the enforcement agency itself. In fully half the states the legislature has no effective role in formulating guidelines.

In Alabama, says the NCSL, "the Administrative Director of Courts reviews the guidelines and makes recommendations to the Alabama Supreme Court." In Arizona, "the Chief Justice of the Arizona Supreme Court appoints a committee to review guidelines. The committee makes recommendations to the Supreme Court for approval." In Arkansas "the Chief Justice of the Arkansas Supreme Court appoints a committee to review guidelines. The committee makes recommendations to the Supreme Court for approval." Even where the legislature formally enacts the rules, it appears to be a rubber stamp for what the courts recommend. In California, "the Legislature statutorily amends the guidelines based on the recommendations of the Judicial Council." And so on down the alphabet. Hawaii cuts the legislature out altogether and places the other two branches in open collusion because "the Family Court establishes the guidelines in consultation with child-support enforcement agency." Nevada openly gives private lawyers who profit from it a formal role in the business: "the Legislature statutorily amends the guidelines based on the recommendations of the State Bar."

This directly violates the most basic principles of American constitutional government: the separation of powers. Rather than being enacted by elected representatives through the legislative process with public input, the formulas are devised by the same unelected judges and bureaucratic police who enforce them and who naturally have a professional interest in making them as burdensome as possible. This is not simply a matter of administrative regulations governing, say, water pollution or broadcast licenses. These guidelines are enforced at gunpoint, with "Wanted" posters and summary incarcerations. One need only imagine if police and courts enacted our other criminal statutes. The result would obviously be a police state, which is precisely how some writers and scholars have described the child-support machinery.[388]

Even without a formal role, enforcement officials are intimately involved in setting guidelines, which they have an obvious stake in making as onerous as possible so as to require criminal enforcement. Virginia guidelines are enacted legislatively, but its reviews in 1999, 2001, and 2005 were conducted by commissions comprised of one part-time representative of parents paying child support and the rest employed full-time by agencies and organizations that benefit directly from divorce."[389] The process is so openly rigged in Virginia that when the fathers' representative in 2001 simply pointed out this fact in a *Washington Times* op-ed column, he was summarily dismissed from the panel for his incorrect "opinions."[390]

"The commissions appointed to review the guidelines have been composed, in large part, of individuals who are unqualified to assess the economic validity of the guidelines or who arguably have an interest in maintaining the status quo, or both," writes William Akins of Georgia. "Of the eleven members of that

Commission, two were members of the judiciary, two represented custodial parent advocacy groups, four were either present or former child-support enforcement personnel and two were state legislators who were up for re-election. Only one, R. Mark Rogers, author of the Minority Report, is an economist."[391] Rogers dissented vigorously from the panel's recommendations.

Jo Michelle Beld, a consultant to the Minnesota enforcement agency, has described how the livelihoods of child-support officials depend on broken homes, how these same enforcement officials set the child-support levels they collect and which they ratchet ever-higher, and how "high child-support orders, in combination with other child-support enforcement policies, have a negative effect on contact between non-custodial parents and their children." She also shows how the child-support machinery virtually obliterates the separation of powers through open "collaboration" and "connections" between the three branches of government. "Legislation, administration, and adjudication," she writes, "are inextricably linked in family policies like child support."[392]

Beld's experience is reflected in a 1999 Minnesota Supreme Court decision, which held that the administrative child-support process created by Minnesota Statute §518.5511 was unconstitutional because it violated the separation of powers by usurping judicial power to an administrative agency and "by permitting child-support officers to practice law."[393] Plainclothes police act as judges and juries.

Georgia illustrates both the process and the predictable results. According to an assistant district attorney, the method of formulating guidelines "violates both substantive due process and equal protection guarantees of the Constitutions of the United States and the State of Georgia."[394] In 2002, a Georgia superior court agreed in a case involving a non-custodial mother, declaring that state's child-support guidelines unconstitutional on "numerous" grounds. "The Guidelines bear no relationship to the constitutional standards for child support of requiring each parent to have an equal duty in supporting the child" and create "a windfall to the obligee," the court ruled.

Characterizing the guidelines as "contrary both to public policy and common sense," the court noted that they bear no connection to any understanding of the cost of raising children. "The custodial parent does not contribute to child costs at the same rate as the non-custodial parent and, often, not at all," the court said. "The presumptive award leaves the non-custodial parent in poverty while the custodial parent enjoys a notably higher standard of living." Though the state appealed and eventually won this decision, the candor with which the court itself characterized its own guidelines was not refuted:

The Guidelines interfere with a non-custodial parent's constitutional right to raise one's children without "unnecessary" government interference. The Guidelines are so excessive as to force non-custodial parents to frequently work extra jobs for basic needs—detracting from parenting without state justification. Low-income obligors are frequently forced to work in a cash economy to survive as a result of child-support obligations that if paid push the obligor below the poverty level. This is the result of automatic withholding of child support with payroll jobs and use of guidelines that presumptively push minimum wage obligors below the poverty level. As these workers are forced to "disappear" into unofficial society, these obligors are deprived of the constitutional right to raise their children without unnecessary government intrusion.[395]

A court in Wisconsin likewise found that state's guidelines would "result in a figure so far beyond the child's needs as to be irrational."[396] A Tennessee court also struck down a portion of that state's child-support guidelines on grounds of "equal protection under the law." The Tennessee Department of Human Services, which regularly jails fathers for minor violations of court orders, ironically announced it would not abide by the court's ruling.[397] All these rulings were quickly reversed on government appeal.

In states where guidelines are enacted legislatively, they often pass by unanimous vote, since not only do legislators avoid questioning any measure advertised as benefiting children, but they can divert the enforcement contracts to their own firms. As was seen in the Arkansas indictments, this is usually considered legal, however questionable ethically, though the participating legislators apparently cannot always resist the obvious temptation to accept personal kickbacks.[398]

The machinery is so rife with such conflicts of interest it might almost appear that it was created to enrich certain groups. The involvement of the private sector shows that this was largely the case. Current child-support guidelines are largely the creation of one man, who is also the founder and primary owner of the nation's largest private collection company.

During the 1980s, Robert Williams was a paid consultant with HHS where he helped establish uniform guidelines in the federal Child Support Guidelines Project. Williams also consulted and still consults with many states. It was during this time that the federally driven approach was developed that led to sharply increased awards. Williams's model was developed in 1987 with a grant from the National Center for State Courts and introduced in his report,

Development of Guidelines for Child Support Orders: Advisory Panel Recommendations and Final Report for OCSE. It was shortly thereafter that Congress passed the Family Support Act of 1988, requiring states to implement presumptive, rather than advisory, child-support guidelines and giving them only a few months of legislative time to do so. Virtually all states met the congressional deadline of October 1989.

"It appears obvious that due to the short deadline required of the states to comply with this new law," writes James Johnston, "most conveniently opted for the very model being espoused by the agency overlooking the whole program." This conclusion is documented in the case of at least one state. "The guidelines were enacted in 1989 to ensure Georgia's receipt of an estimated $25 million in federal funds," writes William Akins. "They were hastily adopted . . . to beat the federal deadline."[399]

A multiplier effect also exacerbated the incentive for states to adopt Williams's guidelines, since states and municipalities tend to follow the lead of not only the federal government but also one another. "Any raises in the child-support guideline he obtains in any state can be used as leverage for raising the child-support guidelines in another state where he has private child-support contracts today, or where he may have them tomorrow," Johnston writes.[400]

One year after joining HHS, and the same year the federally mandated guidelines were created, Williams started Policy Studies Inc. "With his inside knowledge [Williams] has developed a consulting business and collection agency targeting privatization opportunities with those he has consulted," Johnston explains. "In 1996, his company had the greatest number of child-support enforcement contracts . . . of any of the private companies that held state contracts." These findings are consistent with the company's promotional literature, which says PSI operates thirty-one privatized service locations in fifteen states.

The *Denver Business Journal* reports that PSI grew "by leaps and bounds because of the national crackdown on 'deadbeat dads.'" From three employees in 1984, PSI grew exponentially to more than 500 since it began squeezing parents for municipalities. "PSI generally keeps between 10 percent and 15 percent of what it collects," the *Journal* writes, boosting revenues from $9.7 million in 1994 to $21 million in 1996. This was before welfare reform legislation took effect, by which the company "stands to profit even more."[401]

It is not surprising that Williams's profits have soared. For one thing, he collects at least twice: once through the consulting fees he charges government in formulating and implementing the guidelines (including federal tax dollars used to subsidize collection) and again in collecting the resulting arrearages. But more serious than the apparent profiteering is the level of child-support obligation that makes it possible. A collection agency only operates if there are arrearages and defaulters. Williams therefore has a vested interest not only in seeing the child-support levels as high as possible to increase his share in absolute terms, but also in making them so high that they are burdensome and create arrearages. Only by creating a level of obligation high enough to create hardship for fathers can the guidelines create a large enough pool of defaulters to ensure profits and demand for the services of his private collection agency.

"It is to Dr. Williams's benefit to design a child-support formula that calls for high amounts of support which easily create arrearages," Ginger Thomas of the West Virginia Alliance for Two Parents told the state legislature's Domestic Relations Subcommittee. "After all, the more collected, the more profits for his business."[402] Like his counterparts in state governments, Williams's business depends on creating as many fatherless children and "deadbeat dads" as possible.

Likewise in Virginia, Williams and others like him have had a central role in devising and reviewing guidelines. "My most serious concern was with the role of Dr. Robert Williams of PSI," writes Barry Koplen, the sole representative of paying fathers on Virginia's review commission in 1999. "His company's participation in child-support guideline determination and the profit it derives from its child-support collection division points to an obvious conflict of interest. . . . His proposals' higher numbers meant more collections" for his company. According to Koplen's account, Williams was given a continued active role in the periodic review of his own guidelines. "Quickly, it appeared to me that Dr. Williams would dominate our agenda," he recounts. "I sensed that we were being asked to rubber stamp both the continued use of the current guideline designed by Dr. Williams and also the revisions he had proposed to it."[403]

Williams's model raised obligations sharply, leading to "child-support awards significantly beyond the obligor's ability to pay,"[404] write economist Robert and legal scholar Cynthia McNeely. His guideline, along with the only other variation in extensive use in the United States, has been widely and severely criticized for its methods and assumptions. Economist R. Mark Rogers and Donald J. Bieniewicz, a member of an advisory panel to the OCSE, note that the "child-support guidelines currently in use typically generate awards that are much higher than would be the case if based on economically sound cost concepts and with an equal duty of support for both parents."[405]

Rogers also has charged that they result in "excessive burdens" based on a "flawed economic foundation."[406]

Williams himself has admitted "there is no consensus among economists on the most valid theoretical model to use in deriving estimates of child-rearing expenditures," and that "use of alternative models yields widely divergent estimates of the percentages of parental income or consumption allocated to the children."[407] Commenting on this passage, Bieniewicz, who authored alternative guidelines proposed by the Children's Rights Council, writes, "This is a shocking vote of 'no confidence' in the . . . guideline by its author."[408] Shocking indeed, considering that parents who cannot comply are jailed, usually without trial.

Between the conflicts of interest, the bureaucratic aggrandizement, and the financial incentives, it is hardly surprising that child support is set at punitive levels with no allowance for circumstances or fault. The Urban Institute, a left-wing think tank that is far from sympathetic to fathers, reported that the main reason for arrearages is that "orders are set too high relative to ability to pay."[409] As we will see, it is not unusual to find parents living on $500 a month or less while paying two-thirds or more of their salary to wealthy custodians and their parents or boyfriends. Additional factors ratcheting child support still higher that we will examine later, such as "add-ons" and "imputed" income, can result in child-support orders that approach or even exceed a parent's entire income.

"An obligor in Georgia (and in many other states) earning modestly above the poverty level is pushed below the poverty level by presumptive child-support obligations and is forced to make a choice between eating to survive and not making full payment on child support," writes Mark Rogers, who has served on the Georgia Commission on Child Support.[410] The OCSE has admitted that the $90 billion-plus in arrearages it claimed as of 2004 was based on awards that were beyond the parents' ability to pay:

> The best way to reduce the total national child-support debt is to avoid accumulating arrears in the first place. The best ways to avoid the accumulation of arrears are to set appropriate orders initially. . . . Designing a system that establishes appropriate orders will encourage payment of child support.[411]

Child-support enforcement is now a $4 billion national industry in terms of the money expended; in terms of the money it aims to collect, it is a multibillion-dollar enterprise with targets upward of $100 billion. PSI is not the only corporate bounty hunter turning substantial profits from involuntary divorce and fatherless children. Supportkids of Austin, Texas, describes itself as "the private-sector leader" in what the company itself calls "the child-support industry." The company is confident of rich investment opportunities in coming years, optimistic that arrearages will only increase.

"The market served totals $57 billion and is growing at an annual rate of $6 billion to $8 billion per year," enthuses the company founder and CEO. "There is a huge market for the private sector to serve."[412] The size of this "market" is determined not by demand from sovereign consumers but by how many parents can be forcibly separated from their children by government officials and turned into outlaws by impossible child-support burdens.

How much of this windfall the children will see is another matter. Unlike banks, brokerages, and insurance companies, no law requires that private collection agencies (or state ones, for that matter) be audited. The companies are normally paid according to the number of cases they close and amounts they collect, which they self-report.[413]

Kathleen Parker of the *Orlando Sentinel* reports that in Florida during 1998, "taxpayers paid $4.5 million for the state to collect $162,000" from fathers. "The money went to two private companies—Lockheed Martin IMS, a New Jersey subsidiary of the huge defense concern, and Maximus Inc." Lockheed Martin was operating thirty-two contracts in twenty-four states and counties, including a $50 million contract with Baltimore. The companies were paid $50 for every file they closed, plus a commission on money collected. "Lockheed was assigned 101,325 cases and closed 37,270, for which the company was paid roughly $2.2 million," Parker found. "For its efforts during fourteen months, it managed to collect $137,839 in child-support payments. Maximus closed 46,692 of 89,560 cases and was paid $2.25 million. It got twelve deadbeats to cough up $5,867."[414] Maximus has grown by staggering proportions since its founding in 1975 by a former HHS official. In 1998, it reported $244 million in revenue and $15.5 million in net income, averaging a 24.9 percent annual return on capital over three years. Yet in 1994, Mississippi froze a child-support collection contract with Maximus when costs nearly doubled from what the state had spent previously.[415]

Virtually anyone can now become a child-support bounty hunter, giving the general population a financial stake in involuntary divorce, single-parent homes, and fatherless children. As the GAO writes, "Any of thousands of attorneys and collection agencies can collect child support." In addition to state agencies, "about 100 other government agencies and thousands of court-appointed guardians can collect child support." The GAO further reports that "Private attorneys make up the largest group of private entities" collecting support.[416] As we have seen, these are the same attorneys who create the guidelines and who control the appointment of judges who apply them. Government contractors now use the Internet to recruit private citizens as informers and agents, turning the general population into plainclothes police.

Given the conflicts of interest and what some see as the near criminality endemic to child custody and child-support operations (*kidnapping* and *extortion* are the terms used by forcibly divorced parents), it is not wholly surprising that they attract shady individuals and unethical government officials. The federal indictments against lawmakers in Arkansas, examined in the first chapter, included child-support enforcement contracts as well as fees for attorneys *ad litem*. Even before that scandal broke, local child-support offices in Arkansas were under criminal investigation by the FBI and the subject of a six-part series in the *Arkansas Democrat-Gazette*.[417]

The potential of child support to become what one Arkansas official termed a "cash cow" for lawyers and government officials has attracted some of questionable morals. A top adviser to Prince George's County, Maryland, Executive Wayne Curry received consulting contracts not subject to competitive bidding for child-support enforcement within days of leaving the county payroll.[418] Also in Maryland, the office of Governor Parris Glendening announced in March 2002 that it was referring allegations made by a state official against Maximus, which was running Baltimore's enforcement program, to the state attorney general's office for criminal investigation. The allegations included securing court orders for child support by creating multiple cases out of a single valid case, reopening old cases improperly to get credit for obtaining court orders, and collecting money from non-custodial parents even after their children reach adulthood and refusing to refund it. The practices were brought to light by Teresa Kaiser, director of the state's Child Support Enforcement Administration, who bypassed her superiors to ask legislators for an audit. Kaiser noted that the move was "extraordinary" and said it "puts her at risk personally and professionally."[419]

A similar turf war between public and private agencies took place in neighboring Virginia (where Maximus is headquartered) in 1997. R.A.I.D., a private firm that aimed to electronically monitor the home incarceration of allegedly delinquent fathers, aroused the ire of state enforcement officials when it tried to muscle in on their territory. R.A.I.D. was assisted by at least one state legislator who collected a salary from the firm and owned stock in it that appears to have been appreciating. State enforcement officials initially liked the program, until the company became "too aggressive" in pursuit of profit, hardly a surprising development. "Somebody was trying to strong-arm us," said the state's enforcement director, Nick Young. "I got the distinct impression that this was a mill. They were trying to generate money." Young apparently believes his agency should have a monopoly on strong-arm methods. One newspaper depicted the affair much like the turf battles of organized crime syndicates.[420]

Something close to that seems to be what was attracted in Kansas. The *Wichita Eagle* reports that child-support payments collected by a private firm were not being sent to the supposed beneficiaries. MidAmerica Child Support Collections was run by Glenn and Jan Jewett, who are also involved in bingo operations in Las Vegas and who are both ex-convicts. The couple had been awarded a state contract for overseeing child-support collections in Sedgwick County in 1996, but the contract was rescinded after state officials learned that Glenn Jewett had spent five years in federal prison for drug trafficking and Jan Jewett had spent time in federal prison on charges of forgery, concealing stolen property, and writing bad checks.[421]

Allegations of ethical improprieties have been rife throughout the child-support machinery. In Los Angeles, former Deputy District Attorney Jackie Myers said she left office because "I felt we were being told to do unethical, very unethical things." These included processing orders for judgments without even reading the material to justify such a court action. District attorney's operatives, she said, were given a clear directive: "Don't read it, just sign and get the [orders] through the system. . . . They were bringing them to court in boxes."[422] Myers is not the only one to leave her post for ethical reasons. "I got a call from a homeless shelter and was told that I had put a man and . . . his four children out on the street because I had put an enforcement order . . . for 50 percent of his income. I was devastated," ex-Deputy District Attorney Elisa Baker recalled. "That was the beginning of the end for me, because I think that was the first time I was in touch with the ramifications of what I was doing."[423]

Almost a year after the *Los Angeles Times* ran a series of exposés on mismanagement and fraud in the city's child-support system, the Los Angeles district attorney's office was still shooting itself in the foot. In August 1999, the office announced yet another roundup of fathers. "But the sweep, which cost the county more than $600,000, was described by some investigators as a failed and dangerous publicity stunt that produced only a fraction of the targeted arrests and included plenty of blunders." The *Times* continues:

> While [child-support chief Steven K.] Buster praised what he described as "an extremely well organized effort," several investigators involved in the sweep told the *Times* a much different story. . . . Many of those they were sent to apprehend were already in jail or long dead. . . . "I know this is just political," said one investigator, who spoke on the condition of anonymity for fear of retribution. . . . [Said another] investigator, who also insisted on anonymity, "You figure there's got to be some political reason." Deputy District Attorney Robert Foltz agreed: "It was an incredible waste of resources." Foltz . . . criticized the effort as an "ill-conceived plan just for the purpose of making some kind of a media" event.[424]

One woman filed a formal complaint after she was allegedly strip-searched by investigators from the district attorney's office.

Insight magazine has also investigated Los Angeles District Attorney Gil Garcetti's campaign against parents, citing one father whose "take-home pay is approximately $1,200, of which Garcetti often will leave him with $200 to care for a family of four." One month, "Garcetti took all but one dollar" of his paycheck.[425] Why do such practices continue? In addition to the usual incentives, "District Attorney Gil Garcetti's reelection campaign received a total of $15,000 from twenty-one Lockheed Martin IMS employees, most of whom live out of state, a little more than a month before the prosecutor's office recommended that the Board of Supervisors pay the company an extra $2.5 million for running Los Angeles County's child-support computer system."[426] This is the same $171 million computer system that was the subject of a *Times* piece the previous October for having been riddled with problems and eventually collapsing altogether.

As a result of the *Times'* series in 1998, HHS was moved to investigate criminal fraud in the Los Angeles child-support system, but the GAO found that the investigation was perfunctory. The HHS inquiry "consisted of just two phone calls—one of them to the head of the program" whom a confidential source had identified as "one of the D.A. office employees who had engaged in misconduct."[427] According to the GAO, the office of the Inspector General "did not interview any of more than a dozen people who a confidential informant claimed had firsthand knowledge of wrongdoing within the child-support program." The *Times* quotes David Foy, aide to the state representative who requested the GAO review: "The GAO was charged with evaluating the adequacy of the inspector general's investigation and essentially found that not only was it not an adequate investigation, it was no investigation." Federal officials willing to talk about the case insisted on anonymity when they remarked, "It could have been an example of how not to do" an investigation.

In Britain, the *Times* has editorialized that the nation's Child Support Agency has become "a monstrous bureaucracy, chasing responsible parents and wrecking the families it was meant to support." Home Secretary Jack Straw said in a radio interview on July 12, 1998, that "The CSA is a shambles." As elsewhere, the directors promised a "thorough overhaul," yet with the kind of breathtaking illogic that often characterizes the child-support mentality, blame was placed not on the government that created the fiasco but on the very "responsible parents" whose families it was "wrecking." The principal reform proposed by the government and endorsed by the newspaper was not to demand honesty from government officials, much less to question the assumptions on which their operations are based, but simply to shake down any man who happens to be available and is unable to prove his innocence. "In future, absent fathers will have to prove they are not the father of a child," reported the *Times*, apparently oblivious to the *non sequitur*.

Eight years later, the Work and Pensions minister was still saying, "We fully acknowledge that the CSA is not fit for purpose" and that reform would still require "several years."[428]

In Australia, a 1994 parliamentary inquiry into the Child Support Agency (CSA) found "systemic corruption by public servants." Robert Kelso of Central Queensland University said there was "ample evidence" the CSA was "creating false debt by exaggerating incomes of fathers." The chairman of the parliamentary inquiry commission, Roger Price, said no one should have any illusions the CSA was set up to benefit children: "It is not about the best interests of children and never has been."[429] More recently, an independent review described the system as "a costly endeavour with no tangible benefits for children or their parents." It stated that "both the social and economic costs of the scheme defy all logic and are unsustainable." As in the U.S., the study concluded "there are serious flaws in the research which was used to justify the creation of the Child Support Agency and serious flaws in the formula still used to calculate child support." It also found the system untenable in accounting terms: "For every dollar the CSA collects, it costs $5.58 in administration costs, welfare, and lost taxation revenue."[430]

Public ethics and private morals seem equally vulnerable to corruption by child-support extortion and for connected reasons. The profitability and corruption of coerced child support extends even into the family, where not only the program but the children themselves become cash cows. "Children have become the cash prize in Georgia for the parent who has custody," says state Representative Earl Ehrhart in the wake of the superior court decision declaring that state's child-support guidelines unconstitutionally punitive. "The custody issues ought to be about what is best for the child and not cash issues like they are now."[431] The willingness of some women to raise children as "cash crops," as one journalist describes it, is revealed in the savvy career plans of a pre-teen girl: "I'm going to marry a really rich guy, then divorce him and marry for love. But first I'm going to have his kids so I get child support."[432]

PERSECUTING THE IMPOVERISHED?

To the officials, however, it is parents who are the criminals. This is most graphically illustrated in the chilling wanted posters displayed by state governments throughout the United States. On its Ten Most Wanted Fugitives list, even the FBI grants its targets the presumption of innocence by qualifying its accusations with the word "alleged." But the "Ten Most Wanted" child-support list in Virginia and other states simply proclaims citizens collectively guilty, with no presumption of innocence recognized. Newspaper accounts do likewise.[433]

On the version put out by the New Hampshire Office of Child Support, darkened photographs, replete with "distinguishing characteristics" and "a.k.a.," depict the mostly working-class fathers ("janitor," "gas station attendant," "general factory worker") in literally the most sinister light. The determination to portray the fathers as lowlifes seems to override the need to fulfill the deadbeat stereotype, for what the posters reveal foremost is the element of class warfare in the enterprise. Virginia displays the photo of a white "CPA" (who has almost certainly lost his license) at the head of its poster, but the rest are clearly of low income.

Attorney Ronald Henry found similar results with wanted posters in Indiana and other states. "The stereotype of the 'deadbeat dad' is the wealthy surgeon who abandoned his children in poverty to squire his new trophy wife around in a shiny red Porsche," writes Henry, who found on his posters "construction/carpenter," "tool and die worker," "welder/boilermaker," "construction/watchman," and "worked in a sawmill." "Every one of the sixteen names on the Indiana list is an economically marginal blue-collar or occasional worker," Henry writes. "All have hopelessly high arrearages in relation to their economic circumstances. . . . Other state lists are similarly loaded with low-income obligors."[434]

While this shakedown of laboring men by middle-class civil servants is justified in the name of children, figures on the New Hampshire poster reveal that what money they do manage to collect is less likely to go to the children than to the state. One father depicted on the poster was under an order to pay $177 per week and allegedly began to default nine months previously. By this reckoning, he should have owed no more than $6,372. New Hampshire has him owing $32,176. The 400 percent difference—presumably fees, interest, and penalties—is all profit for the state.

Other examples from the same poster: No. 1 actually owes approximately $4,000 but is being billed for $68,000; No. 2 owes about $14,400, billed for $27,904; No. 3 owes about $6,000, but the state claims $37,616; No. 4, $20,800 inflated to $27,300; No. 5, $24,885 versus $54,000; No. 6 owes about $16,000, but the state wants $18,558; No. 7 owes about $20,000, but OCS wants him to pay $42,000; No. 8, total arrearage about $27,500, but OCS is claiming $35,800. "It's a very profitable scam," wrote one correspondent, pointing out these discrepancies to a New Hampshire newspaper. Shortly after the publication of the letter, the state stopped displaying the figures on its posters.[435]

The zealous hounding of low-income fathers—or fathers who are made low-income by involuntary divorce and coerced child support—can be seen in the glee of father-hunters in hot pursuit. "It's just wonderful," enthuses Brian Shea, acting director of child-support enforcement in Maryland. "What you're trying to do in child support is build a box, four walls, around a person."[436] Those troubled by ethical scruples are not so sure about the propriety and wisdom of treating parents like caged animals. Another assistant D.A., who asked not to be identified by name, left his post "to wrestle with my conscience over my past role in child-support enforcement." "The typical 'deadbeat dad' I prosecuted was an unskilled construction worker employed on a seasonal and job-by-job basis," he recounts. "Rarely did these men have the benefit of legal counsel. Yet they faced the full fury of the state's enforcement machinery. . . . These men were frequently jailed for horrid lengths of time—far in excess of the length of time criminals are jailed for substantive crimes."[437]

Within the closed discursive world of the enforcement regime, a father becomes a "deadbeat" if for any reason he fails or refuses to surrender control of his family to the hegemony of the state. "Child support is 'paid' only when it's paid in a bureaucratically acceptable form," writes Bruce Walker of the Oklahoma District Attorneys Council, who claims to have jailed hundreds of fathers. A father is "supporting" his family if he pays by state-approved procedures to state-approved people and has "abandoned" them if he does anything else. "Men who provide non-monetary support are deadbeat dads according to the child-support system," says Walker. "None of the non-monetary support counts, even if the mother and father want it to count and even if they agree in writing that it should count. . . . I had thousands of these cases."

Fathers also get no credit for their expenditures directly on their children, regardless of how substantial. In fact, even fathers raising their children themselves are not immune from pursuit by the state. "Even men who are raising in their homes the very children for whom child support is sought are deadbeat dads," Walker adds. "If the mother gives the father the children because she cannot control them or has other problems, then he is still liable for child support. Most of the fathers I prosecuted said that they would raise their children with no help from the government and with no help from mom, if given the chance."[438]

Parents who have done nothing to forfeit the right to make their own financial decisions about their children have now lost that right to the government. "To allow a party to make payments other than as specified in the support order would lead to continuous trouble and turmoil," according to one court decision.[439] Obviously, it would also undermine the government's power to seize control of children whose parents have done nothing wrong.

Since automatic wage garnishing has been mandatory for all new child-support orders since 1992, the question arises as to how so many fathers supposedly manage to evade their payments. The principal method is by being unemployed. Braver's research confirmed virtually every previous study showing "that the single most important factor relating to nonpayment is losing one's job."[440] Unlike fathers in intact families, forcibly divorced fathers are punished for their unemployment or for failing to earn what government officials decide is enough money. The Dickensian attitude of criminalizing poverty is revealed by Judy Vick, program manager for Nash County, North Carolina, Child Support Enforcement: "They often do not have the wages available to take from them, so we have to take legal action."[441] Despite the stereotype, elsewhere promoted by government officials, OCSE Director Sherri Heller acknowledges that "about two-thirds of the debt and about two-thirds of the people who owe it earned less than $10,000 last year. In other words, it appears that most of the debt is owed by extremely poor debtors."[442]

An ongoing study by University of Texas anthropologist Laura Lein and Rutgers University professor Kathryn Edin has found that "many of the absent fathers who state leaders want to track down and force to pay child support are so destitute that their lives focus on finding the next job, next meal or next night's shelter." "One of the things that really surprised me was how short a job was," Lein told the *Houston Chronicle*. "People really talked about good jobs as jobs that lasted five or six days, or two weeks was really terrific." Their study concluded that the low-income and absentee fathers are often far worse off than their government-assisted families. "They struggle with irregular, low-wage employment. Many of them have faced periods of incarceration. They are affected by disability, illness and dependence on alcohol or other substances," the authors write. "But economically and emotionally marginal as many of these fathers are, they still represent a large proportion of low-income fathers who continue to make contributions to their children's households and to maintain at least some level of relationship with those children."[443]

Fathers who lose their jobs seldom are able financially to hire lawyers to have their child support lowered, and judges rarely reduce the amount anyway. Michigan lawyer Michael Tindall recounts one agent's sworn testimony official to this effect: "The local FOC [Friend of the Court] referee got up on the stand under oath and explained how it was the county's policy that if a child-support payer lost his job, the support payment would not be lowered."[444] Elaine Sorensen of the Urban Institute reports, "Only 4 percent of non-custodial parents whose earnings drop by more than 15 percent are able to get a reduction in support payments."[445] On the other hand, government lawyers will prosecute a father free of charge, regardless of his or the mother's economic circumstances.

It is now a federal crime for a father who is behind in child support, for whatever reason, to leave his state, even if it is the only way he can find work. This law has even been used to prosecute a father whose former wife moved to another state with his children, since he was no longer living in the same state.[446] For all its professed concern about fathers "abandoning" their children, the regime comes down hardest on those fathers who refuse to do so, since fathers who quit their jobs to move to where their children have been taken are given no relief for this sacrifice of their careers and earning power but instead can be prosecuted for being unemployed and losing income. Ontario's Orwellian-named Family Responsibility Office (which operates out of an unmarked building, refuses to give its address, and does not sign the threatening letters it sends to parents it claims are in arrears) confiscated the passport and driver's license of a father who fell behind after he moved to where his children had been relocated and was unable find employment to match the level he had been earning when support payments were set.[447]

Deadbeat Dads or Plundered Pops?

Men who are truly intent on abandoning their progeny have little difficulty disappearing; it is fathers who want to see their children who allow themselves to be snared. This may reveal the cruelest and most cynical side of the child-support machine: its willingness to use a father's love for his children to plunder and destroy him. In September 1998, the *Washington Post* reported on a father who quit his tenured job as a university lecturer in Europe and came to the United States after his wife abducted their children there. He was immediately summoned to court in a jurisdiction where the family had never lived, stripped of all rights regarding his children, and ordered to stay away from them most of the time. He was then ordered to pay two-thirds of his temporary salary as well as the fees of the lawyer hired against him. When his job ends, he will face incarceration for "abandoning" his children. Had he truly wished to abandon them, of course, he could have simply remained in Europe where U.S. courts and child-support authorities would have had no authority over him.[448] Similarly, a Pakistani father ordered by a Virginia judge to pay a full two years of his $10,000 annual Pakistani salary to a lawyer he did not hire could easily remain in Pakistan; he submits to almost certain incarceration to be close to his son.[449]

To the question of why so many ejected fathers are unemployed or penurious, this is not difficult to answer once one understands how the courts operate. Once the children are separated from their father, neither the courts nor the bureaucracy has much incentive to ensure his continued solvency—indeed, a solvent father is a threat—so they can happily reduce him to penury. After all, a fresh supply of fathers is constantly being brought into the system. The myopia was starkly illustrated during periodic controversies over whether to give child support priority over other debts in bankruptcy proceedings, when no one stops to ask the obvious question of why so many allegedly well-heeled "deadbeats" were going through bankruptcy in the first place.[450] In what some have called a policy of "starvation," a federal regulation renders these rich playboys, who otherwise qualify, ineligible for food stamps.[451] Walker relates how he prosecuted a father who was hospitalized for malnutrition because he was not left enough money to feed himself adequately.[452]

Many fathers whose children are seized by the courts also are either ordered out of their homes or must move out for financial reasons, so they are immediately homeless. To what extent child support is responsible for the very poverty it is claimed to alleviate is unclear. It has long been known that the vast majority of the homeless are male. Widespread anecdotal evidence suggests that family courts may be partially responsible for their plight. Mike Yeager of Scranton, Pennsylvania, explained his condition to a local newspaper, saying that when he lost his job, he had to make a choice—pay the rent or pay child support for his three children. "Being in a shelter is better than being in jail," he said.[453] "I'd say 25 to 40 percent of the men in the shelter are veterans," says one shelter director. "Many were married and aren't married now."[454]

Divorced fathers often lose their cars, which may be their only means of transportation to their jobs and children. Those who fall behind in child-support payments, regardless of the reason, now have their cars booted and their driver's licenses and professional licenses revoked, which in turn prevents them from getting and keeping employment. Courts also do not hesitate to summon fathers so often that they lose their jobs and then jail them for being unemployed. It is not unusual for a father to have been summoned to court hundreds of times. It is well known in the business world that fathers under child-support orders, with the threat of jail hanging over their heads, will readily work for lower pay. Aware from wage withholding what fathers have to live on after child support has been deducted, employers are often careful to assign fathers on child-support orders to duties that give them no access to anything they might steal. We do not know how much criminality is driven by child-support obligations, but given the number of young, low-income inner-city men involved in both the child-support system and the drug trade, the overlap is almost certainly substantial.

"The stricter enforcement of child support" discourages legitimate employment among inner-city young men, according to the *New York Times*, which noted that about half of all black men in their late twenties and early thirties who did not go to college are non-custodial fathers. Such debts, the *Times* said, "amount to a tax on earnings . . . and deter them from seeking legal work, since a large share of any earnings could be seized."[455]

Crime in fact is made the less risky option by the ratio of enforcement agents and by incarcerations, which render a father much more likely to be jailed for child support than for drug dealing or violent crime. "Drug dealers know they can make bond and get out of jail," says Etowah County, Alabama, Chief Deputy Todd Entrekin, apparently oblivious to the implications. "On these [child-support] warrants, they're in jail until the support is paid."[456] The logic is also attested by the desperation of even high-income fathers. An air traffic controller earning $130,000 with no prior criminal record claimed he was driven to robbing banks to pay child support. The *San Francisco Chronicle* dismisses the matter by saying the heists resulted from "not managing his money well enough."[457] A Carson City, Nevada, man is said to have "felt pressured by child-support payments when he used a pellet gun to rob a bank" in

2004. His public defender said he "was forced into economic desperation after paying tens of thousands of dollars in child-support payments and also assuming responsibility for supporting his girlfriend's family."[458] Apparently one judge even became compromised. The New York State Commission on Judicial Conduct tried to remove Justice Reynold Mason of State Supreme Court in Brooklyn after finding that "he illegally sublet his apartment to his brother-in-law and, instead of turning the rent money over to the landlord, used it to pay child support."[459]

Evidence of the economic impact is more than anecdotal. A study by PIR Independent Research concludes that child support is the primary driver of unemployment in Australia and that more than 70 percent of unemployed men in Australian are paying child support. "Payers faced with the daunting prospect of losing up to 62 percent of their after-tax wage calculated on their gross wage at marginal tax rates are opting out of the work force," the study found. "On top of high income tax rates cutting in at low levels separated fathers can be left with less than twenty cents in the dollar. This provides strong disincentives to work." Recipients have even less incentive to work. "Payees are receiving considerable monies via parenting payments, family tax benefits, rental assistance and tax free child-support payments from the payer, which can be sufficient to provide a reasonable lifestyle without the need to seek part or full-time work."[460]

When one considers the geographical constraints of having to find work near one's children and of commuting both to a job and to a family and the need to adjust one's work schedule to when a judge decides a father may see his children, not to mention the emotional strains of losing them,[461] it is not difficult to see not only why so many ejected fathers lose their jobs and have trouble finding and keeping new ones, but also why those most committed to remaining in contact with their children are the most likely to have their livelihoods suffer. The comments of a Tennessee judge that "I specifically make it [visitation] so absolutely ridiculous that nobody can adhere to it," was apparently not deemed to be grounds for disciplinary action. "And I hold people in contempt and put them in jail for it," he added.[462]

FOR THE CHILDREN?

Any incentive to reward the mother for bringing another family under the control of the judicial machinery is fair game for the judge to order at the father's expense. Though ostensibly limited by statutory guidelines, in practice a judge is free to order virtually any amount in child support. A judge who decides, on nothing more than his own opinion, that a father could or should be earning more than he does can (and frequently does) "impute" potential income to the father and assess child support and legal fees based on that hypothetical income. The result is that child-support payments may exceed what the father earns. In Wilmington, North Carolina, a disabled veteran was ordered to pay $22 more each month than he earns.[463] In Canada, a child and spousal support award of $3,150 was imposed on a father who was clearing $3,400. When he fell behind, authorities suspended his driver's license. "They removed my ability to earn the very money I was paying them."[464]

At the other end of the income spread is "Michael," ordered to pay $7,153 monthly, or 96 percent of his salary. In figuring his monthly salary the court included one-time and occasional items such as severance pay and bonuses. Michael was left with $302 each month to live on. He lives on borrowed money, and if he goes bankrupt he will lose his license and job as a certified public accountant. "It's 100 percent as a result of this divorce," he says, a divorce for which he gave neither grounds nor consent. "Her only issue is I never spent enough time with her." By court order, his former wife receives $85,836 a year tax-free from him, roughly equivalent to a fully taxable salary of $125,000 a year, according to Donna Laframboise, who wrote a series for the *National Post* shortly before being dismissed from the newspaper.[465]

Even more crushing, though Michael has only occasionally fallen behind, his children are apparently being encouraged to think of him as a deadbeat. "I talked to my sixteen-year-old son when [a *Toronto Star* article on deadbeat dads] came out. You know what he said to me? He said, 'Dad, did you read that article in the *Star*? Well that's what I think of you.'" Laframboise, whose investigation was not challenged or refuted, found that "stories are remarkably similar across the income spectrum" and furnishes these examples:

- In 1997, Denis McKenzie, a Winnipeg postal worker with a take-home pay of $1,900 monthly, was ordered to pay $2,000 in child and spousal support.
- Wayne Archer, a firefighter living in Caledon, Ontario, says that a 1991 child-support order for $750 a month for his son "represented 91 percent of my net pay at the time. . . . In desperation, I bought a camper and put it on the back of my pickup truck."
- Dr. Robert Wright, a British Columbia dentist, fled the country after serving jail time for failing to pay alimony. Although his payments of

$900 a month for child support were up to date, Wright ceased pay-ing the monthly $2,500 in spousal support when he was certified as bankrupt. The judge rejected this evidence and sent him to jail for sixty days.

As Michael's case illustrates, if a father at any point works any extra hours (perhaps to pay child support or legal fees) or receives any other temporary income, he is then locked into that imputed income and those overtime hours, and the child-support level based on them, until his children are grown. In the case of Denis McKenzie, the judge determining the postal worker's income "added additional income he would earn if he delivered extra flyers—thus turning an option of earning more money [by working overtime] into an obli-gation." Fathers like Chris Roney of Urbana, Illinois, are ordered to meet their payments by taking out loans, which are then treated as income in setting their payment level. According to his attorney, money Roney borrowed to pay attor-neys' fees was considered "income" in assessing his level of child support, about $1,400 monthly as of this writing.

If a relative or benefactor pays the child support on behalf of the father, that payment is considered a "gift" and does not offset the obligation, which the father himself still owes. If the payment is made to the father it becomes "income," which can then be used to increase the amount of the father's imputed earning capacity and with it his monthly obligation. Guidelines are formulated "with no consideration for payroll deductions for federal and state income tax, Social Security, mandatory insurance contributions."[466] The non-custodial parent pays all taxes on the money before it is sent to the custodial parent, but all tax deductions and benefits go to the custodial parent alone, as if she were supporting the children by herself.

Custodial parents are not required to spend child support on the children, and—unlike any other government-mandated financial transfer—they are not required to account to either the non-custodial parent or the court for how they spend it. "Dads must pay, but moms are free to squander the money," writes attorney David Butler. "If it is absolutely in the best interests of the chil-dren to require that the support be paid for them, then why should we not also absolutely require that the money be spent for them?"[467]

Judges are not even the only ones who can set or raise a child-support obli-gation. Civil servants can and do arbitrarily increase the child-support obliga-tions of the parents they pursue, sometimes without even informing the obligor. Attorney Tindall was arrested and jailed with no warning when he knew his payments were current. "I found out later that some FOC employee had just upped my support," he told *Michigan Lawyers Weekly*. "There was no order from a judge. They just did it. In court, they admitted that they do this all the time."[468]

In addition to the regular child support, fathers are forced to pay "add-ons," which in most cases include all medical and dental premiums, out-of-pocket medical and dental costs, day care, and extra-curricular activities. Yet there is no precise legal definition of what constitutes a legitimate add-on. "The case law itself is taking completely contradictory views," reads one report. By most formulas these costs are already figured in the basic child support, so the father pays twice. Many add-ons do not even benefit the children but are for costs such as day care, so the children can be stored in an institution against a father's wishes even when he is available and willing to look after them himself.

Edward Kruk, a social work professor at the University of British Columbia, says the add-ons result in the non-custodial parent ordered to pay twice the guideline amount or more. "With preschool children, a lot of dads who are asking for parenting time with their kids are being denied that and the kids are ending up in a day-care setting that fathers then have to pay for as special expenses," he says. "Everyone says child support is about feeding the children," says Mike LaBerge, president of the Calgary chapter of the Equitable Child Maintenance and Access Society, "but it's not." One father is ordered to pay add-ons including $600 a month for skating lessons, $80 for music lessons, and $150 a month for cheerleading lessons."[469]

ABSURDISTAN IN AMERICA

Cases reported in the media are only the tip of an iceberg, but some are typical of the burdens imposed on many involuntarily divorced fathers. What is striking about the media accounts, however, is that they seldom lead to any further investigations to understand why these cases are created. Either these accounts are mistaken, in which case the newspaper should be publishing retractions (though none are being refuted), or they are accurate, in which case something close to a reign of terror is being perpetrated against innocent citizens with no public inquiry. Even extensive investigations, like those of the *Los Angeles Times* and the *National Post*, do not result in any government response or reform.

The *Cincinnati Enquirer* is more forthright than most newspapers when it reports that Christopher Thomas is left with about $500 a month to live on after paying child support. "He sleeps on a friend's couch because he can't afford rent for his own apartment. He doesn't own a car and relies on friends to drive him to work." Yet this startling case prompts no further investigation by the newspaper into why or how the government has made it impossible for this man and others to live.[470] The night after the release of Bobby Sherrill from five harrowing months as an Iraqi hostage, the local sheriff came to arrest him for not paying $1,425 in child support while he was a hostage. Likewise, Clarence Brandley spent nearly ten years in prison, most of it on death row, wrongly accused of murder. After his exoneration and release, the state presented him with a bill for nearly $50,000 in child support that Brandley failed to pay while wrongfully imprisoned.[471]

Similar cases, far from exceptional, are becoming the norm, though they are likely to be publicized in the media only when they reach the dimensions of farce. One custodial father was unaware of forty cents in back child support, "and by the time he found out, the bill had grown to $173.53 for interest and fees." The man "could face up to 180 days in jail." Like many pursued fathers, this one assumes he alone is being treated unfairly and that the rest are the "real" deadbeat dads. "There are plenty of people who owe more or who don't pay at all," he insists. "I paid support every week I was working. I've had my son for almost four years now, and now they come back and say, 'Pay more money?'"[472]

Many share this father's assumption that "there must be some mistake" and that authorities are pursuing an innocent man rather than the "real" deadbeats. But at some point one begins to wonder. If fathers neglecting their children is truly a serious problem, and if officials are as "overburdened" as they claim, they should be concentrating limited resources on serious cases. Instead, the most trivial cases are prosecuted with the full force of the law, reinforcing the suspicion that authorities are doing their best to create as many cases and criminalize as many citizens as they can.

John Hoch of Pennsylvania could not possibly win. When his wife obtained a backdated increase, he found himself with an instant arrearage of $2,600. His request to pay in one lump sum was denied, but instead he was given a payment plan involving an additional $50 each month, permitting the state to charge interest. The same judge who devised the payment plan then froze his bank account for the arrearage. Federal law requires states to seize assets even if a payment schedule has already been established, says the state enforcement director, Dan Richard. "If someone is even a dollar short in a month's payment, assets can be seized."[473]

The Washington, D.C.-based Men's Health Network has compiled a list of patent injustices and absurdities from every state, indicating a pattern less of solicitude for children than of judicial and bureaucratic bullying:

- After a downsizing at a major international airline, an Arizona father was forced to either take a job in a new location outside the state or find a new job and stay near his daughter of whom he had joint custody. He chose to stay in Arizona and seek new employment. A reduction in child support was denied, as it was determined that he left his job voluntarily to seek a lower-wage job.
- A father in Florida accrued arrearages after his child-support order was not modified once he became the custodial parent.
- In Delaware, children received disability payment as a result of their father's injury, but his child support was not modified and he was not credited for the children's share of his disability payments.[474]

The list is infinite. If these were isolated, exceptional, or extreme cases one must inquire why they continue, even after exposure in the media. Partly perhaps because even the media that report them usually accept the official interpretation that individual cases of patent injustice are somehow separate from the pursuit of "real" deadbeats. But the realization of how easily anyone can be turned into a "deadbeat dad" must eventually prompt the question of whether anyone really is. Child-support formulas and enforcement methods are standardized. If one family can be preyed upon by a tyrannical judge and an overzealous goon squad, why should we not assume this is not the case for all 16 million federally "pursued" parents, few of whom presented a problem only a few years ago? We do not normally measure constitutional rights violations by their quantity but maintain a presumption of innocence and assume that a violation of anyone's constitutional rights is a threat to the rights of all. Yet here we assume just the opposite. The official presumption of criminal guilt against all non-custodial parents was revealed by the highest law enforcement official in the land, then-Attorney General Janet Reno, who referred to "$14 billion that is collected from deadbeat parents" *before* her planned crackdown, calling parents who do pay "deadbeats."[475]

The criminalization of the innocent becomes flagrant in "paternity fraud," a common practice whereby men are forced to pay the custodians of children who are acknowledged not to be theirs. A Maryland Court of Appeals was not unusual when it refused to rescind an order against a man who according to

DNA tests could not possibly have been the father of the child he was ordered to support, despite the fact that the mother and the true father joined the falsely accused man in requesting the order be changed. A Nebraska man must pay to support a child born to his former wife as a result of her adulterous affair during their marriage. A Michigan man was ordered to pay child support to the child's biological father after DNA testing cleared him of paternity and the father received sole custody.[476] Such cases have mushroomed. A series in the *Los Angeles Times* reported that in Los Angeles alone 350 new cases are added each month of men required to support children who are established by DNA testing not to be theirs. Eighty percent of paternity establishments there are entered by default judgments, without the alleged fathers ever having a chance to prove their innocence. Yet District Attorney Gill Garcetti insisted he had no intention of overturning orders based on false identifications; on the contrary, he said he would prosecute the men to the full force of the law. "For some reason, the concept of the Bill of Rights does not register with the D.A.'s office of Los Angeles County," says attorney Sam Wasserson.[477]

The rationalization is invariably, once again, the "best interest of the child," thus allowing an evidentiary standard to supercede the presumption of innocence and other due process protections. Yet expanding government power and financial gain are more likely explanations. Here again, federal welfare money provides perverse incentives, requiring states to institute paternity establishment procedures or lose billions of dollars. "Eligibility . . . depends only upon tagging the largest possible number of men, and there is no review or requirement that it be the right men," writes attorney Ronald Henry. Most victims are low-income minority males, and many are young and even underage, with few of the skills or means to defend themselves in a mass judicial "assembly line" that bears little relation to a fair hearing. "The paternity fraud victim is hustled through the formality, often in less than five minutes, and may not even realize what has happened until the first garnishment of his paycheck." Henry estimates that the number of such victims may exceed one million.

In another example of Soviet logic, defenders of the fraud cynically invoke not only the "best interest" but the children's need for fathers. "An attempt to undo a determination of paternity is potentially devastating to a child who ha[s] considered the man to the be father," reads one ruling. "Social science data . . . overwhelmingly establish that children benefit psychologically, socially, educationally, and in other ways from stable and predictable parental relationships." Yet coerced child support is predicated not on uniting children with fathers but on keeping them apart. Despite the touchy-feely language about family and stability and relationships, such decisions have nothing to do "with enforcing anything other than financial obligations," writes Henry. "None of the courts that refuse relief from false paternity establishments is actually talking about maintaining a physical or emotional relationship between the child and the unrelated adult." Nothing prevents the government or the mother from permitting a paternity fraud victim to continue voluntarily a relationship with the child. "Every child-support agency in America knows that it . . . has worked injustice upon appalling numbers of innocent men."[478]

Pushing the divorce machine's criminalization of personal life a step further, Britain's Labour government has responded not by exonerating the innocent but by further criminalizing them for trying to prove their innocence. Labour proposes outlawing home paternity testing kits available from private companies, so men can also be arrested for trying to prove they are not the biological fathers of children they are ordered to support.[479] Similar legislation has been proposed in Australia.[480]

In some jurisdictions stepfathers are now ordered to pay the custodians of their stepchildren. In Australia, this includes adult stepchildren.[481] The Supreme Court of Canada has ruled that a Winnipeg man must pay the custodian of his stepdaughter.[482] Stuart Miller of the American Fathers' Coalition comments wryly that this ruling opens the door to multiple marriages to obtain multiple child-support proceeds from multiple men without the inconvenience of multiple children. This in fact seems to be happening, as judges now allow "double-dipping" whereby both the biological father and stepfather are ordered to pay full child support to the same custodian for the same children.[483] In 2004, the Massachusetts Appeals Court ruled that a mother could collect full child support from two men for the same child.[484]

Viola Trevino did not bother with a pregnancy at all before obtaining a child-support order against her former husband. Steve Barreras was forced to pay $20,000 over five years for a child that never existed. "The child-support system in this state is horrible," an Albuquerque woman in quoted in the local media. "A woman can walk into their office with a birth certificate and a 'sob' story, and the man on that birth certificate is hunted down and forced to pay child support." But the state's Child Support Enforcement Division said it was not responsible for harassing Barreras, because it was "merely enforcing child support already ordered by a judge."[485] New Mexico Governor Bill Richardson ordered an investigation into the case only after an exposé by KRightsRadio host Richard Farr.

Canada also seems to be taking the lead in pursuing what are called "dead-beat accomplices." These are second wives, grandparents, and other relatives who have no legal responsibility for the children but who may now be forced to disclose their finances to the courts.[486] American jurisdictions are following suit. In 1999, Patricia Hill was convicted in Federal District Court of accessory after the fact and harboring a fugitive, both felonies. Ironically, in this case, the "fugitive" (her husband) had not himself violated any law. According to court transcripts, Christopher Cardani, the federal prosecutor in charge of the case, admits to the possibility of prosecuting anyone, including a wife, a grandparent, or a friend, who gives what can be construed as sustenance to a child-support obligor, even if the obligor himself is not in violation of the law. "If the government succeeds in this case, millions of second wives and parents of child-support obligors will find themselves at risk for prosecution," according to Lowell Jaks of the Alliance for Non-Custodial Parents' Rights. "What this amounts to is legalized extortion and blackmail."[487]

In fact, the extortion of family members has long been under way through the incarceration of their men, an effective method of squeezing money out of anyone who loves them or their children. Judges and enforcement agents often comment smugly on how quickly fathers who claim they have no money miraculously manage to come up with it once they are threatened with jail. "We family court judges call [incarceration] 'the magic fountain,'" one unusually candid judge admits. "Of course, there is no magic. The money is paid by his mother, or by the second wife, or by some other innocent who perhaps had to liquidate her life's savings."[488]

Some officials no longer bother with such indirect methods but go directly after the family members' bank accounts. In July 2000, the West Virginia Bureau of Child Support Enforcement cleaned out the bank account of an eighty-five-year-old grandmother whose son allegedly owed child support. Her son paid in none of the $6,450 taken from the account, which comprised her entire life savings. She was also charged a $75 processing fee for the debit.[489] In Iowa, the government confiscated the savings of eleven-year-old Rylan Nitzschke, who earned the money from chores and shoveling snow, because Rylan's father allegedly owed child support (to Rylan) and his father's name was on the boy's bank account. State officials refused to return the money and said the only way Rylan's father can prevent the looting of Rylan's savings in the future is to give the money to the adult with custody.[490]

The claims of some fathers that the child-support system amounts to "kidnapping and extortion" received some verification when it was discovered that mothers are shaking down fathers for extra payments in return for being permitted to see their children. A correspondent to a syndicated personal advice column writes that his former wife was violating a visitation order by refusing to let him see his children but said "I could have time with them if I gave her extra money." Significantly, the authors of the column apparently saw nothing unusual about such arm twisting.[491]

Since it is well known that visitation orders are never enforced, it is very easy for a mother to withhold the children from the father unless he agrees to additional payments. "Desperate divorced dads are secretly paying former partners to buy time with their children," according to the *Herald Sun* of Melbourne, Australia. "The money these dads pay is on top of compulsory child-support payments." The article indicates that Family Court Chief Justice Alastair Nicholson is well aware of such practices. "Most men can't afford to pay, but wouldn't you if it was the only way to see your kids?" one father is quoted as saying.

Child psychologist Michael Carr-Gregg said payments for access to children were unethical. "It's reducing these kids to commodities for sale," he said. "This would send wrong messages to kids who knew they were traded. It's putting a dollar value on their heads." Yet given the nature of the custody system, which is based on a similar principle, such extortion is irresistible. "I'd turn up [for visitation] and they wouldn't be there. I'd see them maybe a fortnight later, maybe not," another father is quoted. "Now I pay the $40. . . . I give her the cash, she gives me the kids."[492]

Some governments are no longer even waiting for a divorce or separation to strip fathers of financial decision-making over their children and bestow monopoly control on mothers. The British government recently implemented the "Child Tax Credit," which automatically deducts money from fathers' pay packets and deposits it in their wives' bank accounts. The measure is based on the presumption "that women are considered more likely to spend the cash on children."[493] No evidence is cited for this presumption.

Perhaps the supreme irony is where children pay child support to grownups; indeed, child molesters can even collect child support from the children they have raped. Courts are now ruling that minor boys statutorily raped by adult women must pay child support to the criminals who raped them. In December 1996, a California appeals court upheld an order that a fifteen-year-old boy statutorily raped by a thirty-four-year-old woman must pay child support. Despite the well-known legal principle that a criminal should never profit from his or her crime, the Supreme Court of Kansas has held that "the issue of consent to sexual activity under the criminal statutes is irrelevant in a civil action to determine paternity and for support of a minor child born of such activity." Likewise, in November 1998 in Walnut Creek, California, a woman accused of giving a sixteen-year-old drugs and then having sex with him sued the boy for child support. According to the Associated Press, "State law entitles the child to support from both parents, even though the boy is considered the victim of statutory rape, Contra Costa district attorney's officials said."

The Michigan Court of Appeals ordered the victim of a statutory rape at the age of fourteen to pay child support to the perpetrator, "even though under state law, the sex act was likely a crime." The court reasoned that "the purpose of child support is to provide for the needs of the child; it is awarded without regard to the fault of either of the parents." The *Detroit Free Press* demonizes the boy as "a man who had sex with a married woman," rather than the victim of a child molester, and makes no mention of the woman being prosecuted for the crime. It also reports that the case files were suppressed.[494]

Child support also renders the elderly and infirm vulnerable to rape-for-profit. A partially disabled eighty-five-year-old man who was sexually assaulted by his housekeeper while recovering from a stroke, and was eventually awarded damages for the assault, was ordered to pay her child support, and his pension was garnished. According to the *National Post*, "He was denied access to the child by the court on the grounds it was not in the best interest of the child."[495] An ironic role reversal takes place when not only children pay child support but grownups collect it. "We've got some forty- to forty-five-year-old 'kids' running around who are owed child support," says Nick Young, child-support enforcement director for Virginia, apparently in all seriousness.[496] In Ohio, a seventy-seven-year-old great grandfather who had always paid was told he owed $45,000 in back child support and had his wages garnished, even though his youngest child was forty-six years old.[497]

In New York, children may legally leave their parents' home at eighteen, but they can receive child support until twenty-one. The result is that such children can collect child support from their own parents. One girl rationalized her suit by saying her mother was "too strict."[498] But it has been left to a divorce lawyer to realize the full potential of the child-support logic (with a contribution from the psychotherapy industry) when he sued his own parents for child support. Judge Melinda Johnson ordered James and Bertha Culp of Ventura, California, to pay their fifty-year-old son David Culp $3,500 a month for living expenses indefinitely because he is incapable of supporting himself. Culp claims to suffer from depression and bipolar disorder. Johnson based her ruling on state Family Code section 3910(a), which she says states that "the father and mother have an equal responsibility to maintain, to the extent of their ability, a child of whatever age who is incapacitated from earning a living and without sufficient means." The most startling feature of the case is that such suits may well have been both foreseen and intended by legislators. (Again, many state lawmakers are divorce lawyers.) Johnson says the statute is "unambiguous," and Culp's lawyer is quoted as saying, "The statute didn't come about by accident."[499]

Obviously innocent or heroic fathers may get a break from the media, though seldom from the authorities. Larry Silvia traveled from Florida to Massachusetts "to donate a kidney to his sister—and ended up in jail on charges of missing $40,000 in child-support payments."[500] The only way the authorities knew he was in the state was because he attended church to see his three daughters. "That afternoon, police showed up . . . with an arrest warrant . . . and took him to jail." The mother's attorney told the court that Silvia was a risk to flee and should go to the hospital in police custody." The judge agreed and set bail at $15,000, which the family of Silvia's sister had to raise to allow her to have her kidney operation.

Once again, there are many unanswered questions and much we do not know in these cases: Who broke up this family? Did this man really owe $40,000? His second wife claims "her husband has records that show he owes only $2,347, and that he only missed four months of payments when he was out of work." Is it likely that this father—who risked and incurred arrest to donate a kidney to his sister and to catch a glimpse of how his daughters were growing up—was another selfish lout who could only be counted on to provide for his children by bringing full force of the penal system to bear on him and subjecting him to criminal penalties for failure to adhere to a judge's determination of how he should handle his family finances?

This is not likely to be the case for Terrance Yeakey, a genuine hero by any assessment. "Four days before he was to receive a medal for his valor in the 1995 Oklahoma City bombing, Yeakey . . . drove to a field near El Reno, where he had grown up, 30 miles from Oklahoma City, and slit his wrists," according to *People* magazine. "Then he staggered half a mile into a gully and shot himself in the head."[501] To the people of his hometown, "Yeakey was a genuine hero: Not only had he pulled three men and a woman from the rubble of the Alfred P. Murrah Federal Building, but he had dedicated himself to helping schoolchildren. . . . He . . . traveled from school to school, counseling students, playing basketball with them, and reading to them." "He loved kids," says a close friend. "That's what drove him, the kids."

Yet among possible explanations for his suicide—which include his military service and the trauma from the bombing—*People* tells us only belatedly that he was a "divorced father" who "apparently fell behind on child-support payments, which forced him to work as many as three extra jobs, at night and on weekends" and that he "missed his kids badly after his bitter divorce." The *St. Louis Post-Dispatch* on May 12, 1996, states up front he "was racked with guilt because an injury kept him from rescuing more victims" (the injury being caused during the rescue) and "despondence over a troubled family life." Only later do we learn that he was "divorced from his wife" and "legally prevented from entering the house the couple had shared with their two daughters, ages two and four." A friend speculated that the suicide was caused by "his love for his two daughters that he could not see." Again the unanswered questions: Why was he forcibly kept from his own children? Was this an emotionally unstable man who had committed some grievous act that warranted being forced to stay away from his children and coerced into paying what government officials decide is necessary for his children? Or was this a heroic father driven to suicide after his children were stolen and abused and he himself effectively enslaved to those who had stolen and abused them? It seems *People* and the *Post-Dispatch* should be telling us one way or the other.

Do these questions matter? Yes, they do matter, because in these questions lies the difference between a father who is pursued because he has abandoned his children and a father who is pursued because he refuses to abandon his children. Courts exist to dispense justice against those who violate the law or agreements. When they abandon this role to become a "social service delivery system" it is much more likely that the justice and penal systems will be perverted to persecute the innocent. While these journalists do not tell us if these parents have done something legally wrong to bring these penalties upon themselves, we do know that according to the law in virtually every jurisdiction in the English-speaking world, they do not need to have done so. By shifting blame from the parent who violates a legal agreement to the deserted parent's imputed and often concocted financial "obligation," the government can arrest a parent whose spouse walks out on him without any legal grounds if he cannot afford horseback riding lessons.[502]

Yeakey's death was unusual only in being covered in the popular press. There are many instances where a punitive child-support award amounts to a summary death sentence. Darren White of Prince George, British Columbia, was ordered out of his home, cut off from all contact with his three children, and ordered to pay $2,071 out of his $2,200 monthly salary in child and spousal support. White was also required to pay double court costs for a divorce he never sought or agreed to. In fact the sentence was even more crushing, since the stress of losing his children also rendered him medically unfit for his job as a locomotive engineer, leaving him $950 a month in disability pay. In March 2000, White hanged himself from a tree. No evidence of any legal wrongdoing was ever presented against him. White's fourteen-year-old daughter writes about her father the government portrayed as a deadbeat:

> My dad was abused by the justice system. . . . My dad was a very good father and wanted the best for all four of his children. All of us children were his life. He wanted everything he could possibly give to his children and what he couldn't. The most important thing he gave his children were his love, and being there for them. He loved all of his kids equally, and with all his heart. He was a kind man who fought a good fight but no matter what he did or said he could never win with this system. Things need to change for all fathers going through this same thing. We need to help; too many kids go without a father because of this, too many kids are hurt."[503]

After White's death, the *Toronto Star* launched a hatchet job, penned by feminist Michelle Landsberg, against a dead man who could not defend himself. (Following in this tradition, the *Kamloops Daily News* proceeded to assassinate the character of Mark Dexel after his body and suicide note were found on January 24, 2003, the first anniversary of the last day he saw his two-year-old son. No friends or family members of Dexel's were quoted in the article, and some were themselves attacked.)[504]

By the testimony of the legal profession that condemned him, Darren White's circumstances and his fate are very common. "There is nothing unusual about this judgment," former British Columbia Supreme Court Judge Lloyd McKenzie was quoted as saying in the *Vancouver Sun*. McKenzie pointed out that the judge in White's case applied standardized guidelines for spousal and child support.[505]

Essentially the same guidelines are used in the United States and elsewhere, with similar consequences. In August 1999, Charles London of New Bedford, Massachusetts, stabbed himself to death with a kitchen knife after being cut off from all contact with his two children and ordered to pay more than 75 percent of his salary in child support, being left with $78 a week.[506] In Britain, the

National Association for Child Support Action has published a "Book of the Dead" chronicling fifty-five cases where they claim the official Court Coroner concluded fathers were driven to suicide because of judgments from divorce courts and harassment by the country's Child Support Agency.[507] One is Terry Brett, who gassed himself in his garage when ordered to pay £1,217 a month from his salary of £1,798. A spokeswoman for the CSA acknowledged that it had been blamed for suicides before.[508] "Back in 1994, when I said people were committing suicide in major part because of family law matters, people were disbelieving," remarks an Australian member of parliament who chairs a parliamentary inquiry into the Child Support Agency and who claims divorced Australian fathers are killing themselves at a rate of twenty a week. "No one disbelieves it anymore."[509]

Yet both researchers and journalists, when they confront this phenomenon at all, treat it as a problem not of justice but of psychotherapy. Professor Pierre Baume, of Monash University found that in Australia, more than 1,000 men aged twenty-five to forty-four take their own lives each year. In language typical of his trade, Baume attributes this alarming statistic (roughly twenty a week) not to the loss of their children and persecution by courts but to "relationship break-ups." For Baume, therefore, the solution is simple: Men do not need due process of law; they need to get in touch with their feelings: "Teaching boys that it is not unmanly to express their feelings," will mean that separated men do not "end up so isolated." Only belatedly do we find that "most of the suicide problems associated with separated men may relate to child access problems."[510]

This at least is Baume's finding as reported in *The Age* newspaper, which may have its own ax to grind. Augustine Kposowa of the University of California Riverside likewise found that the risk of suicide among divorced men was more than twice that of married men (no similar differential was found for women) but came to a rather different conclusion about its cause. Kposowa attributed his finding directly to judgments from family courts. Yet reports of his study by CBS, CNN, and Reuters ignored this conclusion in favor of therapeutic explanations emphasizing fathers' lack of "friends" and "support networks." One reporter told Kposowa flatly that his conclusion was not "politically correct."[511]

Nor does the state necessarily wait for a father to take his own life. Brian Armstrong of Milford, New Hampshire, received what some have called a summary death sentence for losing his job. Incarcerated without trial on January 11, 2000, Armstrong died a week later apparently as the result of a beating by jail guards. "Authorities say he died from a head injury he suffered at the jail," reports the Manchester *Union Leader* and *New Hampshire Sunday News*, but "they have yet to determine how he sustained that injury." Armstrong's parents also said they received no official report or cause of death but believe he was beaten by jail guards and then denied medical attention. His mother was told by medical officials who saw Armstrong days later that his body was covered with bruises and he had suffered a severe brain injury. Another inmate was later transferred from the jail after telling authorities he believed Armstrong was beaten. The inmate said in a jail interview that he saw guards drag Armstrong from his cell into a maximum security unit room from which he then heard screaming he believes was the result of a fifteen-minute beating, before he saw two nurses drag Armstrong off. Armstrong lost his job as a welder and allegedly failed to appear at a hearing on child support. His family claims he was never notified of the hearing, and according to some authorities, failure to appear at a civil hearing is not a legal infraction in New Hampshire. "That didn't mean he didn't love his son. He saw his son. He called him every week," his former wife is quoted as saying. "I'm having a hard time. My son's having a hard time because there's just too many unanswered questions. We want answers."[512]

Mistreatment of prisoners is not limited to parents with child-support orders, of course, though they are the ones most like to have been incarcerated without trial or due process in the first place. The family of forty-nine-year-old diabetic William Barnette claims that his death in jail in February 2002 resulted from the denial of insulin. Barnette had been in jail since December on charges he failed to pay child support.[513] Committing law-abiding citizens to the penal system can have consequences more deadly than for real criminals. On July 24, 2001, Michael Kelly Deal, a former police chief jailed without trial for child-support arrearages, was found murdered by fellow inmates, who feared he would expose their escape plans.[514]

CREATING CRIMINALS

But surely *some* of these fathers must be real deadbeats, as the government tells us? *Some* fathers must be abandoning their children?

Again, no government or academic study has ever shown that significant numbers of fathers are voluntarily abandoning their children, and as we have seen, many studies attest to the contrary. We do not normally suspend the Bill of Rights for an entire class of citizens because of anecdotes propagated by the government and media about what some people of whom we have no knowledge "must have" done. In any case, there is nothing mutually exclusive about protecting the rights of fathers and their children not to be separated without cause and enforcing child-support collection on those men who truly abandon the offspring they have sired. Those who abandon or otherwise abuse their children can be formally charged, tried, and sentenced according to due process of law without suspending the Constitution for the rest of us.

Once one fully understands how the child-support system creates criminals, the elusive deadbeat begins to look like a mythical creature indeed, a creation of those paid to pursue him. Here we have a textbook example of the worst horrors of bureaucratic aggrandizement, creating the very problem it ostensibly exists to solve. With each plundered father comes the demand for more courts, more lawyers, more bureaucracy, more plainclothes police and private agents to "pursue" him—and to plunder more fathers and turn them, too, into impecunious "deadbeats."

It is hardly surprising that some fathers who have been worked over eventually do disappear. Anyone who has had his home and family invaded and livelihood destroyed, who has been looted for everything he has and will ever have, who has been publicly vilified and incarcerated without trial, all on the pretext of supporting children who have been forcibly removed from his care and protection through literally "no fault" of his own and whom he is seldom or never permitted to see, will eventually reach the limits of his endurance. In fact, it is tempting to conclude that this is precisely what the system is designed to encourage, for certainly it does no harm to the enforcement business.

As the repressive features of the child-support regime become conspicuous, public relations campaigns have been devised to put a more acceptable face on it. In most instances all these do is add Orwellian euphemism. Virginia enforcement director Nick Young describes the parents hounded by his office as "clients" and "customers" who "are entitled to have the benefit of child-support services."[515] PSI's Web site advertises "customer service units" where it "teaches techniques for fostering cooperation with each customer": "Specialized customer service centers . . . are an efficient mechanism for increasing responsiveness to customers." These government-employed and government-subsidized entrepreneurs neglect to mention that customers who choose not to patronize their establishments will be arrested. These people are not selling vacuum cleaners; they are bureaucratic gendarmes who do not wear uniforms and who are not trained and disciplined according to the standards and constraints we normally demand of police. As such they are akin to the secret police of totalitarian societies. They often turn up quietly at public hearings and other political events where citizens testify and take notes while refusing to give their own names. Some carry guns and issue arrest warrants. Trying to disguise their police function by portraying them as enterprising service providers does not make them any less dangerous; it makes them far more so.

This repression with a human face allows the machinery to penetrate deeper into the private lives of individuals and families. Some fathers' groups have played into this by insisting that "child support" be redefined more comprehensively to include a father's "emotional" role in the upbringing of his children. This is thunder the state machinery easily steals. David Gray Ross, head of Office of Child Support Enforcement during the Clinton administration, proudly told a conference of non-custodial parents in September 1999 that he changed the mission statement of his office to include encouraging the "emotional support" of children. "Child support is more than money," says the National Child Support Enforcement Association Internet site. "Child support is also love, emotional support, and responsibility." Love and emotional support thus become bureaucratic imperatives, to be assessed by government goons or private bounty hunters and enforced through the penal apparatus.

This is already being realized. The state as emotional counselor has blended law enforcement with psychotherapy, so that the criminal enforcement and penal apparatus becomes an instrument of family therapy. In one program government officials require "clients" (fathers) to "deal with their feelings about the custodial parent and their children." At one point "clients must write their own obituaries as they would be written by their children." "This exercise is very moving," says director Gerry Hamilton. "This helps non-custodial fathers understand why contact with their children is so important."[516]

The amalgamation of psychotherapy and law enforcement reached its apogee in the "responsible fatherhood" programs promoted by the Clinton administration and other governments during the 1990s, which have been re-labeled as "healthy marriage" and "marriage education" by the Bush administration. Under these programs, workshops impart "relationship skills" and introduce methods of "conflict resolution." "Anger management" and "child behavior management" are among the tools of emotional and family engineering which have received the federal imprimatur.[517] Yet while these programs have been promoted as family therapy, holding out the hope that they will preserve and increase the number of marriages, in practice they are mostly devoted to collecting child support.

Deadbeat Dads or Plundered Pops?

In January 2003, HHS announced $2.2 million in grants to faith-based groups to "promote fatherhood and healthy marriage." HHS said the grants "reach out to those who need help in acquiring the skills necessary to build relationships." Yet only 25 percent of the funds were earmarked for marriage; the rest were devoted to deputizing private groups to collect child support ("improve the financial and emotional well being of children"). The Marriage Coalition, a "faith-based organization" in Cleveland, received $200,000 to assist child-support enforcement.[518]

The following May, HHS was again conflating psychotherapy and law enforcement, announcing more grants "to support healthy marriage and parental relationships with the goals of improving the well-being of children." Healthy Families Nampa in Idaho (whose name seems tailored to the federal program) was to use $544,400 for "counseling and other supportive services to parents who are interested in marrying each other." Yet here again, the details indicate that marriage is secondary to child support: "These projects are a sensible government approach to testing and evaluating creative approaches that enhance the overall goals and effectiveness of the child-support enforcement program by integrating the promotion of healthy marriage into existing child-support services." How precisely law enforcement agents can preserve anyone's marriage is not made clear. Almost a million dollars went to Michigan's child-support agency, over and above their regular federal subsidies, "to support children by strengthening marriage."[519] A similar measure in Virginia was announced in July. These disbursements accompany more forthright exercises of police power, wherein HHS reveals that its principal method for rebuilding marriages and "parental relationships" is by arresting parents.

Even as the federal government pays states to separate fathers from their children, it portrays itself as laboring to bring them back, now with the aid of federally funded media campaigns. With the slogan "They're Your Kids. Be Their Dad!" HHS at one point undertook to spend $1.4 million for advertisements to nearly 25,000 newspapers, magazines, and television and radio stations around the country. The spots used actors to portray fathers who "walk out" on their children for no apparent reason. "When Vanessa's Daddy walks out the door today, he's never coming back." "When Michael's father left two years ago . . ." These are naturally infuriating to fathers who are under court orders to stay away from their children. "Goodbye, Vanessa," the mock-father states coldly. "Goodbye, Daddy" says "Vanessa."[520]

The *Christian Science Monitor* sees these ads as "the latest sign Americans—including the government—are waking up to the importance of fatherhood."[521]

161

Perhaps so, but in their fictional depiction of evil deeds by private citizens they are eerily reminiscent of propaganda films. Even the spots themselves reveal the awkward fact that most fathers are absent because the government makes sure they stay absent, since the ads never actually urge fathers to return to their families (which would render them liable to arrest). At one point they let slip that the aim is for fathers to be "close" to their children, but not too close: "It's hard to stay close to your kids when you don't live with them. But you can do it." The disembodied voice does not explain how you can do it when a judge has ordered you to stay away from them on pain of incarceration, when you are working two or three jobs, when your children have been relocated to another city or country, when the court has confiscated your home and booted your car, when you are homeless altogether, or when you are in jail. As columnist Cathy Young writes, "maybe the HHS should launch a new ad campaign directed at the courts and at some custodial mothers, with the slogan, 'They're his kids. Let him be their dad.'"[522]

Yet even critics missed the full import of the campaign. "In March 1999, the department launched a nationwide public service campaign challenging fathers to remain connected to their children even if they do not live with them." In the details, HHS makes clear this means pay child support. Again, the premise betrays the true agenda: not to unite fathers with their children but to keep them apart and to pull them more securely into the government enforcement machinery, extending the bureaucratic hegemony into every corner of their lives. Though invoking therapeutic language about enhancing "relationships" and "encouraging good fathering," in practice HHS makes clear that the relationships they most hoped to enhance were those between fathers and federal officials:

> Activities funded by ACF [Administration for Children and Families] include Fatherhood Development Workshops on effective practices for working with young unemployed and underemployed fathers; the development of a manual for workers to use in helping low-income fathers learn to interact more effectively with the child-support enforcement system; and a peer learning college for child-support enforcement experts to identify systemic barriers these young fathers face in becoming responsible fathers.[523]

Maryland, Virginia, and the District of Columbia have also made creative use of television and children by using both as quasi-law enforcement agents. Television spots feature children reciting a list of Miranda-style rights to their own fathers: "You have the right to remain silent. You have the right to have the authorities give you a break. You have the right to have your past actions not used against you. You have the right to a second chance. You have a right to start doing the right thing."[524] No mention is made of a right—long recognized throughout the Western legal systems—to be left in peace in your own home with your own children and to raise them free from interference by the government.

Michigan Attorney General Mike Cox went a step further in 2004 when he tried to enlist the state's children in an art competition to depict their own fathers as criminals. Cox offered free Domino's pizzas to children who participated in the campaign to create billboards vilifying their fathers. He even invited mothers to express their feelings about their former husbands through their children's artwork. But apparently it was a step too far when Domino's angrily pulled out of the program in response to public outrage, and Cox was forced to cancel the campaign.[525] One political cartoonist showed Cox telling a young child that she could not see her father but she could have a pepperoni pizza.

250,000 PARENTS IN JAIL?

Though the Bureau of Justice Statistics provides official figures on every conceivable category of crime and incarceration, none are reported on the number of parents incarcerated without trial for nonpayment of child support, though this would be simple information to compile. Informal estimates suggest one-third of the American jail population consisting of fathers on contempt-of-court charges connected with child support and similar "family crimes."[526] With the BJS reporting 747,529 inmates in jails in 2005, nearly a quarter-million parents could now be incarcerated for what is supposed to be a civil matter.[527] It is certainly enough to place a serious burden on the penal system. In 1990, the *Post and Courier* of Charleston, South Carolina, reported in one county that on an average day twenty-four jail inmates were held for child support. By 2003, that number had risen to more than 166, about 15 percent of the jail population.[528]

To relieve jail overcrowding in Georgia, a sheriff and superior court judge proposed creating detention camps specifically for fathers.[529] Likewise, the Pittsburgh City Planning Commission has considered a proposal by Goodwill Industries "to convert a former chemical processing plant . . . into a detention center" specifically for fathers.[530] In nearby Lawrence County in 2002, a judge ordered the release of thirty-seven inmates who had been jailed without due process of law, and in December 2003, following a letter from the American Civil Liberties Union, a judge in Montgomery County ordered the release of 100.[531] The sheriff of Polk County, Florida, reports in July 2003 that in the first seven months of that year, "716 persons have been arrested on charges which, at least in part, were related to non-payment" of child support. Even a fraction of this figure throughout the 3,000 counties in America (by no means unlikely) produces an astounding number of arrests.[532]

President Clinton's OCSE chief, David Gray Ross, posted a sign over his office door proclaiming "CHILDREN FIRST" and once told a television reporter, "We really are looking out for the children." It is very easy for those employed by the divorce machinery to pose as the defenders of wronged women and children; the smug sanctimony of judges, lawyers, and enforcement agents is the insult added to the injury for ejected fathers. Yet we should bear in mind that their chivalry costs them nothing. On the contrary, many people now make a comfortable living in the business of hunting down fathers. Yet if we take a moment to consider what it costs fathers to stay in contact with children who have been removed from their care and protection through "no fault" of their own, and who must risk almost certain financial ruin, public excoriation, and indefinite incarceration, we might discover it is not so simple to say who are the villains and who are the heroes.

Chapter 4

BATTERERS OR PROTECTORS?

"When you see children floating down a river, out to sea to drown, human compassion makes us all want to jump in and save them. But we also need to send somebody upstream to figure out who's throwing them into the river in the first place."

— Ronald Henry, Washington attorney

"[F]alse accusations cannot be rebutted and any attempt to secure compensation or correction through the courts is futile."

— Charter 77 (Czechoslovak human rights petition)

For a court to seize control of a family, remove from a parent all decision-making rights over his children, order him to stay away from them most of the time, regulate and micromanage the time he spends with them, and force him to part with his property and savings and future earnings, it is not necessary for the parent to be accused (let alone convicted) of any legal wrongdoing, either criminal or civil. Nevertheless, if the aim is to cut the parent off from his children completely or to have him evicted from the family home, it is helpful to accuse (though not necessarily to formally charge or convict) him of some form of spousal or child "abuse."

Unlike any other area of the law, the accusation is enough. "With child abuse and spouse abuse you don't have to prove anything," the leader of a legal seminar tells divorcing women. "You just have to accuse."[533] Most fathers accused of abuse are never formally charged, tried, or convicted because there is no evidence against them. The purpose usually is not to punish a crime but to gain custody of the children, along with the financial rewards they bring. The result is the parent never receives due process of law or a chance to clear his name, let alone recover his children.

A detailed account by investigative journalist Donna Laframboise describes what is now standard procedure for divorcing women, according to those willing to discuss it:

> Heidi Nabert . . . tells of consulting a lawyer in 1991 prior to filing for divorce: "The lawyer's response to me—and this is precisely what he said— was, 'There's no reason for you to leave [your home]. Can you get him to hit you?'" When a shocked Ms. Nabert replied that her husband of seventeen years had never behaved violently, the lawyer was undeterred. Nabert continues, "He said to me, 'You know, if you do that, we can have him forcibly removed from the home. And you're more than likely guaranteed some form of spousal support.'"

Laframboise quotes Paul Pellman, a family law specialist who has been in practice for seventeen years, who sees at least one case a month where one party seeks unwarranted charges against another to get him out of the home. "You spend a night in jail almost automatically. And your bail conditions restrict you from ever attending at the home again except to get your goods. So it's an easy way to kick somebody out."[534] A *Detroit News* article with a typically "he said/she said" approach recounts matter-of-factly and with no hint of irony or shock how easy it is for a discontented mother to criminalize her children's father:

> Missing Michigan, they returned to Grand Rapids. Charles's initial job offer fell through, and he found work as a night security officer.
>
> They initially thought it a good idea to work opposite shifts, cutting out a need for day care. Then, the couple who had spent years before and during their marriage working side by side daily, drifted farther and farther apart.
>
> "I just became extremely angry," says Kelly, who is 37. "I was ready to move on and have some kind of a normal life."
>
> Charles, who is 47, was frustrated, too. "I wasn't out sitting on a bar stool and chasing women," he explains. "I was working."
>
> Eventually, Kelly sought the advice of a divorce attorney, who suggested she file a restraining order against her husband and kick him out of the house. . . .[535]

Among legal practitioners it is now common knowledge that patently trumped-up accusations are frequently used, and virtually never punished, in divorce and custody proceedings. Attorney Thomas Kasper has described how abuse accusations readily "become part of the gamesmanship of divorce."[536] Elaine Epstein writes that "allegations of abuse are now used for tactical advantage" in custody cases.[537] "Whenever a woman claims to be a victim, she is automatically believed," says Washington state attorney Lisa Scott. "No proof of abuse is required."[538] Jeannie Suk characterizes domestic violence accusations as a system of "state-imposed *de facto* divorce that subjects the practical and substantive continuation of the relationship to criminal sanction."[539]

Open perjury is readily acknowledged in family law circles. "Women lie every day," says Ottawa Judge Dianne Nicholas. "Every day women in [domestic] court say, 'I made it up. I'm lying. It didn't happen'—and they're not charged."[540] Bar associations and even courts themselves regularly sponsor seminars counseling mothers on how to fabricate abuse accusations. "The number of women attending the seminars who smugly—indeed boastfully— announced that they had already sworn out false or grossly exaggerated domestic violence complaints against their hapless husbands, and that the device worked!" wrote an astonished Thomas Kiernan in the *New Jersey Law Journal*. "To add amazement to my astonishment, the lawyer-lecturers invariably congratulated the self-confessed miscreants."[541]

It is divorce and child custody that now bring most fathers into the massive industry of "domestic violence" and "child abuse." These words are now red flags, political buzzwords that are driven by misinformation and whose reality is largely disconnected from what they connote to most people. Attorney and scholar David Heleniak describes domestic abuse as "an area of law mired in intellectual dishonesty and injustice."[542] Suk has detailed the sophistries by which American courts use domestic violence hysteria to rationalize evicting American citizens from their homes without a shred of evidence that they have committed any legal infraction.[543] Responding to the politicization of the law and perversion of scholarship by domestic violence activists to serve an ideological agenda, some scholars are now in open revolt against this dishonesty. Domestic violence has become "a backwater of tautological pseudo-theory and failed intervention programs," write Donald Dutton and Kenneth Corvo. "No other area of established social welfare, criminal justice, public health, or behavioral intervention has such weak evidence in support of mandated practice."

The bureaucrat/activists of certifying agencies and "batterer" treatment programs have become "true believers," disregarding research that does not support their views. They are enthralled with the power that comes with having one's philosophy hold sway and the control they feel from influencing criminal justice policy. Ironically, they often attribute these very "power and control" motives to abusive men.[544]

"Domestic violence" is now a vast industry, funded through numerous interlocking government programs at the federal, state, and local levels and by private foundations and transnational organizations. Yet there is little indication of any serious problem other than what is connected with divorce and custody. "There is not an epidemic of domestic violence," Judge Milton Raphaelson has stated (after his retirement). "There is an epidemic of *hysteria* about domestic violence."[545]

In some ways, the domestic violence regime simply codifies the *de facto* criminalization of private life and parenthood created by involuntary divorce and sole custody. "In this regime," writes legal scholar Suk,[546] "the home is a space in which criminal law deliberately and coercively *reorders* and *controls* private rights and relationships in property and marriage—not as an incident of prosecution, but as its goal." Though ostensibly criminalizing violence (which is already criminal), domestic violence law results "not only in the criminalization of violence proper, but also in the criminalization of . . . an alleged abuser's presence in the home." Indeed, it amounts to the "criminal prohibition of intimate relationships in the home." Potential spouses and sexual partners "cannot contract around the state's mandates without risking arrest and punishment."[547]

The premise on which most of the industry is based is that domestic violence is a political crime perpetrated exclusively by men against women. Yet this misconception has been subjected to so much scrutiny that the truth is finally beginning to reach general awareness. That women perpetrate domestic violence, including severe violence, as much as men has been established by so many studies as to require no further treatment here.[548] "A surprising fact has turned up in the grimly familiar world of domestic violence," writes Nancy Updike in the left-wing magazine *Mother Jones*, hardly a bastion of male chauvinism. "Women report using violence in their relationships more often than men." This surprising fact has been well known among researchers in the field for at least a quarter century, yet *Mother Jones* approaches it defensively. "This willingness to pay attention to what was once considered reactionary nonsense signals a fundamental conceptual shift in how domestic violence is being stud-ied," Updike writes. "Money and ideology are at the heart of the problem."[549] While feminist polemicists refuse to acknowledge this truth, its theorists admit and even celebrate it. "Women are doing the battering," writes Betty Friedan, "as much or more than men."[550]

While the data from detached researchers is clear, inaccuracies continue to be promulgated by both advocacy groups and government officials. The U.S. Department of Justice states that "Strategies for preventing intimate partner violence should focus on risks posed by men."[551] "In 95 percent of domestic assaults," officials claim, "the man is the perpetrator of the vio-lence."[552] Such statements are false, but they also reveal the mentality that propagates them. Even were they true, what precisely are the implications for public policy we are expected to draw? That membership in a group estab-lishes guilt?

In a larger sense, of course, it does not matter what percentage of which group commits the preponderance of a particular crime; the important public issue is due process of law for every individual. Even if one gender were shown statistically to commit the preponderance of domestic violence, this obviously does not justify punishing the innocent members of that gender, which is pre-cisely what is happening. Yet even official government documents now use phrases like "violence against women" and "male violence," as if responsibil-ity for crimes is assigned to categories of people rather than the individuals who commit them. The fact that such presumptions of criminality are propa-gated not only by feminists but by politicians, journalists, and scholars indi-cates how unhealthy and politicized the issue has become, how many interests have developed a stake in obfuscating rather than illuminating the truth, and how far we have gone toward accepting doctrines of collective guilt that were once associated with totalitarian regimes.

The very designation of a special category of "domestic" violence, separate from other forms of assault—a category defined by the relationship between the parties rather than the nature of the deed—raises questions as fundamental as what precisely is the subject under discussion. It is important to realize from the beginning that none of the statistics purporting to quantify family violence are based on convictions through jury trials or even formal charges; they are based on "reports" and are therefore not necessarily substantiated. As we will see, substantial incentives exist not only for women but also for federally funded interest groups and governments to manufacture false accusations and exaggerate incidents.

Compounding the problem of definition is the willingness of those who would make domestic violence a political crime to blur the distinction between what is truly violent and illegal and what is not. The power to criminalize peaceful private behavior, personal imperfections, and routine family disagreements is concisely conveyed in the term "abuse." It is ambiguous and elastic enough to be stretched beyond what is physical and criminal. "You don't have to be beaten to be abused," is now a standard slogan of abuse advocates and even ostensibly objective journalists, such as the Jacobin-sounding "public safety correspondent" of the *St. Louis Post-Dispatch*: "Abuse also means name-calling, put-downs, control and isolation. Abuse means an intimate partner constantly refusing to let you have money, intimidating you by shouting, giving you negative looks or gestures, forcing you into sex acts, or ignoring your opinions."[553] This reporter's opinions help explain why accusations of such "abuse" against citizens guilty of no legal infraction are reported uncritically by news media as if "negative looks" and "name-calling" constituted crimes liable to arrest and prosecution. A group as conservative as the Irish Bishops Conference includes "social control" and "economic abuse," which it defines as "depriving her of clothes" and "harassing her over bills."[554]

Even more serious, these definitions are now employed by law enforcement agencies. A poster on the New York subway urges women to call the city's domestic violence hot line if they have suffered "emotional abuse," such as being called "fat" or "stupid."[555] Another issued by the Alexandria, Virginia, Domestic Violence Program encourages women to call if their partners "negate your words, abilities, ideas, and actions." With some $1 billion annually from the Violence Against Women Act, the highest law-enforcement agency in the land, the U.S. Department of Justice, declares that "undermining an individual's sense of self-worth and/or self-esteem" is a federal crime. "Domestic violence can be physical, sexual, emotional, economic, or psychological actions or threats of actions that influence another person," says DOJ. Among the "crimes" in DOJ's definition of "violent" assault are "constant criticism, diminishing one's abilities, [and] name-calling" or "attempting to make an individual financially dependent by maintaining total control over financial resources."[556] The British Home Office explicitly states that domestic "violence" need not be violent. "Domestic violence is not restricted to physical violence," it states; "it may include psychological, emotional, sexual, and economic abuse."[557]

By these criteria, "violence" becomes whatever a self-proclaimed "victim" says it is. If true violence were really a major problem, one would expect those concerned about it to focus scarce resources on the most serious cases and resist this cheapening of the language whereby the stuff of lovers' quarrels and ordinary family friction opens citizens to arrest. Instead activists and officials use vague terms to imply lawbreaking and violence where none has taken place. In her book *The Battered Women*, psychologist Lenore Walker excuses a women who violently attacked her husband because he "had been battering her by ignoring her and by working late."[558] Social scientists now study, and the media credulously report, what they term "psychological" or "mental abuse" of grown women, consisting not of physical violence but the ordinary anxieties of life.[559] "Violence has been redefined into meaninglessness to include anything that causes anyone displeasure," writes author Melanie Phillips:

> One study included "feeling threatened" as evidence of violence. Even the Home Office some years back widened the definition to include the slippery "emotional abuse." That now embraces insults or rows. In America, it includes an "overprotective manner" or not helping the children with their homework. . . . To call it abuse is to batter the language. To equate it with violence is dishonest. To accuse only men of doing it is despicable. To encourage children to "inform" on their fathers for doing it is beyond belief.[560]

While name-calling and undermining someone's self-esteem are not usually considered chargeable offenses, the Justice Department has been devising methods for punishing them—separate from the usual due process procedures. A document funded and disseminated by DOJ contains a blueprint for a campaign of public propaganda and child indoctrination and an institutionalized reign of terror against parents who are not even formally charged with any offense:

- Establish a Family Violence Coordinating Council.
- Do not allow mediation between domestic violence victims and perpetrators.
- Do not allow joint custody under any circumstances.
- Do not allow mutual restraining orders unless there are supporting findings.
- Do not allow couples counseling.
- Implement visitation centers.
- Implement parenting classes in every junior high school.

- Implement a massive community education program.
- Implement court appointed special advocates and guardians *ad litem* programs to provide advocacy, support, and representation to children.
- Implement mechanisms to enforce child support.
- Allow for permanent or indefinite restraining orders and orders of protection.
- Fast track domestic violence prosecutions through priority docketing, specialized domestic violence courts, and vertical prosecution.
- Develop and implement a coordinated response with strong advocates from criminal justice, victim services, childrens services, and allied professions.
- Conduct mandatory and frequent training of all professionals . . . including orientation training, continuing education, and multicultural awareness.

DOJ claims that "batterers" can be identified not by evidence of physical violence but as males who "project image of a caring, concerned partner or father." Such citizens should be punished with:

- Punitive conditions.
- Financial assessments.
- Apology to victim.
- Community service.
- Nonjail loss-of-liberty confinement.
- Electronic monitoring [*e.g.*, ankle bracelets to track movements].
- Intensive supervision.
- Mandatory treatment that is "batterer-specific" provided by professionals who are specialists.
- No couples counseling.
- Mandatory alcohol and other drug treatment, with a mandate of abstinence.
- Restitution (including direct and indirect for replacement costs of damaged property, medical and counseling bills, and attorney costs).
- Ongoing child support.
- Mortgage or rent payments.
- All payments should be made through the court or correctional institution.

- Forfeit of weapons, particularly guns and rifles.
- Ordered to submit to warrantless searches of their persons or homes.
- Supervised at maximum intensity.
- Satisfy special protective obligations when children are involved such as custody, visitation, etc.[561]

What is clear from this agenda—and what is underestimated even by some critics of the domestic violence industry—is how much of the hysteria is fomented specifically for the purpose of removing children from their fathers. "All of this domestic violence industry is about trying to take children away from their fathers," says *Irish Times* columnist John Waters. "When they've taken away the fathers, they'll take away the mothers."[562] Feminists themselves point out that most domestic violence occurs during "custody battles," and the vast preponderance of domestic violence cases arise among divorced and separated couples with children.[563]

So overwhelming is this connection that it is almost certainly the main thrust behind the growth of the domestic abuse industry, politicizing both criminal justice and private life. While generalizations about domestic violence are almost impossible to quantify—again, because of definitions so broad as to be effectively meaningless—it is fairly obvious that family dissolution and disputes over child custody are chiefly responsible for the flood of allegations. In New Hampshire, divorce attorneys commonly refer to restraining orders as "silver bullets" because of their efficiency and effectiveness in securing custody. One marital master testified, "Requests for *ex-parte* relief are based upon many circumstances, some of which are made only for the purpose of obtaining an advantage in litigation."[564]

This is further evident from the words of advocacy groups themselves, who constitute the most vociferous opponents of divorce and custody reform.[565] Federally funded domestic violence programs openly promote divorce with resources and links to referral services for divorce lawyers. Moreover, their literature is dominated by complaints not that allegedly violent assailants are avoiding prison and walking the streets but that they are retaining custody of their children after their wives divorce them. Indeed, so pointed is this complaint that custody, rather than safety, is the principal grievance concerning men who are portrayed, without evidence or trial, as violent criminals. A special issue of *Mother Jones* magazine ostensibly devoted to domestic violence focuses, almost from the first paragraph, largely on securing child custody.[566] A widely criticized film on domestic violence broadcast by PBS in October 2005 and its promotional literature contained the following assertions:[567]

- "All over America, battered mothers are losing custody of their children."
- "One third of mothers lose custody to abusive husbands."
- "Batterers are twice as likely to contest [custody] as non-batterers. And they often win sole or joint custody."
- "Seventy-five percent of cases in which fathers contest custody, fathers have history of being batterers."

These statements are untrue.[568] But the claims themselves are revealing. Were they true, one would expect the principal concern to be that men are beating their wives and not being prosecuted, with custody as secondary. If duly convicted criminals are incarcerated as expected, after all, questions of child custody should not arise. Instead, custody is the principal complaint, confirming that the alleged "batterers" have not been convicted of battering or any other crime.

Ostensibly scientific feminist scholarship is similarly revealing. Fathers trying to see their children following unproven accusations is described as "further violence" and the "threat of kidnapping"; simply responding to court proceedings is described as "violence." One highly influential feminist scholar claims to have examined 100,000 cases where women "reported" that "the batterer threatened to kidnap their children," "batterers had threatened legal custody action," and "the battering man used court-ordered visitation as an occasion to continue verbal and emotional abuse of the woman."[569] This is not violence; it is fathers trying to recover their children through the same legal processes by which their children were removed and which, in most cases, they themselves did not initiate.

These distortions directly influence government policy. The late Senator Paul Wellstone successfully championed federal spending using figures apparently from this article. "Some perpetrators of violence use the children as pawns to control the abused party and to commit more violence during separation or divorce." But the Senator's evidence for this "violence" tells another story altogether. "In one study, 34 percent of women in shelters and callers to hot lines reported threats of kidnapping, 11 percent reported that the batterer had kidnapped the child for some period, and 21 percent reported that threats of kidnapping forced the victim to return to the batterer."[570] In other words, "more violence" consists in the fathers predictably wanting their children back.

Wellstone continues: "Up to 75 percent of all domestic assaults reported to law enforcement agencies were inflicted after the separation of the couple." This is another way of saying that an intact family is the safest place for women and children, divorce and separation create the circumstances most conducive to domestic violence (especially when children are involved), false charges are more likely to be leveled during custody disputes, and fathers who may have become violent did so, not surprisingly, when their children were taken away. And all this is evident only from Wellstone's spin.

The American Psychological Association, whose members frequently testify in family court proceedings and provide what is ostensibly balanced scientific expertise, toes a similar political line.[571] "A large proportion of reported domestic violence happens after the partners are separated," the APA says, quite rightly. "Since threats and violence are control strategies used by the batterer, the woman's leaving may threaten his sense of power and increase his need to control the woman and children." What it certainly does threaten is the safety and well-being of his children and his natural desire to see them protected and cared for. "Child custody and visitation arrangements also may become an ongoing scenario for intimidation, threats, and violent behavior," the APA report continues. "Threats may be made to hurt the children and other family members." These blanket assertions of what "may" happen are a favorite device for smearing innocent citizens who have been neither convicted nor charged with any legal infraction and are guilty of nothing more than wanting their children back, since of course anything "may" be true. "Fathers who batter their children's mothers can be expected to use abusive power and control techniques to control the children, too." Not violence exactly, if one reads carefully, just "power and control techniques."

Can fathers "be expected" to want to control their children because controlling one's children is part of what parenthood is all about? Do "techniques to control the children" now constitute crimes? Or do these terms perhaps mean having their children within their care and protection or exercising ordinary parental discipline? Insisting they go to bed or arrive at school on time, that they brush their hair and teeth, that they be taught basic civility and manners, or any of the other basic tasks of parenthood that are generally neglected in the children of divorce? Might they mean protecting the children from the neglect and abuse that (as we will see shortly) is most likely in precisely the kind of single-mother home that is being created?

"In many of these families, prior to separation, the men were not actively involved in the raising of their children," the APA confidently asserts. "To gain control after the marital separation, the fathers fight for the right to be involved." How the APA is privy (and by what right it should be) to what takes place within the private homes of "many of these families" is neither explained nor justified. What is clear is that the issue here is not violence but custody. "Most people, including the battered woman herself, believe that when a woman leaves a violent man, she will remain the primary caretaker of their children," would seem to be a fairly clear admission, couched in the appropriate code, of the real motivation. "Recent studies suggest that an abusive man is more likely than a nonviolent father to seek sole physical custody of his children and may be just as likely (or even more likely) to be awarded custody as the mother." No evidence or documentation is provided for this assertion by an ostensibly scientific organization, and none is possible, since no such "studies" exist. And in any case what can it possibly mean? That a "nonviolent" father is defined as one who simply allows his children to be taken away?

Even judges, who are obligated to be impartial and apolitical, turn out to be zealous advocates for women. The National Council of Juvenile and Family Court Judges, whose members are supposed to administer "equal justice under law" to all parties, seems to have already concluded that male litigants are "dangerous" criminals and regard their role as helping mothers obtain custody. In a paper funded by the Justice Department and formerly posted on its Internet site, the judges advocate that government officials help women fill out paternal termination forms. They also call for terminating fathers' rights to see their children with no evidence of violence, ignoring any officials who question the truthfulness of abuse allegations, ignoring visitation orders, eliminating mediation, eliminating consideration of mothers alienating children against their fathers, and re-"education" of judges."

The group describes its purpose as "to identify . . . the overlap between domestic violence and child custody and visitation." Mothers are throughout presumed to be the only victims of violence (which need not be "physical" but can be "emotional"), and fathers are described not as "defendants" but as "batterers." The judges openly acknowledge that false allegations are used to secure custody and lament the possibility that the lack of formal convictions "can have a negative impact on battered women and their children in later custody and visitation decisions."

The ostensibly impartial and apolitical judges also attack citizens who criticize the government. "Fathers' rights groups often focus on the rights of fathers instead of their responsibilities," the federally funded judges inform us. The judges acknowledge that they and their courtrooms have become so politicized that their mandate is less dispensing impartial justice than implementing ideology against political opponents: "Fathers' rights groups . . . couch their message against a backdrop of real fear that social structures will disintegrate if fathers are not present in their children's homes, or at least an active presence in their lives."

Might such statements raise questions about the impartiality of judges who sit in judgment on actual cases? Can fathers who must appear in the courts of these politicized judges expect "equal justice"? Do fathers attacked from a federal Internet site get space to provide their side of the issue? The judges go on to reveal that they are less concerned with dispensing justice than promoting feminist ideology and divorce:

> In recent years there has been a shift away from the safety concerns of battered women and their children to a focus on re-establishing patriarchal values. With this shift has come an assumption that whatever is good for fathers is good for children, *with a corollary message that divorce is always harmful to children.*[572]

The true agenda emerges in the emphasized words: A federally funded paper claiming concern for victims of "violence" is in reality a manifesto for judges to create fatherless homes.

RESTRAINING-ORDER MADNESS

Even without a formal charge or accusation, fathers are summarily and peremptorily removed from their homes through "*ex parte*" restraining orders. These orders, separating fathers from their children for weeks, months, years, and even life, are issued without the presentation of any evidence of legal wrongdoing. They are often issued at a hearing at which the father is not present and about which he may not even be notified, or they may be issued over the telephone or by fax with no hearing at all. A father receiving such an order must immediately vacate his home and make no further contact with his children. "This is so even if the [alleged] victim initiates contact or invites the defendant to come home."[573]

Restraining orders or "orders of protection" are a radical legal innovation and the logical culmination of what some decry as "judicial activism" or "judicial legislation": They do not punish criminals for illegal acts they are proven to have committed but prohibit law-abiding citizens from otherwise legal acts. "Once the restraining order is in place, a vast range of ordinarily legal behavior," most often contact with one's own children, is "criminalized."[574] Judges can simply legislate new crimes with the stroke of a pen. "It criminalizes conduct that is not generally criminal—namely, presence at home," writes Suk. "The protection order thus enables the creation of a crime out of the ordinarily innocent behavior of being at home."[575]

But it is only a crime for the recipient of the order, who can then be arrested for doing what no statute prohibits and what the rest of us may do without penalty. A woman who obtains a restraining order against a father "can make him the only man in the world who is specifically prevented *by law* from spontaneously seeing his children without her permission."[576] Because violent assault and other statutory crimes are already by definition punishable, the only people effectively restrained from anything are peaceful, law-abiding fathers who are prohibited from seeing their children. Restraining orders thus codify the presumption of guilt begun with the divorce decree and the custody order.

"The order identifies the subject of the order as an abuser even if he has not been convicted," writes Suk. Even when no evidence exists to convict him, "the protection order can provide the basis for new criminal liability on the more easily proven crime of violating the order." The purpose of the order then is to create a criminal, and it is the order itself, rather than any violent act, that creates the crime. "Indeed, part of the reason the order exists is to be violated, so as to set in motion criminal prosecution," Suk continues. "After all, violating the court order is a crime even if the conduct the order prohibits is ordinarily not a crime."[577]

The orders are issued virtually for the asking. Elaine Epstein, past president of the Massachusetts Bar Association and of the Massachusetts Women's Bar Association, accuses her peers of caving into the "media frenzy surrounding domestic violence" and of doling out restraining orders "like candy." "Restraining orders and orders to vacate are granted to virtually all who apply," and "the facts have become irrelevant," she writes. "In virtually all cases, no notice, meaningful hearing, or impartial weighing of evidence is to be had."[578] Attorney Paul Patten of Fall River, Massachusetts, also says they are "issued like candy," adding, "It's a rare case that they won't be issued as long as somebody says the magic word, 'I've been hit' or 'I've been threatened.'"[579]

Representative Barbara Gray told journalist Cathy Young that "judges grant the restraining orders without asking too many questions"—and apparently saw nothing wrong with that.[580] "As a judge for ten years, I issued hundreds of restraining orders after hearing one only one side," First Justice of Dudley, Massachusetts, District Court Milton Raphaelson confesses.[581] Connecticut attorney Arnold Rutkin charges that many judges view restraining orders as a "rubber-stamping exercise" and that subsequent hearings "are usually a sham."[582] "No objective proof is required," writes Minnesota attorney Daniel Butler. "If the petitioner simply says she is afraid, the order for protection will commonly be issued giving her the home, the children, child support, maintenance, etc."[583]

In Missouri, a survey of judges and attorneys revealed complaints of disregard for due process and restraining orders widely used as a "litigation strategy."[584] "I don't think there's a lawyer in domestic relations in this state who doesn't feel there has been abuse of restraining orders," says Massachusetts attorney Sheara Friend. "It's not politically correct—lawyers don't want to be pegged as being anti-abused women—but privately they agree."[585] Massachusetts judges issue 60,000 restraining orders yearly, though an analysis by the state itself found that fewer than half involve even an *allegation* of violence.[586] According to the U.S. Justice Department, a restraining order is issued every two minutes in Massachusetts.[587]

Restraining order recipients who attempt to contact their children or spouses can be arrested for "stalking," an offense the federal government defines as "nonconsensual communication."[588] "Stories of violations for minor infractions are legion," the *Boston Globe* reports. "In one case, a father was arrested for violating an order when he put a note in his son's suitcase telling the mother the boy had been sick over a weekend visit. In another, a father was arrested for sending his son a birthday card."[589] Arresting fathers for attending public events such as their children's musical recitals or sporting competitions—events any stranger may attend—is a practice many find difficult to believe, but it is very common. National Public Radio broadcast one story about a father who was arrested in church for attending his daughter's first communion. During the segment, an eight-year-old girl wails and begs to know when her father will be able to see her or call her on the phone. The answer, because of a "lifetime" restraining order, is never.[590]

Even accidental contact in public places is punished with arrest. "Fathers hit with restraining orders based on trivial or uncorroborated allegations have been jailed for sending their kids a Christmas card, asking a telephone operator to convey the message that a gravely ill grandmother would like to see her grandchildren, or returning a child's phone call."[591]

The trial of Harry Stewart is a textbook example of restraining order abuse. Contact between Stewart and his children was criminalized by a restraining order. Yet if anyone was violent it appears to have been Stewart's former wife. In September 1997, Stewart was featured on a local news report on battered husbands. For twelve years, he claimed he was repeatedly assaulted and terrorized by his wife. The specific violations with which Stewart was charged constitute a litany of the petty and trivial:

- Opening an apartment complex foyer door so his five-year-old son could ring the bell for his mother on a visitation return.
- Picking up his children on foot when his car was broken. (The restraining order said he had to stay in his vehicle at pick-ups and drop-offs.)
- Picking up his children when his visitation was temporarily suspended during a court investigation. Miscommunication by court officials led Stewart to believe he was in compliance with the court requirements that needed to be met for the resumption of visitation.
- Exiting his car at his children's school to pick them up for a scheduled visitation. (The restraining order stated he must remain in his car when returning the children to school after visitation.)
- Exiting his car to help his son with a package during a visitation exchange.
- Exiting his car to pick up his son who had fallen down while running to his car for a visitation pick-up.

Though Stewart was never charged with any physical assault, he faced a possible ten years in prison. Mark Charalambous of the Massachusetts Fatherhood Coalition comments, "It is incomprehensible that a loving father who has never even been accused of domestic violence should be facing ten years in jail."[592] Stewart had already been jailed for six months not for committing any crime but because he refused to confess to one.

Like domestic violence generally, restraining orders have become a lucrative industry. Massachusetts "has hundreds if not thousands of . . . specialists," according to the *Massachusetts News*. "Training in getting restraining orders, and in helping and urging women to get them occupies a significant amount of the curriculum at Northeastern University's Domestic Violence

Institute internship program. Federally paid advocates in many if not all district and probate courts in the state are also trained to assist women in getting restraining orders."[593]

Massachusetts has been relatively well documented and publicized, but authoritarian enforcement methods elsewhere defy both constitutional protections and common sense. The punishment of a Pennsylvania father was so arbitrary that the Associated Press and CNN seemed to regard it as a joke, though the man could spend years in prison: "Next time, Blaine Jeschonek may want to consider taking a bus," the news services commented wryly.

> Jeschonek, 44, was arrested and charged with criminal contempt for allegedly violating a court order that forbade him from having any contact with his estranged wife or his daughter. . . . Judge Thomas Ling . . . called police after learning Jeschonek had carpooled with his wife, Beth. The Jeschoneks had traveled together to court to ask Ling to dismiss the restraining order. . . . "You're violating my order right under my nose," Ling said.[594]

In Maine, a father acquitted on child abuse charges was re-arrested for telling his children he loved them. The father "was arrested because he poked his head into the victim-witness advocate's office before the verdict and told his children that he loved them and that he was sorry they had to go through the ordeal. Assistant District Attorney Rick Morse then had [him] arrested for violating conditions of his bail, which included no contact with the children."[595]

The epidemic of knowingly false accusations is now worldwide. A survey of judicial magistrates in New South Wales found that "almost 90 percent believe domestic violence orders were used by applicants—often on the advice of a solicitor—as a tactic in family court proceedings to deprive their partners of access to their children."[596] In Alberta courtrooms, "judges routinely hold five-minute hearings at the start of the day and make *ex parte* orders without any inquiries as to why the opposing party cannot be notified."[597] When an activist documented the practice and other abuses in a twelve-page report, police (who did not dispute the report) modified their policies. The standard procedure was indicated by a February 11, 2002, headline in the *Edmonton Sun*—"False Abuse Accusers Will Be Charged"—an admission that previously they were not.

Restraining orders issued on these terms obviously constitute a serious violation of due process of law. "The restraining order law is one of the most unconstitutional acts ever passed by the Massachusetts legislature," says attorney Gregory Hession. "A court can issue an order that boots you out of your house, never lets you see your children again, confiscates your guns, and takes your money, all without you even knowing that a hearing took place." A defendant charged with the most heinous violent crime "has all his or her rights preserved and carefully guarded when before a court," says Hession. "Not so with restraining order hearings, where a defendant may lose all those things, with no due process at all." Hession describes the process as a "political lynching":

> In a criminal trial, defendants . . . are presumed innocent. They have a right to a trial by jury. They have the right to face their accusers and have evidence presented and cross examine any witnesses. They may not be deprived of property or liberty without due process of law. The Commonwealth must prove guilt beyond a reasonable doubt. The law has to be clearly defined. They have a right to a lawyer, and to be provided one if they cannot afford one.
> The abuse law throws out all of those protections.[598]

According to the New Jersey family court, to allow abuse defendants due process protections "perpetuates the cycle of power and control whereby the [alleged?] perpetrator remains the one with the power and the [alleged?] victim remains powerless."[599] Describing accused fathers not as "defendants" but as "perpetrators" and "batterers," while omitting the word "alleged" is the norm not only in feminist literature but in media reports and, most seriously, in state and federal statutes. David Heleniak identifies six separate denials of due process in the New Jersey statute, which he terms "a due process fiasco": lack of notice, denial of poor defendants to free counsel, denial of right to take depositions, lack of fully evidentiary hearings, improper standard of proof, and denial of trial by jury.[600] Fathers enjoy fewer constitutional protections than accused criminals.

Yet the judiciary has shown little proclivity to even consider passing constitutional review on these practices. On the contrary, orders are issued by the very judges who are expected to protect constitutional rights from violation by others. In fact the same judges who issue them openly acknowledge their unconstitutionality—and their own indifference. "Your job is not to become concerned about the constitutional rights of the man that you're violating as you grant a restraining order," Ocean City, New Jersey, Municipal Court Judge Richard Russell instructed his fellow judges at a government training seminar in 1994:

Throw him out on the street, give him the clothes on his back and tell him, "See ya around." . . . The woman needs this protection because the statute granted her that protection. . . . They have declared domestic violence to be an evil in our society. So we don't have to worry about the rights.[601]

"Grant every order," Russell advises his colleagues. "That is the safest thing to do."

Judges who attended this seminar were willing to speak candidly only with anonymity. One called the restraining order law "the most abused piece of legislation that comes to my mind." Another readily acknowledged the irony of judges violating the constitution: "The constitution is being ignored," he said. "If the judiciary should feel that it is obliged to close its eyes to constitutional considerations in order to assist the legislature in attaining a currently popular objective, it will have prostituted itself and abrogated its responsibility to maintain its independence and its primary responsibility of upholding the Constitution." Yet Russell expressly renounced this function: "Am I doing something wrong telling these judges they have to ignore the constitutional protections most people have, I don't think so. . . . I am doing my job properly by teaching other judges to follow the legislative mandate." Those naïve judges still attached to old-fashioned concepts like the Bill of Rights were apparently whipped into the party line by their instructors.

"Those with no background express disbelief, until we explain the intent of the legislation," Russell acknowledges. A reporter notes that "Judges who have seen the training presentation say that if anyone objects, they keep it to themselves." Concludes another judge, "I would never approach the topic by saying, 'Look, these people are stripped of their constitutional rights,'" though he acknowledges that is what is happening.[602] Subsequent reports indicate the advice is being practiced: "For years, Essex County men arrested for violating such orders have been denied due process by languishing in jail . . . without a Superior Court hearing, a bail review or counsel."[603]

Though clearly an abuse of authority, it is important to recognize the political and bureaucratic pressure on judges. Federally funded feminist groups lobby judges to grant not only restraining orders but custody and child support at the same time—without the father present to defend himself—and publicize the names of judges who try to observe due process.[604] A Maine judge was removed from the bench for "lack of sensitivity" to women applying for restraining orders—"which, the judge's many defenders said, meant simply that he listened to both parties."[605] Another judge spoke candidly only upon his retirement, when, as he told a college audience, there was nothing "they" could do to him. "Few lives, if any, have been saved, but much harm, and possibly loss of lives, has come from the issuance of restraining orders and the arrests and conflicts ensuing therefrom," Judge Raphaelson of Massachusetts writes. "This is not only my opinion; it is the opinion of many who remain quiet due to the political climate. Innocent men and their children are deprived of each other."[606]

Precisely what purpose is served by arresting a father for seeing his children in a public place, where it is highly unlikely any "abuse" will occur without witnesses and intervention? Is a father who shows up unauthorized at his daughter's school play "stalking" anyone, or does he simply want to see his little girl perform? "Fathers whose only crime was falling out of favor with the mothers of their children are being jailed for trying to telephone their kids," says Charalambous. "What is the logical conclusion, a world where everyone has a protection order against anyone they find annoying?"[607]

It is fairly clear that restraining orders serve as another tool to enforce divorce and sole custody; by keeping parents apart they keep the divorce as belligerent (and profitable) as possible. "Mediation and communication counseling are critical in a divorce," says Sheara Friend, a family counselor. "The 209A non-contact order prevents that. Especially if it's a divorce that involves children, you need the parties talking with each other. The 209A completely stops that. It's a very divisive thing to do right at the time the parties need to talk."[608] Once again it appears that restraining orders protect not safety but power. They are not an instrument of justice to prevent wrongdoing but a tool of the divorce industry to keep itself in business.

To understand the logic, one need only imagine an involuntarily divorced father who runs into his children at the zoo or at church or goes to a school performance or some friend's house or a day-care facility where he knows the children will be at a specific time. Anyone can go to the zoo or to church, because this is, as children used to say, a "free country," right? Not exactly. Anyone can go to the zoo or the church and see this man's children, except their father. If this father runs into his children at the zoo, they may be delighted, but the regime of unilateral divorce and single-parent custody will be severely threatened by this man exercising his right of free movement to be with his own children. So if this father runs into his children at the zoo, he will be arrested. The media will say nothing about how he was trying to see his children but report faithfully that he was charged with "stalking" his former wife, and his name can end up on a register of "sex offenders." If there is no restraining order against him already, there soon will be. Then if he runs into his children on the street, even accidentally, he can be sent to the state penitentiary for years. This is how the divorce industry protects itself from the threat posed by personal freedom and ordinary family associations. It is also how unilateral divorce and sole custody threaten our most basic constitutional freedoms, including the private sphere of life itself.

Some suggest that judges must "balance" the rights of the accused with the genuine need of women for protection and that protective orders are issued on the principle of "better safe than sorry." Yet this begs important questions. We do not adopt such logic anywhere else in the law. We do not restrain citizens from their basic constitutional rights, including the right of free movement and free association (especially with their own children), before they have committed any offense, merely because someone asks us to. Our criminal justice system is predicated on the assumption that people should be punished for what they have done, not for what someone says they might do. We assume citizens are innocent until proven guilty, that they should enjoy their basic freedom until evidence of legal wrongdoing is presented against them, and that knowingly false accusations against them should be punished. Restraining orders overturn all this.

Yet the most telling (and seldom asked) question is how precisely protective orders can prevent violence at all. Violent assault is already illegal and punishable by incarceration. Anyone intending to violently attack someone is unlikely to be deterred by a protective order, since violating a protective order need not add anything to the punishment for violent assault. "Where there is genuine abuse, an order doesn't do any good, anyway," says Hession. "Can you stop a fist or a bullet with a piece of paper?"[609] The only people deterred are those who obey the law. One father whose wife obtained a restraining order against him was "enjoined and restrained from committing any domestic violence upon her."[610] But is he not thus enjoined and restrained to begin with, along with the rest of us? Once again, the orders seem designed not to prevent or punish crime but to eliminate fathers.

Also unclear is how taking away people's children can prevent violence. Common sense suggests that taking away a man's children will provoke precisely the kind of violent response it ostensibly intends to prevent. "We hear that some brute attacked his estranged wife despite a court order prohibiting him from coming near her," writes Paul Carpenter in the *Morning Call*. "Such stories never suggest that perhaps the guy flipped his wig because of a [protective order]. . . . It's amazing there aren't more rampages."[611] In the run-up to

Fathers' Day 2001, the *Washington Post* launched a gratuitous attack on fathers with a front-page article on some that allegedly became violent. By ranging through twelve states over several years the *Post* managed to find twelve violent fathers, most of whom were said to have violated protective orders.[612] This self-fulfilling tendency of protective orders gives the impression of vindicating their use when the orders may in fact be having precisely the opposite effect. Those who argue that bureaucratic government develops an interest in creating and exacerbating precisely the problem it ostensibly exists to address could hardly find more striking evidence to validate their theory. Here again the conclusion seems inescapable that the purpose is not to protect anyone from violent fathers but to protect the power of the divorce industry from peaceful ones.

VISITATION OR INSTITUTIONALIZATION?

The logical result would seem to be that fathers and their children—when they are permitted to be together at all—are isolated from mothers and the rest of the world and allowed to see one another only under the gaze of officials in an institutional setting. This is precisely what is now taking place in the growing and lucrative system of "supervised visitation centers" in which fathers must pay to see their children. "These centers not only get state funding, they also charge fathers for the privilege of seeing their own offspring." Rates run as high as $80 an hour. "People yell at you in front of the children. They try to degrade the father in the child's eyes," says Jim O'Brien. "No matter what you do, you're doing it wrong. I wish I'd never come here. . . . They belittle you." When O'Brien asked his daughter if she'd made her first communion in the six years since he had seen her, the social worker jumped in and said, "You're not allowed to ask that!"

Rick Brita is another father who has been forced to use an institution. It seems Brita was never convicted of any child abuse, and what was supposed to be a three-week arrangement was turned into a three-year fiasco. "It's like being in jail," says Brita's friend Joseph Rizoli:

> Everything the father does on the visitation has to be permissioned. Even hugging your own children could end your visit. In Rick's case, three years has given him permission to pass this hoop and he can hug his kids now. But he can't take the children out to a park or anything else outside the center. . . . He can't even take pictures of his own children.[613]

Are fathers and their children subject to this humiliation because the father is dangerous, or is it because the centers get federal money for each case committed to them? "Are these contract centers concerned with the children or the funding?" asks Stan Rains of Victoria, Texas, who has witnessed similar ordeals:

> Children are acutely aware of the ever-present, note-taking case workers and of the cameras located every ten feet along the walls. I have seen a parent and child cling to one another and stare back at the narrow-eyed, stern visages of several caseworkers studying this parent and child clinging to one another in terror and desperation. They reminded me of two neurotic and traumatized research monkeys reacting to the observations of white-frocked researchers, conditioned to the fact that these white-coated observers had the power to inflict pain, anguish, and even death. With this parent-child pair, their desperate, mutual clinging to one another, seemed to be viewed negatively by the case workers. . . . The demeaning of the "visiting" parent is readily visible from the minute that a person enters the "secured facility" with armed guards, officious case workers with their clipboards, and with arrogant, domineering managers. . . . The child's impression is that all of these authority figures see Daddy as a serious and dangerous threat. . . . It leaves a child with an impression that their love for Daddy is dangerous and bad, and so is Daddy. . . . Caseworkers . . . correct parents and children alike, openly, for all to hear . . .[614]

This too has become a major industry. "Visitation centers are becoming so popular among family court judges, probation officers, and some lawyers and parents that certain centers . . . have waiting lists up to a year long," the *Boston Globe* reports.[615] "That has led to visits being cut short to accommodate other families." The system is promoted by the Supervised Visitation Network, a group whose membership has mushroomed since its founding in 1992. The *Massachusetts News* describes it as a "matrix of lawyers, judges, social workers, academics, and domestic violence activists" who "have networked, talked with each other, served on various commissions, boosted each other's careers, and helped to expand the definition of domestic violence, and the size of state and federal funding massively."

SVN's "Standards and Guidelines" makes it clear that supervision is not limited to cases of violence or potential violence by the non-custodial parent against the children, which it clearly regards as exceptional, but is available in any circumstances of "conflict" between the parents. SVN's definition of "family violence" also indicates that it need not be physical or illegal: "Family violence is any form of physical, sexual, *or other abuse* inflicted on any person in a household by a family or household member."[616]

In Virginia, Michael Ewing is one of the few fathers' advocates ever to run a federally funded non-profit visitation center. In his program's first year, the Norfolk-area courts made more than 700 case referrals. "We solved all of the problems but two," Ewing said. "Only two families required supervised visitation." Ewing says the supervised visitation idea has been "beefed up with phony statistics" and there is very little need for it. As will be seen, it is well established that child abuse is overwhelmingly perpetrated by single mothers and their live-in boyfriends, and Ewing wonders why natural fathers, "who in reality are quite unlikely to abuse their own children," are targeted for supervision. "I think there's another agenda here." Ewing's center lost its funding in the second year. He thinks a local social worker who had lost clients because of Ewing's success complained to an influential state senator.[617]

'COURTS' WITHOUT DUE PROCESS?

The logical next step is special courts to expedite convictions. This is precisely what is now happening with "integrated domestic violence courts." Some 300 now operate in at least twenty-three states and more in Canada. New York City has two different levels of domestic violence courts, in addition to family courts.[618] Proponents openly acknowledge that these courts exist not to administer justice as such but to facilitate conviction and punishment: "to make [alleged?] batterers and abusers take responsibility for their actions," in the words of New York Chief Judge Judith Kaye.[619] These courts bear little relation to most Americans' understanding of due process. There is no presumption of innocence, hearsay evidence is admissible, and defendants have no right to confront their accusers. One study found there was no possibility that a defendant can be found innocent, since all persons arrested for non-felony domestic violence received some punishment: fine, jail, and/or treatment.[620]

The "fast-track" program of El Paso County, Colorado, "is designed to mete out swift justice to [alleged?] perpetrators who [allegedly?] abuse their partners, based on the theory that holding offenders immediately accountable will help prevent future offenses." Critics say "it coerces defendants into pleading guilty by depriving them of essential constitutional rights, including the right to post bond and the right to be represented by an attorney." "It's just butchering the Bill of Rights," according to attorney Kevin Donovan.[621] Previously, domestic violence defendants were treated like any other, but district attorney Doug Miles concluded that "domestic-violence perpetrators are very slick" and therefore merited special procedures to deal with their slickness. *Mother Jones* magazine, which applauds these suspensions of due process, notes that "conviction rates have risen" and "guilty pleas are way up, suggesting that prosecutors were able to build more substantial cases, leading to more plea bargaining." In other words, the near-certainty of conviction pressures the innocent into pleading guilty.[622]

Sending people to prison apparently is now a virtue in itself. In San Diego, two lawyers report with glee that suspending due process protections "obtains convictions in about 88 percent of its cases."[623] New York City reports conviction rates comparable to those in the Soviet Union, over 90 percent "even before the specialized domestic violence courts were established."[624] Convictions are supposed to be based on an impartial weighing of evidence in each individual case. Nowhere else in the law do we regard convicting people of crimes—thousands of people of whose guilt or innocence we can have no first-hand knowledge—as a virtue for its own sake.

In Canada, special domestic violence courts are empowered to seize the property, including the homes, of men accused of domestic violence (though not necessarily convicted or even formally charged) and to do so *ex parte*, without the men being present to defend themselves. Again, the "violence" need not be physical.[625] "This bill is classic police-state legislation and violates just about every constitutional principle that anyone with even a minimal familiarity with our Constitution might think of," according to Robert Martin who teaches constitutional law at the University of Western Ontario.[626] Walter Fox, a Toronto lawyer, describes these courts as "scary and pre-fascist," saying there is no presumption of innocence or burden of proof.[627]

In Britain, centuries-old protections for the accused are set aside in the zeal to convict those who are labeled not as "defendants" but as "abusers." "Special domestic violence courts" allow third parties such as civil servants and feminist groups to use "relaxed rules of evidence and the lower burden of proof" to bring "civil actions" against those they target as batterers, even if their alleged "victim" brings no charges. "Victim support groups," who say women "should be spared having to take legal action," can now act in the name of anonymous alleged victims—with no proof that such victims even exist—to loot men who have been convicted of nothing.[628]

Special courts to try special crimes that can only be committed by certain people are a familiar device totalitarian regimes adopted to replace blind justice with ideological justice. New courts created during the French Revolution led to the Reign of Terror and were consciously imitated in the Soviet Union. In Hitler's dreaded *Volksgerichte*, or "people's courts," write Carl Friedrich and Zbigniew Brzezinski, "only expediency in terms of National Socialist standards served as a basis for judgment."[629] In her authoritative study, Rosemary O'Kane emphasizes that the essence of the revolutionary Reign of Terror "lies in summary justice," typically executed by "newly appointed law courts" or "extraordinary courts and revolutionary tribunals."[630]

Forced confessions are a common feature of domestic violence or "batterers" programs, extracted on pain of losing one's children or incarceration. In Warren County, Pennsylvania, and elsewhere fathers like Robert Pessia are threatened with jail unless they sign pre-printed confessions stating, "I have physically and emotionally battered my partner." The father must then describe the violence, even if he insists he committed none. The documents require him to state, "I am responsible for the violence I used. My behavior was not provoked."[631] Again, the words of Friedrich and Brzezinski are apposite. "Confessions are the key to this psychic coercion," they write. "The inmate is subjected to a constant barrage of propaganda and ever repeated demands that he 'confess his sins,' that he 'admit his shame.'"[632]

ONE-STOP DIVORCE SHOPS

"Battered women's shelters" are another institution of the divorce industry. Erin Pizzey, who founded the first shelter in London in 1971, attests that many of the women were "as violent as the men" they left "and violent towards their children." Pizzey says feminists "hijacked the domestic violence movement, not just in Britain, but internationally."[633]

Shelters have been described as "one-stop divorce shops" because of their willingness to assist women in custody proceedings—even when the women have not been the victims of any violence—by manufacturing abuse and incest accusations against fathers. Shelters supply "letters of endorsement" for use against fathers in court, according to Louise Malenfant, an activist in Canada, and Donna Laframboise, who investigated shelters for the *National Post*, "despite the fact that the shelter employees have never met the men involved, have only heard one side of the story, and have only known the women for a short time under highly artificial conditions."[634]

Batterers or Protectors?

One woman used help from a shelter to produce a ten-page affidavit alleging not that her husband was physically abusive, but that he had health problems. "I got the restraining order and soon after I got full custody of my children, with no visitation for my husband." Judges are "most definitely swayed" by letters from shelters, says a lawyer who uses the tactic. "You've got sort of a 'professional' now saying he shouldn't see his kids." As we have seen, judges seldom require much convincing in the first place, since separating children from their fathers is in their own bureaucratic interest. The lawyer said she represented a woman who "came in with this two- or three-page letter . . . and [the father] was denied access on that basis." "Relationships between fathers and children are being ripped asunder in some cases merely on the say-so of a shelter worker," writes Laframboise, who recounts these examples:

> A shelter worker wrote a letter to a family court on behalf of a woman who "had been a victim of abuse in her childhood and now as a adult" and who was "intelligent, insightful, and sincere." But it turned out the woman had already made seven sexual abuse complaints involving eleven different people, including her father, brother, and sister with whom she continued living. All were dismissed or acquitted.

> A counselor at a shelter wrote a letter declaring client to be a "loving and devoted mother" and expressing the "strong feeling" that custody should be awarded to her rather than to the husband she was leaving. But four years earlier, the Children's Aid Society had found she was a danger to her son and an older daughter. A Children's Aid worker told a court that both children "admitted being afraid of their mother much of the time." The courts awarded custody of all three children to the woman.

> A shelter worker wrote that a woman had been "physically and emotionally" abused by the husband she was leaving, and since "her children are her life," she should be assisted in gaining custody. However a psychologist noted that she had told him her husband "has never struck her physically." Custody was awarded to the mother.[635]

Battered women's shelters throughout the United States and Canada also have had "a long history of financial disarray, weak accountability, criminal charges, lawsuits, mass resignations, and vicious infighting," the *National Post* reports. "A growing chorus of critics say the highly politicized character of many facilities means that the clients' needs take second place to the agenda of . . . zealots concerned with dogma who are overtly hostile to men, male children, and heterosexual relationships."

The politicization of these centers is described by workers who signed a letter saying that "the workplace [was] used to further extreme militant feminist philosophy" and that lesbian employees received preferential treatment while heterosexual ones were told not to "discuss their wedding plans or their wedding days with their co-workers." Ironically for institutions ostensibly sheltering women from violence, the centers themselves have experienced "violence against women." The atmosphere in one Ontario shelter "became so acrimonious that police were called in after a staffer tried to prevent the chair of the board from entering the building. Residents witnessed some pushing and shoving." At another, a woman "was charged with assault while a stalking charge was laid against another."

"They politicize clients that are really supposed to be into healing," says Jeannette McEachern, who ran a center for seventeen years. She says of the center's volunteer manual that "three-quarters of it was [devoted to] strong feminist philosophy." A lawyer who helped establish a rape crisis center resigned because the male-bashing got too blatant and the attacks from colleagues too personal. "Women who go for help get this philosophy: that you have to hate men or you're lost." One woman whose husband "didn't beat me up or nothing, we just had an argument," says shelter workers ignored her actual situation and pressured her to conform to their agenda. "They asked me if I was abused, and I said, 'No.' They wanted me to get a lawyer, and I said, 'For what?'" She maintains shelter employees tried to "trick" her into making incriminating statements about her husband. "Everything negative about him, they wrote it down. If I said something nice about him, they wouldn't write it down. I kept telling them, 'No, he didn't hit me.'" She was offered incentives such as housing and furniture to leave her husband. "They said, 'If you leave him, we can help you find a place right away.' But I said, 'I don't want to leave him.' . . . They wanted that so bad. They were trying to break up a family, and I didn't want that."

Another woman describes the shelter as "an experience from hell." The message was: "You believe what we believe, you do what we say, or get out of here."[636]

COURTS AND CHILD ABUSE

Logically, a story about the war against fathers should contain some account of the very real terrors and injuries endured by men who are violently attacked by women. A substantial and growing body of scholarly literature has now documented this problem: shootings in the back, hired killers, midnight castrations, and more.[637] Further, the media have even begun to publicize such cases. Such coverage is certainly overdue; the domestic violence industry vehemently resists recognizing that men can be victims of attacks by women. Yet in keeping with its voyeuristic, soap opera fixation on the "he said / she said" approach to family problems, even the media's emerging balance may be selective. In simply placing men alongside women as "victims," the academy and media may be further feminizing our perceptions of domestic violence and once again covering up more than they are revealing.

Not only does violence against men seldom elicit much sympathy among the public; it is not foremost among the terrors of fathers themselves, most of whom would willingly endure unrelenting fear of the most gruesome physical assault in preference to the emotional horrors of losing their children. "The most common theme among abused men is their tales not of physical anguish but of dispossession—losing custody of children due to accusations of physical and sexual abuse," writes Patricia Pearson.[638]

Philip Cook, author of *Abused Men*, says this is the main reason men remain in violent relationships. "If they have children, there is grave concern, and unfortunately rightly so, that they may never see their children again. They don't feel that they will get a fair shake in the courts regarding custody no matter what happens or what she does," he relates. "And it's actually true. There are many cases that I know of in which a woman was actually arrested for domestic violence still receive custody of the children [*sic*]."[639] In fact the greatest danger lies not only in the loss but in the very real possibility of the physical destruction of their children as well. "A battered man knows that if his wife has been abusing him, she has often been abusing the children," writes Warren Farrell. "Leaving her means leaving his children unprotected from her abuse."[640]

Here we arrive at the crowning achievement of the divorce regime and the one most thoroughly disguised by politically correct politicians, journalists, and scholars: the massive and even institutionalized epidemic of child abuse—emotional, physical, and sexual—for which it is largely responsible and on which it may even be said to thrive. For the incontrovertible fact is that divorce and single-parent homes are not precipitated by child abuse, as the courts, bar associations, and feminists would have us believe, but the other way around.

Though not usually classed as a form of child abuse, the emotional devastation inflicted on children by divorce itself is arguably at least as serious as the effects on grown women of the "abuse" recounted by domestic violence groups ("depriving her of clothes"). The psychological trauma and emotional damage of divorce on children has been understood for centuries, however fashionable it has become in recent years to deny it. Judith Wallerstein and Sandra Blakeslee have called divorce the "single most important cause of enduring pain in a child's life."[641] Wallerstein and Joan Kelly found that children of divorce "expressed the wish for increased contact with their fathers with a startling and moving intensity." "The most striking response among the six- to eight-year-old children was their pervasive sadness," they write:

> The impact of separation appeared to be so strong that the children's usual defenses and coping strategies did not hold sufficiently under the stress. Crying and sobbing were not uncommon . . . and many children were on the brink of tears as they spoke with us. . . . Particularly striking . . . was the yearning for the father. More than half of these children missed their father acutely. Many felt abandoned and rejected by him and expressed their longing in ways reminiscent of grief for a dead parent. . . . In confronting the despair and sadness of these children and their intense, almost physical, longing for the father, that inner psychological needs of great power and intensity were being expressed.

Adolescents also "reported feelings of emptiness, tearfulness, and difficulty in concentrating, chronic fatigue, and very troublesome dreams. "I cried and I begged and begged," said one.[642]

"The effects of this tidal wave of divorce are devastating, for our children and for our nation's future," writes Katerine Kersten of the Center on the American Experiment. "Children of divorce are at far greater risk for a host of ills than their peers from intact families," including crime, drug and alcohol abuse, depression or hyperactivity, and aggressive or impulsive behavior":

> Children of divorce tend to have intercourse earlier, to have more sexual partners and sexually transmitted diseases, and a greater number of out-of-wedlock births. . . . Children of divorced parents tend to perform more poorly in math and spelling than their peers from intact families. . . . These children have significantly higher high-school dropout rates and lower rates of college graduation. . . . Divorce frequently impedes a child's ability to

sustain family life as an adult. It tends to weaken parent-child relations, diminish trust of others, promote destructive ways of handling conflict, change children's expectations of marriage, and lead to higher rates of cohabitation and divorce as children reach adulthood.[643]

When this cruelty is inflicted by both parents there is probably little that public policy can do to remedy it. But as we have seen, and contrary to what divorce advocates present, this is relatively rare. When we recall that 80 percent of divorces are inflicted on the children by only one parent—who can do so over the objections of the other—it is not unreasonable to class divorce itself as a form of preventable child abuse.

But the psychological abuse is only the beginning of the nightmare for the children of divorce. Beyond it is the physical and sexual violence to which children in single-mother homes are exposed far more than those in intact families. For contrary to misleading statements propagated by the child abuse branch of the divorce industry, the uncontested and inescapable fact of central importance in understanding the causes of child abuse is that it is overwhelmingly a phenomenon of single-parent homes.

As with domestic violence between adults, one must always be cautious about figures and assertions about child abuse, however "scientific" they purport to be. Here too the designation of a category of "abuse," separate from violent crime, raises problems of definition similar to those that beset domestic violence, rendering determinations highly subjective at best and subject to considerable manipulation. Like domestic violence, child abuse is not usually adjudicated as violent assault, so no objective measure of its incidence is available. Consequently, vague definitions and subjective methods of verification create uncertainties even about what precisely is the subject under discussion. Further, they likewise raise serious questions about due process of law.[644]

None of the government studies purporting to quantify child abuse bases its figures on convictions in jury trials or even court actions, even when the cases are classified as "confirmed" or "substantiated." (The exceptions prove the rule: For parents who do receive jury trials, "A verdict of not guilty in a criminal court will not effect the 'true [substantiated] finding' in Juvenile Court because that finding is based on a different and lower evidentiary standard.")[645] At best, such studies are based on "reports" by social workers, and some apparently represent nothing more than interviews conducted with non-specialists about alleged abuse they chose *not* to report.[646] Most of the literature on child abuse provided from official sources and from government-funded scholars and advocacy groups is carefully selected, and some is highly questionable.

As if to highlight the dangers, waves of child abuse hysteria swept America and other countries during the 1980s and 1990s. Though almost universally proven groundless, the result was torn-apart families, hideous injustices, and ruined lives. The "witch hunt," as the American Civil Liberties Union termed it, in Wenatchee, Washington, is only the most well-known example of how parents of both genders were deprived of their children and unjustly incarcerated by setting aside constitutional safeguards while the media and civil liberties advocates (including the ACLU itself) looked the other way.[647] Similar cases came to light in California, Massachusetts, North Carolina, Ontario, Saskatchewan, the north of England, and more recently France. Yet even today it is not clear that we have learned any lessons from these miscarriages of justice or that the hysteria has subsided so much as it has been institutionalized.

The abuse and exploitation of children by the very people and programs who claim to be protecting them is now so common and has been exposed in so many scholarly studies and popular accounts that one wonders why it is permitted to continue. Since at least the 1980s, scholars like Douglas Besharov have warned that a "flood of unfounded reports" endangered truly abused children.[648] In recent years, serious questions have been raised by critics from both the left and right about whether innocent parents are losing their children because of false or exaggerated accusations of abuse. "There is an antifamily bias that pervades the policies and practices of the child welfare system," according to Jane Knitzer of the Children's Defense Fund. "Children are inappropriately removed from their families."[649]

Part of this debate has raged within the child welfare profession itself, where some have alleged that children are removed unjustly and unnecessarily from parents in "staggering proportions." A California commission concluded that "the state's foster care system runs contrary to the preservation of families by unnecessarily removing an increasing number of children from their homes each year."[650] "Children everywhere are often removed from their parents without a warrant when one should be obtained," says California attorney David Beauvais. "Parents are often tricked or intimidated. . . . Courts too often rubber-stamp CPS [child protective services] recommendations and hearings are confidentially held. There is no public access and no media scrutiny. Once in the system, parents are well on their way to losing their parental rights."[651]

Batterers or Protectors?

Writers such as Ross Parke and Armin Brott, Dorothy Rabinowitz, Richard Wexler, Dean Tong, Dana Mack, and Sylvia Ann Hewlett and Cornel West have demonstrated the political and financial incentives that induce prosecutors, family courts, and child protective services to exaggerate and even fabricate charges of child abuse against parents in order to take away their children. "By far the most powerful incentive to rubber-stamp an abuse charge is financial," argue Parke and Brott.[652] A San Diego grand jury investigation revealed "a system out of control, with few checks and little balance." This system, where justice is blocked by "confidential files, closed courts, gag orders, and total statutory immunity [for judges and social workers], has isolated itself to a degree unprecedented in our system of jurisprudence and ordered liberties."[653]

Like child-support enforcement agents, child protective services blur the distinction between social work and law enforcement. In effect, they constitute another form of plainclothes family police. "Although spoken of in terms of social services," writes Susan Orr, "the child-protection function of child welfare is essentially a police action." Yet because they are not called police, these social workers are not required to follow due process procedures, nor are the courts before which parents accused by them are summoned. Orr calls child protective services "the most intrusive arm of social services," because of their power to remove children from their parents. Yet because the parents are seldom charged criminally, they are not afforded due process protections and are unable to defend themselves in proceedings that are often secret and without public record. "The child protection system is built upon the notion that child maltreatment is remediable with the right therapeutic treatment," Orr observes. "By forsaking the courts of criminal law, in which determinations of justice and injustice are made and punishments meted out, child welfare agencies took on the much larger task of attempting to heal family members who have gone wrong." This system of therapeutic law enforcement, applied in the cases Orr describes mostly to single mothers and some intact families, is precisely what fathers face on a much larger scale in the same courts and bureaucracies through involuntary divorce.[654]

The San Diego grand jury report also emphasizes the role of social workers as plainclothes police that in practice eclipse the regular police. "We found that some police officers abdicate their role as fact finders to the social worker," they write. "Detectives will integrate elements of the social workers' investigation into their own reports, instead of performing an independent investigation." Police are generally held to higher standards of evidence than social workers, who can pursue cases even when police conclude that insufficient evidence exists. "When police determine that they cannot find sufficient evidence to charge, the criminal case is usually dropped." Yet the "civil" case may proceed in the juvenile or family court in the absence of evidence.[655] "Most state agencies that deal in the areas of child protection are primarily autonomous, with little if any supervision from or accountability to anyone," writes Dean Tong. "While they can remove children from a home and file a charge without presenting any evidence, they cannot be held personally responsible for their actions."[656]

This is aggravated by a bureaucratic culture that threatens both fathers and mothers, including intact families. Some have suggested the rise of "a new class of professionals—social workers, therapists, foster care providers, family court lawyers—who have a vested interest in taking over parental function."[657] Government bureaucracies that have assumed the role of protector over children whose fathers have been forced away also develop a professional interest in eliminating their competitors. "These are people who . . . are given an enormous amount of power," says Melvin Guyer, a psychiatry professor at the University of Michigan and a practicing attorney. "And they routinely abuse that power."[658]

The San Diego grand jury's report also emphasizes that "social workers are perceived to have nearly unlimited power" and quotes one witness as saying: "Power corrupts. Absolute power corrupts absolutely. Total immunity [enjoyed by social workers] is absolute power." They are even empowered to punish their critics. "Parents and therapists have testified that in many cases social workers have even been allowed to retaliate."[659] On September 21, 2004, an "Order of Arrest" was entered by a magistrate in Georgia against Stephen Lee Johnson, for his Web site criticizing the state's child protective service. The order followed threats of lawsuits by state officials against Johnson.[660]

This lack of due process protections in the "child abuse industry," as one social worker calls it, has resulted in a presumption of guilt similar to that pervading domestic violence and child support. "When I started working, we tried to prove a family was innocent," she recounts. "Now we assume they are guilty until they prove they are not."[661] In Massachusetts, as elsewhere, allegations are "substantiated" not by a court proceeding, let alone a jury trial, but by administrative personnel in the Department of Social Services, which issues letters stating, "At least one person said you were responsible for the incident and there was no available information to *definitively indicate otherwise*."[662]

Here again, "The burden of proof, contrary to every other area of our judicial system, is on the alleged perpetrator to prove his innocence."[663]

The San Diego grand jury describes the Soviet logic by which justice is rigged against fathers and anyone who stands by them. "Ironically, 'denial' is taken as evidence of guilt," they found. "Unlike any other area of our judicial system, in Juvenile Court the alleged perpetrator . . . does not have to be proven guilty in order to achieve a true [substantiated] finding":

> If a father denies molest and a true finding is made, he suffers the ultimate Catch 22: He can either admit and take a chance that the department will allow him to begin reunification with his family, or he can deny and no reunification will occur.
>
> If the spouse supports her husband's denial, she is "accommodating his denial" . . . and she too will not be allowed to reunify with the child. . . .
>
> If the child denies the molest, this can be seen as part of a "child abuse accommodation syndrome" and an additional reason why the child should have no contact with the parents.
>
> Thus, all members of the family can deny a false molest allegation and, in each instance, the system uses the denial as evidence of guilt.

As with domestic violence, accused parents must undergo a therapy program that requires confessing. "The only way to complete Parents United is to admit the molest," in San Diego. "Not complying . . . is grounds for . . . termination of parental rights."[664] Documented cases also exist of social workers falsifying transcripts of interviews with children to frame fathers.[665] Also like domestic violence, there is little doubt that bypassing due process procedures (not to mention holding someone's children) creates pressures for guilty pleas by the innocent. The grand jury describes the "likelihood that a charge will produce a plea to a lesser offense":

> Penalties for conviction are very high, and the cost of a defense prohibitive. . . . Numerous defense attorneys testified that they allow and even encourage their clients to plead to a minor charge even when they are certain of the client's innocence in order to facilitate the reunification of the family.[666]

Here again, the "better safe than sorry" rationalization for these procedures is not wholly plausible, since such practices may create more abuse than they prevent. The Children's Project of the American Civil Liberties Union reports that children in foster care are ten times more likely to be maltreated while in the custody of the state than in their own homes.[667] Similar findings of widespread abuse in foster care are well documented.[668]

A FATHER'S PROTECTION

Yet when all allowances are made for false reports, it can hardly be denied that child abuse has become a serious problem. Contrary to what the industry suggests, it is clear that the child abuse explosion has coincided with the divorce revolution and the rise in single-parent homes. In the seven years between two federal studies, 1986-1993, physical abuse of children was found to have nearly doubled, sexual abuse apparently more than doubled, "and emotional abuse, physical neglect, and emotional neglect were all more than two and one-half times" their earlier level. The estimated number of "seriously injured" children "essentially quadrupled" in this short period.[669] Since the divorce revolution began well before 1986, this is likely a slice of a much larger trend.

Like domestic violence, child abuse is often laid at the door of fathers by divorce operatives eager to justify involuntary divorce and exclusive mother custody. A PBS documentary, *Breaking the Silence: Children's Stories*, aired in October 2005, asserts without evidence and contrary to known data that "Children are most often in danger from the father." The verbal smoke and mirrors used to disguise the truth is sometimes flagrant. "Adult domestic violence and child maltreatment often occur together," says Meredith Hofford, director of the family violence department of the NCJFCJ, "with the same assailant responsible for both."[670] No documentation is provided for this statement, but to the extent it is true, the "assailant" is overwhelmingly likely to be the single mother.[671] Hofford reveals this in calling for more government money to "support" what she describes as "battered women who maltreat their children."[672]

A huge body of feminist literature has developed using misleading assumptions purporting to connect domestic violence with child abuse, all with the transparent purpose of rationalizing the removal of children from their fathers. "This literature consistently assumes that the source of the abuse is the father," though hard data show otherwise.[673]

There is no evidence that the child abuse epidemic has anything to do with fathers except insofar as they are prevented from protecting their children or that allegations made against fathers during divorce proceedings are anything other than a smokescreen to disguise the real abuse. In addition to one million ostensibly "substantiated" cases of child abuse annually, an additional two million reports are never substantiated,[674] and as the quantity of reports has increased, "substantiation rates have plummeted."[675] As with domestic violence, most unsubstantiated reports are made during divorce proceedings for the transparent purpose of obtaining custody and preventing fathers' visitation.

"There is no dispute within the Juvenile Dependency System that false allegations of sexual molest during custody disputes occur," reports the San Diego grand jury. "The Jury has found that a parent making a false allegation of abuse or molest during a custody dispute is very likely to achieve the desired result. These accusations are made primarily to avoid visitation and joint custody provisions and the accuser frequently succeeds."[676] A variety of studies has found that 75 percent to 80 percent of allegations of child abuse made during divorce (95 percent of which are made by women) are "completely false."[677] "Today's system for responding to allegations of child sexual abuse is one that in the majority of cases exacts no negative consequences from the individual filing false allegations," writes Tong.[678]

Despite undisputed evidence about the protective value of intact families with fathers, the habits of child protective officials seem to be to further marginalize them. One study of several hundred cases concludes that "An anti-male attitude is often found in documents, statements, and in the writings of those claiming to be experts in cases of child sexual abuse." These scholars document techniques by social service agencies to systematically teach children to hate their fathers, including inculcating in the children a message that the father has sexually molested them. "The professionals use techniques that teach children a negative and critical view of men in general and fathers in particular," they write. "The child is repeatedly reinforced for fantasizing throwing Daddy in jail and is trained to hate and fear him."[679] These are the same social workers who report child abuse figures to the federal government.

Even allowing for this, it is still clear from the figures they report that it is not fathers but mothers—overwhelmingly single mothers—who are by far the most likely to injure and kill their children. Data from the Department of Health and Human Services, an agency strongly pervaded by a feminist culture, consistently show that women are much more likely than men to be perpetrators of child maltreatment: "almost two-thirds were females," the 1996 report states, and subsequent studies contain similar findings.[680] Given that "male" perpetrators are not usually fathers but much more likely to be boyfriends and stepfathers, fathers emerge as by far the least likely child abusers.[681]

While fathers are often thought more likely to commit sexual as opposed to physical child abuse, sexual abuse is much less common than severe physical abuse (though it receives far more attention and is most likely to be raised in custody battles) and much more likely to be perpetrated by boyfriends and stepfathers. "Children are seven times more likely to be badly beaten by their parents than they are to be sexually abused by them," according to the National Society for the Prevention of Cruelty to Children. Their study found that father-daughter incest is "rare, occurring in less than 4 in 1,000 children," and that three-fourths of incest perpetrators are brothers and stepbrothers rather than fathers.[682] Likewise, a University of Iowa study found that "father caretakers" were almost four times as likely as biological fathers to sexually abuse children, and another study found that a preschooler not living with both biological parents is forty times more likely to be sexually abused.[683] Ralph Underwager has estimated that roughly 2.5 percent of parents who are accused of sexual abuse are likely to be guilty, but this is almost certainly much too high.[684] Figures from HHS indicate that between 1 and 1.5 out of 1,000 child-abuse investigations "end up being a *substantiated* case of *sexual* abuse by the *natural* father," and even these are not necessarily determined by convictions in jury trials.[685]

The most dangerous place for a child is the home of a single mother. The HHS studies confirmed the already well-established fact that children in single-parent households are at much higher risk for physical violence and sexual molestation than those living in two-parent homes: "Children of single parents had a 77 percent greater risk of being harmed by physical abuse, an 87 percent greater risk of being harmed by physical neglect, and an 80 percent greater risk of suffering serious injury or harm from abuse or neglect than children living with both parents."[686]

Children in mother-only households were three times more likely to be "fatally abused" (murdered) than children in father-only households. Females were 78 percent of the perpetrators of "fatal child abuse" (murder), 81 percent of natural parents who seriously abuse their children, 72 percent of natural parents who moderately abuse their children, and 65 percent of natural parents who are inferred to have abused their children. Natural mothers were the perpetrators of 93 percent of physical neglect, 86 percent of educational neglect, 78 percent of emotional neglect, 60 percent of physical abuse. When the perpetrator is a non-natural parent, "males" (that is, boyfriends and stepfathers) are the perpetrators of 90 percent of physical abuse, 97 percent of sexual abuse, 74 percent of emotional abuse, and 82 percent of educational neglect. Children are twenty times more likely to be "fatally abused" (murdered), twenty-two times more likely to be "seriously" abused, twenty times more likely to be "moderately" abused, and eighteen times more likely to be sexually abused in households earning less than $15,000 per year (households without fathers) than in households earning more than $30,000 per year (households with fathers).[687]

Some suggest that HHS seriously underreports the difference between single-parent homes and intact married families.[688] A British study found children are up to thirty-three times more likely to suffer serious abuse and seventy-three times more likely to suffer fatal abuse in the home of a mother with a live-in boyfriend or stepfather than in an intact family.[689] "Contrary to public perception," write researchers Patrick Fagan and Dorothy Hanks, "research shows that the most likely physical abuser of a young child will be that child's mother, not a male in the household."[690] "The person who is least likely to abuse a child is a married father," notes Canadian Senator Anne Cools. "The person who is most likely is a single, unmarried mother."[691] Maggie Gallagher sums up the reality: "The person most likely to abuse a child physically is a single mother. The person most likely to abuse a child sexually is the mother's boyfriend or second husband."[692] A two-parent family is "the safest environment for children."[693]

Shorn of ideological euphemism, what these figures effectively demonstrate is that the presence of the second parent, usually the father, constitutes the principal impediment to abuse. At one time all this would have been considered common sense, because two parents check each another's excesses and the father was traditionally recognized as the children's natural protector. "Although, as a literary theme, the 'good father' protecting his children from the 'bad mother' is almost unheard of (so idealized has mothering become)," writes Adrienne Burgess, who heads the British government's Fathers Direct program, "in real life fathers have often played the protector role inside families."[694]

This is confirmed by academic research, however diffident scholars have become about stating it. "The presence of the father . . . placed the child at lesser risk for child sexual abuse," concludes a recent study of low-income families, defensively. "The protective effect from the father's presence in most households was sufficiently strong to offset the risk incurred by the few paternal perpetrators."[695] In fact, the risk of "paternal perpetrators" is minimal. "It is solidly clear that an ongoing, co-residential social and biological father decreases, by far, the dangers to that child of being abused."[696] From the perspective of the father, it would appear that the real child abusers have thrown him out of the family so they can abuse his children with impunity.

Murder especially is an acute danger for children living in single-mother homes.

Women accounted for 78 percent of child murders according to HHS and mothers for 55 percent according to a Justice Department report.[697] Between 1986 and 1993, as the number of single-mother households increased dramatically, fatal child abuse increased 46 percent.[698]

Homicide is the single largest killer of infants (22.6 percent)—surpassing "accidental" suffocation, motor vehicle accidents, fire, drowning, choking, "other unintentional injuries," and "injuries of undetermined intent"—according to the National Institute of Child Health and Human Development at the National Institutes of Health.[699] The study found that infants were more likely to die from injuries if their mothers were young and unmarried.

Even this may understate the extent of the killing, since such studies generally take "accidental" and "unintentional" deaths at face value. Yet some researchers believe that what is diagnosed as "Sudden Infant Death Syndrome" may often be murder. Michael Green from Sheffield University's Department of Forensic Pathology writes in the *British Medical Journal* that up to 40 percent of babies registered as "cot deaths" may have been killed by their "parents" or another adult. Dr. Green, a leading pediatric pathologist, goes so far as to suggest that SIDS be abolished as a legitimate attribution for cause of death.[700] Professor Sir Roy Meadow of St. James University Hospital, Leeds, likewise says that "doctors and coroners have in some cases overlooked signs of bleeding, broken bones, and foreign bodies blocking the airway because they were under pressure to resolve unexplained cases swiftly and without controversy," according to the *The Independent*. "In doing so, they may have helped parents get away with murder." Though the newspaper tried to sanitize the phenomenon with the word *parents*, it eventually revealed that this usually means single mothers:

> Meadow's view is based on a study of the records of eighty-one children judged by criminal and family courts to have been killed by their parents. In forty-nine cases, the children had initially been certified as dying from SIDS and a further twenty-nine were classified as dying from other natural causes. The mother was responsible for the death—usually smothering—in more than 80 percent of cases. In twenty-four of the families, more than one child had died, and in five of them, three children had died.

The acceptance of so many children dying of unknown causes was characterized by Meadow as a "national scandal": "If one out of every 1,000 twenty-one-year-olds died suddenly and unexpectedly without an identifiable cause, there would be a national outcry."[701]

In the United States, some allege that child murders could be twice as frequent as official statistics indicate, owing to a willingness to attribute many to SIDS.[702] SIDS was considered a genetic affliction that ran in families, based on an influential 1972 article in *Pediatrics* magazine by Alfred Steinschneider. For years Steinschneider's article prevented coroners and doctors across North America "from entertaining suspicions when multiple babies perished in a family," writes Patricia Pearson. But twenty-two years later the housewife he used as the case study confessed to smothering all five of her children.[703] The number of young children who die in the United States at the hands of "parents" or other caregivers is underreported by nearly 60 percent, according to one team of researchers.[704]

Yet mothers are seldom punished for injuring or killing their children. "Even child killers can get sympathy if they can claim victimization by a male," writes Cathy Young, who quotes one feminist activist as saying, "When a woman [is] so alone that she wants to kill herself and her children, it's not her fault."[705] Judges seem to agree. "Most women aren't incarcerated for infanticide," writes Patricia Pearson:

> Of those who are even convicted, about two-thirds avoid prison, and the rest receive an average sentence of seven years. In England between 1982 and 1989, fewer than 10 percent of mothers convicted of manslaughter for killing their children (at any age) were imprisoned; only two of the mothers who'd committed infanticide were. British fathers were more likely to be charged with murder than manslaughter. More than half of the fathers convicted of manslaughter went to jail. Three times as many mothers as fathers are deemed to be mentally ill for killing their children.[706]

In July 1999, Marie Noe, who admitted to murdering eight of her children, was sentenced to probation. Even the *Washington Post*, notoriously sentimental when it comes to mothers, marveled that a serial killer who pleaded guilty to eight murders could be sentenced to twenty years' probation:

> The victims were eight of her children, each of whom she smothered as infants. These deaths, which occurred between 1949 and 1968, were then

believed to be cases of what is now called SIDS—Sudden Infant Death Syndrome. They were not. Ms. Noe now admits that it was she, not any disease, who killed eight members of her family.[707]

Latrena Pixley is another case that has baffled the public. Pixley was given custody of one child after having been convicted of murdering its half-sibling. Pixley was the mother of three children by three different fathers when she was convicted of killing her baby girl. The judge suspended Pixley's sentence and ordered her to spend weekends in jail for three years.[708]

Stories of mothers (again, usually single mothers) murdering their children are now so common that there is no need to multiply examples. Those reported in the media, such as the sensational Andrea Yates case, are only the tip of the iceberg; many are not reported at all. Even once the problem becomes too conspicuous to ignore, the media will often put a politically correct spin on it. The *Chicago Tribune* would have us believe that Marilyn Lemak was the victim of a legal system so uncaring and insensitive that it refused to let her throw her children's father out of the house on nothing more than her own whim. Her only recourse, naturally, was to kill the children. The *Tribune*'s account defies paraphrase, not to mention belief:

MOTHER'S PATH FROM DESPAIR TO TRAGEDY
Divorce records reveal inner conflict preceding slayings
14 March 1999
Jaban Hanna / Ted Gregory / Abdon Pallasch /
Lisa Black / Michael Ko

Six months ago, Marilyn Lemak went before a Divorce Court judge to show that living with her husband was causing her emotional problems. If she could prove that, the judge might grant her request that her husband, David Lemak, move out of the big Victorian home in Naperville where they were raising three young children. Marilyn Lemak told the judge that she felt "ignored as a parent and as a wife."

"Feelings of just, well, I was just feeling very stressed," she said in September. "I felt like I was always either being ignored or my authority overrided or just my concerns belittled."

She said she was suffering physical symptoms due to the stress of the household: severe headaches, neck and back tension, and jaw clenching, which was causing pain in her face. She said the symptoms were lessened when David Lemak was not around.

But the Divorce Court hearing did not go her way.

No matter how hard she and her attorney tried, Marilyn Lemak could not muster enough evidence to prove to the judge that she was suffering emotional distress because she was sharing the house with her husband.

To her, though, the evidence apparently was overwhelming.

Today, Marilyn Lemak is in a DuPage County Jail cell—at times nearly catatonic, her attorney says—charged with murdering her three children.

Nowhere in the lengthy article with five contributing writers does it mention that Marilyn Lemak's husband had in fact already moved out of the house when she embarked on her killing spree. One might conclude his real failing was not being present to protect his children from their homicidal mother.[709]

Yet had he been present he would have risked being blamed for her killings or for "controlling" her. This was the defense of "a wisp of a woman" charged with six counts of strangling her own children and defended by a battered women's group "based on their belief that her actions were the byproduct of domestic violence." "We see this as the response of a woman who was abused and exposed to violence," said Pacyinz Lyfoung of Asian Women United of Minnesota. "We are not condoning what was done, but we are supporting Khoua Her in this difficult time in her life." This formulaic wording—"abused and exposed to violence"—reveals that she was not actually the victim of any violence. Yet the *Boston Globe* gives more attention to her failed suicide attempt than to the murders, before turning its guns on the father for a "combative relationship."[710]

The recognition that fathers might actually protect their children apparently serves only to reinforce the double standard of punishing fathers for the crimes of mothers. Alba Ingrid Scarpelli, convicted of "multiple counts of child abuse for tying up and torturing her five-year-old son," was sentenced to eighteen months on work release. Yet the boy's father, who apparently stood by while she committed the abuse, received eight years in prison. The judge explained, "You are going to receive a substantially more severe sentence because you were substantially more culpable." The judge pointed to the father's former job as a volunteer firefighter and certification as a medical technician. "You were in a superior position to intervene and stop this."[711]

Observers find such decisions baffling. But contrary to the language of some fathers' groups, the judge who issued this ruling is neither ignorant nor insane, and he is not simply "biased." The only plausible explanation is political pressure exercised by bar associations dominated by feminist groups who can ruin a judge's career. A Brooklyn judge, described as "gutsier than most" by the *New York Law Journal*, was denied reappointment when he challenged social service agencies' efforts to remove children from their parents. A lawyer close to the Legal Aid Society said that "many of that group's lawyers, who [claim to] represent the children's interests in abuse cases, and lawyers with agencies where [allegedly?] abused children are placed, have been upset by Judge Segal's attempts to spur family reunifications." Though no evidence indicated that his rulings resulted in any child being abused or neglected, "most of the opposition [to his reappointment] came from attorneys who represent children in neglect and abuse proceedings."[712] An Edmonton, Alberta, judge was forced by feminists to apologize for saying, "That parties who decide to have children together should split for any reason is abhorrent to me." The case involved a divorcing mother whose two young sons were hospitalized for heat stroke after she left them in a hot parked car.[713]

STORY OF ANNA RATH

These pressures explain the politics behind journalistic anecdotes, which in themselves prove little and are almost always incomplete. Still, journalistic accounts do reveal the assumptions of both reporters and our society. They are also sometimes consistent with more systematic and authoritative investigations that reveal a pattern consistent with the politics we have described. In case studies investigated by the San Diego grand jury (which it claims are typical of many others it encountered), the same pattern recurs in almost every case:

- The mother ends the marriage either by leaving or committing adultery.
- The mother is given custody.
- The mother may subject the children to neglect or physical or sexual abuse.
- The father is accused of sexual abuse, though no physical evidence is produced.
- The father passes extensive psychological testing.
- Social workers and court therapists make negative reports about the father and support the mother.
- The children are taught to hate and fear the father and make wild allegations against him that are inconsistent with the physical evidence. The children are found to "have been heavily coached" and

their stories are "incredible, potentially exaggerated, and maybe even sometimes fantasized."

- Because "the children now fear their father," therapists oppose "forcing the children to visit with him."
- The father is denied visitation, and the children do not see him for years.

"In all three of these cases the children have been deprived of their fathers for extended periods of time," the Jury concludes. "Their relationships with their fathers are probably irreconcilable."[714]

An example of how the accusation can be more abusive than the father is reported by LifeSite news. "Four-year-old Anna Rath was taken from her parents . . . and is being held by B[ritish] C[olumbia] social workers on the basis of an unfounded accusation of sexual abuse against her father . . . apparently by a disgruntled acquaintance who threatened Rath with revenge." The account of how feminist social workers physically, psychologically, and sexually abused a four-year-old girl is worth quoting at length:

Social workers arrived at the Rath home with police and apprehended Anna, taking her to a hospital where she was subjected to an invasive "rape exam." The doctor informed the social worker that there was "no evidence of sexual assault," but the provincial bureaucrat refused to return the child to her parents. Instead, she placed Anna in a foster home to await another, more invasive rape exam. . . . Despite these desperate attempts to find evidence of sexual abuse, medics found nothing that could justify the accusations. . . . During one of the interviews, RCMP constable Berube subjected the four-year-old to horrific questioning attempting to lead the child to agree that she did sexual things. The child had no idea what he was referring to. The constable admitted in court that he had no training in interviewing cases of sexual abuse, or in interviewing children. . . .

In court, [Anna's father] wept openly over this state-sanctioned violation of his child's innocence, devastated that a government bureaucracy allegedly committed to the protection of children could inflict so much harm on his young daughter.[715]

Such horrors are now well documented. What is seldom appreciated, however—and what reveals these cases as preventable—is how often, even in cases involving intact families, as in the Rath case, it is allegations directed at the father that lead state agents to invite themselves into the underpants of children. Abusive "investigations" and "examinations" are one of the most common methods. University of Michigan social work professor Kathleen Faller, who promotes the use of anatomical dolls in child interrogations, is alleged to have "emotionally abused a young child during an investigation." Larry Champney told the *Detroit Free Press* videotapes of interviews with his three-year-old-daughter showed that an interviewer at Faller's clinic used repeated and suggestive questioning to get the child to say something bad about her father: "The interviewer used anatomical dolls and nude drawings and allowed the mother to participate in the interview." Champney's lawyer said Faller's clinic destroyed parent-child relationships with its work. "Faller and her people are part of the industry of false validations that hurts every child who has really been abused and devastates families."[716]

Regardless of who actually perpetrates it, the bureaucratic pressure is to place blame for child abuse on the father. A California father who reported that his daughter had been molested by a babysitter was himself arrested and accused of sexually abusing his two girls. "The investigators put us through these long interviews, going over and over the same things. The two people questioning me kept trying to pound it into my head that it was Grandpa and Dad who abused me, not the babysitters," recounts one of the girls. "They kept saying, 'Why don't you just tell the truth?'" On the basis of coerced testimony from one of the daughters the father spent fifteen years in prison. "I kept saying, 'But they didn't do anything.' Now I realize they were trying to get me to say things that weren't true. They said that if we didn't tell them Dad had molested us, we wouldn't be able to see our families ever again."[717]

The experience of Heidi and Neil Howard illustrates where the logic of the multi-faceted divorce machine is moving, as forced divorce, restraining orders, and child confiscations reinforce one another to create a semi-totalitarian nightmare: If the mother cannot be enticed to divorce the father with financial and emotional incentives, then threaten her with child abuse charges. Heidi Howard was told by social workers at the Massachusetts Department of Social Services to divorce her husband or they would take away her children. This is standard procedure at DSS, according to the *Massachusetts News* and attorney Gregory Hession. *News* reporter Nev Moore says she has seen hundreds of similar cases.

The Howards' ordeal began when they had a terminally ill baby. A home visit by a nurse, who was also a DSS agent, resulted in a series of scurrilous reports with wild allegations of sexual abuse and mutilation of their sons, though no evidence was ever presented. The Lowell District Attorney ignored the allegations, but DSS pursued the family anyway. A social worker told Heidi she was a battered woman. When Heidi said Neil was never violent the social worker replied, "You don't need to be beaten to be battered," saying he kept the family checkbook to gain "power" over her, which constitutes violence. Under pressure of losing her children, Heidi agreed to a restraining order but later recanted and moved to vacate it. Neil was arrested, Heidi was locked in a psychiatric ward, and their children were seized by DSS and placed in foster homes. Visitations varied from one to two hours a month. DSS stopped one visit because the parents hugged their children. The parents began finding bruises on the younger son, as well as missing and chipped teeth, crushed fingernails, and a broken arm. According to DSS files, day-care workers also noticed marks on his buttocks and back. When the infant Faith died on her first birthday the grieving parents were restored custody of her. DSS refused to permit the younger son to attend her funeral. The older son attended with two social workers.

Shortly after another daughter was born, the Howards were ordered to bring her to DSS and fled their home. They were arrested and shackled at the wrists and ankles, and the baby was seized. In a closed session a judge awarded custody to DSS based on psychological evaluations that the parents were "under stress." Using logic with which many family court litigants are familiar, the judge acknowledged the stress was due to DSS taking their children but allowed DSS to keep the baby anyway. No abuse of the new baby was ever alleged. In fact there was never a hearing before a judge on any abuse allegation against the Howards. DSS planned to put the boys up for adoption. The Howards must attend parenting classes and therapy.

Hession says such cases are mushrooming. Financial incentives and adoption quotas have created a "child protection racket" rife with "baby stealing and baby selling," where children are "shoehorned into adoption." "I am just appalled by how many times this pattern is repeated," he reports. In a family court he visited, the hallway was clogged with parents and children being adopted. "You could hardly walk. You had never seen such mass adoptions before." David Grossack, an attorney who has filed federal class action suits on behalf of parents, also attests that the Howards' experience is common. "Inexplicable decisions and nonsensical restraining orders are the rule, not the exception."[718]

IGNORING COMMON SENSE

What is striking about all this is how self-generating it is. By refusing to face the ideologically incorrect solution of simply allowing the father to remain in his family, government bureaucracies can present themselves as the solution to the very problems they themselves create. The more child abuse that takes place—whether by "parents" or by the social work bureaucracies themselves—the more the proffered solution is to further expand the child abuse bureaucracy. Waxing indignant about a string of child deaths at the hands of social workers in the District of Columbia, federal judges and the *Washington Post* seem to find solace in the D.C. government's proposed solution: hire *more* social workers (and lawyers too, for some unspecified reason). "Olivia Golden, the Child and Family Services' latest director, said she is overhauling the agency and will use her increased budget to recruit more social workers and double the number of lawyers to back up her new team of managers."[719] No mention is made of why the fathers of these children are not present or what precisely the increased contingent of lawyers will do other than make more work for themselves. But apparently lawyers, not fathers, now protect children.

Or lawyers protect children from fathers. This is the message of a particularly vicious advertisement circulated by the Indiana State Bar Association. With a graphic photo of an apparently badly bruised child, the Indiana lawyers depict themselves as knights in shining armor, rescuing the pitiable tots from their brutal fathers, by juxtaposing the wicked deeds of a fictional father next to the selfless altruism of the attorneys:

Her father takes his anger out on her.
A lawyer has him stopped.
The state charges her father in criminal court.
A lawyer protects her interests.
Welfare places her in a foster home.
A lawyer finds a permanent one.
Her father almost killed her.
An Indiana lawyer saved her.[720]

These Indiana Joneses do not mention that their selfless chivalry in separating children from their parents is remunerated at rates upward of $250 an hour.

By depicting fathers as killers, the promoters of compassion and self-described champions of children can ignore the one efficacious, common-sense solution of returning the father to the home and instead respond to the escalating child abuse crisis by increasing the number of personnel and agencies that are perpetrating it. The *Atlanta Journal-Constitution* investigated reforms undertaken to the Georgia child protective machinery ten years earlier and found that the problem has only become worse. "Nearly ten years later, children are continuing to die. Then, it was at the rate of one a week. Today, it's nearly triple that number."

The article leads off with three grisly stories of child abuse within "families," with no mention in any of a father, either as perpetrator or as present to protect the children. Yet the failed reforms include hiring hundreds more caseworkers to implement ever-more invasive and authoritarian measures, such as "a computerized tracking system . . . to help police and child welfare workers keep tabs on potentially abusive parents." No mention is made of allowing fathers to return to the homes, where we know most of this abuse is taking place, and guaranteeing the integrity of the two-parent family, which we know to be the safest environment for both women and children. Instead, family court judges lobby "to make higher salaries and lower caseloads for caseworkers among their top legislative priorities," posturing as defenders of children but also increasing the reach of their own patronage. "And they will throw their weight behind funding for more specialized foster-care homes for the growing number of disturbed youngsters damaged by years of abuse."[721]

Whether it is evicting the father from the home, establishing visitation centers where he may see his children under the surveillance of social workers, protecting the children from the abusive single mother and her boyfriend, treating the emotionally devastated children with drugs or psychotherapy, or removing them altogether into the control of state-sponsored foster homes and (as they grow older) juvenile detention facilities—the solution to the problems created by each bureaucracy is to create more bureaucracy.

One can venture further, since it is apparent that much of the abuse takes place not despite government programs, but because of them. Legally speaking, it is the courts that create the single-mother homes where the bulk of child abuse takes place and that force the fathers away from the children. Again, some maintain that judges who summarily award sole custody to mothers on the merest accusation of abuse, even when they know full well that the father has done nothing wrong, are acting on the principle to "err on the side of caution."[722]

Yet this explanation is more charitable than tenable, since it is clear that the judges are erring on the side of danger, and it is difficult to believe they do not realize it. Judges are well aware that the most dangerous environment for children is precisely the single-mother homes they themselves create. Yet they have no hesitation in creating them, secure in the knowledge that they will never be held accountable for any harm that comes to the children. On the contrary, if they do not they may be punished by the bar associations, feminists, and the social service bureaucracies whose existence and funding depend on a constant supply of impoverished and abused children. The harsh but unavoidable truth is that child abuse is very good for the family law business and for the massive bureaucratic machinery connected with it, since the more abused children the more demand for courts and child protective services.

It is an established principle that bureaucracies create business for themselves by perpetuating the very problems they ostensibly combat. "Bureaucracies everywhere have a remorseless drive to expand—to widen their client base," write Hewlett and West. [723] Appalling as it sounds, the conclusion seems inescapable that we have created a huge army of government officials with a vested professional interest in encouraging as much child abuse as they can.

MORE VIOLENT THAN CRIMINAL COURT

Not only has the father's role as his children's protector now become politically incorrect; the divorce machine has perverted it into a fault. Such "male violence against women" as does occur is almost certainly the result of child stealing more often than it is the cause, since common sense suggests that fathers with no previous proclivity to violence could well erupt when their children are taken. "A significant percentage of domestic violence occurs during litigated divorces in families who never had a history of it," according to Douglas Schoenberg, a New Jersey divorce attorney and mediator. [724] At the risk of laboring the ideologically incorrect obvious, one is tempted to say this is precisely what fathers are for: to become violent when someone interferes with their children.

This question has not been systematically investigated, though a study by Anne McMurray of Australia's Griffith University School of Nursing that began with the express purpose to "provide definitive explanations for the violent behaviors of certain *males*," concluded that "regardless of the male's propensity toward violence" the circumstances most conducive to it arose "during the process of marital separation and divorce, particularly in relation to disputes over child custody, support, and access." "These men," McMurray found, "from a range of socioeconomic backgrounds and age groups, freely discussed episodes in which they had either planned, executed, or fantasized about violence against their spouses in retaliation for real or perceived injustices related to child custody, support, and/or access." McMurray's subjects recounted that abuse "had not been a feature of the marriage but had been triggered by the separation."

For most people, the only thing surprising about this finding is that it requires the trappings of social science to state what some might consider common sense: that normal people become violent when you take away their children. Despite the preconceptions of her study, McMurray mentions that mothers who had lost custody also "discussed murdering their husbands over coffee one day." Given the emotional horror experienced by virtually all parents upon the loss of their children—including severe depression, increased alcohol consumption, and thoughts of suicide and violence—the wonder is that more do not explode. McMurray expresses "the need for all health professionals to advocate for changes that would help to correct injustices in the family court system."[725]

Unlike fathers, mothers who act on such fantasies can apparently cite them as extenuating circumstances. One woman who phoned her husband, told him her van had broken down, asked him to pick up their two daughters, and shot him when he arrived, was sentenced to one day in jail for assault. The "extreme departure from the federal sentencing guidelines" was warranted, the judge said, "by her depression and desperate fear that her husband would take away the children in their impending divorce."[726] Characteristically, the newspaper does not mention if (as is statistically likely) it was the mother who initiated the divorce in the first place.

When fathers snap, it is invariably picked up by the media, even though statistically there is little warrant for it. In an al-Qaeda-style suicide, "A pilot whose small plane crashed into a house was the home's owner," and "it appeared that the crash was deliberate." Investigators seemed to think they could explain the suicide by rummaging through the rubble. "For days, investigators have picked through the ashes and wreckage of Mr. Joy's home, his plane, and his life searching for what might have driven Mr. Joy, a successful business consultant and motivational speaker, to suicide." But the Associated Press conveys the motivation fairly clearly when they tell us that Joy's wife "had obtained a restraining order against him the day before the crash" keeping him away from his daughter. On what grounds? Neither the judge nor the AP is willing to tell us, since Judge William Drescher, who granted the restraining order, "sealed the court documents in which Ms. Joy explained why she wanted the order." Though a citizen was forcibly removed from his own home and separated from his child by a government official without a trial and is now dead, the AP is apparently willing to honor her request for "privacy."[727]

Likewise, the *Wichita Eagle* expresses bafflement at a murder-suicide even as it manages to convey the obvious reason. A man suspected of killing his wife and himself "was upset over a pending divorce," writes the *Eagle* in language that trivializes the stealing of people's children, and "worried about how much time he'd get to spend with his daughters." Neighbors described the father as "very mild-mannered." "He appeared to enjoy spending most of his time with the kids, said next-door neighbor Mary Herrin. 'I thought he was just the greatest dad,' she said. 'I just don't know what happened.'"[728] Any parent with a modicum of sense who can imagine how they would respond to someone taking away their children should have little difficulty understanding "what happened."

We have already seen that suicide is a major problem among divorced fathers. One study found that the suicide rate for divorced men was five times higher than for married men and significantly higher than for divorced women.[729] "For some men," the directors of a support group for divorced fathers write, with understatement, "it is the loss of their children (more than the loss of their marriage) that may literally make a difference . . . between life and death."[730] That these cases are more than anecdotes is attested by a female family law attorney with no personal interest in exculpating fathers, who simply states what some might think should not have to be stated:

> I have noticed that not only are suicides on the rise, but there is an ever increasing flow of fathers committing very violent acts of domestic violence, including killing the wife and sometimes even the children. I really feel that there is a direct correlation between family court and these acts of violence. . . . Although I don't condone domestic violence, I can understand why men feel so trapped with nowhere to turn but to violence against the wife, children, or themselves. . . . I myself can't imagine how some of my clients hold it together. If I put myself in my clients' shoes and I was denied seeing my child, I would go crazy. . . . The courts need to stop what they are doing to fathers. The courts are perpetuating violence. . . . I really would like the court to open their eyes, look at the damage their unfairness to fathers has done to this society. It's now resulting in murder-suicides at an enormous rate.[731]

Few press pieces report the strains under which the father is put and how domestic violence claims connected with custody disputes may become self-fulfilling. Incidents such as that reported in the Associated Press that "A man who recently lost custody of his daughters shot his ex-wife to death during her morning jog Monday and then killed himself" are not as common as the press implies, but there is no need for them to be happening at all. In a rare example of a newspaper reporting the background to such atrocities, the *Denver Post* recounts that "the father of Simon Gonzales, the 30-year-old man who shot and killed his three daughters last month before dying in a gun battle with Castle Rock police, said Monday that part of the blame for the tragedy lies with his son's estranged wife." The *Post* quotes the grandfather:

> "I think he was just so afraid that those girls were going to be taken away from him that he just snapped," Leroy Gonzales said. "The sun rose and set on those girls in my son's life," he said. "He rented an apartment so he could see his kids as often as he could. He was in love with his children. He was always hugging them, making them smile, making them laugh. They adored him. They looked at him with adoring eyes." . . . "The financial burden was just tremendous," Gonzales said. "And she's the one who made him that way. He was just killing himself, working around the clock, paying all her bills and then she tells him she's taking the kids and she's going to take him for everything that he's worth."[732]

Fathers of course should no more be excused for killing their spouses or children than mothers, but the common factor in both instances is the intervention of the divorce machinery. In this case at least some of the blame would seem to lie with the legal system.

In her book *The Assault on Parenthood*, Dana Mack reports that in interviews and focus groups with parents throughout the United States, when she posed the question of "how to improve the lives of children," she consistently received one recurring reply: "Shoot the judges and lawyers!" (To which some added, "Shoot the lawyers first, and then if the judges don't get the message, shoot them.") "This refrain was uttered almost word for word in several cities I visited, as if parents had gotten together and rehearsed it before talking to me." By speaking of "parents," Mack is able to dismiss their fury by saying, "Of course they were joking" and approach their bitterness with a measure of sympathy. Had she reported what she elsewhere reveals, that most of these "parents" are in fact fathers, she would have had to condemn the brutes.[733]

These parents are not joking in the slightest. The government has taken their children and everything else that is dear to them—including their homes, savings, and freedom. Many are cornered and desperate men who live in constant fear of arrest. They exist like rats in a cage, poked with sharp objects by an assortment of people, and they are merely acting out the logic of their situation.

This is clear from violent attacks against judges and lawyers, which have gone largely unreported in the mainstream press. "Statistics are scarce, but judges and lawyers nationwide agree from all the stories they hear about fatal shootings, bombings, knifings, and beatings that family law is the most dangerous area in which to practice," reports a law journal.[734] A legislative investigation in Nevada found that "more family court judges are shot by their litigants" than in any other area of the law.[735] As if to illustrate the legislature's findings (and refusal to act on them), a family court judge in Reno was shot near a courthouse in June 2006.

The year 1992 was "one of the bloodiest in divorce court history—a time when angry and bitter divorce litigants declared an open season on judges, lawyers, and the spouses who brought them to court."[736] On July 6 of the same year the *Washington Post* reported that "Two attorneys were killed, and two judges were among three people wounded . . . when a gunman stood in a courtroom spectators' gallery and opened fire with a handgun." Later the same day the man turned himself in. "It's a horrible, horrible thing I did today," the man is quoted as saying. "I have sinned and am certainly wrong, but someone needs to look into what happened to me." The press portrayed the incident as just another lunatic with a gun, but most lunatics with guns do not say, "I have sinned and am certainly wrong." In fact, the gunman was an attorney who was trying to call attention to the loss of his child and "blamed a legal conspiracy for allegations he had molested his boy." Despite his professional status and absence of any previous criminal record, he was executed within months by a legal system in which death-row inmates with no resources or education are able to drag out their sentences for years. Some allege the execution was expedited because he threatened to blow the whistle on family courts.

As a result of this incident and others like it, security measures were increased in courthouses throughout the country. Most people mistakenly assume metal detectors were installed in courthouses because of criminals and terrorists. In fact what they fear is fathers. According to the *Boston Globe*, judges now carry guns under their robes to protect themselves specifically from fathers. "The potential for violence," the *Globe* reports, comes "not in criminal sessions, but in probate and family court, where shocked husbands angered over unfavorable divorce and child custody settlements take their wrath out on those who decided their fates." The director of a judges' group says, "The decisions they make in probate court strike much more toward ego—taking away children, taking homes away."[737] A parent's response to having his children taken away is dismissed as simply an affront to puerile male "ego." Dakota County, Minnesota, District Attorney James Backstrom agrees that family court produces far more violence than criminal court. "We're most concerned about the people in family court—the child-support and divorce cases," he said. "They pose a greater risk than the criminal defendants because they're more emotional."[738]

"The most volatile court in the nation, where judges are killed on the bench, is family courts," according to Bruce Howell, administrator for Montgomery, Alabama, Juvenile Court. "When you're dealing with people's children, they get real upset. Family court is where it all happens, and judges get killed right on the bench. People whip out guns and start shooting them in front of the courtroom."[739] The ABC television magazine *20/20* has also reported on the killing of judges by fathers. Not one father was quoted on the show, but fathers generally were portrayed as little better than dangerous animals. One of the many lawyers interviewed remarks, "You really don't know what monsters lurk behind regular people." It can hardly surprise anyone that interfering with their children is one way to find out. A father with no history of violence trying to keep his children from being taken away is now a "monster."[740]

Among the most sensational media stories of recent years—including violent deaths—have grown directly out of family law. The O. J. Simpson case, the Washington Beltway sniper, the Laci Peterson killing(s), the school shootings in Jonesboro, Arkansas, the Lew Barbar shooting in Alexandria, Virginia, plus cases like Elian Gonzalez and possibly the Chandra Levy death were all occasioned by the workings of American family law. And in every case, while questions of race or gun control or communism were aired *ad nauseam*, the media ignored the role of family law.

Of course it is obligatory to register the standard piety that such violence must never be condoned. Yet in other circumstances we expect a father to use any means at his disposal, including violent ones, to protect his children against anyone who interferes with them, and we would condemn a father who failed to do so. "By design," writes Bai Macfarlane, "one of the most instinctive, adamant, forceful urges of human beings is to protect their own children."[741] "What would you do if I came along in the street and took your children from you?" writes Matt O'Connor in a Church of England newspaper. "You would do everything physically in your power to defend your children. You would probably injure me and maybe even kill me to protect your own flesh and blood. And yet fathers are somehow supposed to walk away."[742]

Once a father is designated a "divorced" father, even if the divorce was through "no fault" of his own, and when his children are taken away by government officials, we call him a "monster" and a criminal for doing what any normal parent is expected to do. We may do more to diminish the violence by airing the perhaps obvious question of what judges and lawyers expect when they set about the business of taking away people's children. On the principle of laughing to keep from crying, it may be worth recalling the irreverent Darwin Awards, "given annually to those individuals who did the most for the human gene pool by removing themselves from it." One cannot help but wonder if the young man who went bungee-jumping using household elastic cords taped together to a length exceeding the distance separating himself from the ground or the youths who carelessly launched their July 4 fireworks from atop a fuel distillation storage tank are any less deserving of our sympathy than those who adopt as their mission in life the practice of interfering with other people's children.

Chapter 5

FATHERS AND FEMINISM

Feminism is a revolution.

— Gloria Steinem

Revolutions are very hard indeed on privacy.

— Crane Brinton, *Anatomy of Revolution*[743]

The essence of revolutionary reigns of terror lies in summary justice. . . . Reigns of terror and virtue are essentially characterized by committee dictatorship. . . . At the top rests a committee . . . below which is an "extemporized," freshly recruited bureaucracy, newly appointed law courts, supplementary organizations ("extraordinary courts and revolutionary tribunals"), and last but not least a secret police. . . . Each Terror was . . . similar enough in construction of its coercive institutions for the administration of summary justice: institutions to gather information and to round-up suspects, courts or tribunals to administer revolutionary justice, and the growth of a system for the detainment, correction, or execution of the accused.

— Rosemary H. T. O'Kane, *The Revolutionary Reign of Terror*[744]

F amily law and feminism are natural allies. Family law inserts the coercive power of the state directly into the private lives of individuals and families. Feminism's central idea is that "the personal is political" and therefore subject to state scrutiny and control.[745] Not all feminists necessarily advocate using the criminal justice system to enforce feminist ideology within private households and personal relationships; many do not seem to realize it is happening, and some are genuinely horrified when they discover it is. But the

221

ideologues who control organized feminism today have found that the penal apparatus provides an effective instrument for waging gender warfare on the most personal level, institutionalizing feminist ideology within private life, and criminalizing individual men (and sometimes women) who fail to measure up to the feminist ideal of ideologically correct behavior in their personal lives.

It is logical that the first targets of the feminist Terror should be fathers, the living embodiments, after all, of the hated "patriarchy." Like feminism itself, "Family law has been driven for at least thirty years by a specific animus against marriage and against men," writes Melanie Phillips.[746] Fathers today are marked off as official villains and demonized in the mass media by their own government; their children are removed; their property is confiscated; their constitutional protections are stripped away; and they are rounded up in pre-dawn raids and incarcerated without charge or trial. As citizens in Eastern bloc countries once did, it is now fathers who live in fear of the "knock on the door."

Child custody is not the only area where feminists have discovered they can commandeer the criminal justice system to punish ideologically incorrect private behavior, and certainly it is not the best known. Their agenda in more politically salient issues such as date rape and sexual harassment has commanded far more media and scholarly attention (where it is frequently characterized as "totalitarian"). "Feminism today, in its erasure of the boundaries between public and private, is writing a new chapter in the dystopian tradition of surveillance and unfreedom," observes Daphne Patai, " . . . whereby one's every gesture, every thought, is exposed to the judgment of one's fellow citizens."[747]

Yet while the trends are connected, the intrusive tendencies of law governing sexual harassment or date rape are minor compared to the invasiveness government-enforced feminism has already realized in family law. Yet this receives no comparable scrutiny from critics of feminism, let alone from the mainstream media or civil libertarians. As recently as 1996 a scholarly critique of "feminist jurisprudence" did not address family law at all. Nevertheless, we were warned then that "through the use of civil rather than criminal law for purposes of censorship, and under the guise of legislating equality, large areas of speech are becoming *per se* illegal, unbeknownst to the majority of Americans."[748]

An indication of where we may be going is provided by a law proposed in Germany that "would require husbands to pay pocket money to their wives," according to one account. "Failure to pay pocket money . . . could result in the offender being hauled into family court and ordered to pay."[749] Apparently

Fathers and Feminism

German feminist groups have also lobbied for a bill that would provide for the arrest of men who fail to do half the housework. Spain actually passed such a law in 2005. Significantly, the first line of enforcement is not jail but divorce and loss of children, who once again serve as the weapons. "It will be applied in divorce proceedings: Men who don't do their share could be given less time with their children."[750]

Conventional criminal sanctions are not necessary when control of children already gives virtually absolute power over the family and its finances. If a mother is dissatisfied with the performance of her children's father for any reason, a phone call will have him quickly removed, kept away by the police, and eventually jailed. She will thereby at the very least seize control of his movements and his finances. Since gender roles tend to emerge with the appearance of children,[751] this affects fathers much more than other men.

Thus far we have not discussed feminist ideology or the relationships between men and women because the central issue in the criminalization of parents is the abuse of power by the government, not individuals' political beliefs or personal relationships. Yet feminism is the ideological subtext of all that has gone before. The feminization of politics, along with allied fields such as law, journalism, and academia, so often billed as imparting a new "compassion" to the hard world of masculine power, has in reality had a much more dangerous effect: It has transformed the political arena into a national soap opera that opens the private lives of not only public figures but all citizens to the eyes and ears of the public and the heavy hand of the state.

Ironically, the area in which organized feminism realizes its intrusive, authoritarian potential has not been a conspicuous part of its political agenda. Child custody has not been politically visible for the simple reason that it has not had to be: Women had already won this battle before the war began.[752] The emergence of divorce as a political weapon has occurred largely invisibly, because it politicized professions already dominated by women, while the media and intellectuals were focusing on feminist challenges to male-dominated spheres. It is only recently that the National Organization for Women, for example, has felt threatened enough by fathers' groups to begin adopting conference resolutions attacking them and smear campaigns to discredit them.[753]

The connected, even more gaping irony in feminism's defense of automatic and sole mother custody is striking to anyone uninitiated in the politics of the custody system. One of the earliest and most fundamental planks in the feminist platform urged fathers to take a more active role in child-rearing. Accordingly, groups such as NOW at one time even advocated presumptive joint custody laws. Some feminists do remain consistent, such as Karen DeCrow, past president of NOW, who says that "part of ending sexism involves eliminating the inhuman practice of awarding a parent 'visitation' to his or her own child."[754] Betty Friedan, to an uncertain extent, also seemed to see the inconsistency and claimed to be upholding feminist principles. "Women have had too much power in the home, and it's not been good for the family," she said. "It's really better for the family that women get some power in society, and then they don't need to have all that power in the home. It's better for children and better for husbands and fathers to share the power in the parenting."[755]

Feminist journalist Maureen Freely, pointing out that "family courts are closed courts and not required to explain their mysterious ways to the public," that "they almost always decide in favour of the mother," and that fathers "have next to no rights," objects: "As a feminist—in other words, as someone who believes in equal rights—I find this appalling." But the sisterhood does not and is prepared to excommunicate those who do: "I'm even more appalled, though, by the all too common assumption that you have to abandon feminism in order to say this."[756]

Many fathers embarking on their ordeal with the custody regime innocently expect sympathy from feminists. They are soon disabused. "I rather naively thought that this issue would bring feminists to my aid. After all, what I was asking was that this somewhat overlooked dimension of their revolution be attended to," writes columnist John Waters. "But what I found was that, far from getting support from feminists, the only significant resistance was coming from feminists and the political leaders who live in fear of them."[757] Among organized feminism, idealistic principles were long ago replaced by the self-interested pursuit of power. Women's groups have joined lawyers and judges as the main opponents of divorce and custody reform and promote measures to institutionalize gender bias.

Cathy Young observes the irony: "Feminists who resent any suggestion that a mother belongs with her children often insist, when it comes to child custody, that children belong with the mother."[758] It is not difficult to see why. Through divorce, children have become today's most effective political weapons and the most formidable source of power for feminist politicos and their allies in government. It is hardly new in the history of revolutions that, when forced to choose, most revolutionaries readily take power over principles.[759] In the world of child custody, both genders are equal, but one gender is more equal than the other.

Fathers and Feminism

The degeneration of feminist idealism is visible in Canada, where feminists refused to attend government consultations on child custody. Sitting next to fathers, they said would lead "to the further subordination of women" and create an "adversarial" atmosphere. The feminists, who once clamored for admission to male venues, demanded their own, female-only hearings. Most ironic of all, the Canadian sisters objected to proposed changes in custody law "because they are deliberately gender neutral" and did not "make one single reference to women."[760] Those who foolishly thought that feminists advocated (with equal stridency) gender neutrality in the law clearly need to be re-educated. "The best interest of children is inextricably linked to all aspects of women's equality," they now insist.

So while some might criticize the "best interest of the child" standard as vague, feminists know precisely what it means: "The best interests of children," says Eileen Morrow of the Ontario Association of Interval and Transition Houses, "can only be met by ensuring the well-being of their mothers."[761] This interesting formulation has become the slogan of feminist-dominated social work bureaucracies, the ones that specialize in removing children from fathers and married mothers. The Massachusetts Department of Social Services states epigraphically on its Internet site: "The best interests of children cannot be separated from the best interests of their mothers."[762]

Incidentally, though the Canadian government's "consultations" that did include fathers reportedly cost taxpayers $1.5 million, they were not true public hearings. Reporters were excluded, and no verbatim public record was taken. Liberal member of Parliament Roger Gallaway called the meetings an "affront to Parliament" and an effort to delay reform. "It's an expensive joke," he is quoted as saying. "This isn't a consultation of ordinary Canadians. . . . It's consultants consulting consultants." Feminist groups were also given advance copies of a government survey days before it was available to members of Parliament and the public. "It's outrageous that one group had advance knowledge of it," he protested, adding that fathers' groups do not receive government funding to assist their lobbying efforts, though feminist groups do.[763]

Feminist principles are now put to novel use by government officials who invoke sexual harassment law to insulate themselves from public criticism. Virginia Secretary of Health and Human Resources Louis Rossiter accuses private citizens of creating a "hostile work environment" for public officials by criticizing them. In a letter defending the dismissal of a member of a state child-support guideline review panel for a column the panelist published in the

Washington Times, Rossiter justifies his action by saying, "This Office already has one board, the Board of Social Services, with state employees who do not wish to attend meetings because they feel there is a hostile work environment from people who sometimes behave rudely (they all happen to be men)."[764] These citizens "happen to be" men because they are fathers whose children have been taken away, and the "state employees" who are taking away their children are the largely female social workers whose livelihood depends on a steady influx of fatherless children. Civil servants apparently may now be excused from performing their duties or being answerable to the citizens they ostensibly serve if they deem those citizens to be deficient in etiquette, and criticizing civil servants now amounts to harassment.

Social workers in San Diego likewise seem to consider themselves above criticism because it might hurt their feelings. Noting that "social workers are perceived to have nearly unlimited power," and can "retaliate" against the children of citizens who criticize them, an investigating grand jury reports that it "was warned repeatedly by DSS [Department of Social Services] and by some members of the judiciary about the importance of focusing on the positive aspects of the system . . . and that any criticism must be heavily leavened with positive observations."[765]

It is tempting to conclude that this degeneration of the feminist revolution was inevitable, simply following others before it. It is an inescapable truth that politics is foremost about power, and public policy is about the use of coercive force—including ultimately the power to kill. Sincere and ideologically pure as some early feminists undoubtedly were, feminist politics has not transcended this truth by turning the political arena into a fuzzy, family-friendly nursery with warm and cuddly feelings all around, as some of its theorists at one time promised. On the contrary, it has merely politicized the family with a ruthless logic that is more than a little totalitarian in its ability to use police and prisons as instruments for adjudicating ordinary family differences and to transform the most personal relationships into calculations of power.

A few years ago feminist political theorist Kathy Ferguson envisioned a world where male-dominated power politics would be supplanted with the more feminine politics of "empowerment." Male power brokers would be replaced by quasi-Platonic female "caretakers" whose claim to leadership would be their capacity for compassion and suffering. In this feminist utopia the only remaining problem would be who would relieve the suffering of these saintly souls. "For a feminist community, then, Plato's question 'Who will guard the guardians?' might be rephrased as 'Who will care for the caretakers?'"[766]

Ferguson would have been more perspicacious if she had asked, "Who will guard the caretakers?" For her dream of a syndicalist rule of caretakers is now the reality, and the caretakers have run amok.

"Caretakers Routinely Drug Foster Children" trumpets a headline in the *Los Angeles Times.* The article claims that "children under state protection in California group and foster homes are being drugged with potent, dangerous psychiatric medications, at times just to keep them obedient and docile for their overburdened caretakers."[767] Backed by the power of the state and its bureaucratic police, the caretakers are criminalizing parents, confiscating children, indoctrinating children to inform on their parents, and drugging or incarcerating those who have learned they do not have to obey their parents or anyone else. They are also standing as gatekeepers between fathers—and increasingly all parents—and their children.

Sylvia Ann Hewlett and Cornel West (hardly reactionaries) write of "a new class of professionals—social workers, therapists, foster care providers, family court lawyers—who have a vested interest in taking over parental function."[768] A horrified spokeswoman for this "new class" validates their point: "There's this whole group of people out there caring for kids, and nobody is watching them," says Nina Auerbach, of Child Care Resources in Washington. "We just can't ignore this whole segment of care anymore." The "people" Auerbach is referring to are their families.[769]

Overwhelmingly, these professional watchers are female, and their agenda is avowedly feminist. "Female professionals dominate the maternal and child health, family support, and income security systems," observe fatherhood advocates Ron Mincy and Hillard Pouncy. "Those of us who are trying to promote responsible fatherhood among unwed and disadvantaged parents and children . . . must . . . articulate a message about male/female roles and relationships that these professionals can hear."[770] Less well known is the domination of the newer child-support enforcement machinery by female gendarmes with an agenda. "The vindictiveness with which my state enforced child-support obligations, and the methods we employed, could not have been better designed to embitter men against their children and utterly destroy any helpful relationship between them," a former Virginia district attorney writes to HHR Secretary Rossiter. "Most of the child-support bureaucrats I worked with were divorced women with a score to settle against the male gender."[771]

Yet despite numerous exposés of abusive government bureaucracies from writers on both the left and right, the feminist-inspired politics of children shows no signs of being brought under control. None of the prosecutors or judges who have railroaded parents into jail on spurious charges without due process of law has been prosecuted. Indeed, one of them was made attorney general of the United States. Following her career as a state attorney general in Dade County, Florida, where, in the words of left-wing journalist Nat Hentoff, she "orchestrated some horrendously unjust convictions," including using child abuse hysteria to send one innocent man to prison for five consecutive life terms (he was exonerated by a federal appeals court after twelve years of confinement), Janet Reno became U.S. attorney general, and "this grim part of her record was ignored."[772] From this position she managed to use questionable rumors of child abuse to launch a violent assault against American citizens in Waco, Texas, resulting in the deaths of twenty-four children whom she was ostensibly protecting.

Such episodes indicate how the destruction of fatherhood might be seen as part of a larger and growing trend of politicizing children in pursuit of other agendas. Marian Wright Edelman has admitted she founded the Children's Defense Fund in the early 1970s upon realizing that the country was weary of the broader New Left agenda: "I got the idea that children might be a very effective way to broaden the base for change." Edelman "put children squarely in the front of almost every domestic policy debate."[773] She and her strategy were influential in high policy circles during the 1990s, and this trend toward casting an array of political causes in terms of their purported benefit to children now reaches well beyond traditional family issues and extends to the highest levels of government. "Children, it can be fairly said, have been an obsession for this administration," writes sympathetic columnist Richard Cohen of the Clinton presidency.[774] His point is borne out by the words of its officials. "Government has got to ensure that parents are old enough, wise enough, and able to care for their children," Reno declared. Former Health and Human Services Secretary Donna Shalala envisions a future kindergartener's day: "Renata will play gender-neutral games in government day care and think of herself as part of the world, not just her town or the United States."[775]

The philosophy of turning children over to state control and denying a sphere of family privacy is succinctly conveyed in Hillary Clinton's aphorism, "There is no such thing as other people's children." Hillary rejects the notion that "families are private, nonpolitical units whose interests subsume those of children" and believes instead in "the status of children as political beings."[776] Commenting on these passages and others like them, the late Barbara Olson wrote, "For Hillary, children are the levers by which one forces social change."

Fathers and Feminism

Historian Christopher Lasch likewise observed with respect to Hillary's philosophy of "children's rights": "The notion that children are fully capable of speaking for themselves makes it possible for ventriloquists to speak through them and thus to disguise their own objectives as the child."[777] Even proponents seem to acknowledge the totalitarian implications, while remaining determined. Praising Hillary's book, *It Takes a Village*, for its message that "each of us—society as a whole—bears responsibility for all children, even other people's children," Stewart Friedman and Jeffrey Greenhaus insist that we "must be prepared to make the most of the *brave new world* lying in the future." "Success in the *brave new world*," they add, "requires skills found more among women than men."[778]

This trend can be seen as an extension, writ large at the level of high politics, of the "best interest of the child" rationale that has been routinely invoked in family court for years as a justification for removing children from their parents. The prophecy of political scientist Jean Bethke Elshtain would seem to be fulfilled: "The replacements for parents and families would not be a happy, consensual world of children coequal with adults but one in which children became clients of institutionally powerful social bureaucrats and engineers of all sorts for whom they would serve as so much grist for the mill of extra-familial schemes and ambitions." Elshtain fears not only the harm to children but the threat to democracy from questionable attempts to erode parental authority under the guise of democratizing the family. "Any further erosion of that ethical life embodied in the family bodes ill for democracy," she warns. "The resulting vacuum would not be filled by some perfect democratic consensus that covered children as well as adults unambiguously. Instead one would get more coordination and control from those . . . for whom democracy and all that sustains it are as much a nuisance to be combated as an ideal and way of life to cherish."[779]

Yet the cause of "children's rights" continues, with open calls from the feminist legal community for traditional parental authority to be replaced by government bureaucrats. "For those who would like to have the State use its power and resources to improve the lives of children, parental rights constitute the greatest legal obstacle to government intervention to protect children from harmful parenting practices and to state efforts to assume greater authority over the care and education of children." These words are published in a respectable law review article that asks "why parents should have any child-rearing rights at all." "Parental child-rearing rights are illegitimate," declares James Dwyer. "No one should possess a *right* to control the life of

229

another person no matter what reasons, religious or otherwise, he might have for wanting to do so. Children are persons, intimately bound up with but nevertheless distinct from their parents." Dwyer cites no legal precedent or any authority other than his own opinion. Indeed, his logic leads him to call for abolition of not only parental authority and the family but, in an apparent rush of legal nihilism, the bedrock principles from which our legal system has derived its authority for centuries: "The evolution of our social attitudes toward, and legal treatment of, children in recent decades would afford the Supreme Court an adequate rationale for departing from the rule of *stare decisis* and for overruling *Yoder* and *Pierce* precedents to abolish parental child-rearing rights."[780]

While the politicization of children has been promoted at the expense of both parents, it is fathers who are usually the first casualties. Part of this owes its inspiration directly to feminists, many of whom "look at children as comrades in suffering at the hands of an oppressive patriarchy," in the words of author Kay Hymowitz. "Women and children share a similar victim status in that both groups are dependent upon another group of people from whom rapists or abusers are drawn," she quotes one feminist as saying. "Just as women have traditionally been dependent on men, children are dependent upon adults."[781]

This liberation jurisprudence has been institutionalized by feminist lawyers. "Family law tends to justify the domination of women by men and the oppression of children by parents," writes lawyer and family law professor Frances Olsen. "Family law reinforces the most common forms of male domination and parental oppression."[782] Thus children, like women, are designated an oppressed minority and enlisted as political comrades, and their natural rebellious impulses become politicized as a force for revolutionary change.

Not surprisingly then, children are also learning to use the divorce courts as a means of liberation from parental oppression, and judges are obliging them by granting children "divorces" from their parents. In Melbourne, Australia, a fourteen-year-old boy was permitted to divorce his mother on grounds of "irreconcilable differences." Family lawyer Elizabeth Dowling defended the practice as protecting children, "especially those in minority groups." "She said a girl raised in a religious sect might not share her parents' views and divorce would be the only way she could leave a situation intolerable to her," reports the *Herald Sun*. "Divorces also could be an escape for homosexual children whose parents refused to accept them."[783] In Massachusetts, fourteen-year-old Patrick Holland was granted a divorce from his father.[784] In both cases, it appears that the child was following the example of the mother, who had already divorced the father with whom the child then had no contact. "I just couldn't live there," said one boy. ""It is probably a bad decision, but I don't think I could live with her for a long period."

Despite protestations to the contrary, hostility to the family in general and fathers in particular is clearly manifest in many feminist writings. "Patriarchy's chief institution is the family, within which men hold the power to determine the privileges, statuses, and roles of women and children," write Esther Ngan-ling Chow and Catherine White Berheide. "Such a structure is buttressed by traditional gender-role ideology and is further institutionalized and reproduced in gendered power relationships throughout society."[785] This rejectionism elaborates on an older Marxist contempt for the family going back to Friedrich Engels. "The family is often the site of hideous violence, abuse, and oppression," writes Colin MacLeod in an ostensibly scholarly journal with an openly Marxist slant. "A child's earliest lessons in bigotry often begin at home. . . . Patriarchy and misogyny are frequently nourished and perpetuated in the traditional family."[786] Amy Gutman believes government officials should censor parent-child communication by intervening against parents who "bias the choices of children toward some disputed or controversial ways of life and away from others."[787]

Similar language was used in the Soviet Union, where in fact the world's first no-fault divorce system was implemented. Propagandists inveighed against "narrow and petty" parents who were "only interested in their own offspring." "The worker-mother must learn *not* to differentiate between yours and mine," wrote Marxist agitator Alexandra Kollontai; "she must remember that there are only *our* children, the children of Russia's communist workers." She added that children must be raised by "qualified educators" so that the child can grow up a "conscious communist" who recognizes the need for "solidarity, comradeship, mutual help, and loyalty" to the collective: "In place of the individual and egoistic family, a great universal family of workers will develop, in which all the workers, men and women, will above all be comrades."[788]

Mainstream feminist academics openly express disdain for family privacy and for a private sphere of life beyond the limits of state interference. Chow and Berheide sneer at "the ideology of the family as a bastion of privacy." Political theorist Carol Pateman insists that denying "the dichotomy between the public and the private . . . is, ultimately, what the feminist movement is about." Susan Moller Okin, another leading feminist political theorist, writes of the "artificial nature of the dichotomy between the sphere of private, domestic life and that of the state." She believes the "separation of private from public is largely an ideological construct. Public policies must respect people's views and choices . . . only insofar as it can be ensured that . . . for those who choose it, the division of labor between the sexes does not result in injustice. . . . The protection of the privacy of a domestic sphere in which inequality exists is the protection of the right of the strong to exploit and abuse the weak."[789]

And again, the remedy for such perceived "inequality" is divorce. Okin's book, *Justice, Gender, and the Family*, highlights how the "divorce culture," to use Barbara Whitehead's phrase, has permeated the core of academic discourse, not only of fields such as sociology and psychology, but also political science, to the point where divorce becomes an instrument for radical political change. Purporting to be a work of political theory and engaging with canonical works of political thought and contemporary theorists, Okin's work is in fact a manifesto for divorce-driven government regulation of private life. For what is striking about Okin's utopian vision of a state-enforced "society without gender" is the vanguard role played in her anti-patriarchal revolution by divorce and the state divorce machinery, which will rectify the gender inequalities she insists inhere in the family.

Okin marshals the standard clichés about paternal abandonment, deadbeat dads, and domestic violence. But more significant is that the economic injustices and disadvantages she insists women suffer within the family only become a reality once the family is dissolved. Indignant that housework is unpaid, she acknowledges: "This may at first seem a matter of little importance. If wives, *so long as they stay married*, usually share their husbands' standards of living for the most part, why should it matter who earns the income?" The answer, of course, is divorce, as well as bargaining leverage in expectation of it during what Okin calls the "predivorce situation" (the marriage).[790] What appears as a work of detached scholarship is closer to a highbrow version of the myriad advice books now on the market instructing women how to dissolve their marriages. Okin's book won a feminist award from the American Political Science Association, but its page on the Internet site of the Barnes and Noble bookstore informs us that customers who bought this book also bought not other scholarly works of political science, but the following self-help manuals: *What Every Woman Should Know about Divorce and Custody: Judges, Lawyers, and Therapists Share Winning Strategies on How to Keep the Kids, the Cash, and Your Sanity*; *Joint Custody with a Jerk: Raising a Child with an Uncooperative Ex*; *Divorce and Money: How to Make the Best Financial Decisions during Divorce*.[791]

Fathers and Feminism

Two conservative scholars follow a similar logical path and arrive at a similar conclusion, with even more striking implications. Broadening the argument from economics to politics, John Lott and Larry Kenny argue that the enormous growth in the size of government machinery during the twentieth century resulted directly from women acquiring the vote. Women, far more than men, voted to create the welfare state. Lott and Kenny then proceed to the obvious question: "Why would men and women have differing political interests?" The premise of their question invites the answer: "*If there were no divorces* in society and women and men married early in life, the interests of men and women would appear to be closely linked together." The answer again is now brutally familiar: "As divorce or desertion rates rise, more women will be saddled with the costs of raising the children."

> Divorced women may seek legal guarantees to some portion of this expected higher income through alimony, but, besides difficulties in tracking down the man to ensure payment, relatively risk-averse women may in addition prefer some guaranteed minimum income over the risky return from the particular man that they were originally married to. While the evidence indicates that welfare leads some fathers to desert their families, some women may also view welfare as a means of allowing them to remain at home and raise their children when their husbands leave them.[792]

Both conservatives and feminists, one from prejudice and the other from ideology, insist on presenting the resort to government power as a defensive move by women to protect themselves from the costs of divorce, credulously attributed to male desertion. But we have seen that male desertion is not a major cause of divorce; not only are most divorces initiated by women, but (as we will see shortly) the divorce revolution itself was driven largely by feminists. The growth of government power therefore is not a defensive measure at all. Divorce is a political weapon and an *offensive* one at that, promoted by the same ideological and bureaucratic groups that have simultaneously been expanding the power and reach of the state to deal with its consequences.

Next to divorce, the other items on the feminist agenda, which have commanded the vast bulk of media and academic attention—equal pay, job discrimination, sexual harassment—are politically trivial. It is divorce that has simultaneously increased both female and governmental power, with no voice of opposition. This is true whether the actual wielders of government power are female or male. "Divorces led to bodies of men (called legislatures) protecting women collectively as other men (called husbands) failed to protect women individually," writes Warren Farrell. "This meant raising taxes mostly on other men to provide money mostly for women. When divorces deprive women of husbands to protect them then, our collective unconscious still wants to protect women."[793] With the growth of the welfare state, women have in effect married the state, which becomes surrogate husband and assumes the principal paternal roles of protector and provider. Subtly and gradually, by playing on male chivalry and the misconceptions of both left and right, divorce has not only politicized and institutionalized the battle of the sexes, but possibly revolutionized the governmental structure of every modern state and vastly expanded the reach of government power.

This is consistent with the findings of other scholars. During the nineteenth century, writes Barbara Whitehead, "divorce became an increasingly important measure of women's political freedom as well as an expression of feminine initiative and independence." Though she never says so outright (her argument depends on the implied culpability of men), the therapeutic and narcissistic "divorce culture" she describes is by her own depiction overwhelmingly a feminine culture, and her acclaimed book of the same name is a chronicle of how women have used to divorce to leverage power. Whitehead's divorce culture has tended to expand during periods of political radicalism. The American Revolution, for example, was accompanied by a "burst of divorce," and "The association of divorce with women's freedom and prerogatives, established in those early days, remained an enduring and important feature of American divorce."[794]

In fact, it was feminists who really created the divorce revolution. The National Association of Women Lawyers claims credit for pioneering no-fault divorce, which it describes as "the greatest project NAWL has ever undertaken." According to NAWL, the National Conference of Commissioners of Uniform State Laws had attempted to produce such a bill since its founding in 1892, but it was NAWL that provided the initiative as early as 1947, when its convention voted to draft and promote a bill that would embody the ideal of no-fault divorce. Working through the American Bar Association, Matilda Fenberg convinced NCCUSL, which produced the Uniform Marriage and Divorce Act. As NAWL proudly notes, "By 1977, the divorce portions had been adopted by nine states" and "the ideal of no-fault divorce became the guiding principle for reform of divorce laws in the majority of states."[795]

The link with feminist doctrine is documented by a team of Dutch sociologists, who emphasize that their results are in line with findings in American divorce literature: "Women with modern attitudes toward gender—as reflected in participation in women's liberation groups, using one's maiden name, voting for far-left political parties, and so on—have a higher risk of divorce [in fact, 52 percent higher] than more traditional women."[796] Germaine Greer has said the high rate of divorce should be celebrated as the major sign of feminist progress: "Exactly the thing that people tear their hair out about is exactly the thing I am very proud of."[797]

Today, the liberalization of divorce continues as one of the first platform planks to be implemented when leftist and feminist governments come to power throughout the world, often disguised among measures for "human rights." When the socialist government came to power in Spain in 2004, the three priorities on its domestic agenda were legalized abortion, same-sex marriage, and liberalized divorce. Iranian feminist Emadeddin Baghi writes in the *Washington Post* that "a 20 percent increase in the divorce rate is regrettable and worrisome, but it is also a sign that traditional marriage is changing as women gain equality."[798] Turkey was required to withdraw a proposal to criminalize adultery in order to gain favorable consideration from the European Union, but the liberalization of divorce in the same program counted in its favor.

CUSTODY AS A 'SHOW OF FORCE'

Despite the posturing of everyone involved in the politics of children, we should remember once again that "custody" is not primarily about the needs of children; it is foremost about the power of adults. "What a sense of power!" one mother exults upon absconding with her children. "*I finally was in control of my life. I was finally the one who could make my life's story turn out good or bad.*"[799] Noting that "the question of custody absolutely swamps all the other variables," in determining which parent files for divorce, researcher Margaret Brinig translates: "Custody is a way for women to achieve a real show of force over men."[800] She and co-researcher Douglas Allen explain in the more politic language of the scholarly reviews: "Having custody of children may . . . be a way of asserting control over a non-custodial parent, either personally or through the child support that usually goes along with the children," they write.

> Divorce . . . allows the woman to exercise control over household spending when she is awarded custody. If the court names her primary custodian, she makes most, if not all, of the major decisions regarding the child. As custodial parent, she will be able to spend the money the husband pays in child

support exactly as she pleases—something she may not do during marriage. Finally, although the court will usually have ordered visitation, she can exert some control over her former husband by regulating many, although not all, aspects of the time he spends with the child. In the extreme, she can even "poison" the child against the father.[801]

In the extreme, she can have the father taken away in handcuffs. Simply by filing for divorce, the mother is designated, in effect, family dictator. Men "should forget all that psychobabble about active listening and validation," concludes one study of marriage. "If you want your marriage to last for a long time . . . just do what your wife says. . . . The marriages that did work all had one thing in common—the husband was willing to give in to the wife."[802]

And the principal weapon in exercising this power is, once again, the children. Even before divorce, as men become more aware of what they will face, the threat becomes a source of leverage within the family. "If I have an argument with my wife, she spreads the divorce papers out on the living room table and begins to fill them out," says a thirty-eight-year-old engineer. "There's no compromising with her. I either accept her decisions or she threatens to divorce me. If she does, she'll get custody of my little girl and I doubt she'll even let me see her, much less play an active role in raising her."[803] After divorce, mothers can and do "orchestrate men's relationship with children," writes sociologist Judith Seltzer. "Mothers are reluctant to relinquish authority over children . . . to the children's father. . . . For many women, divorce is a step toward autonomy and greater independence from men. . . . By facilitating divorced fathers' independent involvement with children, divorced mothers may fear that they will lose many of their own decision-making rights."[804] Fathers are often accused of drifting away after divorce, but in addition to the financial disincentives we have already discussed are the emotional ones. "Many women overtly prevent fathers from parenting," John Gray, author of the best-selling book, *Men Are from Mars, Women Are from Venus*, explains:

> They will do all sorts of things to prevent the father from taking care of the children, then they'll turn around and say the father doesn't participate. The man does something with the children, and the woman is immediately there to tell him what he is doing wrong and how he should do it better. She will start interrogating him . . . not allowing him to take charge and feel more responsible for the kids. She's coming from a place that he doesn't know

how to do it, so she'll have to do it. But what man wants to have his wife or ex-wife correcting him all time, particularly in front of his children? So, quite automatically then, many men back off from the situation.[805]

Though control of a man's children is often control enough, as Brinig and Allen indicate it is child support that provides the financial and political leverage for control over the father. Despite official rhetoric, the money benefits not the children, who almost always suffer from divorce, but the mother, who is accountable to no one for how she spends the tax-free windfall. "Remember that money is never 'awarded' but merely redistributed within the family," writes Judge Mary Lou Benotto. "Thus, by definition, the family can never be better off after divorce."[806] Conservative Maggie Gallagher adopts ironically quasi-feminist language to describe the domestic politics of divorce. "The divorce revolution can more accurately be described as a *shift in power* . . . a game heavily weighted in favor of the unfaithful, the immature, the betrayer," she writes. "The spouse who decides to divorce has a liberating sense of mastery . . . with its psychic echoes of the original adolescent break from family."[807] Overwhelmingly when children are involved, as we have seen, this "spouse" is a mother. Sentimental attachment to motherhood seems to inhibit conservatives like Gallagher from acknowledging this fact, but feminists readily admit and even celebrate it. "Contrary to the widespread notion of marriages mutually breaking down," writes Rosalind Miles, "the vast majority of petitions for divorce are brought by wives."[808]

A growing literature now informs mothers how to use their children and the legal machinery to wreak vengeance on their children's fathers, with book titles like *The Courage to Divorce, Learning to Leave: A Woman's Guide, How to Heal the Hurt by Hating, The Woman's Book of Revenge: Getting Even When "Mr. Right" Turns Out to Be All Wrong, The Good Divorce, Get Rid of Him*, and *The Woman's Book of Divorce: 101 Ways to Make Him Suffer Forever and Ever*. In her aptly titled 1997 book, *Cutting Loose: Why Women Who Leave Their Marriages Do So Well*, Ashton Applewhite offers a revealing portrait of the kind of woman who takes full advantage of this opportunity. His book is an extended indulgence in the intoxication that comes with power: "I feel great," she enthuses, "in full possession of myself, responsible, sexy, independent, and powerful." And while she never says so outright, the power comes from the children. She is not, after all, urging women never to marry or have children in the first place. No, it is essential first to get the children and the emotional, legal, and financial leverage that comes with them.

Within this genre, divorced is reified and romanticized, as if divorce itself is somehow a spiritually enriching experience. "Few events in life open the door to the new and unexpected as widely as divorce," writes Mavis Hetherington. "After divorce, to a great extent individuals influence their own destiny."[809] Why after divorce, rather than before marriage? The only possible answer is the coercive power bestowed by the legal system and backed by the state, using children as the weapons. A bizarre kind of logic seems at work here, where divorce begins to sound so good that it is almost worth marrying solely to acquire the benefits of divorce. Psychotherapist Mira Kirshenbaum apparently believes "there may be too few divorces, not too many."[810] Whitehead describes the extensive therapeutic literature targeting divorced women with language emphasizing "feelings" and "relationships" and the "emergence of self" brought by divorce. Romantic "themes of protest and revolt" and "notions of rebellion" characterize the divorce literature.[811] Divorce seems almost apocalyptic, ushering in a new stage of history and the egalitarian utopia long envisioned by feminists. Hetherington conjectures that "divorce may be a social adjustment to a world where female needs are considered the equal of male needs."

But men are not in the habit of talking about their "needs." The enthusiasm of Hetherington and others seems to render them oblivious to the inescapable fact that their brave new world is, by its nature, predicated upon a deception, raising the question of how long they can expect it to continue before the deception is discovered.

This already seems to be happening. There is mounting evidence that as men discover the terms of marriage and divorce today, they are engaging in a marriage boycott or marriage "strike": refusing to marry or start families, knowing they can be criminalized if their wife walks out and how attractive the divorce industry has made it for her to do so. "Have anti-father family court policies led to a men's marriage strike?" ask two writers. Likewise, "Australian men are avoiding marriage because of the financial ruin marital break-ups bring," according to one account, which ignores the emotional ruin of losing one's children. Sonja Hastings of Fathers-4-Equality says that "no matter how decent, hardworking, and caring you may be as a father, that in the event of separation, you will more than likely not get custody of your child, you will lose up to 80 percent of all your assets, you will have to pay up to five times the cost of raising a child, and most importantly you could never see your child again." In Britain a fathers' group tours university campuses warning young men not to start families. Even one attorney writes a book concluding that the only effective protection for men to avoid losing their children is not to start a family in the first place.[812]

Depicting marriage as a man's ball-and-chain used to be a joke, but any man who glances at one Yahoo.com discussion group will certainly have second thoughts about placing his head in a noose. Discussants are candid about celebrating the power of women to use their children and the divorce courts to turn their husbands into "slaves." The group describes itself as:

> A serious and supportive discussion forum for divorced or legally separated women to discuss how they have used divorce, child support, alimony, and the courts to make their ex-husbands their financial slaves. Also how ex-wives have used the psychology of divorce to turn their ex-husbands into servants and slaves for their own amusement and enrichment." A forum for women to share their success stories in humiliating and bankrupting ex-husbands—and then moving on, with their ex's money, to better relationships with more attractive men. Humiliation. Revenge. Female power. Female financial domination. No doubt about it, for many women, divorce can be the road to the easy life—and wealth and riches. And the beauty of it all is that it's all done at the expense of your ex, who now is your financial slave. This list is about placing your ex in psychological and financial bondage. Discuss the tactics—and laugh about it—here.[813]

The latest pop trend in Britain is the rise of the "Sarah" ("single and rich and happy"). Close Wealth Management, an investment group, reports there are 200,000 of these "mass affluent" females. The source of their wealth is divorce courts.[814]

What provides the ideological thrust to the divorce "revolution" is not simply feminism but organized and doctrinaire feminism of a particularly vicious kind, one that thrives on angry mothers of whose vindictive tendencies the divorce industry is more than happy to take full advantage. Judith Wallerstein and Joan Kelly found that 85 percent of divorced mothers expressed anger and bitterness toward their ex-spouse. "In general, more women than men hung onto the anger they felt towards their ex-spouses," they write. "Half of the mothers continued to make extremely critical, or disparaging, remarks about their husbands, whereas only one-fifth of the fathers were so intensely critical in front of the children."[815]

Sociologist William Goode reported that 48 percent of the more than 500 women he interviewed thought their former husbands should be punished for what they had done to them, even it involved no legal infraction.[816] "Many women wish their former husbands some unspeakable torture," observes attorney David Chambers with apparent regret that he and his colleagues cannot oblige the sisterhood further. "In this country the county jail is about the best we have to offer." Chambers himself seems to have no objection to "cutting off fingers or branding foreheads," but laments that such measures "would be regarded as barbaric" by others.[817]

What is invariably presented in public policy literature as concern about "abandoned" children and "absent" fathers often has little to do with the needs of children or the actions of fathers but proceeds more from the desires of mothers, often for needs that are no more tangible than "self-esteem" and "self-fulfillment." Correspondents to an Internet message board at Women.com spelled out in clear detail the reasons for ending their marriages and using trumped-up domestic violence allegations to do so:

> . . . You are so unhappy . . . but I am in a marriage with 2 children (married 13? years) and my kids are hurt by the fact there is a lot of stress and unhappiness in our home . . . I live with emotional and verbal abuse . . . I didn't feel I had a right to complain, because there are no "visible" scars and I couldn't PROVE he was hurting me and the kids . . . but I have come to realize, I deserve better and after meeting some friends on another board here at women.com . . . I got the courage to call the local Domestic Violence shelter (mine is free of charge) to find out where the most appropriate place would be for me and my kids to get some help coping and perhaps leaving . . . It turns out I can find help THERE . . . It is hard and scary, but it helps to see that I am not the only one unhappy and to hear stories of how much better things are for many after they finally got brave and took steps to find their own happiness and build their (and their children's) self-esteem.[818]

The authors of an Australian study say their finding that mothers initiate the overwhelming majority of divorces "reflects the importance of 'emotional closeness' and companionship in modern relationships. It also suggests people continue to have higher expectations of self-fulfillment in marriage and less tolerance for unsatisfying relationships."[819] Yet this ever-elusive search for "emotional closeness" and "self-fulfillment," all gushy and sentimental as it is intended to sound, can now be pursued by wielding the deadly force of the penal system, with its jails and detention facilities, against spouses and even children who disappoint our expectations, hurt our feelings, or otherwise prove "unsatisfying."

Indeed, the divorce-liberated mother's love for not only her spouse but also her children becomes conditional and problematic. Far from being moved by their needs, she becomes the most dangerous threat to their physical safety, as we have seen. "The power that these little beings—our children—have over us and the fact that they can validate our existence makes us 'hate their guts,'" writes Anne Wilson Schaef. "We love our children, but we hate what they stand for."[820] The divorced mother no longer need endure any check on this hate, and her identification with the child not only to "validate" her "existence" but also to provide coercive state-backed power can have terrifying consequences for the children. It "may result in a variety of reactions toward the child: overprotection, unconscious seduction, resentment, neglect, hatred," Leontine Young wrote years before single motherhood became fashionable. "Whatever the specific expression, they are all crippling for the child and deeply damaging to the mother. It is not surprising that desertion is a recurrent problem in this group."[821]

The single mother who has discovered she can commandeer the police and jails to remove the father—perhaps especially one who is willing to avail herself of this power—can indulge her resentment and give it free rein, especially when it is given voice by feminist ideology. Boys especially seem to have become the objects of this resentful rage within the sisterhood, with the result that young boys are the majority of abused children. If the reasons are not obvious, feminism makes them so. "A mother may love her son dearly, but he is nevertheless a member of a class that has controlled and oppressed her," writes Schaef. "As a result, she cannot help but feel rage and hostility toward him."[822]

Women who indulge this rage to the point of murder can now expect defense from organized feminism. In the summer of 2001, National Organization for Women officers in Texas and Washington came to the defense of Andrea Yates, who confessed to murdering her five children. On ABC's *Good Morning America*, television personality Rosie O'Donnell expressed "overwhelming empathy" for Andrea Yates.[823] "One of our feminist beliefs is to be there for other women," Deborah Bell, president of Texas NOW, told the Associated Press. "We want to be there with her in her time of need."[824] As Dave Kopel pointed out with reference to mass-murderer Nikolay Soltys, "Imagine the outrage if a 'fathers' rights' group formed a legal defense fund for Soltys, claiming, 'One of our fatherly beliefs is to be there for other men.'"[825]

NOW President Patricia Ireland, said the Yates case revealed America as a "patriarchal society" where "women are imprisoned at home with their children." Children and fathers who have been liberated from their prison-homes by the divorce industry and who really are incarcerated may have a different view of what constitutes a "prison." In *Newsweek* magazine, Anna Quindlen wrote, "Every mother I've asked about the Yates case has the same reaction... . She gets this look. And the looks say that at some forbidden level she understands."[826] Mothers who understand the appeal of killing their children are the ones to whom judges universally and automatically grant immediate and exclusive custody when they file for divorce without giving any reason.

A similar trend seems to be developing with sexual abuse. While feminists refer to fathers' groups as "pedophiles," it is feminists themselves who are most likely to push the frontiers of sexual experimentation. No feminist group has ever documented a fathers' group defending a proven child sexual abuser (though they are constantly trying to find one). Yet prominent feminist Andrea Dworkin writes favorably of incest:

> The incest taboo ensures that however free we become, we never become genuinely free. The incest taboo, because it denies us essential fulfillment with the parents whom we love with our primary energy, forces us to internalize those parents and constantly seek them, or seek to negate them, in the minds, bodies and hearts of other humans who are not our parents and never will be.
>
> The incest taboo does the worst work of the culture: it teaches us the mechanisms of repressing and internalizing erotic feeling. ... It demands that we place the nuclear family above the human family. The destruction of the incest taboo is essential to the development of cooperative human community based on free-flow of natural and androgynous eroticism.[827]

HARDSHIP FOR DAUGHTERS, SECOND WIVES

While feminist groups frame child custody as an issue of women's rights, the divorce system in fact pits women against one another and creates hardships for huge numbers of women and girls. The most obvious victims are daughters, who are denied the right to see their fathers whenever they wish, deprived of a healthy marital example and male role model, and often grow up in the poverty that, feminists rightly point out, frequently accompanies single motherhood.[828] Second wives and their children are also treated as second class and suffer the financial hardships of the men on whose incomes they depend. Grandparents are another group whose lives are often devastated when they are not only denied contact with their grandchildren but find themselves having to take in and support grown sons who have been evicted from their homes and cannot possibly support themselves on what is left after child support. We have seen that efforts are now being made to prosecute second wives and grandparents, and in practice many are already extorted into paying child support. They too can have their homes and financial accounts invaded by officials with no show of wrongdoing on the principle that it is "for the children" and the ends justify the means. Second wives and grandparents are regularly denied admittance to family courts to witness or influence decisions that may profoundly affect their lives. "Fathers" groups report that half their members are women, and both second wives and grandparents are now organizing political groups of their own.

One might include among the victims mothers themselves, who often end up betrayed by lawyers who they eventually realize have no concern for their children and whose rosy prognoses often include the expectation of child support and legal fees that their bankrupted ex-husbands simply cannot pay. "Women are particularly vulnerable to lawyers," writes journalist Melinda Blau, ". . . only to discover that they are not the knights in shining armor we had hoped for—far from it. Many women felt that their attorneys . . . didn't understand (or couldn't care less about) the needs of their children."[829]

Perhaps recognizing this, some feminists try to distance themselves from the worst and even claim that women are "oppressed" by lawyers and judges. Some undoubtedly are, especially those with politically connected former husbands. Yet Sanford Braver found that divorcing women are far more satisfied by the legal process than men. In his study, 75 percent of the men and 35 percent of the women believed the system in divorce cases was slanted toward mothers; fewer than 10 percent of the women and no men said it was slanted toward fathers.[830]

But gender bias in this is case unimportant, we are told, because feminists know that fathers do not care about their children. Just as "many" fathers "may be" batterers and pedophiles (though it is clearly documented that a very tiny number in fact are), so a similarly nebulous "many" fathers take little interest in caring for them. "Many of the fathers who rail the loudest at the unfairness of the system are the same fathers who, while the domestic relationship was intact, couldn't find two hours a week to spend with their children," divorce lawyer Tim Tippins confidently informs us.[831] How Tippins is able (much less entitled) to peer into the living rooms of so "many" citizens to observe and evaluate how they conduct their private lives is not explained. But apparently every parent in America is now answerable to Tim Tippins for how many hours each week they spend with their children. Those who fail to spend what Tippins regards as the requisite time apparently have no grounds to complain if their children are taken away by the government at the request of Tippins and his colleagues. Do parents who must be away from home for extended periods because of, say, job demands or military duty thereby forfeit the right to their children if they cannot manage to fit in Tippins's minimum weekly requirement? And how are parents to prove to Tippins and the government that they have spent the requisite number of hours with their children? Must they supply documentation? Witnesses? Yes, that is precisely what they must do, and they must hire a lawyer like Tippins at extortionate sums to present it in court.

Under pressure from feminist lawyers, courts are developing new, ostensibly gender-neutral doctrines to justify taking children from involuntarily divorced but legally innocent parents. Yet the cost is further invasions of citizen privacy and increased government regulation of private lives. "One of the factors to which the courts often look is which parent was the primary care-giving parent prior to the onset of legal hostilities," Tippins points out. The term "primary caregiver" or "primary caretaker" is another novel piece of legal jargon that has become popular in family court. Fathers' groups object that it is one more ruse for ensuring automatic mother custody, regardless of her actions and contrary to (feminist-instigated) laws mandating gender neutrality.

"The 'primary caretaker' theory is first, foremost, and always a change-of-name device designed to maximize the number of cases in which the court will be compelled to preserve the bias of maternal preference and award sole custody to mothers," writes attorney Ronald Henry. "Every definition that has been put forward for this term has systematically counted and recounted the types of tasks mothers most often perform while systematically excluding the ways that fathers most often nurture. No effort is made to hide this bias." So if one parent risks his life on a construction site or in the armed forces to provide for his children, government officials are not likely to decide that this qualifies as "primary care-giving." But it is more than just the difference between earning wages and changing diapers; it creates imbalances between duties that are equally hands-on or hands-off. "The primary caretaker theory aggressively asserts that traditional 'women's work' is meritorious while 'men's work' is irrelevant," Henry continues. "The typical definition of the primary caretaker gives credit for shopping but not for earning the money that permits the shopping; for laundering the little league uniform but not for developing the interest in baseball; for vacuuming the floors but not for cutting the grass."[832]

Yet even could fairer criteria be determined, there is still a more fundamental and serious objection to the "primary caretaker" doctrine in cases of unilateral divorce. This is the assumption that it is a legitimate role for government officials to look into private homes and pass judgment not on legally recognized and actionable offenses but on how citizens conduct their personal lives. It allows officials to place a government imprimatur on how family members divide the household labor. Regardless of whether you agreed to or gave grounds for a divorce, if officials do not approve of what you do within your home, they have license to march off with your children. So if one parent drives the children to soccer games while the other gets up with them when they are sick in the night, if one takes the children to school while the other takes them to the doctor, evidence and witnesses must be provided documenting who did what to the satisfaction of government agents, who will apportion the children accordingly. Even assuming it were possible to create a fair standard between mothers and fathers, how can state officials determine who is the "primary caregiver" of children without conducting a highly intrusive inquisition into what people do in the privacy of their homes? Obviously they cannot, which is precisely why such inquisitions—with all their attendant violations of constitutional privacy protections—are already the regular and principal business of these dangerous and tyrannical courts.

This is a prescription for government so invasive that the term "totalitarian" cannot be avoided. No parent can possibly defend himself (or herself) against this kind of innuendo once a battery of officials sets to work conducting such an inquisition. But equally troubling is the use of the courts to enforce a political ideology within private households. This blanket dismissal of fathers, many of whom have proven their love for their children through heroic sacrifice against overwhelming obstacles to be with them, is now rampant not only in feminist polemic but also in the literature of judges, lawyers, psychotherapists, and other ostensibly objective professions who profit from divorce. Aside from ignoring the contributions fathers make for their children outside of personal care-taking,[833] using imprecise stereotypes to justify acts of coercive state intervention against citizens who have done nothing legally wrong raises serious questions of how far we are to allow state officials to regulate private family life (using children as their tools) in the name of institutionalizing gender equality. The question is not how far a stereotype may be illustrated with anecdotes, but since when do we deny the constitutional rights of an individual because of a generalization about "many" members of a group to which he belongs? Do "many" black youths rob liquor stores? Do "many" Jews lend money at interest? Even could it be shown statistically that they do, does this justify expropriations of citizens who are members of these groups or incarcerations without trial?

Possibly there is some truth to the stereotypes about fathers, but even the truth they contain may result from the self-fulfilling tendency of all stereotypes. One hesitates to enter the vapid "he said/she said" technique of displaying private lives in public and calling it journalism or scholarship. Yet even feminists acknowledge that extent of father involvement, even within intact families, is often decided by mothers. "The truth of the matter is that women are themselves very reluctant to yield their prime role in the caring of children to men," writes Melanie Phillips. "With very few exceptions . . . women allow men to play a caring role with their children only under sufferance."[834]

Perhaps this too is only a stereotype, though if so, it is one to which feminists confess to sharing. "If I'm honest—and I think feminists have to be honest on these matters—I never felt we were quite equal," admits Angela Neustatter. "I, as the mother, the one with the biological bond, had primacy."[835] Again, we must not condemn all mothers (if condemnation it is) for assuming this superiority; no doubt many mothers do not take on this role of "gatekeeper" to the children. "Parenting can be pretty territorial," says Montreal psychotherapist Vikki Stark. "A lot of women are giving lip service to equal parenting, but they really want to keep control."[836] The point is that, however each of us might vary in our opinions about this assignment of gender roles, with the advent of family law such matters are no longer matters of personal preference to be worked out by family members in private among themselves with the give-and-take inherent in family relationships and in the necessary spirit of cooperation and compromise, trust and love. Unilateral divorce now allows mothers who wish to assert their supremacy to call in government gendarmes to enforce it at gunpoint and to take Dad away in handcuffs if he objects.

There is even reason to believe that fathers who are most involved personally with their children may be the ones most likely to inspire resentment from their children's mothers over encroachments on their turf and so most likely to fall victim to enforced divorce and separation. "Be careful what you wish for because you might get it," another mother confesses. "In my case, I did get a husband who was involved, creative, energetic, instinctual in his parenting. . . . And you know what? I hate it. I'm ashamed, but I hate that I am not the center of my child's universe."[837] Is a mother who feels this way more likely or less than the average to avail herself of the open invitation offered by the government divorce machinery to grab the children and go, secure in the knowledge that she can blacken the father's reputation in court and in public by asserting that she was the "primary caregiver" and he was typical of "many" fathers who are uninvolved? Perhaps not. But there is little reason to assume she is any less likely to do so.

Empirical evidence supports this possibility that involved fathers threaten mothers. It is well established that about half of mothers either see no value in the father's contact with his children and actively tried to sabotage it or resent his visits.[838] But even more striking, "Fathers describing themselves as having been relatively highly involved with and attached to their children and sharing in family work tasks during the marriage were more likely to lose contact with their children after divorce, whereas those previously on the periphery of their children's lives were more likely to remain in contact," writes sociologist Edward Kruk. "Now-disengaged fathers consistently scored highest on all measures of pre-divorce involvement, attachment, and influence."[839]

For that matter, is the father likely to be given any credit for his direct involvement with his children and the sacrifice of his career that most likely entailed? Or is he more likely to be told that his sacrifice was a voluntary loss of earnings, that he should be earning more money than he does, that his child-support obligation will be based on what he should be earning, and that he is now liable to incarceration for his past commitment to caring for his children and his present inability to pay what the government tells him he "owes"? If he does receive any leniency it will be only at the price of signing over his children's patrimony to government officials and opening his private life to their inspection and approval.

The cynicism with which judges promiscuously invoke both feminist doctrines and traditional gender roles—or for that matter any justification that happens to be available for eliminating the father—is revealed by British Lord Justice Matthew Thorpe's decision to remove custody from a father "who had raised the children in their £1 million home while his wife enjoyed a successful career on a salary of £300,000," because of "the realities involving the different roles and functions of men and women." Notwithstanding the new rhetoric about "primary caretakers," Thorpe said it was "not uncommon" nowadays for those who have "sacrificed the opportunity to provide full-time care for their children in favour of a highly competitive profession to think again about their priorities." A mother who stays home with her children has "sacrificed" her career, and one who works has "sacrificed the opportunity to provide full-time care" for her children. The father who actually raised the children apparently sacrificed nothing but, like most fathers, was just being selfish.[840]

The contradictory demands of feminism—and increasingly the rest of society as well—are such that fathers often cannot win. When they are simultaneously criticized, as they are by Sara Ruddick, for being both "absent" and "controlling" one is reminded of the joke about the bad restaurant where the food is inedible and the portions are too small. Cathy Young has shown how feminists who once criticized fathers for not being personally involved in child-rearing now excoriate those who are. "Absent and emotionally distant fathers already have a mesmerizing effect on their children," sneers Phyllis Chesler. "Present and emotionally intimate fathers probably have twice the mesmerizing effect."[841] Such cheap shots may make for mildly amusing farce on a television comedy. When they become part of a real-life drama in the family law courts—where too little or too much involvement with one's children are equally (and even simultaneously) used as grounds for state officials to take children and parents into "custody"—it makes for an inquisition into private life for which terms like *Kafkaesque* and *totalitarian* are hardly exaggerations.

The blanket accusation that fathers have no interest in seeing their children, despite widespread (but largely ignored) complaints from non-custodial fathers that what little visitation they are granted by the courts is never enforced—takes a particularly ugly (but also revealing) form when it involves money. "Some fathers, who previously would gladly have agreed to allow the mother to assume the burdens of custody, have been motivated to fight for custody or greater custodial time in an effort to avoid or diminish their child-support obligation," contends attorney Tim Tippins.[842]

Aside from the question, once again, of how Tippins can peer into the minds of "some" individuals to know what they would "gladly" do in circumstances that do not exist, this argument is a favorite smear that shifts the burden of proof onto a parent to convince government officials that he loves his children to their satisfaction as the price for keeping or even seeing them. Yet beyond this, it is also an open admission that child-support payments exceed the costs of raising children. "If child-support awards actually reflect true child costs and cross-crediting takes place to accurately reflect each parent's incurred child costs, then there is no monetary incentive to ask for increased shares of parenting time," write Mark Rogers and Donald Bieniewicz:

Only when child-support guidelines exceed true costs (representing a profit from custody) do parents ask for or seek to prevent changes in parenting time for financial reasons. Curiously, any argument that a [non-custodial parent] is asking for increased parenting time to reduce child support is at the same time an argument the [custodial parent] is making a profit from child support."[843]

This is not the place to take on the huge problem of negative cultural and media stereotypes of men and fathers. These have already been thoroughly documented and refuted by Warren Farrell, Ross Parke and Armin Brott, and others.[844] What is worth emphasizing is that such stereotypes are no longer limited to amusing and harmless pokes at male foibles in the popular media but now involve vicious attacks in otherwise respectable public policy and academic forums where bigoted remarks against any other group would meet with pointed disapproval and carry adverse political consequences. In August 1999, a California assemblywoman is reported to have suggested on the floor of the chamber that most fathers were "drunk and hungover."[845] This followed an ostensibly scholarly article in *American Psychologist* specifically attacking fathers as unnecessary and suggesting, without evidence, that they were detrimental to families by a tendency to squander family funds on alcohol and gambling.[846]

Men are not usually inclined to object to negative stereotypes about themselves for fear of appearing petty. This danger is real, since it is common for men's grievances to be dismissed, even by those unsympathetic to feminism, as the mirror image of feminist "whining." "The last thing we need in America is yet another victim group, this one made up of seriously aggrieved males," writes columnist John Leo, who nevertheless devoted a column to the dangers of male-bashing.[847] It is easily forgotten that we are presented here with an entirely different level of "discrimination." Stereotypes about women may be unfair and perpetuate gender roles, but they are not likely to result in mothers losing their children, let alone being rounded up at gunpoint in pre-dawn raids and jailed indefinitely without charge or trial. (Some of this does happen to mothers, but it is less likely to be because of stereotyped gender roles than because of feminist campaigns against them; nor are such women defended by feminists.) As Patricia Pearson observes, "Men can be committed to prison on the strength of stereotypes about *them*."[848] For most men, the full realization of this possibility hits home only when a judge orders them to stay away from their children on pain of arrest.

The no-win situation in which fathers are placed is not limited to feminists. The more fathers attempt to live up to the feminist ideal, the more they are then taken to task by conservatives. Norman Podhoretz accuses New Age men of "avoiding the responsibilities of fatherhood," which he sees as "providing food, shelter, and moral authority."[849] Podhoretz may or may not have a legitimate point about the proper role of the male parent, but like most armchair commentators he seems oblivious that fathers who try to assume this edifying paternal model risk losing their children altogether in divorce court for not being the "primary caregiver" or should a judge or social workers disapprove of how they exercise "moral authority."

Fathers who try to take their moral authority into the political arena by organizing advocacy groups are only likely to be caricatured in the media and by politicians. One is far more likely to hear about fathers' groups from the hostile commentaries of their opponents than from their own spokesmen, since they are seldom permitted to publish their own writings, speak in the media on their own behalf, or testify on legislation pertaining to fatherhood. (One need only ponder when a fathers' advocate was last seen on *Larry King Live* or the PBS *Newshour*. The answer is never.) When fathers groups are mentioned in the media, expressions like "rabid" and "foaming at the mouth" are invoked to dehumanize them and depict them as animals. "A crusade of angry dads with an extreme right-wing view" is how one Sunday magazine supplement portrays them, with no pretense of objectivity, though in fact activist fathers span the political spectrum.[850]

A newspaper as eminent as the *Boston Globe*, in the same article reporting the massive abuse of unconstitutional restraining orders against legally innocent parents, evidently feels the need to take a gratuitous swipe at law-abiding citizens, comparing the exercise of their constitutional right to peacefully protest government policy with the violent rampage of a fictional man. "Recall that in the original Angry White Male movie, *Falling Down*, it was partly a restraining order preventing him from seeing his little girl that launched the Michael Douglas character on his slash-and-burn rampage through downtown Los Angeles," writes Kate Zernike. "Many divorced fathers' groups are about as subtle."[851]

Even defenders of fathers must be circumspect. Cathy Young notes that "Many of the defendants [of restraining orders] are clearly not choir boys."[852] This may be diplomacy or the strictures of editors (I have been instructed by editors to write such things as the price of getting published). But since when does the Bill of Rights apply only to choir boys? Do constitutional protections depend on citizens being saints? "If men were angels," wrote the principal author of the U.S. Constitution, "no government would be necessary."[853]

'RESPONSIBLE FATHERHOOD' OR GOVERNMENT INTRUSION?

Perhaps the most revealing indicator of the depth of enmity against fathers in public life today is provided not by feminists but, ironically, by self-styled advocates for fatherhood. As we have seen, today's two most prominent scholarly promoters of fatherhood, David Blankenhorn and David Popenoe, both go out of their way to insist against all evidence (and without providing any of their own) that the main cause of the problem is fathers abandoning their children.[854] It is unlikely that these polemicists are unaware of the truth.

In a volume entitled *The Fatherhood Movement*, which amounts to a manifesto of "responsible fatherhood," Wade Horn admits that some of his fellow fatherhood promoters "are tempted to designate absent fathers as the 'enemy.'" To his credit, Horn rejects this, but even broaching the possibility of a "fatherhood movement" in which fathers who are driven away from their children are then designated as the "enemy" indicates that non-custodial fathers themselves have no voice in this movement. Former Senator Dan Coats has no hesitation in vilifying men who have no platform to reply: "The most serious problem is absent, irresponsible fathers," he declares flatly. "The abandonment of children, particularly by fathers, is . . . a form of adult behavior with profoundly destructive consequences." Yet the senator evinces not a single study or any evidence that large numbers of fathers are willfully abandoning their children. He apparently knows first hand "millions of single mothers who raise their children in hard circumstances . . . examples of sacrifice and commitment" against "the suffering of children caused by absent and irresponsible fathers."

Mitchell Pearlstein likewise deplores (also without proving) the "masculinization of irresponsibility," "abandoned kids," and "missing men." By his own admission, Pearlstein is reluctant to offend groups that are politically influential, while he is willing to demonize those who are not. Pearlstein confidently reports knowing that "millions" of single mothers are rising their children "heroically and successfully with little help from men." Yes, "some" men are "honorable and responsible," Pearlstein acknowledges. Apparently it is honorable and responsible to allow your children to be taken away, provided you pay those who take them.[855]

Affiliated with Blankenhorn's Institute for American Values is Dana Mack, another scholar who risks inconsistency for the sake of attacking fathers. Mack describes the pressures besieging those who try to be good "parents," how social workers confiscate children from parents on the barest pretext, how family courts are "shrouded in secrecy, and the standards for bringing evidence and making convictions are far more lax than in the criminal court system," how "hearsay evidence is admitted [and] defense attorneys can be denied access to investigative records," and how "allegations of physical or sexual abuse have skyrocketed" during divorce. Then, with no hint of irony, Mack suggests out of the blue that "the only way a child can be rescued from the ravages of post-divorce animosity is to allow the parent with primary custody full power to determine visitation rights." She invokes feminist and Freudian social engineers Joseph Goldstein, Anna Freud, and Albert Solnit to the effect that a "visiting or visited parent has little chance to serve as a true object for love, trust, and identification" when children "maintain . . . contact with two . . . parents who are not in positive contact."[856]

In other words, creating fatherless children justifies itself: Sealing children off completely from their fathers is acceptable because children cannot have a meaningful relationship with a father from whom they have been forcibly separated. This logic would be peculiar enough from a feminist. But it comes from a scholar claiming to defend parenthood and affiliated with an organization ostensibly devoted to strengthening fatherhood.

Though feminists and advocates for "responsible fatherhood" claim to repudiate one another's agendas, there is clearly a delicate *pas de deux* going on here, since both groups do have a vested interest in demonizing at least some fathers and in preventing them from being heard on their own behalf. Moreover, both groups have a financial stake in having children separated from their parents, since both are generously subsidized by taxpayers' money, which would dry up were they to question the extensive government programs targeted at fathers. Significantly, feminists attack legislation promoted by fatherhood advocates for doing precisely what feminist groups themselves have long done on a much grander scale: procuring government money for their own organizations.[857] Though a case of the pot calling the kettle black, there is some justice in the charge that "responsible" fatherhood programs have created another vested interest group subsisting on the public dole.

In 1999, as Texas governor and presidential candidate, George W. Bush announced that the National Fatherhood Initiative "has been awarded a grant of $416,000 to create the Texas Fatherhood Initiative . . . the largest such effort in the country."[858] NFI in turn lauded Bush and his state: "Texas, by creating the most ambitious statewide fatherhood promotion project to date, has taken a leadership role in the nationwide fight against father absence." This sounds edifying and is no doubt well-intentioned, but it is not clear precisely what it means. The Texas initiative promised the following:

- To implement a statewide public education campaign to heighten awareness of the critical role fathers play in ensuring the well-being of children and communities.
- To conduct a series of fatherhood forums throughout the state designed to facilitate strategic planning by community leaders.
- To establish a Texas Fatherhood Resource Center to provide training and technical assistance to community-based organizations developing local fatherhood programming.

Though no doubt valuable as a means to "heighten awareness," it is not clear in what tangible way any of these measures can reunite a child to a father who is forcibly kept away by a court order. Will this return children to the care and protection of their fathers and guarantee the integrity of the family unit from forced dissolution by the state? Or is it jobs for the boys (and girls)? Fatherhood promotion groups are no more immune than anyone else from the allure of government money, which can easily end up fueling the patronage and the problem rather than providing the solution. When Bush became president, HHS adopted similar language to create federal programs to encourage "healthy marriage." Yet whatever their good intentions, both fatherhood and marriage programs have also been used to promote child-support enforcement, which acts as an incentive *against* marriage and to keep fathers away.[859]

Revealingly, while high-profile feminist groups like NOW publicly castigate "responsible fatherhood" organizations for their "patriarchal" values, feminists in the trenches of the gender war seem to recognize the value of this promotion. In its attack on independent fathers' groups which are funded entirely by members' contributions and receive no government money, the National Council of Juvenile and Family Court Judges (itself government-funded) and the U.S. Justice Department suggest countering the message of fathers' advocates by offering financial payments to fatherhood organizations willing to toe a government-approved line and join in the vilification of fathers: "To counter these harmful messages [of fathers' groups], the voices of 'responsible' fatherhood groups must be heard on the subject of domestic violence and child custody—and there must be an increase in resources to these groups so their voices can be heard."[860]

This paper, itself funded by the Justice Department and published on its Internet site by an association of judges who command six-figure incomes, claims that ragtag groups of impecunious men who live in constant fear of arrest "have considerable resources—money, time, and institutional power—to accomplish their goals." One might bear in mind that these same judges wield the power to reduce the money and time at the disposal of these men by confiscating their savings and earnings and by incarcerating them without trial, and they do not hesitate to exercise it. Whatever their resources, these groups are not given free space to answer this attack on the Internet site of the Justice Department.

The same judges who tell us that fathers convicted of nothing should be presumed dangerous to their children, invoke the rhetoric of "responsible fatherhood" to insist that fathers should be forced to take what the judges regard as a sufficient interest in their children: "Children should have a right to responsible parenting," the judges insist, "and batterers who have court-ordered visitation rights should face consequences if they fail to show up for visits." If they are dangerous "batterers" why is it so essential that they show up? To provide revenue for supervised visitation centers? And what if impediments exist to their ability to "show up"—as for example when they must work to avoid being jailed for non-payment of child support, or they cannot afford a car, or they must travel thousands of miles to where the children have been relocated, or when they show up and are not permitted to see their children?

To realize what is at work here one need only imagine if the civil rights movement had been led by white people promoting "responsible black people." (The comparison is not far-fetched in fact, since the racial component is conspicuous in "responsible fatherhood" organizations, which concentrate on minority fathers, while traditional civil rights groups remain strangely silent.)

We should be skeptical about government programs to "promote" and "restore" anything so private as a parent's relationship with his own children. What is advertised as a program to facilitate "access and visitation" of fathers with their children is likely to mean more supervised visitation centers, where fathers must pay to visit their children in institutions.[861] "Encouraging good fathering" often means more government-sponsored advertisements demonizing fathers in the mass media and state regulation of their relationship with their children. In Massachusetts the state has even drawn up a list authorizing "Five Principles of Fatherhood," approved by the government. Among the list is "Give affection to my children," and "Demonstrate respect at all times to the mother of my children." Officials believe that "men forced to pay support are more likely to take an emotional interest in their children,"[862] or at least a government-approved emotional interest. One cannot help but wonder what penalties the state will bring to bear on fathers who fail to demonstrate sufficient "emotion" and "respect." State-approved "parenting" or "anger management" classes? "Mental examinations"? These (and the fees for them) are already forcibly imposed on fathers who have done nothing legally wrong. Perhaps politicians will soon be calling for jail time, house arrest, and electronic monitoring for the insufficiently emotional and respectful.

This is not far-fetched at a time when some jurisdictions are seriously considering requiring "parenting licenses" and mandatory "parenting courses," without which it would be a crime to have a child.[863] If the Canadian Bar Association has its way, that country's federal government will legislate parental duties, not making clear that the law would necessarily even be restricted to divorced parents. "The CBA advocates legislating a list of parental responsibilities." In case anyone misses it, the list includes child support three times:

> Such responsibilities would include maintaining a loving, nurturing and supportive relationship with the children; financially supporting the child; meeting the child's day to day needs; consulting with the other parent on major health, education, religious, and welfare issues; encouraging the child to respect the other parent; providing financial support . . .[864]

Some idea of the truly totalitarian world to which the logic of government-as-father is leading can be glimpsed from a letter published in a prestigious legal affairs newspaper, the *Los Angeles Daily Journal*. The correspondent, who identifies himself as a child-support official of twenty-four years, argues for the forced sterilization of all persons, including married ones, who create a pregnancy without government approval. "The father of the child, even if the mother is married to him, should have to sign a pre-pregnancy agreement with county child support stating how he plans to provide financial support for the child . . . should he no longer be with the mother of the child," writes Paul Bloomberg of Los Angeles. Not if he willfully abandons the child: if he no longer lives with the mother, regardless of the reason. By the wording, this official plainly shows his awareness that the state can confiscate a man's children at any time for any reason and then force him to pay for it. The mother too is subject to control and even terror by the state. "Women should shake with fear at the thought of getting pregnant if they have not planned for the child properly," Bloomberg adds. "The county should review all the data and issue an opinion as to whether it is advisable for her to get pregnant or whether the county will consider a pregnancy child abuse."

That such a letter could be published in a respectable journal of the legal profession indicates the Orwellian dimensions now assumed by the child politics industry. "If, after six months, officials prove that the financial needs of the child are not being met, the child should be removed from the home . . . until the parents can prove that the financial needs of the child can be met," Bloomberg concludes. "The mother and father of the child should be forcibly sterilized if the pregnancy occurred without the county's consent." A government program of forced sterilization is conceptually (and politically) easier to countenance than simply allowing children to have their fathers.

Possibly this letter is a hoax, planted by some fathers' rights activist to make divorce practitioners look like Nazis. Evidently the *Los Angeles Daily Journal*, a mouthpiece of those practitioners, did not think so. Bloomberg's concern for children comes through as sincere enough to make the letter convincing: "Too many children are found in garbage cans or in homes where they are tortured and beaten to death to take pregnancy as just a trivial right." Indeed they are, but would it not be simpler just to allow the father to remain in the home in the first place where, in the absence of state intervention, most fathers manage to provide for their children? Of course such a policy would probably render officials like Bloomberg unnecessary.[865]

Apparently one judge has already taken Bloomberg's suggestions to heart and begun to implement this measure, so beloved of segregationists, Nazis, and Stalinists. Kentucky Family Court Judge D. Michael Foellger orders fathers with child-support arrearages to pay up or be sterilized. No statutory authority exists in Kentucky for such punishments, which were never debated by any elected legislature; Foellgers "thought of the idea himself." Still, he has no fears anyone will question his unilateral scheme for solving societal ills or his power to invent new punishments at his own whim. "Foellger believes he can legally give the ultimatum because the men are in contempt for not paying the child support, and a judge has wide latitude to enforce his orders. In such instances, the child-support cases are civil, not criminal." So no trial is required before mutilating citizens, because forced sterilization is a civil matter.[866] The judge claimed the ultimatum applied only to men who had fathered children with several women, but court secrecy prevented journalists or scholars from verifying this, consulting the litigants, or otherwise investigating the matter.

One could hardly ask for a more glaring example of government creating a problem for itself to solve. In a time of supposedly tight budgets, governments are willing to lay out expenditures for questionable, counter-productive, and even dangerous programs to deal with the problems created by existing government agencies rather than taking the morally straightforward but politically difficult step of not creating the problem in the first place. Our entire approach to the fatherhood crisis is fundamentally self-contradictory and self-defeating, and it is especially ironic that its promoters should describe themselves as encouraging "responsible" fatherhood. For government itself has become a huge caricature of precisely the irresponsible father it excoriates. In assuming the role of political paterfamilias and *parens patriae*, our governments have transformed themselves into institutionalized versions of a figure we all naturally hold in contempt: the weak and cowardly father who will lavish out any amount of money futilely trying to appease his wayward children, because he lacks the courage simply to tell them firmly that what they are doing is wrong.

Chapter 6

THE POLITICS OF FATHERHOOD

The attack on the family in modern political thought has been sweeping and unremitting. . . . The abolition of the child stands alongside the abolition of the family as part of the agenda of political thought. . . . If the family is to survive as an institution . . . the major thrust of modern politics must be altered.

— Philip Abbott[867]

The fathers' rights movement is the civil rights movement of our era. Some belittle the plight of fathers, saying "Oh, they're men, they're privileged, what have they suffered compared to other groups?" The answer is this— whatever horrors blacks or women or other groups have endured in the past fifty years, nobody ever took their children away. What discrimination and what injustice is worse than that?"

— Melanie Mays[868]

n his essay "Totem and Taboo" (1913), Sigmund Freud postulated that civilization was built upon the collective murder of a primal father. This killing was perpetrated by the sons, who both feared and envied his power. Freud argued that the civilized order began with the self-imposed prohibitions and rituals the sons then instituted to prevent themselves destroying one another over the spoils, which consisted of both the father's political dominance and his monopoly of access to the women of the horde. Among these observances was the ritual feeding on the body and imbibing the blood of the sacrificial victim, which Freud saw exemplified in the totem meal of primitive peoples. This eating and drinking at once commemorated the deed and bequeathed to the sons the life and strength of the father. The father was thus made to bear the guilt for the community's sins, which was absolved for each participant in the ritual feeding.

Today we seem to have come up with a novel variation on the Freudian theme. As a society we seem intent on dismantling civilization by ganging up on all fathers, on whom we heap all our sins and whom we make to atone for all the ills of society. Their very absence, we are told, is at the root of all our society's problems. Yet when present they seem to serve only as victims for a new form of human sacrifice. The temples of this diabolical sacrament are courtrooms, where political priests in black vestments mutter formulaic incantations before they break the body and pour forth the blood, initiating a kind of communal feeding frenzy.

Our modern revolt may also have been initiated by the sons, if one goes back a few years, though today power has been assumed by officials who act in their name and claim to represent their interests: judges, lawyers, psychotherapists, social workers, mediators, counselors, bureaucratic police, and a swarm of other human parasites who derive powerful political sustenance and lucrative financial nourishment from the cannibalized father. In the Freudian scheme, the sons ambivalently mix love and hate toward the patriarch. In our grotesque inversion, hate alone triumphs against each individual father, whose very destruction fosters contempt for his weakness. In contrast to the Freudian theory, our version does not halt the killing cycle but infinitely perpetuates it. With the destruction of each father a new generation of children learns contempt and hatred for all fathers, and so the cycle is renewed and the practice passed down. If any child seems to have validated Freud's Oedipal theory it is our collective modern state, which eliminates the fathers and marries the mothers.

Freud is discredited these days with just about everyone, fathers' groups as well as feminists. Perhaps this is for the best. The horrors that continue to be perpetrated in the name of psychoanalysis and psychotherapy have wrought destruction nowhere so much as in the family.

Yet any writer who places a revolt against the father at the center of his theory is one we might pay at least some attention to today. In this, by far his most brilliant and enduring work (perhaps because it is less psychoanalysis than political theory), Freud seems to have tapped into something fundamental. Today's worldwide attack on fathers lends a renewed plausibility to Freud's patricide theory that was not evident a few years ago. Nothing less than the unleashing of a powerful primal urge, buried for eons in some deep and unexplored recess of our collective subconscious, would seem to account for the virulence of father hatred in our society today. Certainly other groups have served as scapegoats and objects for hate-mongers; if Freud's explanation—that these groups serve as displaced father figures—is obviously self-justifying, it might nevertheless not be dismissed too quickly.

Only time will tell if this hatred, potentially the most intrusive of all, becomes as politically total as others of our recent past. But no hatred is today given official sanction other than the hatred of men in general and fathers in particular. Moreover, few hatreds are as self-generating and self-perpetuating across the generations. One cannot help but wonder if hatred of fathers is such a powerful force that, unchecked, it could indeed unravel our civilization.

Freud was not the first to theorize about the role of fathers in civil society, nor was he entirely original. Fatherhood and paternal authority—and revolts against them as well—form an intimate part of our political culture, and theorists much more revered in the Anglophone political canon, including some of our intellectual and political founding fathers, were moved by ideas not wholly unlike those Freud articulated in the scientist vocabulary of psychoanalysis. The social contract of John Locke, arguably the seminal influence in modern and especially American political thought, was a theory of the family as much as of the state and was likewise predicated on the dethroning of a primal father figure. Locke's principal political writings were a sustained polemic against "patriarchalist" theories which held that kings reigned by a divine right passed down from father to son since Adam, both the first father and the first ruler. Locke did not deny that such a primal patriarchal monarch had existed, nor that political authority originated in paternal rule.

"If we look back as far as history will direct us, towards the original of commonwealths, we shall generally find them under the government and administration of one man," he wrote. "The government commonly began in the father." Yet against the patriarchalists, Locke insisted that whatever early father had come to occupy political primacy as a monarch, he had been stripped of any special claim to political authority derived from his fatherhood alone, and Locke's central contribution to political thought was his insistence that this authority was not a divine mandate but exercised merely by the consent of the community: "The beginning of politic society depends upon the consent of the individuals to join into and make one society."

In the male-dominated society of Locke's time and every age before and since (at least until recently), this meant ultimate political authority passed to his sons. "This was not by any paternal right," Locke insisted, "but only by the consent of his children." Whatever office the father might hold was merely for the sake of convenience and "not any regard or respect to paternal authority."[869] According to Locke's revolutionary theory, later invoked by Jefferson in justification of his own revolution, the sons could revoke their consent at any time, and the revolutions of the seventeenth century, like those of the eighteenth, were declarations that they had done so. Modern civil society required that the first father's political rule be overthrown.

Unlike Freud, Locke did not require that the political father be killed; it was acceptable that he continue to reign so long as he understood that ultimate authority from that time forth lay with the sons. Hence Britain's "constitutional monarchy," which dates from Locke's Glorious Revolution of 1688-89. The sons became patriarchs in their own right within their own households; none could ever become supreme over the others, but all acting together could revoke or reconstitute the monarch's mandate at any time. But while Locke's theory did not necessarily require patricide or regicide, it did derive from, defend, and in turn inspire revolutions in which political father figures were indeed being killed, and with great sacramental fanfare. The killing of kings— not in the corners of dungeons as had occasionally occurred in previous centuries but in the publicly displayed trials and executions of 1649 and 1793 (or the more gentle renunciation of their authority in 1776)[870]—was justified by first denying their paternal status. It was their public trial and execution at the hands of their own subjects that effectively (and sacramentally) devolved the patriarchal image from the monarch to the heads of individual families.

Like Freud's primal patricide, Locke's social contract allows the political power of the father to live on, albeit in diffused and circumscribed form. It is shared out among the rebels but only with appropriate safeguards to ensure that none can ever again assume exclusive power over the others. In our history these safeguards have taken two forms: the less visible but perhaps more important on the popular level are religious sacraments, as Freud recognized; since Locke's time though they have also taken the form of secular constitutionalism. Like the God on whom he is modeled, the first father is no longer expressly represented in our political system, but his image is re-embodied in individual fathers who together constitute the sovereign body of citizens.

In the Protestant political culture that Locke and his readers until recently presupposed, these fathers' authority is buttressed by, among other things, the sacrament of God's "son." More clearly than Freud's totem meal, the communal eating and drinking in the Christian eucharist commemorates the sacrifice of the body and blood. This sacramentalism featured centrally in a political movement that was largely responsible for two events of inestimable importance in modern history: one was the world's first true political ideology and first true revolution; the other was the seminal political culture of what came to be the United States. In the English Revolution of the 1640s, puritan intellectuals politicized eucharistic symbols to instigate and justify what was in effect an act of political patricide: revolution against a divinely anointed king. As Christ sacrificed his body and blood to save his saints, so they were expected to sacrifice theirs on the battlefields of England to erect his throne on earth.

Not accidentally, it was the puritans who also insisted that the family function as effectively the lowest administrative unit of the church, with fathers exercising essentially sacerdotal and sacramental discipline within families. The puritan belief in the family as "a little commonwealth" anticipated our modern conviction that families constitute the building blocks of "civil society."[871] And since feminist scholars are quick to point to this as evidence of a resurgent "patriarchy," it is worth noting that women were drawn to puritanism (as they have been to more recent instances of religious radicalism) in disproportionately large numbers.

The seeds of republican constitutionalism also existed in this revolution, as they did in the puritan colonization of New England, and from Locke's time became more expressly political with the intentional fragmentation and decentralization of power and division of sovereignty which Locke prescribed in general terms and which are most clearly manifest in the American Constitution. In no other political document is the concern to control and channel patriarchal authority so clearly apparent: the "checks and balances" and the federalist bifurcation of power whose main aim was to prevent the return to monarchy or an equivalent tyranny by concentrating power in any one man or body of men. It is little wonder that many observers have characterized the U.S. Constitution as secular scripture and the American political system as a series of secular sacraments, starting with the ten commandments in the Bill of Rights, proscribing to the government what "thou shalt not" do.

The republican political thought of the American and French revolutions—in essence secularized puritanism[872]—might be seen as the political institutionalization of the religious prohibitions that Locke and Freud, in their different ways, saw as marking the birth of civilization. The prohibitions on "titles of nobility" are another of the more obvious features. These revolutions' obsession with republican "virtue"—a word understood as connoting "manliness" and often consciously opposed to the "effeminacy" and "foppery" (homosexuality) that republican theorists equated with the decadence of the royal court—is another, more clearly gender-derived manifestation of this.

Did these anti-monarchical revolutions then unleash a pent-up hatred of the father? They are often said to have ushered in modern secular society and with it a kind of renunciation or even hatred of God the Father: a sort of regicide as deicide.[873] Locke and his predecessor Thomas Hobbes are among the philosophers most frequently said to have "secularized" political thought, removing God from the political system. Yet it is more likely that, to the extent that our citizenship is defined by puritanism-republicanism, it is also defined by patriarchy. The rebellions against the king that gave birth to our republican ideas and institutions were rebellions circumscribed by patriarchal rules.

This at least is what feminist political theorists have told us.[874] What they have not done is to demonstrate any alternative. If patriarchy is so firmly embedded in our political culture, after all, perhaps it serves some useful purpose, with which we tamper at our risk.

One suggestion of why this may be so is supplied by Locke's predecessor in contract theory and revolutionary political thought. Hobbes attributed to patriarchy a central role in the process of leaving the state of nature and entering into civil society. Hobbes saw the transition from nature to society as coinciding with the shift in sovereignty over children from the mother to the father. For Hobbes, the development of married fatherhood as a social role marked nothing less than the beginning of civil society and civilization itself. In the state of nature, "the dominion is in the mother," Hobbes argued:

> For in the condition of mere nature, where there are no matrimonial laws, it cannot be known who is the father, unless it be declared by the mother. And therefore the right of dominion over the child dependeth on her will and is consequently hers.[875]

Only in civil society—where "matrimonial laws" do operate—is sovereign authority over the children shared with the father. Civilization requires fathers.

It was precisely the program of the radical puritan intellectuals—whom Hobbes disliked and whose name has become popularly synonymous with repressive sexual morality—to, as they saw it, renew and resurrect this civilization by jettisoning the remnants of paganism and imposing strict sexual control on the citizenry. In fact, it is no exaggeration to say that one of the top priorities of the world's first revolutionaries was to control sexual license—and especially, as feminists have pointed out, the sexual license of women. Puritanism and other Calvinist political movements popularized sexual repression (of both men and women) as a political platform and made it a requirement for modern citizenship.[876] The republican revolutions of the next century in America and France left the sexual issues largely in the background but made the political implications even more explicit.[877]

Ironically but not accidentally, it was in these same sexually repressive revolutions that feminism, like all political radicalism, also originated. Early feminism was far from sexually (or politically) libertine, and its advocates generally shared the puritanical republican ideology of their male comrades (a puritanical strain some detect in feminism to this day).[878] Mary Wollstonecraft consistently defended her feminism by juxtaposing republican "virtue" (again, etymologically connected with masculinity) with the decadent "pleasure" connected in the puritan-republican mind with the effete culture of the royal court, with its associations of not only tyranny and corruption but also frivolity, homosexuality, and the sale of political influence for sexual favors. "Pleasure is the business of woman's life, according to the present modification of society," Wollstonecraft pointed out, "and while it continues to be so, little can be expected from such weak beings." Women have "the liberty of running from pleasure to pleasure," she complained. "Women seek for pleasure as the main purpose of existence."

Wollstonecraft's feminism rebelled against "false refinement," "immorality," "vanity," "corruption," "libertine notions of beauty," and "frivolous productions." "The seeds of false refinement, immorality, and vanity, have ever been shed by the great," she wrote. "Weak, artificial beings, raised above the common wants and affections of their race, in a premature unnatural manner, undermine the very foundation of virtue and spread corruption through the whole mass of society." Most serious for revolutionary purposes, Wollstonecraft was keenly aware that women's available sources of power carried inherent potential for both corruption and tyranny. "This artificial weakness produces a propensity to tyrannize, and give birth to cunning, the natural opponent of strength." Virtue, she wrote, is "an acquirement to which pleasure must be sacrificed."[879]

It may not be fanciful to suggest that Wollstonecraft's feminism had at least as much in common with a strain of apparently antifeminist writing that had arisen at the inception of modern political thought as it does with today's feminism. The influence of feminine wiles within the political system, after all, had been associated with tyranny and terror at least since the time of Mary Tudor and Mary Stuart, when John Knox issued his *First Blast of the Trumpet*

Against the Monstrous Regiment of Women. It became especially vivid with the revolutions we have been discussing, which adopted among their most vociferous grievances the political influence of consort queens Henrietta Maria and Marie Antoinette.[880]

In short, our political identity, "patriarchal" as it may be, was born in rebellion and revolution, and so was its matriarchal nemesis.

Radical politics has come a long way since the eighteenth century, and this is not the place to trace its development. But Wollstonecraft's puritanical contempt for "pleasure" contrasts sharply with the political hedonism of modern feminists like Carole Vance:

> Feminism must put forward a politics that resists deprivation and supports pleasure. It must understand pleasure as life-affirming, empowering, desirous of human connection and the future, and not fear it as destructive, enfeebling, or corrupt. Feminism must speak to sexual pleasure as a fundamental right, which cannot be put off to a better or easier time.[881]

There are sound reasons why every civilization insists on repressing sexual promiscuity, and Wollstonecraft's prose indicates how difficult it was to dismantle centuries of habituated moral repression. While Western movements such as puritanism have been largely egalitarian between the genders, it is foremost the sexuality of women that society demands to be brought under control. "The suppression by cultural forces of women's inordinately high sexual drive and orgasmic capacity must have been an important prerequisite for the evolution of modern human societies and has continued, of necessity, to be a major preoccupation of practically every civilization," observes Mary Jane Sherfey. "It is conceivable that the *forceful* suppression of women's inordinate sexual demands was the prerequisite to the dawn of every modern civilization and almost every living culture."[882]

This recognition is contrary to the sentimental assumptions about women held by many conservatives today,[883] who insist on blaming social havoc on uncontrolled *male* sexuality. Yet it is echoed by modern defenders of patriarchy such as Daniel Amneus, who supports his argument largely by drawing on feminist writings. Like Hobbes, Amneus insists that fatherhood is nothing less than the defining feature and prerequisite of civilized society. Matriarchies govern the societies of mammals and uncivilized peoples—the "state of nature," in the language of political theory—according to Amneus. Only civilization requires and creates nuclear families with the constant, active presence of a father. For Amneus therefore it is the female, not the male, whose promiscuity threatens the social order and whose new economic independence in recent decades creates the material basis for that promiscuity. Amneus bases his theory on an observation of social anthropologist Robert Briffault: "The female, not the male, determines all the conditions of the animal family. Where the female can derive no benefit from association with the male, no such association takes place."[884] Divorce and single parenthood therefore, are the inevitable result of female economic emancipation, including income subsidies such as welfare and child support.

Amneus's argument has enormous force. Intellectually it is the most powerful response yet to the current crisis of fatherhood. Also like Hobbes, though, Amneus is intellectually innovative while remaining politically conservative. (He is even less happy about the feminist revolt than Hobbes was about the puritan.) There is nothing wrong with this, of course, and his analysis of the problem may well penetrate deeper and endure longer than anything I can offer here, just as Hobbes continues to be read today while most puritan writings remain in obscurity. As a program for practical action, however, it has limitations; his express advocacy of father custody has a nineteenth-century ring that will make it difficult to find acceptance beyond the fringe of political debate. Without denying Amneus's brilliance, therefore, I propose to play the puritans to his Hobbes: the radicals to whom he was temperamentally and politically opposed but with whom he also had much in common. To do this it is necessary to return to our own time.[885]

EROSION OF CIVIC VIRTUE

As we saw at the start, fatherhood and marriage have become the rage in recent years among policymakers, some academics, and media. Presidents Bill Clinton and George W. Bush and aspirants like Al Gore, members of Congress, governors, mayors, and scholars like David Blankenhorn and David Popenoe—all these people tell us, quite rightly, about the importance of fatherhood and the destructive social consequences of marriage breakdown and single-parent homes on both children and society.

Yet we have also seen that these policymakers and advocates have either failed or refused to tell us why this problem has arisen, finding it easier simply to heap the sins of society on fathers rather than summon the resolve to confront the much more formidable government machine that is in fact responsible for it.

But the fatherhood and marriage promoters have failed on another score too, even within their own frame of reference, for they have been unable to explain precisely why fatherlessness has such a devastating effect on both children and society and the reasons for the connection with violent crime, substance abuse, truancy and lowered scholastic performance, and other social-psychological pathologies. Though almost everyone today accepts that an important link exists, no coherent explanation has been offered for what precisely it is. Armin Brott notes that "dads play a unique—and very important—role from the start" but acknowledges that "the experts haven't yet figured out exactly why fathers have such a major impact on their children's development."[886]

I do not believe we are likely to find the answer from the experts, because it most likely will emerge in precisely the moral dimension the forensic psychotherapeutic experts are determined to ignore. So long as we insist upon viewing children as laboratory animals, whose needs can be interpreted and whose destiny is determined by a priesthood of forensic social scientists, we make ourselves part of the problem rather than the solution. Not until we learn once again to see children as future citizens who must one day face moral choices of their own—choices inseparable from their own upbringing and family life—will we fully come to terms with the crisis of fatherhood and the various crises its destruction has brought.

Richard Gardner and Barbara Whitehead provide a hint at the problem of the wayward children of divorce with the suggestion that "It is not too fanciful to see these behavioral responses . . . as a kind of protest activity, a way for children to register their strenuous objections to divorce."[887] If this is true, then a more effective therapy than sessions with the school counselor may be moral leadership from at least one parent in refusing to accede to the divorce.

Some fatherhood advocates do emphasize fathers as figures of moral authority. We are told, sensibly enough, that only a father can teach a boy how to be a man and show a girl what to expect from one. We are also told, more disturbingly, that children whose fathers are missing due to death or duty do not lash out in the same destructive behaviors as do the children of separation and divorce.[888] There must be something more then, something inherent in the process of separation and divorce that devastates many children. That something, I want to suggest, is a code of social and civic morality and of fundamental justice without which not only can no family function, but no democracy and no civilization can either.

By expunging justice from family courts, we are institutionalizing injustice not only in our political system but also in the raising of our children. In previous decades, "When children lost their intact family, their innate sense of justice was not violated," writes Bai Macfarlane. "One of their parents had done certain things that were considered morally wrong, and everybody understood that." Modern no-fault divorce altered that fundamentally. Under the new laws, "When a child's intact family was destroyed because one parent simply . . . gets divorced, the children are told by social workers, court-ordered psychologists, and court-ordered children's attorneys that it is lawful, good, and even natural for . . . the one who was responsible for breaking up the family . . . to take the children from the other parent," Macfarlane adds. "Children innately know this . . . is unjust, but the legal community tells them they are mistaken."[889]

The words *divorce* and *custody* have become so common as to be rendered banal. Though we have no shortage of quasi-scientific studies affirming that they are highly destructive of children, it may be more instructive to set aside the psychotherapeutic hocus-pocus and approach the matter in plain terms that we all as citizens not only can but must understand. In civic terms, the essence of divorce and custody is to bring the power of the state into the home for use against family members: ultimately it is the power to have family members arrested. This basic fact is now covered over by layers of euphemism and administration, but the essential truth is that whenever the state is involved in any matter the ultimate sanction, as Locke pointed out, is prison and death. When we recall that the family members against whom the power of the state is marshaled may well be legally blameless, we can begin to grasp the full horror of what we have created and the extent to which the divorce machinery has been fashioned into an instrument of terror.

The inherently authoritarian implications of mobilizing the criminal justice system to punish family members for ordinary family differences can be seen as, almost literally, a declaration of war. It returns the family to something like a Hobbesian state of nature with its "war of all against all," or at least to the pre-political society of the blood feud. (It was Hobbes who pointed out with respect to the state of nature what we saw through recent research on domestic violence: that physical strength counts for little, and women can and do inflict injury and death on their children's fathers just as easily as the reverse.)[890] The terms we regularly invoke to describe a divorce involving children—custody *battle*, *warring* parents—reflect the political environment Locke also termed the "state of war." Without children, the fallout from the most acrimonious divorce is usually manageable. But when one parent takes the children from the other, it creates very unstable and dangerous conditions indeed—conditions that make violence not only possible but logical. This may be why mothers who snatch the children and seek restraining orders against fathers before the fathers have done anything wrong can tell the court so convincingly that they are "in fear" from him: They know what *they* would do if someone took their children.

As most of us know (but as the divorce regime labors to make us forget), this is nothing more than the natural and predictable and even expected response of any parent when someone interferes with their children. "People in marital conflict are fighting over the most important matters in their lives," writes solicitor Adrian Pellman, with British understatement, "their children and all they have worked for, and . . . such fundamental issues can only be resolved by conflict."[891] No, not just conflict: *violence*. What results is much more serious than simply a state of mutual animosity. When it involves children for whom most parents—and perhaps especially fathers—will readily die and kill (and in other circumstances are expected to do so without hesitation), the result is a highly unstable state where, as in Hobbes's state of nature, it is hardly an exaggeration to recognize that neither parent is entirely safe so long as the other is alive. One parent, at a minimum, must be physically restrained.

In these circumstances, the militarization of the family, with children becoming both the weapons and spoils, is virtually inescapable. Attorney Bob Hirschfeld describes the atmosphere surrounding children torn between family factions. "I recall . . . a Hatfield-McCoy exchange in which the child was transferred on an apartment house parking lot. On one side, stood members of the mother's family, wielding baseball bats. On the other side of the lot, were the father's family, similarly armed. . . . A bloodless exchange finally took place."[892] Anyone who doubts the seriousness of what is involved need only imagine what would happen were the police and jails not available to be used against fathers (or for that matter mothers) whose children have been forcibly removed. This thought helps explain why the father whose children are taken is immediately treated as a quasi-criminal—his movements are controlled, his private life is monitored, he is interrogated behind closed doors, his home is entered, his personal papers are examined, he is placed under restraining orders, his savings are confiscated, his wages are attached, his name is entered on various government "registers"—even before he has done anything wrong. The state knows that by taking a man's children it has created an outlaw. When one adds the ever-present threat of imminent arrest through false accusations or impossible child-support burdens, it is not difficult to see that what the media and police seem to insist on treating as another lunatic with a gun may in reality be a cornered father simply acting out the logic of his circumstances.

The bottom line is that the criminalization of the father is, quite simply, unavoidable so long as we are willing to enforce unilateral divorce with children. With the father an outlaw, the children may be in the immediate "custody" of the mother (a term suggesting incarceration), but it is more accurate to say that ultimately they have become wards of the state, which establishes what amounts to a puppet government within the family. In fact, it is not unreasonable to see the custodial parent at this point as effectively and functionally a government official. She[893] is paid to care for her children with money that comes directly from the state (after being confiscated from the father). Indeed, the jargon now used by courts and feminists to justify her supremacy indicates that what we once called a "mother" has been replaced by a gender-neutral government-appointed and government-funded "primary caretaker." Moreover, by giving the custodial parent—at whose invitation the state usually justifies its intervention—the power of judge in her own case, the state turns the family into a kind of satrapy. Knowing she has virtually absolute power over the child, and through the child over the non-custodial parent, it is not surprising that the custodial parent starts to behave like a petty dictator.

The family becomes in effect government-occupied territory. The children experience family life not as a nursery of cooperation, compromise, trust, and forgiveness. Instead they receive a firsthand lesson in tyranny. Backed by the courts, police, and jails, the custodial parent now "calls the shots" alone—issuing orders and instructions to the non-custodial parent, undermining his authority with the children, dictating the terms of his access to them, talking to and about him contemptuously and condescendingly in the presence of the children as if he were himself a naughty child, perhaps engaging in a full-scale campaign of vilification—and all with the blessing and backing of the government.[894]

The children cannot help but pick up on these messages. They witness how their father has in effect been declared a public enemy on whom the full force of the government is brought to bear. Eventually they come to understand that the force keeping him away is the police, who are the guarantors of the mother's supremacy. Thus the message the children receive about both the family and the state is that they are dictatorships, ruled by an arbitrary power which can be marshaled against private enemies for personal grievances. If Daddy disagrees with Mommy or has different ideas on, say, how the children should be raised, we no longer have to listen to him or compromise with him because a telephone call will have him removed, and the police and jailers will make sure he stays away. And if the police can be used to arrest Dad because he does something Mom doesn't like, what will they do to me if I do something Mom doesn't like? On the other hand, perhaps someday I too can marshal the police and jails against family members with whom I have differences or against anyone who hurts my feelings.

The children's fears are not unfounded. After witnessing this dictatorship over their father, they may then experience it themselves. Lacking firm authority that is in any sense moral, as well as any effective restraints on her behavior, the custodial parent now exercises unchecked power over the children as well, a relationship that becomes increasingly strained and acrimonious as the children grow older, less credulous, and more rebellious. In extreme (but not uncommon) cases this opens the way to physical abuse, as we have seen, a phenomenon many times more common in single-parent homes than in intact families. As the children react adversely to this destruction of their home and father, or as the cute and cuddly children turn into rebellious adolescents, they can be turned over to foster care by their mothers, as large numbers now are, with additional federally funded incentives. If more vigorous instruments are required, various arms of the state—psychotherapists, police, and penal institutions—can be marshaled against the children as well. Thus the drugging and institutionalization of children in foster care, psychiatric institutions, juvenile detention facilities, and jails that has now become increasingly familiar. *The Progressive* magazine has detailed how many "parents" are now voluntarily turning over the troublesome teenagers they cannot control to the police. Overwhelmingly, though the politically correct article does not point this out, these parents are single mothers.[895]

All this can be done without the knowledge or consent of the father, whose voice in his children's welfare was long ago silenced. Zed McLarnon is one of many fathers who lost custody of his son to an adulterous wife and her new husband (who was also a state-employed social worker), only to find that the couple later turned the unruly youth over to the custody of the Massachusetts Department of Social Services, without informing his father.[896] In the single-mother household, "Wait till your father gets home," has been replaced by "I can turn you over to Social Services."

In the occupied family of forced divorce, parental and political authority are unnaturally intertwined, a process that results in both kinds of authority being simultaneously abused and weakened. Discipline and civility are the first casualties, since it is difficult to teach children to say "please" and "thank you" when we simply issue orders (or court orders) to Dad. Thus the lines of authority are confused and tangled. "Parents are no longer the rule-givers but, rather, the rule-breakers," writes Barbara Whitehead. "Living in unstable families with unreliable parents, the literary children of divorce have been robbed of their traditional prerogatives to push against and even subvert the rules and boundaries. Rascality now belongs to the grownups." On the other hand, through divorce the children are "empowered to get the parent into legal trouble any time the parent does something the child does not like."[897]

In destroying the authority of the non-custodial parent, the custodial parent and the courts are in the long run undermining their own as well. "When the child's father is not present, maternal authority and discipline can be compromised," notes Whitehead. "In both divorced and intact families, studies show, children comply more readily with fathers' than with mothers' demands."[898] Eventually the children develop a contempt for all authority. "First, the father's authority is challenged," observes attorney Jeffery Leving. "Soon after, the children become discipline problems for mothers, teachers, counselors, and coaches. Later in life, a chronic inability to respect the authority of employers, the police, and the courts is common."[899]

This peaks in adolescence, when natural rebelliousness coincides with the full realization of how one or both parents have abused their authority by setting their own desires above the needs of their children. Politically precocious adolescents will sense something similar about the public authority that has engineered the destruction of their home for its own purposes while cynically proclaiming their "best interests." It is this adversarial relationship imposed on the children toward virtually every form of authority that I believe best accounts for the horrifying statistics on juvenile emotional and social problems that correlate more strongly with divorce and single-parent households than any other factor. In different though no less certain ways than their father, the children too are eventually and effectively placed in the role of outlaws.

Further, while many children are materially impoverished by the institutionalized destruction of their family, in other cases the systematic bribery dispensed by the divorce regime extends to the children themselves, who may be rewarded for their cooperation with material opulence, forcibly extracted from their father, and used to corrupt his children and also give them a stake in his plunder and criminalization. A growing theme among social commentators today is how adolescents are often flooded with more money than they know what to do with and more than is probably healthy for them to have.[900] How many of these are children of divorce, where the state has forcibly removed spending decisions from the father and placed them with the unsupervised adolescent? Perhaps this accounts for why "relative to other youth, youth receiving child support but who rarely see their fathers are more likely to smoke and engage in sexual intercourse and criminal activity than other youth."[901] The advice to parents given in *The Best of Life's Little Instruction Calendar* on November 14-15, 1998, is indicative of growing opinion among many: "To help your children turn out well, spend twice as much time with them and half as much money." The divorce machine forces fathers to do precisely the opposite.

It is not difficult to see that this is a highly unhealthy system to have in any society; it is especially threatening to a democratic one, and it is no accident that we are now seeing not only devastating social consequences but violations of civil rights and civil liberties as well, coupled with public, media, and official indifference. In fact, the logic of involuntary divorce and sole custody is reminiscent of another system of domestic dictatorship that once tried unsuccessfully to co-exist with free civil government, and the complaints of fathers that they are reduced to "slavery" may be valid in ways even they do not fully realize. Politically, the most powerful argument against slavery—and what eventually did more than any other to bring about the realization of how threatening it was to democratic freedom—was not so much its physical cruelty as its moral degeneracy: the tyrannical habits it encouraged in the slaveholder, the servile ones it fostered in the slave, and the moral degradation it engendered in both. Such dispositions were said to be incompatible with the kind of republican virtue required for free self-government.

Abolitionist Charles Sumner's warning of slavery's impact on the moral development of white children growing up in slave societies was at least as alarming as concerns about cruelty to black ones. "Their hearts, while yet tender with childhood, are necessarily hardened by this conduct, and their subsequent lives perhaps bear enduring testimony to this legalized uncharitableness," he wrote. "They are unable to eradicate it from their natures. . . . Their characters are debased, and they become less fit for the magnanimous duties of a good citizen."[902] Something similar may be seen today in the confiscated children of government-enforced divorce. No people can remain free who harbor within themselves a system of dictatorship or raise their children according to its principles.

CAN FATHERHOOD BE RESTORED?

In these circumstances how can we realistically speak of "restoring" fatherhood? Can the same government apparatus that has forced the father away from his children and seized control over them restore his fatherhood—and for that matter his children's childhood? It could voluntarily withdraw, of course, but how far and for how long? "Freedom is never voluntarily given by the oppressor," ran the refrain preached by Dr. Martin Luther King Jr. throughout the civil rights years, "it must be demanded by the oppressed."[903] King could be so categorical because he knew that what the state giveth, the state can taketh away. This is why he emphasized it must be demanded *by* the oppressed. The connected truism of those years was that no oppressed people can be liberated by others; almost by definition, they must do it for themselves. Only in the process of gaining what is rightfully theirs can a people learn to hold on to it, use it responsibly, and pass it on to their children.

Some advocates for fatherhood do seem to have an inkling of this when they suggest that fatherhood is the basis of public morality. "Fathers can be a powerful influence in making better citizens," writes Don Eberly of the National Fatherhood Initiative. The argument needs to be taken much further, but Eberly makes a good start. "A democracy requires of its citizens . . . that they possess enough faith, energy, imagination, and self-control to work actively together to solve common problems, to help one another, and if necessary to sacrifice for their own future well-being and the nation's," he writes. "Fathers play a key role in developing and sustaining the kind of personal character on which democracy depends."[904]

An important and indisputable point, but the question must be posed as to whether this civic virtue can be instilled or imposed from without—say, by a government program or a non-profit organization such as Eberly himself has founded. Perhaps it can, but in the past it was usually because pressure from citizens themselves was behind it. Civic virtue that is enduring and dependable enough to serve as the foundation for a stable democratic society has usually been the product of substantial human sacrifice. Historically, this sacrifice has often been inspired by the most prominent and problematic answer the modern world has furnished to tyranny and oppression, and that is rebellion. At some point the upstanding citizens become militant activists. At some point they rebel.

Eberly and his colleagues among the advocates for "responsible fatherhood" will not go this far. Fatherhood as a model for "citizenship" is wholesome, whereas "activism" raises red flags. They are right to be cautious, for rebellion always carries enormous dangers, as the modern world has become terribly aware. After all, we have already hypothesized that unleashing adolescent rebellion accounts for much of the destructive behavior in the children of divorce (and the mothers of divorce too). Can rebellion be a source of civic virtue, much less a sound principle on which to raise children?

We have also noted that modern citizenship in the English-speaking world and much of the West was born in rebellion and revolution. Further, as most of us know from personal experience, rebellion is also an almost unavoidable part of childhood and adolescent growth. But even beyond this, I want to suggest that fatherhood too plays a role in rebellion, or at least in our attitude toward it. The first rebellion most of us learn is rebellion against our parents, and I think for most that means rebellion against our fathers. As a student of political thought, rather than of psychoanalysis, I again see one insight in the much-maligned (and often rightly maligned) Freud: that rebellion against paternal authority is an inescapable fact of life and an essential part of the generational cycle. Fathers who fail or refuse to exercise authority (or are forcibly prevented from doing so) deprive their children of many things, which are so obvious and so frequently recounted by conservatives as not to need any further mention here. But they also deprive them of something that should be dear to the liberal left. They deprive them of the lessons of rebellion. They also deprive the rest of us of something, for rebellion is not only part of growing up; in our liberal republican democracy, for better or worse, it is an ingredient in the development of responsible citizens.

The ability to rebel constructively and responsibly, to question and challenge authority without seeking to destroy it altogether, to respect and even (as some recent rebels have insisted) love one's opponents—these are part of the maturation process of citizenship that most of us begin to learn when for the first time we stand up to the authority of our fathers. Learning to rebel against someone we love, it might be said, is essential training for learning to love those against whom we rebel. This "love" is explicit in the political philosophies of Gandhi, King, and other practitioners of nonviolent resistance. But acknowledging our connection and maintaining our loyalty to the society we criticize and the government from whose policies we dissent in the most vehement terms is an essential habit in any stable civic order, and it is also a theme of the best leftist political philosophy.[905]

To be sure, the overly authoritarian father runs the risk of his children denying or attempting to escape from his authority altogether, of producing young anarchists. But the father who abdicates his authority risks creating a thirst for it in his children. He will not avoid a rebellion; chances are it will become an authoritarian rebellion.

Collective rebellion that seeks to overthrow the entire "patriarchy," however, is another matter altogether. When we as a society collectively rebel against fatherhood itself and fathers as a group and seek their destruction, we may be killing the goose that lays the golden egg; we certainly embark on a very dangerous course. I do not necessarily rule out that it may be done; perhaps it may even be, as feminists promise, the beginning of a new and more glorious stage in history. But if it is to be done without destroying our civilization, we had better understand a little better precisely what we are doing.

The feminist revolt against patriarchy has not bothered to do this. On the contrary, whatever its merits as envisioned by ideologically pure theorists, popular feminism has itself often been closer in temperament to adolescent rebellion, which is rebellion for its own sake. "Women have to demand a great many things which may not necessarily be good in themselves simply because these things are forbidden," wrote Katherine Anthony during feminism's own adolescence. "They have also to reject many things which may not necessarily be evil in themselves simply because they are prescribed. The idea of obedience can have no moral validity for women for a long time to come."[906] It is these naughty girls—who are so far from understanding or wishing to understand the responsibilities that accompany authority that they rebel against authority essentially for the thrill of doing so—who have now procured for themselves virtually monopoly control over the raising of children. And once again (it cannot be emphasized enough), they are backed with the lethal force of the state.

Without denying the potential validity of the feminist program when it has been forced to explain itself in the harsh glare of public debate, the secret rebellion feminism has perpetrated, without ever having to justify it, in the hidden world of family law appears as less a reasoned and refined program of constructive reform than a putsch of spoiled brats. And the spoiled brats are raising our children. "Spoiled children make bad spouses and worse parents," observes critic Leon Kass. "Necessity, not luxury, is for most people the mother of virtue and maturity."[907] Can a political movement (or an individual mother) that indulges in rebellion for is own sake—and that uses children as its principal weapon and source of power in the revolutionary struggle—be entrusted with imparting to those children the responsibilities of adulthood, including the exercise of civic leadership? Or can it teach only the permanent rebellion with which modern history has become so familiar, with its seemingly inexorable march toward nihilism and terror?

Some indicators are not encouraging. The hatred often expressed by the children of single mothers for their "absent" fathers—even when the breakup was beyond the father's control—is now writ large on the political agenda and may well come to be directed at the entire civic order. "America's ability to maintain her freedoms may ultimately depend on there being some kind of massive national healing," writes Bob Just, who speaks for the children of divorce now coming of age. "We are not even talking about a few million Americans," he warns. "A huge, if not dominant, portion of this country's electorate will soon be 'adult children of divorce.'" They may also be the next generation of rebels:

> Our fear, our anger, our sense of betrayal, our self-loathing, fear of failure, fear of success, and our often deeply depressive nature may cause us to harken to the angry demagogue politicians who outwardly echo our internal pain. In that sense, we are a "mob," full of dark emotions and looking for a leader. A political tsunami is coming . . . perhaps even a nation-killing problem. . . .
>
> Who are we? We are often ready to believe the worst about America and about our fellow Americans because our experience with "family" is not good. . . . We don't just "question authority," we often distrust, even hate authority. (Look for us at all those angry demonstrations.) Why do you think politicians get such resonance by crying "victim"? What child of divorce doesn't feel like a victim? . . . The disaster that befell us was completely out of our control.[908]

Just's point is reinforced by theories which link sexual radicalism such as feminism and homosexuality—today's most rapidly growing ideological complex—with weak or absent fathers.[909]

What fathers must devise (and while others can help, it is the fathers and non-custodial mothers who must create it themselves) is a rebellion that restores rather than destroys moral and constitutional authority and, yes, one according to whose principles they can actually raise their children. Precedents are available for such a rebellion, not only in the earliest revolutions of the seventeenth and eighteenth centuries, which we have already discussed, but more recently in the nonviolent "velvet" revolutions that brought down the governments of the institutionalized left. Their "nonpolitical politics" were in fact reminiscent of the anti-partisan politics of the early American republic.[910] Their rule was necessarily transitional, somewhat naïve, and in the long run inevitably ill-suited to the mundane task of governing. But generally they succeeded in bringing down tyranny without themselves absorbing its poison and thus avoided the terror that would have tainted the legitimacy and integrity of subsequent government.

Beyond their obvious significance in the geopolitics of our own time, the anti-communist revolutions of 1989 are historical because they seem to have defined the limits of modern radicalism. The totalitarian politics against which they rebelled had previously been seen by much of the Western intellectual elite as the legitimate if wayward heirs of our own "bourgeois" revolutions. Since 1989 it is no longer tenable to accept this without extensive qualification. The experience of communism, its corruption, and implosion demonstrated globally what some have long told us but what may require the further degeneration and corruption to make clear in the domestic politics of the Western democracies: that human nature is not infinitely malleable, and in moral and political terms there is a limit to how far humanity can "progress." The admonition long issued to the West by the rebels in those revolutions constitutes a challenge with which we may still be forced to reckon. "Do we not in fact stand as a kind of warning to the West," asked Vaclav Havel in the years before those systems collapsed, "revealing to it its own latent tendencies?" What Havel calls this "global crisis" of bureaucratic power did not collapse in 1989:

Totalitarian regimes are not . . . some kind of an avant-garde of world progress. Alas, just the opposite: they are the avant-garde of a global crisis of this civilization. . . . It is the total rule of a bloated, anonymously bureaucratic power . . . a power grounded in an omnipresent ideological fiction which can rationalize anything without ever having to come in contact with the truth. Power as the omnipresent monopoly of control, repression, and fear; power which makes thought, morality, and privacy a state monopoly . . . ; power which . . . swallows up everyone, so that all should become integrated within it, at least through their silence. No one actually possesses such power, since it is the power itself which possesses everyone; it is a monstrosity which is not guided by humans but which, on the contrary, drags all persons along.[911]

CONCLUSION
Ending the War

The empty court is locked up. If all the injustice it has committed and all the misery it has caused could only be locked up with it, and the whole burnt away in a great funeral pyre—why so much the better.

— Dickens

I t has become commonplace that the family is the building block of civil society, and many have warned that its dissolution portends the destruction of not only social order but civic freedom and, indeed, civilization itself. Today we see precisely how this principle operates as it unfolds before our eyes. Yet some of the very people who have issued the warnings now avert their eyes from the fulfillment of their own prophecies.

Ironically, too, some want to use this principle to politicize the family even further. To say that the family is a "public" institution and the foundation of our civic order is not to say that it necessarily supports—or must be supported by—the coercive power of government. On the contrary, the civic importance of the family is precisely that it is *not* political in the ideological sense. "Of all alternate communities, the family is clearly the greatest danger to the movement and the state," writes unorthodox socialist Michael Walzer. "That is not only because of the force of familial loyalty, but also because the family is a place of retreat from political battles: we go home to rest, to sleep."[912] The public and political contribution of the family is to reserve a zone that is private and apolitical. The threat it poses to state power need not be explicitly political; against the totalitarian claims of the modern state the ordinary business of family life is a threat. "Marriage is . . . the true reservoir of liberty,"

281

writes Allan Carlson. "Every new marriage of man and woman is also an act of defiance against ambitious political and ideological powers that would reduce human activity to their purposes."[913] Almost a century ago, G. K. Chesterton suggested that the family serves as the principal check on state power and predicted that someday the state and family would directly confront one another.[914] The argument of this book is that that day has arrived.

Chesterton was arguing against the liberalization of divorce, and despite all the current attention to just about every *other* threat to the family, divorce is the most direct and serious. Summoning citizens who are charged with no legal wrongdoing and seizing control of their children, homes, property, movements, and persons is not justice or the rule of law. It is something close to terror. Some contend this is an unavoidable part of the divorce process, but if so we need a thorough discussion of precisely how much government intrusion and coercion we are willing to accept in the name of divorce and how far we are willing to impose repressive measures on citizens whose only offense is their refusal to cooperate in the abrogation of their marriages or the confiscation of their children.

In January 2002, the late Pope John Paul II issued what many saw as a surprisingly strong statement against divorce that specifically singled out legal practitioners for criticism. For his pains he was attacked by lawyers, journalists, and politicians from both the left and right. Yet his characterization of divorce as a "festering wound" with "devastating consequences that spread in society like the plague" is as accurate politically as it is socially, and for similar reasons. What Frederick Douglass once observed of the slave power's menacing expansion throughout the political system can now be seen in the cancerous spread of the divorce regime: It is "advancing, poisoning, corrupting, and perverting the institutions of the country, growing more and more haughty, imperious, and exacting."[915]

We cannot even begin to think of effective remedies until we first challenge certain assumptions that have governed "family policy" since the term gained salience. As we saw at the start, public discussion of these topics even now is dominated by therapeutic disciplines which are themselves branches of the divorce industry. One place to begin, therefore, is to recognize that we are confronted here with a question not of social science but of constitutional government. Nowhere in public life today has social science created for its practitioners such a tyranny over not only democratic decision-making but individual rights and private life as in family policy. The first step, therefore, might be to loosen the grip of the social "scientists" in circumscribing the parameters within which we may act. "Some researchers have contended that divorce does not constitute a serious problem for children because it does not cause long-term damage in a majority of the children who experience it," notes Barbara Whitehead, who comments that "this sets an unusually demanding standard."[916] But even she fails to state what seems obvious to those outside the academy: It is for parents, not researchers, to decide what is good and bad for their children. In their influential study on fatherless children, *Growing Up with Single Parents*, sociologists Sara McLanahan and Gary Sandefur propose "an empirically grounded effort to shed light on several unresolved and hotly disputed questions" about divorce and children. They are the wrong questions:

- Was divorce's impact on children significant enough to warrant public concern and attention?
- Or should it be viewed as a private choice that had few negative consequences for children or the society?
- Was the damage caused by divorce economic and therefore reparable by increased income?
- Or was there something about the disruptions of divorce that created non-economic forms of loss and disadvantage and thus might be reparable only by reduced levels of divorce?
- Were children "better off" living with two married parents, even if the parents didn't get along, or would they lead happier lives in a single-parent or stepfamily household?[917]

Most people can answer these questions with common sense. Most people can also see that, despite the pretense of objectivity in this ostensible "science," the scientists have worded their query to invite the answers they prefer. But even granting these scholars the answers they are seeking and that the divorce regime prefers—that the impact of divorce on children is not great, that the impact on society is minimal, and so forth—the questions themselves are not the ones we should be asking. More compelling ones need to be addressed:

- Do we really expect parents to simply acquiesce as the government takes away their children because two social scientists say it will not harm their children?
- Do we really expect any loving parent to say, "Sure, take my children and do with them as you wish. McLanahan and Sandefur have

a study that says my children may not suffer severe long-term damage by being taken away from me. And you want two-thirds of my income to pay for them? By all means, take that too"?

- How far are we prepared to marshal the criminal justice system as an instrument of repression against parents who refuse to respond as the social engineers think they should?

It should be apparent that what we are confronted with here is much more serious than simply "unfairness" to men or "gender bias" against fathers in divorce courts. Such language—the jargon of our generation's political discourse—obscures far more than it reveals. The power to seize control of the private lives of its citizens is the most dangerous power any government can possess. Never before has an American government claimed the power to summon citizens who are simply minding their own business, impose arbitrary orders on them that amount to a personalized criminal code circumscribing and regulating the most personal and private corners of their lives, and incarcerate them without trial when they cannot meet its impossible terms.

Everyone today seems to agree that family law and family policy are in chaos, and there is no shortage of proposals for reforming them. Yet unless we appreciate the full extent of the problem, our remedies could very likely make matters much worse. One theme that has recurred throughout this study is that the divorce regime, in good bureaucratic fashion, has been very adept at convincing not only policymakers but the media and public that the solution to the ills it generates is to increase the size and scope of the machinery generating the ills: more courts, more judges, more lawyers, more psychotherapists, more child protective services, more child-support enforcement agents, more fatherhood programs, divorcing-couple education programs, marriage promotion schemes, parenting classes, domestic violence units, batterers' programs, supervised visitation centers, anger management classes, children's therapy classes, and on and on. At some point we must ask, "Where does it all end?"

Until we accept that these governmental institutions are not a very effective solution but more likely to be part of the problem, we will never rein in the government's war on the family, fathers, and the Constitution. "In liberal societies," writes a political scientist, "the professionalized service state stands above the family and threatens to 'help' it out of its very existence."[918] Nothing in the findings of this or any other study indicates that any of the abuses it describes would be alleviated by increasing any governmental or quasi-governmental apparatus. On the contrary, there is considerable evidence that such growth in government power would only perpetuate and exacerbate the problems and result in further losses of privacy and freedom. The government's voracious divorce-custody machine is not "inefficient," "overburdened," "under-funded," or any other of the self-serving clichés propagated by its practitioners. Judges and their patronage clients are not underpaid or poorly trained; they are not stupid or ignorant, and they do not need to be further "educated." They are part of an ideologically driven bureaucratic machine that is highly effective at executing its purpose, which is to seize control of children from their parents and use them to extend the scope and power of the state over the private lives of adults.

Almost everyone in public life today professes concern for children. Child-support officials post signs in their offices proclaiming "CHILDREN FIRST," and the same slogan is emblazoned on police cars in the District of Columbia and license plates in Virginia. An advocacy group calls itself the Children's Rights Council and avoids being identified with parents' or fathers' rights. Barbara Whitehead and David Popenoe write of such groups, "their rhetoric is pro-child . . . but their agenda is pro-divorced dads."[919] The implication is that Whitehead and Popenoe are the ones who are truly "pro-child." Clearly we have come a long way since W. C. Fields, responding to the question of how he liked children, could reply, "Parboiled."

Yet for all the pieties, there is little evidence that the lives of children are better now that they have armies of officials claiming to look out for their interests than in the days when they were expected to be seen and not heard. On the contrary, it is evident that their lives have deteriorated markedly and that most of that deterioration is the result of divorce and single-parent homes. It costs nothing to proclaim one's concern for children of course; many people today derive substantial income through the industries ostensibly devoted to children. Yet we should be very wary of the claims of those who profess to be moved by pity for other people's children. Using children to tug on our heartstrings is not only a weakness of the sentimental; it may also be a ploy by those cynical and unscrupulous enough to exploit children for their own agenda. Children are now a major source of political leverage not only for feminist ideologues but for a host of government officials, journalists, and academics. "The state must declare the child to be the most precious treasure of the people," insisted none other than Adolf Hitler, who understood that "as long as government is perceived as working for the benefit of children, the people will happily endure almost any curtailment of liberty."[920]

It is not necessary to believe that all the officials who staff the vast bureaucratic empire now administering the lives of children are mindless zealots or ruthless Nazis; doubtless many are conscientious individuals, sincerely doing their best in difficult circumstances. But this is not the point. In the long run there is a more important consideration than whether a particular judge or social worker may be honest or whether a specific government program is appropriate. Much more serious is that we have turned over control of our children to officials who are not and can never be held responsible for what happens to them. Regardless of whether officials make the "right" or "wrong" decisions in particular instances, whether they implement "good" or "bad" policies (even assuming such things can be ascertained), the fact remains, and will probably always remain, that these officials can walk away from the consequences of what they do with impunity. Were every civil servant selflessly devoted to the welfare of children, and were every government program lovingly designed and administered purely out of altruistic concern for children, they would still—by the very nature of what they are doing and by the very fact of making public what should be private—constitute a massive bloc of unaccountable power.

I do not mean simply that officials are almost never punished by the law when the children under their control are harmed or harm others, or that judges and lawyers and social workers protect one another's misdeeds, though this is true and should alert us that something is seriously wrong. When a child is harmed or harms others in the custody of a parent, that parent can be held liable. Judges and civil servants can always claim that they had too big a caseload and need more "resources." So children die in the care of social workers, and the social workers insist the solution is to hire more of them. Families are destroyed in ugly "custody battles," so the judges say we must create more courts and hire more judges to process more custody battles. Few stop to question whether some vitiating fallacy or flaw may exist at the inception of the process. And again, that inception is almost always the removal of the father. The father's removal initiates the problems for the state to solve, and because the state and its operatives are then perceived as the solution rather than the problem, their mistakes and misdeeds justify the continued existence and limitless expansion of the problem-solvers.

It is true that from time to time attempts are made to hold officials accountable, by pointing the finger at this judge or that social worker and demanding to know why a certain child went missing or died. But there is little evidence that these histrionics constitute anything more than posturing by self-righteous journalists and politicians who raise their own profile by moral grandstanding. Perhaps even more sobering is the realization that these officials will never and can never be held accountable by the children themselves. No child will ever grow up and say to a government official, "You failed to protect me, or provide for me, or teach me right from wrong." And much as they might pretend otherwise, few officials would be greatly bothered if they did.

Parents do not have that luxury, for parents are by definition responsible for their children. Certainly parents make mistakes, as any parent or child can testify (and as judges, attorneys, and social workers seem to delight in pointing out). But unlike civil servants, parents must live with the consequences of their mistakes, and in the long run that fact alone is far more important than this or that mistake. Parental responsibility is the basis of all social and even civic responsibility. Destroy that, and we have undermined the hierarchical structure of all accountability throughout society and the state. Replacing parents with judges and bureaucrats and police is not only bad for children and families: It is bad for democracy. It creates an army of officials who have power without responsibility.

Something similar might apply to those who claim to be the watchdogs of the government and hold it to account, and it may explain why the watchdogs have become lapdogs. Not only the "liberal media" but the conservative media too have often acted as cheerleaders in the government's war against parents and families. "The biggest problem I see in this country today isn't winning the war against terrorism," proclaims Oliver North. "The biggest problem . . . is men not being responsible for the children they create."[921]

Conservative pundits can indulge in this armchair wisdom because, much like their liberal counterparts, they too have power without responsibility. Their opinions are different (and I am more inclined to agree with them than I used to be), but the rightness or wrongness of their opinions is less important than the fact that their opinions have few consequences for themselves. The central abuse in today's media pundits is less their biases than the fact that they have only opinions, but no responsibility for those opinions. Unlike the parents they attack (who have no similar platform from which to reply), they can vent their opinions, move on to the next topic, voice more opinions, and then move on again.

The media today traffic in opinions. We have become a very opinionated society, and the media thrives on airing our opinions. Daytime television and talk radio are mostly the airing of opinions. Public opinion polling is big business, and politicians are not the only ones who watch polls. Standard college political science textbooks now invariably contain a chapter on "public opinion."

But opinions do not cost anything. If opinions turn out to be wrong (or inconvenient), we can easily change them. "Those are my principles," we can say with Groucho Marx. "If you don't like them, I have others." If they hurt people in the meantime, that is of no consequence to us, because we can walk away from the consequences with impunity, along with the opinion leaders and opinion mongers.

Some eighty years ago, in his great work on the subject, Walter Lippmann warned that democracy cannot allow itself to degenerate into the rule of public opinion. "The only meaningful public is composed of those people directly interested in an issue," he believed.[922] Lippmann was concerned primarily with the great issues of war and peace. Yet his observation is equally valid in the microcosmic world of family politics, since no one's "interest" is more legitimate as a basis for public policy over what used to be private life than that of parents. One benefit to our democracy of reasserting parental authority may be reining in the tyranny of not only the media but also our own opinions, which are weapons we supply to a media priesthood that can manipulate our views to the point of telling us what we believe.

For parents, how their children are raised and government's power over their children are more than matters of opinion; often nowadays they are matters of life and death. Traditionally, the family has served as a realm protected from the prying eyes not only of government but also of the opinionated, who often yearn to marshal the state to forcibly enact their opinions. Certainly parents have long benefited from support (and pressure) from extended families, neighborhoods, churches, and local schools—all institutions, incidentally, that have been eclipsed and supplanted by government power.[923] Yet ultimately it is the very nature of parenthood to declare to the world: "Your opinions about my children are of no consequence. You do not love my children, and you are not responsible for them. If your opinions about what is best for my children turn out to be wrong, it is my children and I who must live with the consequences, not you. I am not required to conform to your opinions about what is best for my children, and I am not answerable to you for how I raise them."

For this reason, parents may be today's single most significant challenge to the media's role as gatekeepers of the public agenda and public debate and the single most important check on government power. Yet they seem to have abdicated this role. We have all witnessed the sad spectacle of mothers or fathers on daytime television, recounting the stories of their divorce or some other experience by which their children were removed and reduced to demeaning defenses of themselves, pathetically insisting they have been "good" and "involved" parents and laying out details of their private lives as evidence of their claim. We yearn to hear them declare that their parenting is none of the government's business—and for that matter none of the media's or the public's business either. The heart of our malaise over not only the family, but perhaps much of today's politics, may not be this or that government policy so much as the fact that not enough parents are willing to stand up and make this declaration.

The irresponsibility of the media is widely perceived today across the political spectrum and agreed upon by people who do not agree on what precisely is irresponsible about it. This results in frustrated and counterproductive demands that the media be regulated by government. Yet if our aim is to return the media to its essential role as watchdog of the government and wean it of its soap opera voyeurism into our private lives, this end might be more effectively achieved without the abridgement of press freedom by parents standing upon their own authority and ejecting the media from their homes.

The ubiquitous accomplices, the hired muscle in the tyranny of the media and public opinion, are the "experts." While advice may be welcome, parenting is not a skill that can be scientifically imparted, like engineering or computer programming. "No child can be raised 'by the book,'" writes Jennifer Roback Morse, "despite what some child-development experts might lead us to believe."[924] The high priests of scientific child-rearing have not only perpetrated their deception through books; they now wield state power and impose their unproven theories on parents by force of law and, for parents who resist, at gunpoint. "It shouldn't surprise anyone who has raised a child . . . that in spite of millions of words, common sense is still the best teacher," a survey of modern child-rearing manuals concludes, "and most common sense, emerges during a parent's on-the-job training. Many experts rely on common sense, too, though they are loath to admit it because no one would buy their books if they did."[925] Parenting is a complex and evolving experience, involving the interaction of countless factors, including changing personalities and relationships and emotions: not only love but trust, loyalty, morality, experience, authority, and more—all of which are unique in every family and between any two members of a family. There is no such thing as a "best" parent apart from these considerations, and no outsider can observe and evaluate these things without changing them in the process. This is precisely why, for centuries, we have left parents to speak for and make decisions about their own children without government interference.

Accepting this principle for parenthood may also help restore our civic life, for it also applies to citizenship. If we accept the assumption that there is one "best" president and a "best" Congress, separate from the present demands of a complex society, we could simply turn the difficult choices of self-government over to the experts of the American Political Science Association and be done with it. We do not allow this with our democracy, and we must not allow it with our children.

It is perhaps a legacy of the Enlightenment that today both liberals and conservatives seem to worship at the altar of the meritocracy. But when it comes to imperfect people, in the long run merit is less important than accountability. Democracy can survive temporary rule by the mediocre and incompetent (surely that, of all things, has been empirically proven), and children can survive being raised by parents that some of us may view as less than perfect. What neither children nor democracy can survive is being ruled by the unaccountable. Destroying the institutions of accountability in pursuit of the ideal commonwealth or the perfectly raised children, and we destroy the good in pursuit of the perfect.

And when it comes to legal accountability, as we see from the punitive measures now adopted by governments, this is true mostly for fathers. Whether we wish to admit it or not, it is mostly men that are held responsible. For all the demonizing of men by divorce practitioners, and for all the hatred of the "patriarchy" by the feminists, these groups—like some conservatives— pay fathers a tribute they refuse to pay women: They hold the fathers responsible. Some states are now enacting laws that permit mothers to legally abandon their infants, on the rationale that so many are doing it anyway. No such provision extends to fathers. Some fathers' rights groups complain this is unfair. But allowing fathers to dispose of their children the way mothers can, while perhaps more "fair," is not going to rescue the family or the children. Even now we can see that it is very likely more men who will have to sacrifice their lives before the divorce regime is brought under control.

Yet as the authoritarian noose of the divorce regime tightens, non-custodial mothers face similar repression as fathers. Fox News recently broadcast a story on "deadbeat moms," demonstrating the network's concept of balance is that credulously demonizing mothers on the word of the government apparently makes it acceptable to demonize fathers. But Fox apparently still will not entertain the possibility that the government might be wrong.

We may find that in the end, it is parents—and perhaps above all fathers— who must rescue their children from exploitation by the divorce regime. For all the effort to "restore fatherhood" through government programs, ultimately the only ones who can restore fatherhood are fathers themselves. When we understand the political dimension of the family crisis, fathers become, almost by definition, the only ones who can truly "save the children" by re-creating the family with themselves in it.

Yet fathers' groups have received hostility from liberals and a mixed reception from conservatives. Some perceive it as one more special interest group, clamoring for rights which become special protections enforced by the government: what Allan Carlson has described as "abstract or imaginary 'rights' that are divorced from a sense of duty and from the authentic human affections toward kin and neighbors."[926]

Yet Carlson's wording describes precisely what the voices of fathers need not be. In fact, they may be the only political group today whose aims are not "divorced from authentic affections toward kin," however awkwardly they express it at times. As such, they may hold the key to redeeming not only families but a political culture that for forty years has been sinking into the mire of permanent rebellion. Indeed, their current plight indicates how the divorce "revolution" has brought us all to a brave new quasi-Freudian world where not only traditional authorities and institutions are attacked and brought low, but so now are private individuals, simply because they hold the most basic position of human authority, the head of a family. Through fathers we can hope to restore a civic culture that originates from the family upwards. And so they may be the ones to lead us in restoring our freedom and constitutional government as well. Imagine founding fathers once again.

ARE MARRIAGE CONTRACTS FRAUDULENT?

The increase in the number and power of officials charged with overseeing and administering children is the silent revolution of the last century. Their present assault on fathers and assumption of control over families did not arise out of nowhere. Though the immediate origins may be traced to the rise of family courts, no-fault divorce, and organized feminism, it may also be seen as the culmination of trends that have developed over many decades. For more than a century we have been gradually "institutionalizing childhood," as one scholar puts it, resulting in what another calls the "bureaucratization of children's lives."[927]

Most of the governmental divorce machinery was originally created and justified as ancillary to the welfare system, which decimated the urban black family by driving fathers from the homes of poor children with a logic similar to that by which family courts are now driving out the fathers of the middle class. Many of those fathers and children ended up incarcerated in our newly burgeoning prison and juvenile detention system, whose dramatic growth directly coincided with the rise of the welfare state; today, the prison system continues its exponential expansion alongside the divorce revolution and the government's campaign against fathers. Divorce and family courts also have their antecedents in juvenile courts, which were originally created to deal with crime. Like most measures institutionalizing family relationships, special treatment for children in the criminal justice system was promoted as a reform that would afford greater humanity to minor defendants. In retrospect, it was a major step in blurring the distinction between criminal justice and psychotherapy[928] and in opening the way for the criminalization of family conflict.

In this connection, it is no accident that, along with the criminalization of fathers, we now see more and more instances of the criminalization of children, especially boys. This is not only because some are committing more serious crimes at younger ages, but also because of the expanding number of acts (many of them semi-sexual) for which children may be prosecuted. The juvenile justice apparatus also arose alongside the psychotherapeutic professions and the psychotherapeutic state. As we have seen, these practitioners continue to maintain a highly influential presence in family court proceedings, where they have the backing of the state, including the power to institutionalize and incarcerate without due process of law both parents and children they claim are in need of their "services."

The institutionalization of children and child-rearing can also been seen in the expansion of government and private day care, federally funded foster care, and the proliferation of organized activities for children in ever-younger age groups.[929] Most of these developments are driven by the state, and they are all greatly accelerated by the removal of fathers from the home.

The linchpin in this expansion of government power over private life and politicization of children has been the judiciary, whose own politicization is likewise a phenomenon that accelerated throughout the twentieth century. Several generations of Americans have now come of age habituated to seeing judges as knights in shining armor, riding in to rescue oppressed minorities when politicians lacked the will or the courage. Yet ironically, the judiciary today has become so politicized that it is itself now widely perceived as the chief violator of the rights it once protected.[930]

Conclusion

It is likely within the next few years that America will face an unprecedented constitutional crisis, as a bureaucratic judiciary aggrandizes to itself ever more powers in contempt of common citizens and as pressure increases on elected officials to impose some limit. Indeed, part of the argument of this book is that this crisis has already manifested itself less in the visible and exalted circles of high judicial politics (where its most eminent critics still insist upon finding it) than in the humble realm of family court (where it drastically alters the daily and personal lives of millions of citizens).

As with some erstwhile defenders of the family, most critics of the judiciary have ignored this. They charge the courts with being an insulated and undemocratic elite, issuing edicts from on high in contempt of the wishes of ordinary citizens who must live with the consequences of judicial self-righteousness. Yet the critics themselves also may have become somewhat insulated from the concerns of ordinary people. Pretend as we might, relatively few citizens are likely to lose sleep over rulings on affirmative action, school prayer, or even abortion, compared with those who must deal with courts that have taken away their children. The most eminent exception to this omission is Phyllis Schlafly, who has eloquently set the tyranny of family courts in the larger context of judicial aggrandizement.[931]

As the courts increasingly avail themselves of their power to scrutinize democratic decisions for consistency with the Constitution, it is worth remembering that they are not the only branch of government granted that authority. Our elected officials at all levels, both legislative and executive, are also obligated by a no less constitutional oath, to protect and defend (and therefore to interpret) the Constitution. Moreover, the separation of powers does not leave the political branches defenseless. The judiciary is still the "least dangerous" branch, in Alexander Hamilton's phrase, because it must depend upon the executive branch to enforce its decisions and the legislative to finance that enforcement. While the executive backs up its authority with the "power of the sword," and the legislative wields a similar sanction in the "power of the purse," the judiciary commands no comparable physical leverage. Its sole authority is the respect in which it is held, and that respect is wearing thin. If the judiciary can refuse to apply laws and validate acts it deems inconsistent with the Constitution, nothing requires elected officials to enforce judicial decisions they deem to be in similar violation.

Can we therefore allow elected officials to interpret the Constitution and refuse to enforce court decisions they regard as constitutionally unsound? Certainly, there are dangers in this course. Yet at some point we must insist they do so. For while the judiciary has at times done an admirable job of protecting our liberties from encroachment by others, no mechanism protects freedom from encroachment by the judiciary itself except the other two branches. That is precisely what checks and balances is all about. And there could hardly be a more appropriate place to begin than with the orders of courts that are so invasive and so clearly contrary to the Constitution that the courts themselves openly acknowledge the fact.

Yet our elected officials have shown little inclination to fulfill the oath our Constitution requires of them for its own preservation. And when it comes to the divorce courts, their diffidence often extends to protecting and assisting the unconstitutional and intrusive practices of the judiciary. It is hardly surprising that the same authorities that have the power to rip apart families can also rip up the Bill of Rights and other protections. As Douglass observed, tyranny cannot forever remain isolated and contained within one sector of society but must inevitably fester and spread and poison all government.

In this instance, however, there is something grimly appropriate and almost diabolically sacramental about the violation of one oath leading to the violation of others. The divorce industry, after all, is a governmental regime founded upon the betrayal of an intimate trust, and its existence requires the widespread violation of what most people still hold to be the most sacred trust or at least the most solemn promise one makes in life. It is no accident that public officials whose livelihoods depend upon encouraging citizens to betray their private trust will have little hesitation in betraying the trust conferred upon them by the public. This is all the more likely when the public itself, who in a democracy must hold officials accountable, is increasingly comprised of citizens whose private and marital morals the government has had a hand in corrupting. One need not believe in the entanglement of church and state to recognize that a society that fails to enforce its contracts or otherwise value one's word is a society that will lack the moral authority to hold anyone—including public leaders—to their promises. And that is a society which can only function by substituting ever-greater applications of police power.

Maggie Gallagher's observation that marriage has become "the only contract where the law now sides with the party who wants to violate it" raises the question of how far we are willing to allow our government to be an active party to deceit and faithless dealing.[932] No more consequential example exists today of the link, so beloved of conservatives (and now so ignored by them), between personal morality and public ethics—between the fidelity of private individuals and the faithfulness of public servants—or the connection of both with the civilized order.

Our present divorce system is not only unjust but fundamentally dishonest. For all the talk of a "divorce culture," it is not clear that most people today enter the marriage contract with the intention of breaking it. "If the marital vows were changed to ' . . . until I grow tired of you,' or ' . . . for a period of five years unless I decide otherwise,' and the state were willing to sanction such an agreement, then divorce would not be such a significant event from a moral point of view," attorney Steven Varnis writes. "But there is no evidence that the content of marital vows or marital expectations at the time of marriage has changed."[933] Varnis may be only half right, but even so, the point is that the marriage contract has become not simply unenforceable, as Gallagher describes it, but fraudulent. Until it is made enforceable, it is pointless and even irresponsible to preach at young people to entrust it with their lives and the lives of their unborn children.

It may be arguable that government should not enforce the marriage contract, or any contracts for that matter (though the Constitution holds otherwise). I am not aware of anyone who suggests the government should be forcibly abrogating contracts, let alone luring citizens into contracts that it then tears up. If we truly believe our present divorce policy is appropriate, we should at least have the honesty to tell young people up front that marriage provides them with no protection against government seizure of their children and everything else they have. Let us inform them at the time of their marriage that even if they remain faithful to their vows, they can lose their children, their home, their savings and future earnings, their freedom, and even their lives. Not only will the government afford them no protection; it will prosecute them as criminals, though without the due process of law afforded to formally accused criminals. And let us then see how many young people—let us be honest, young men—are willing to start families.

To do otherwise is a clear prescription for precisely what this book has described: the transformation of free government into a criminal regime. "Governments operating protection rackets are nothing new," observes Thomas Sowell.[934] It is one thing to tolerate divorce. It is another altogether to hijack the criminal justice machinery to forcibly separate children from their parents. In a free society, courts exist to dispense justice. When courts stop dispensing justice, they will start dispensing injustice; there really is no middle ground. Without justice, asked St. Augustine, "what are kingdoms but great robberies?"

RECOMMENDATIONS

The traditional mechanisms for reinforcing families and sorting out marital difficulties were the extended family, the congregation, and the local community. In retrospect, it would seem to be the failure of these institutions to assert the moral authority they once exercised over couples that has led the state machinery to fill the vacuum with its coercive force. In the long run, there is no substitute for reinvigorating these social and cultural institutions alongside the family if that institution is to recover and retain its vitality.

Attempts to reinvigorate them are beyond the scope of this essay, but they are essential. The current trend toward ascribing social deterioration to the corruption of "culture" conveys an important truth. Provided it does not become a substitute for concrete legal and political reform, the movement to recapture our shared understanding of the cultural and civic importance of the family is imperative.

Reducing the divorce rate in the first place is of course the most desirable goal. Accordingly, some now endeavor to revive principles of pastoral counseling and the role of churches and other faith-based and local communities in supporting and preserving marriages. Initiatives such as Marriage Savers have demonstrated highly impressive results in rescuing individual marriages, substantially reducing local rates of divorce and cohabitation, and restoring the integrity of traditional marriage.[935] Given the poisonous legal environment within which these efforts must operate, with its active hostility to the family, the results they show are all the more startling. Some parents' groups are tempted to dismiss such campaigns, but they represent the politically invisible methods by which marriages and families were sustained in the days before large-scale meddling by state officials, which must again be available once the state machinery is reformed.

Concerning the efficacy of modern psychotherapeutic techniques (which are now often blended with traditional religious ones) in reinforcing marriage, these too are beyond the scope of this work and my expertise. While I have been highly critical of the psychotherapy industries, my criticisms are directed not at the substance of these fields but specifically at their *forensic* practitioners: those dependent on government largesse who have become highly mercenary to the government agenda.

Claims by government officials to assume the roles of pastoral counselor or family therapist must be treated with extreme caution. Government programs to promote marriage and "responsible fatherhood" have supported worthwhile projects. Yet they also come with other agendas, about which well-

Conclusion

intentioned authors of those projects themselves may not be aware. As we have seen, some such programs have even become tools of repressive federal law enforcement practices.[936] Some object that government should not be involved in private life at all and that compelling couples to undergo counseling, mediation, education, and similar therapeutic hurdles ostensibly designed to discourage divorce further infringes upon personal freedom and involves the government in private family life. As we saw in the first chapter, this concern is not groundless. In any case, government therapy is unnecessary, since the goal of restoring marriage and the family and giving children their fathers can be achieved far more effectively with less government intrusion by a combination of private initiatives and substantive legal reform.

Given the central role of law and government in actively invading private life and forcibly sundering family relationships, it is not sufficient to limit ourselves to restoring the culture of marriage and the personal relationships of individual couples. If we are to bring under control the abuses described in this book, legal and political reform is critical.

While parents are the first ones who must demand change, this too might involve the churches, which have a political as well as a pastoral role. The clergy should not involve itself in politics lightly, but in the United States and throughout the English-speaking world church leaders have readily mobilized against major social injustices such as slavery and abortion (injustices in which they themselves were not required to participate). Political action to defend marriage and family integrity may be even more appropriate for church leaders, because these institutions directly involve their own offices in consecrating marriages, which are being desecrated and nullified by state edict. A family is initially legitimized (usually) through marriage, which is witnessed by a congregation. These must not only be the marriage's first recourse in times of trouble but, in turn, its principal defenders against encroachment from the state. Marriage is the one occasion when churches still directly affect the daily lives of most people and the foremost one on which the churches are conspicuously failing them. There is no more critical challenge before the churches today, nor any greater opportunity to reverse the mass exodus, than to defend their own ordinances from demolition by the state.

Many reform proposals have been put forth in recent years. The most celebrated—moderate attempts to slow the divorce process through "covenant marriage" laws and extended mandatory waiting periods preceding divorce—while a step in the right direction, appear too weak to make more than a marginal difference.[937]

Truly substantial reforms have largely been blocked by the strident opposition of government-funded feminists, bar associations, and other divorce industry operatives—a confirmation that such measures are indeed likely to address the problem effectively. Three such reforms deserve extensive debate and implementation:

1. Reasonable limits on "no-fault" divorce when children are involved.
2. Shared parenting for children of divorce or separation.
3. Restoring and enforcing the traditional rights of parents to the care, custody, and companionship of their children.

Alongside these changes, two areas of government policy demand immediate attention:

- The precise purpose of child support must be publicly determined, and enforcement programs must be narrowly designed to serve only that purpose, observing due process of law.
- Both domestic violence and child abuse must be adjudicated as criminal assault, observing due process protections, and government funding for programs addressing these issues must be made contingent on such protections.

Before considering each, it is worth emphasizing that different parents, victimized by different mechanisms of the divorce machinery, will seek different forms of redress. The precise combination of these reforms is a matter on which reasonable people may disagree. What is critical is that we expand the public discussion of the family and initiate a major national dialogue on divorce and custody reform and on guaranteeing the parent-child bond. It is to provoke that dialogue that I offer these prescriptions.

LIMITING "NO-FAULT" DIVORCE

Reforming "no-fault" divorce laws to allow divorce *by mutual consent* (which is how these laws were originally advertised) but placing reasonable controls on unilateral and involuntary divorce is imperative *when children are involved.* "If a couple marries and divorces . . . before there are children, that is sad but not tragic," writes Michael McManus of Marriage Savers. "What's tragic is a divorce with children whose innocent lives will be scarred."[938]

Conclusion

Some object that forcing people to remain married violates their civil liberties, but no prominent voice seriously advocates prohibiting divorce to the extent of controlling anyone's personal associations. "The alternative to liberal or 'no-fault' divorce is not no divorce," writes Robert Whelan, "but divorce which is granted only . . . after due legal process to establish fault."[939] Requiring married partners to accept responsibility for abrogating an agreement into which they entered without compulsion is hardly an unreasonable restriction on liberty.

"The essential point of fault is to make sure that one is held accountable for misconduct and is not allowed to escape the consequences of his or her own acts," writes legal authority Harvey Golden. "Just as a criminal is held accountable for his behavior by our criminal justice system, and just as a tortfeasor is held responsible for his intentional or reckless or negligent deeds, so too should a seriously misbehaving spouse be required to bear the consequences of his or her acts in largely contributing to the breakup of the marriage."[940] This would seem all the more compelling in light of the constitutional clause requiring the enforcement of contracts and what many see as a public interest in maintaining stable families.

The obvious counter-argument—that imperfections can be found on both sides in any marital dispute—does not justify abandoning all standards for what constitutes legally recognized fault. Taking this logic to its conclusion would undermine the very principle of justice. "There is fault on both sides in every human relationship," Fred Hanson acknowledged when the new divorce laws were being drafted. "The faults, however, are far from equal. No secular society can be operated on the theory that all faults are equal." Hanson was the dissenting member of the National Conference of Commissioners of Uniform State Laws, which presented "no-fault" laws to the states. "To do justice between parties without regard to fault is an impossibility," he warned. "I wonder what's to become of the maxim that no man shall profit by his own wrong—or woman either, for that matter."[941] Today we have the answer to that question.

The tautology that marital conflict makes unrestricted divorce self-justifying is not necessarily valid. In 25 percent of marriage breakdowns, writes Margaret Brinig, the man has "no clue" there is a problem until the woman tells him she wants out.[942] A British study found that in more than half of divorce cases there was no recollection of major conflict before the separation. Divorce has become a political weapon, and its ready availability almost certainly produces more rather than less conflict. "The assumption that parental conflict will cease at divorce is not only invalid," writes Patricia Morgan, "divorce itself *instigates conflict* which continues into the post-divorce period."[943]

The simple assumption that divorce in itself indicates preexisting parental conflict that harms children is also seldom valid as far as children are concerned, as any child will testify. Judith Wallerstein and Sandra Blakeslee found that hardly any were pleased with the divorce, even when severe conflict existed in their families. "Children . . . can be quite content even when their parents' marriage is profoundly unhappy for one or both partners," they write. "Only one in ten children in our study experienced relief when their parents divorced. These were mostly older children in families where there had been open violence and where the children had lived with the fear that the violence would hurt a parent or themselves."[944]

Both socially and psychologically, divorce and separation almost always have a more detrimental effect on children than even high-conflict marriages, and the effects are exacerbated when one parent is removed or marginalized from the children's lives through sole custody. "For kids, the misery their parents may feel in an unhappy marriage is usually less significant than the changes [the children] have to go through after a divorce," says Neil Kalter, a University of Michigan psychologist. "They'd rather their parents keep fighting and not get divorced."[945] Several British surveys of children of divorce found that most children recalled a happy family life before the breakup.[946]

Yet reforming unilateral divorce and restricting it to cases of mutual consent will not in itself necessarily address the problem of children. As Chesterton once pointed out, limiting divorce may in practice mean no more than preventing remarriage. Even with fault divorce, a parent could still separate and live with the children and a new partner in permanent adultery. Moreover, judges have shown themselves ingenious when it comes to finding excuses to reward separation of spouses and children from their parents; judges could grant a fault divorce and then, invoking the "best interest" standard, grant custody to the guilty spouse. Reinstating fault grounds is part of a remedy, but without addressing child custody specifically, it is not sufficient.

SHARED PARENTING

By far the simplest and most modest solution—and the one that will ameliorate the problem of fatherless children in the short run because it is consistent with the no-fault nature of existing divorce law—is a rebuttable presumption of shared parenting (once known as "joint custody"), whereby divorced or unmarried parents divide time and authority over the children equally. Shared parenting de-escalates conflict by replacing adversarial litigation, with its winner-take-all mentality that inflames conflict and turns children into weapons, with a guarantee that both parents will have a meaningful role in the lives of their children.

Like no-fault reform, evidence suggests that such a measure would help reduce the problem in the first place by bringing the divorce rate itself under control. "If a parent is able to forecast that they have total ownership of the child post-divorce and almost all of the child's time, as usually happens in sole custody, there is little deterrent to divorce," according to John Guidubaldi of John Carroll and Kent State universities.[947] We have already seen that the parent who anticipates gaining custody is the one most likely to file for divorce. That study's authors also suggest that shared parenting would result in fewer divorces.[948]

Divorce rates appear to decline in states where courts retain custody of children to both parents, since that reduces the potential to use the children as weapons. Guidubaldi and Richard Kuhn found that states with higher levels of shared parenting awards "have shown significantly greater declines in divorces in the following years . . . compared with other states." Overall divorce rates declined nearly four times faster in high shared-parenting states compared with states where shared parenting is relatively rare. A significant factor is that shared parenting "removes the capacity for one spouse to hurt the other by denying participation in raising the children."[949]

There is also evidence that it is better for children. All "studies" purporting to quantify children's psychological conditions in terms of their "adjustment" and "self-esteem" should be treated with caution. Nevertheless, as Robert Bauserman reports in a survey of scholarly research, children in shared-parenting arrangements are consistently found to have fewer behavioral and emotional problems and better family relationships than those in sole-custody situations:

> Children in joint physical or legal custody were better adjusted than children in sole-custody settings, but no different from those in intact families. More positive adjustment of joint-custody children held for separate comparisons of general adjustment, family relationships, self-esteem, emotional and behavioral adjustment, and divorce-specific adjustment. Joint-custody parents reported less current and past conflict than did sole-custody parents. . . . The results are consistent with the hypothesis that joint custody can be

advantageous for children in some cases, possibly by facilitating ongoing positive involvement with both parents.[950]

Such findings could be multiplied almost indefinitely:

- "Single custody subjects evidenced greater self-hate and perceived more rejection from their fathers than joint physical custody subjects. . . . Higher father-child contact was associated with better adjustment, lower self-hate, and lower perceived rejection from father; lower father-child contact was associated with poorer adjustment, higher self-hate, and higher perceived rejection from father."[951]
- "Children in joint custody families had fewer behavioral adjustment problems with externalizing behavior than children in mother custody families."[952]
- "Children from intact families reflected the most positive father relationships, followed by children in joint custody, with children in single custody scoring considerably lower than the other two groups."[953]

But the case for allowing legally innocent parents to keep their children, and children to keep their parents, does not rest on measurements of children's psychological conditions following divorce imposed upon them and one of their parents. No burden of proof should be required to show that children "fare" or "adjust" well to being allowed to remain with their parents. The burden of proof should be on those who claim that children are better served by removing them from their parents, a test that has never been remotely met. "Even those researchers who currently oppose joint custody do not argue that sole custody leads to better adjustment of the children (one can find little evidence for that proposition)," one scholar points out. "[They] merely argue that children in sole custody do not do any *worse* than children in joint custody."[954]

Like divorce reform, custody reform provokes vehement opposition from divorce operatives, whose arguments appear designed to protect the interests not of children but of grownups. Indeed, the strident defense of existing practice proceeds from a dialectic that ironically combines sexual liberation with tyrannical government power, a combination succinctly expressed by Jo Ann Schulman of the National Center on Women and Family Law: "Forced joint custody, like forced sterilization and forced pregnancy, is a denial of women's right to control their lives."[955] And to control the lives of others. This is a peculiar argument, given that Ms. Schulman has little to say about forced divorce or forced separation from one's children or one's parent, or how much control a parent has over his life when his movements are controlled by government order or when he is incarcerated without trial. "When one parent says, 'Let's share custody' and the other parent says, 'No, I want sole custody,' which one is demanding to be in control?" asks attorney Ronald Henry. "Who's trying to exercise power? . . . Who is it that wants to be the one who's dominant?"[956]

The very fact that the divorce industry opposes it so aggressively indicates that shared parenting offers hope to involuntarily divorced parents and their children. "My experience with presumptive joint custody as a domestic relations lawyer in Louisiana was almost uniformly negative," says National Organization for Women President Kim Gandy, who seems to embody the alliance. It is not surprising that "as a domestic relations lawyer" Ms. Gandy should have had this response. She lists NOW's political allies in their campaign against shared parenting: "the bar association, child psychologists, social workers, family law experts, judges, lawyers"—the very people who profit from unilateral divorce and fatherless children.[957] A shared parenting proposal in the Kentucky legislature prompted a similarly revealing admission from Jo Ann Wise of the Kentucky Bar Association's family law committee: "Judges and lawyers alike, the people who do this for a living, were opposed."[958] The opinions of divorce profiteers evidently trump those of the children's parents.

As we have seen, domestic violence and child abuse are the other bugbears invoked by feminists and divorce lawyers to oppose divorce and custody reform. NOW asserts that joint custody "is dangerous for women and their children who are trying to leave or have left violent husbands/fathers," without saying why. Violent spouses can be prosecuted under assault laws and are precluded from custody under shared-parenting provisions. Using custody law to punish alleged criminal assault is as illogical as it appears. Yet so pervasive is anti-father propaganda now that feminist organizations regularly use the terms *batterer* and *pedophile* as synonyms for *father*. "Policies that make divorce more difficult, can be dangerous and even deadly for battered women," asserts Family Violence Prevention Fund Executive Director Esta Soler, also without explaining why.[958]

As we have also seen, these groups have very fluid definitions of words like *battered* and *violence*. A 1996 NOW resolution asserts that fathers' groups which challenge current custody practices are "using the abuse of power in order to control in the same fashion as do batterers."[959] Feminists claim that "false accusations by women are in fact rare"[960] (and oppose penalties for making them). But their own political agenda indicates otherwise. By using unproven abuse allegations against men to secure automatic child custody for women, feminists are openly practicing in the political arena precisely what they claim is not happening in the courts: unfounded accusations of "battering" to separate children from fathers who are guilty of no such thing.

Similarly revealing are the self-justifying arguments feminists invoke to rationalize sole mother custody, saying "joint custody works best when both parents want it and agree to work together," but it "is unworkable for uncooperative parents."[962] This tautological reasoning simply extends platitudes invoked as self-justification for unilateral divorce. After all, if an intact family or shared parenting require "agreement" and "cooperation" between parents, the most effective method for the parent who expects sole custody to sabotage either is to be as disagreeable and uncooperative as possible.

"It is . . . possible for a mother who wishes to exclude a father from a significant co-parenting role to create a conflictual situation in a variety of ways . . . and end up with sole custody of her children," writes family scholar Michael Friedman. The circular logic becomes palpable in light of the fact that almost all divorce-related conflict is precisely over the children: "At the center of most post-divorce conflicts involving children is the issue of custody/access." To make conflict over custody and access grounds for denying custody and access is obviously to reward the parent that creates conflict by trying to impede the other's custody and access. "Power inequality is a very important context of post-divorce conflict," writes Friedman. "Disregarding the power inequality that often prevails in custody arrangements can obscure the fact that one parent is often fighting for more equitable access which the other parent is blocking."[963]

It is a platitude of divorce literature that parents should cooperate for their children's welfare, but cooperating for the children's good is different from cooperating in their confiscation. No parent can be expected to cooperate willingly in the removal of his or her children. To arbitrarily take away someone's children, and then rationalize that action because the parent objects or refuses to "cooperate" with the stealing of his or her children, is logic from the pages of Kafka. Yet this is precisely what the courts do.

As with domestic violence and child abuse, the kind of marital conflict feminists claim justifies not only unilateral divorce but also single-parent custody is much more likely to be the result than the cause of these actions. The very act of excluding a parent from his or her child is itself an act of "conflict" and will naturally create conflict in the excluded parent. "Those of us serving as mediators, evaluators, and special masters have noted a fair number of cases in which one parent is more angry and clearly more responsible for creating conflictual situations to which the other must respond," writes one practitioner. "In such cases, it is perhaps unfair to reflexively label the couple as in high conflict, rather than focus on the 'troublemaker.'"[964]

The entire point of arrangements such as marriage and shared parenting is that they require parents to cooperate and compromise (and to set an example of such for children); allowing one parent to simply exclude the other removes any constraint on that parent to moderate his or her behavior. In fact, shared parenting repeatedly has been demonstrated to reduce parental conflict for precisely this reason. Judith Seltzer has concluded that joint custody, even when imposed over the objection of one parent, reduces post-divorce conflict.[965]

Another study team found that "joint legal custody had considerable benefits for children, increasing their paternal visitation and enhancing their well-being." The team also found that "both child-support compliance and paternal visitation were highest in those cases where joint custody was awarded against the mothers' wishes but in conformity with the fathers' wishes." The authors concluded that these results demonstrate "the value of joint legal custody even when the couple does not initially agree to it. Joint custody appears to enhance paternal involvement, child-support compliance, and child adjustment."[966]

GUARANTEEING PARENTAL RIGHTS

Taking this logic a step further, some comprehensive combination of divorce and custody reform could help return us to the long-established legal principle (still largely honored elsewhere in the law) that legal innocence is sufficient justification for simply being left alone by the government—and in this case, left alone *with one's children*. As a rule governing when children may be taken away from their parents, we must replace the vague, subjective, and permissive "best interest of the child" criterion with a more precise policy explicitly and categorically stipulating what constitutional case law over many decades has asserted: that no child may ever be forcibly separated from a parent or have their relationship with their parent interfered with without legally recognized grounds of civil[967] or criminal wrongdoing or, at a minimum, without agreement by that parent to a divorce or separation.

Granting that divorce is a legal right, it need not necessarily follow that that right entails protection from all its consequences or the power to shift the liabilities and costs onto an innocent or involuntarily divorced parent. Neither must the right to divorce necessarily extend to abrogating the right of legally innocent citizens to be left in peace in their own homes with their own children. Still less does it necessarily confer the right to marshal the courts, police, and prisons to criminalize parents who do not willingly cooperate. Going further, there is nothing authoritarian about requiring parents who choose to desert marriages they freely entered or who commit recognized marital faults such as adultery to accept the costs of that decision, including the presumption that the departing or guilty parent has put his or her own wishes before the needs of children and is therefore less fit and responsible than the parent who remains faithful to the family. On the contrary, it is the current practice of ignoring justice and allowing that burden to be imposed on the parent who remains faithful that has produced dangerous intrusions into private life.

Such a policy would mean that "custody" (with its authoritarian connotations) would not be actively awarded to anyone but simply passively left to remain with the innocent parent of either gender. "If . . . the interests of the children are paramount," asks Melanie Phillips, "why shouldn't the behaviour of the parents be one of the factors taken into consideration when custody is awarded?"[968] That this is consistent with most people's understanding of basic justice is evident when it arises from quarters not normally involved in divorce and custody discussions. "There's really not much we can do about people—male or female—who will selfishly turn their spouse and children's lives upside down by ripping apart a family without even offering a coherent reason," observes Tim O'Brien of the Michigan Libertarian Party. Yet we could greatly reduce the consequences, "by simply amending our no-fault divorce law to give the (rebuttable) presumption of custody of any minor children to the defendant [who is innocent or does not wish to divorce], regardless of gender." O'Brien elaborates on what must seem unexceptionable to the uninitiated:

It is, after all, reasonable to presume that "the best interests of the child" will be better served by remaining with the parent who does not abandon commitments for frivolous reasons and wants to maintain the family. The spouse/parent who still wishes to leave may, of course, do so—with his or her clothes and any other personal belongings. The more dedicated, responsible party should keep the children, home, property, and claim on future child support.

"The immediate effect of such a change would undoubtedly be a plummeting divorce rate, reducing the necessity for child-support orders," O'Brien adds. "The difficulties of collecting in the few remaining cases would be significantly reduced since the only parents who would incur such obligations are those who have voluntarily taken them on in exchange for being released from the marriage contract."[969]

As O'Brien indicates, custody reform will obviate the need for most government-coerced child support. The precise purpose of child support has never been made clear or publicly debated. Most people assume that coerced child support is for parents who have abandoned their children or at least agreed voluntarily to live apart from them. It was certainly never intended to subsidize the forced removal of children from loving, innocent parents or to force parents to pay for the stealing of their own children. The precise purpose of forced expropriations under the name of "child support" must be publicly debated and determined, and enforcement programs must be narrowly designed and restructured to serve only that purpose.

Divorce practitioners now invariably resist all these substantive reforms with the same refrain: that they "may" trap women (but not men, apparently) in "bad marriages" with "abusive" spouses. In the case of physical violence, this is clearly not true, since physically violent abuse has long been recognized as legitimate grounds for divorce. In fact, very few marriages, "good" or "bad," are characterized by violence at all. According to one study, "86 percent of unhappily married adults reported no violence in their relationship (including 77 percent of unhappy spouses who later divorced or separated)."[970]

As for "bad" marriages, this is a meaningless phrase. A marriage is what two people make it. "The question is whether ordinary women married to ordinary men should make the effort so sustain their marriages," writes Jennifer Roback Morse. "Any one of us can unilaterally create a high-conflict marriage by starting quarrels or overreacting to perceived slights. We can easily deceive ourselves that we are entitled to a divorce because of the very conflict that we created ourselves."[971] No one in the Western democracies today is forced to marry and make the lifetime commitment it entails. If we do not have the courage to stand up to hysteria of those who lobby for protecting and institutionalizing faithless behavior, then our professed concern for children is mere posturing.

Still, it must be recognized that one likely consequence of any effective reform will be an increase in the already exploding number of fabricated spousal and child abuse accusations made during divorce proceedings. The solution is to demand from the criminal justice system a clear distinction between behavior that is criminal and behavior that is private. One of the nation's leading authorities on child abuse recommends that it be categorically adjudicated as criminal assault—not only to protect children more effectively, but also to ensure that accused parents receive due process of law and those not formally charged can be left in peace with their children until evidence of criminality is presented against them.[972] This would also make possible what should not require saying: that knowingly false accusations themselves be prosecuted as criminal offenses.

Similarly, adjudicating domestic violence as violent assault like any other, including criminal standards of evidence, would at once protect the victimized, the accused, and the integrity of our justice system. "The criminal prosecution of those family members who are alleged to direct violence toward any other member of the family would be more effective in holding accountable both the perpetrators of violence and those who falsely allege abuse than at present, particularly in those cases where allegations of abuse are dealt with exclusively within the family court arena," writes social work professor Edward Kruk. "The use of family courts as 'quasi-criminal courts' that do not have the resources to apply due process when abuse allegations are made," is what endangers both civil liberties and families.[973]

Such reforms are not likely so long as the federal government pays states to violate constitutional protections. Given that gender-neutral laws already prohibit violent assault in every jurisdiction, the precise purpose of federal programs to protect only named groups is not clear. Such funding must be made contingent on observance of constitutional provisions or curtailed.

Theoretically, new laws should not be necessary to protect the rights of parents and children. Enforcing existing civil rights and civil liberties—including the Bill of Rights and the substantial body of federal and state case law recognizing parenthood as a fundamental constitutional right—should be sufficient to protect the rights of citizens to their children, property, and freedom. Enforcing existing protections could also offer a more effective and safer method of preserving family integrity than extensive "social engineering" in the form of yet more changes in laws governing marriage and custody. An advantage in defending existing parental rights through litigation rather than legislation is that such rights would be retroactively applicable to millions of parents who are already separated from their children and living in criminal or semi-criminal status.

Unfortunately, the branch of government charged with enforcing constitutional protections—the judiciary—not only refuses to do so in the realm of family law but has itself become their principal violator. The argument of this book is that this refusal proceeds from deeply entrenched conflicts of interest that are not likely to correct themselves. Past civil rights violations on such a massive scale have been rectified only through the mobilization of all three branches of the federal government, with the federal judiciary often taking the lead.

Conclusion

Many are understandably reluctant to encourage federal involvement in domestic relations law, which is traditionally the province of states. This is all the more reason to address the problem as one of constitutional rights rather than family policy. The two principal mechanisms for criminalizing parents—child-support enforcement and domestic violence law—are now both effectively federalized, with no corresponding federal protection for the accused. The two political branches of the federal government are both deeply involved in domestic relations through child-support and domestic-violence funding, plus more recent fatherhood and marriage promotion programs, with the result of huge and growing federal bureaucracies. (And this leaves aside the enormous and connected issue of federal welfare programs, both driven by and driving family dissolution.)

Guaranteeing the right of parents and their children not to be forcibly separated without cause in the first place carries few financial costs and could reduce the need for expensive and invasive federal programs that thrive on family destruction by addressing its symptoms rather than its cause. These rights are unlikely to be protected by the same state court systems that are violating them. Even the federal judiciary itself, whose increasing involvement in child-support and domestic violence cases contributes to its "activist" proclivities, might be more likely to return to first principles and regain its rightful place as defender of the Constitution were it to face squarely the constitutional implications of forcibly removing children from legally innocent parents. For this to happen, the arbitrary and indefensible "domestic relations exception" and all other barriers to due process in family law must be declared invalid and federal courts must actively scrutinize family law cases, as they would any other, for violations of human and constitutional rights.

Yet recognizing that the willingness of the federal judiciary to review practices of lower courts (where federal judges often begin their careers) is far from dependable, the legislative and executive branches of government at both the state and federal levels may be more willing to exercise leadership. These policy changes could be effected by legislation at the state level, since that is usually considered the proper jurisdiction for family law. A number of states have already been debating statutes or constitutional measures that would guarantee the rights of parents to supervise the upbringing of their children without government interference. This must become a national debate, and federal measures too could reinforce recognized rights without necessarily establishing new ones.

Several years ago, Congress began to do something like this. The Parental Rights and Responsibilities Act of 1995 declared that parents' rights to direct the upbringing of their children are fundamental rights which the government can curtail only under conditions of "compelling interest." It stipulated that "No Federal, State, or local government, or any official of such a government acting under color of law, shall interfere with or usurp the right of a parent to direct the upbringing of the child of the parent."[974]

Fatally, the proposed law exempted parents who lose their children through involuntary divorce. In other words, it stipulated that the government could not interfere with your children unless your spouse asked it to through divorce, in which case the government could seize them with no further explanation. A substantial constituency that could have been mobilized to support this measure was thus excluded from its protections. A more vigorous law, one encompassing all parents, including "non-custodial" ones, could mobilize a powerful coalition of parents.

For those who question whether Congress possesses this authority, a stronger alternative exists, one to which some advocates for marriage are already resorting. If the U.S. Constitution needs an amendment today to protect family integrity from pressures that could not have been foreseen two centuries ago, the most direct and comprehensive approach would be an amendment guaranteeing the privacy and inviolability of the family and codifying traditional rights of parents to the care and custody of their children and to direct their upbringing free from arbitrary state interference.

From homeschoolers, to victims of false child abuse accusations, to parents whose children are put on psychotropic drugs without their consent, to divorced fathers and mothers, it is parents who are being besieged by an increasingly repressive state apparatus and denied basic due process protections. Such an amendment would also reinforce the marriage bond in the most critical cases—those involving children—without the allegedly intolerant or exclusionary implications of amendments that have been proposed to limit same-sex marriage, and it would do so much more effectively.

Finally, given the proclivity of the judiciary to interpret legislative language into meanings far removed from the legislative intent, stronger measures may be appropriate. Government officials who knowingly violate the constitutional rights of American citizens by seizing their children without cause are committing criminal acts. Congress and state legislatures or federal and state inspectors general should launch formal investigations of family courts and their bureaucratic accessories with a view to identifying, curtailing, and prosecuting widespread and serious violations of the basic civil rights of American parents now being perpetrated under color of law.

NOTES

Introduction: The Crisis of Fatherhood and Marriage

1. Daniel Patrick Moynihan, *The Negro Family: the Case for National Action* (Washington: United States Department of Labor, March 1965).

2. Wade Horn and Tom Sylvester, *Fathers Facts* (Gaithersburg: National Fatherhood Initiative, 2002), pp. 15, 26.

3. Patricia Morgan, *Farewell to the Family* (London: Institute of Economic Affairs, 1999), pp. 189-190.

4. Attempts to attribute these behaviors to poverty or racial discrimination have been refuted by studies that control for these variables. See Urie Bronfenbrenner, "Discovering What Families Do," in David Blankenhorn, *et al.* (eds.), *Rebuilding the Nest: A New Commitment to the American Family* (Milwaukee: Family Service America, 1990), p. 34; Ronald Angel and Jacqueline Angel, *Painful Inheritance: Health and the New Generation of Fatherless Children* (Madison: University of Wisconsin Press, 1993), p. 188. Even left-wing scholars concur: Norman Dennis and George Erdos, *Families Without Fatherhood* (London: Civitas, 2000).

5. Horn and Sylvester, *Father Facts*, p. 15.

6. Elaine Ciulla Kamarck and William Galston, *Putting Children First* (Washington: Progressive Policy Institute, 1990), p. 14.

7. Clinton is quoted in Horn and Sylvester, *Fathers Facts*, p. 17; Gore is quoted in Jeffery Leving, *Fathers' Rights* (New York: Basic Books, 1997), p. 47; "President Bush Speaks at the Fourth National Summit on Fatherhood," White House press release 7 June 2001.

8. David Blankenhorn, *Fatherless America* (New York: Basic Books, 1995), p. 1; Louise Silverstein and Carl Auerbach, "Deconstructing the Essential Father," *American Psychologist* (June 1999).

9. Stephen Baskerville, "The Real Danger of Same-Sex Marriage," *The Family in America*, vol. 20, no. 5-6 (May-June 2006).

10. *Why Marriage Matters* (New York: Institute for American Values, 2005), p. 32.

11. *Turning the Corner on Father Absence in Black America* (Atlanta: Morehouse Research Institute and Institute for American Values, 1999), p. 6.

Notes

12. Nomination acceptance speech at the Democratic National Convention in Madison Square Garden, New York City, 16 July 1992.

13. Blankenhorn, *Fatherless America*, pp. 1, 22-23. Blankenhorn produces no evidence for these statements.

14. David Popenoe, "Life Without Father," in Cynthia Daniels (ed.), *Lost Fathers* (New York: St. Martin's, 1998), p. 34.

15. John Tierney, "New Look at Realities of Divorce," *New York Times*, 11 July 2000. Tierney is nonetheless skeptical.

16. Daniels, *Lost Fathers*, introduction, p. 2; Robert Griswold, "The History and Politics of Fatherlessness," in *ibid.*, p. 19.

17. George Gilder, *Men and Marriage* (Gretna, Louisiana: Pelican Publishing Co., 1993), p. 53.

18. Danielle Crittenden, *What Our Mothers Didn't Tell Us* (New York: Simon and Schuster, 1999), p. 106.

19. Leon Kass, "The End of Courtship," *The Public Interest* (http://www.thepublicinterest.com; n.d.; accessed 26 March 2002).

20. Bryce Christensen, "The Strange Politics of Child Support," *Society*, vol. 39, no. 1 (November-December 2001), 63.

21. Nomination acceptance speech at the Democratic National Convention in Madison Square Garden, New York City, 16 July 1992.

22. Marguerite Roulet, "Child Support and the Media," Center on Fathers, Families, and Public Policy, 2003 (http://www.cffpp.org/publications/child_media.html).

23. See chapter 2.

24. Kathleen Parker, "Alabama Support Law Dogs Dads," *Orlando Sentinel*, 14 February 2001.

25. "Bipartisan Blather," *Washington Post*, 22 December 2000, p. A33.

26. There is also no evidence for the peculiar assumption among policymakers that receiving or not receiving child support has anything to do with deviant behavior by fatherless children. William S. Comanor and Llad Phillips, "Family Structure and Child Support: What Matters for Youth Delinquency Rates," in Comanor (ed.), *The Law and Economics of Child Support Payments* (Cheltenham: Edward Elgar, 2004).

27. "Why We Don't Marry," *City Journal*, Winter 2002.

28. "Happy Person Day, Dads," *Calgary Herald*, 17 June 2001.

29. *Bias: A CBS Insider Exposes How the Media Distort the News* (Washington: Regnery, 2001), p. 136.

30. *The War Against Parents* (Boston and New York: Houghton Mifflin, 1998), p. 173. Noting that many fathers have neither custody nor visitation rights, they add (p. 177), "It seems strange to call them by the pejorative term 'absent' when they have no right to be present."

31. "Dads are the last subculture in America whom it is permissible to bash and malign with impunity. . . . You can depict dads as stumbling, bumbling doofs all you want and receive not a single shred of flak for it. . . . Too often, family TV comedy is all about what dad did to screw up the day/night/event/situation. Fathers are mere dummies at the mercy of everyone, their children included." Wendy Touhy, "Sins of the Father," *The Age, The Green Guide* (television guide and commentary), 23 December 2004, p. 8.

32. Sanford L. Braver with Diane O'Connell, *Divorced Dads: Shattering the Myths* (New York: Tarcher/Putnam, 1998), p. 6. This book is "probably the most important work of conservative social science in a decade," though I am not sure there is anything specifically conservative about it. Robert Locke, "Deadbeat Social Scientists,"

FrontPageMagazine.com, 2 July 2001 (http://frontpagemag.com/columnists/locke/2001/locke06-29-01.htm).

33. "Women Who Banish Fathers Seen as Heroines," *Irish Times*, 6 October 1998.

34. Melanie Phillips, "The Rape Reform That Makes All Men Guilty," *Sunday Times*, 4 July 1999.

35. Susan Shell, "The Liberal Case Against Gay Marriage," *The Public Interest* 156 (Summer 2004), pp. 5-7.

36. Margaret Mead, *Male and Female: A Study of the Sexes in a Changing World* (New York: Dell, 1969), p. 198.

37. Dana Mack, *The Assault on Parenthood* (New York: Simon and Schuster, 1997); Hewlett and West, *War Against Parents*.

38. Anna Keller, "Parenting Post-Divorce: Problems, Concerns," in David Levy (ed.), *The Best Parent is Both Parents* (Norfolk: Hampton Roads Publishing, 1993), p. 56.

39. I will generally use the feminine gender to refer to custodial and the masculine for non-custodial parents, in keeping with the norm in roughly 85 percent to 90 percent of cases. There are significant instances where the genders are reversed, however.

40. Wayne Anderson, *The Custody Hoax* (Goodland, Kansas: Vindicator, 1992), p. 1.

41. Judy Parejko, *Stolen Vows: The Illusion of No-Fault Divorce and the Rise of the American Divorce Industry* (Collierville, Tennessee: InstantPublisher, 2002), p. 99.

42. *In Re Gault*, 387 U.S. 1, 27-28 (1967).

43. Robert Samuelson, "Hustling the System," *Washington Post*, 23 December 1992, p. A17; *Wall Street Journal* editorial, 24 June 1999; Walter Olson, "Lawyers, Gums, and Rummies: Why Do We Hate Attorneys," *Reason*, July 1999. The American Bar Association confirms that the public regards lawyers as "greedy, manipulative and corrupt." Mary Gallagher, "ABA Survey Finds Lawyers Among Lowest-Regarded U.S. Professions," *New Jersey Law Journal*, 7 May 2002.

44. John Caher, "Court Restructuring 'Long Overdue,' Official Tells Matrimonial Commission," *New York Law Journal*, 5 November 2004, p. 1.

45. One exception is Phyllis Schlafly, *The Supremacists* (Dallas: Spence, revised edn., 2006). Both Samuelson and Olsen, as well as Stuart Taylor, Robert Bork, Edwin Meese, Tod Gaziano, Bruce Fein, and other eminent legal critics, both liberal and conservative, have told me they were unaware of what takes place in family courts.

46. Helen Alvare, "Types and Styles of Family Proceedings," Report of the United States to the XII World Congress, International Association of Procedural Law, 2003, p. 1. Informal estimates by lawyers, judges, and litigants based on case dockets are more like 50 percent-60 percent.

47. Maureen Freely, "A Secret World of Suffering Children," *The Independent*, 18 October 2001.

48. *Liberty*, August 2002, letters to the editor, p. 4.

49. Barbara Dafoe Whitehead, *The Divorce Culture* (New York: Vintage, 1998), pp. 70-71.

50. John Stapleton, "'Problem' Parents Doing Time," *The Australian*, 8-9 April 2000, p. 26.

51. John Campion, *Marriage and Fatherhood: Important Information for Young Men* (Cheltenham: UKMM Publishing Group, 1997), p. v.

52. Richard Cohen has sympathetically termed this the "feminization of journalism." "What Powerful Men?" *Washington Post*, 12 July 2001, p. A27.

53. Online: http://crcw.princeton.edu/papers.html.

54. The Urban Institute, February 1995 (online: http://harbpress.com/files/NonCustPay.htm; accessed 6 July 2002).

55. Self-described "liberal" Irwin Garfinkel is candid about the source of his funding, the ideological slant of his scholarship, and even the biases proceeding from his personal life in the introduction to *Assuring Child Support* (New York: Russell Sage Foundation, 1992).

Chapter 1 / Judicial Kidnapping

56. Jed H. Abraham, *From Courtship to Courtroom: What Divorce Law Is Doing to Marriage* (New York: Bloch, 1999), pp. 49-52, where some of the points made here are described. See a typical account in Warren Farrell, *Father and Child Reunion* (New York: Tarcher/Putnam, 2001), p. 35 and *passim*.

57. Abraham, *From Courtship to Courtroom*, pp. 170-171.

58. *Ibid.*, p. 6.

59. *Ibid.*, pp. 4, 6; Karen Winner, *Divorced from Justice* (New York: ReganBooks, 1997), p. xx.

60. Abraham, *From Courtship to Courtroom*, p. 138.

61. Journalism has only begun to expose these abuses; see: Cathy Young, "The Sadness of the American Father," *American Spectator*, June 2000; Melanie Phillips, "The Rape of Justice," *Spectator*, 10 June 2000; Paul Craig Roberts, "Men the Greater Casualties," *Washington Times*, 3 September 2001.

62. Donald C. Hubin, "Parental Rights and Due Process," *Journal of Law and Family Studies*, vol. 1, no. 2 (1999), p. 136.

63. Justice Mary Southin of the British Columbia Court of Appeal: "The legislature. . . has decreed that fathers have no rights." Quoted in *The Province* (Vancouver), "Dad 'Feels Like Dirt': Father Has No Right to Give Own Sons His Surname," 24 May 2001. Canada's Justice Minister Martin Cauchon has stated that, "Parents have responsibilities, they don't have rights." Quoted in "Rights and Responsibilities," *Ottawa Citizen* editorial, 31 March 2003.

64. A similar assessment is quoted in Sanford L. Braver with Diane O'Connell, *Divorced Dads: Shattering the Myths* (New York: Tarcher/Putnam, 1998), p. 121.

65. Maureen Freely, "A Secret World of Suffering Children," *The Independent*, 18 October 2001.

66. Melanie Phillips, *The Sex-Change Society: Feminised Britain and the Neutered Male* (London: Social Market Foundation, 1999), p. 282. Attorney Wayne Anderson describes it as a "hoax." "The uninitiated layman usually finds it difficult to accept the fact of the custody hoax," he says, noting that many find it "just too horrible to consider." *The Custody Hoax* (Goodland, Kansas: Vindicator, 1992), p. 3.

67. David Blankenhorn also connects these problems with fatherlessness, which he calls, without citing any evidence, "the flight of males from their children's lives." *Fatherless America* (New York: Basic Books, 1995), p. 2.

68. Correspondence from Ernie Allen, President, National Center for Missing and Exploited Children (n.d., received December 2000). The number has apparently more than doubled since the publication of their *Family Abduction* (Arlington, 1994), p. vii.

69. Robert Seidenberg, *The Father's Emergency Guide to Divorce-Custody Battle* (Takoma Park, Maryland: JES, 1997), p. 38.

70. Cynthia McNeely, "Lagging Behind the Times: Parenthood, Custody, and Gender Bias in the Family Court," *Florida State University Law Review*, vol. 25, no. 4 (Summer 1998); Christopher Tillitski, "Fathers and Child Custody: Issues, Trends, and Implications for Counseling," *Journal of Mental Health Counseling*, vol. 14, no.2 (July 1992); Jeffery Leving, *Fathers' Rights* (New York: Basic Books, 1997), chap. 2; Seidenberg, *Father's Emergency Guide*, chap. 1 and *passim*. Recent literature is surveyed in Sanford L. Braver, *et al.*, "Experiences of Family Law Attorneys Regarding Current Issues in Family

Law: Results of a Survey Conducted at a Bar Association Conference," *Family Relations* (forthcoming).

71.   *State ex rel. Watts v. Watts*, 350 N.Y.S. 2d 285 (N.Y. City Fam. Ct., 1973), *Commonwealth ex rel. Spriggs v. Carlson*, 368 Atl. 2d 635 (Pa., 1977).

72.   McNeely, "Lagging Behind the Times," pp. 952-953. "Judges and County Clerk Loretta Bowman in the past agreed to not record the gender of litigants, thereby making it impossible to probe and lay to rest charges of judicial gender bias," according to a week-long investigative series by the *Las Vegas Sun*. Yet the court acknowledged that its computer system "(which tracks hundreds of thousands of domestic, criminal, and civil cases) is capable of recording such detail." Rachael Levy, *et al.*, "Court Statistics on Gender Not Compiled," *Las Vegas Sun*, 19 January 1997.

73.   Joan Kelly, "The Determination of Child Custody in the USA," *Future of Children*, vol. 4, no. 1 (Spring/Summer 1994).

74.   Geoffrey Miller, "Being There: The Importance of the Present Father in the Design of Child Support Obligations," New York University School of Law, Public Law and Legal Theory Research Paper Series Working Paper No. 22, July, 2000, p. 11, note 17.

75.   McNeely, "Lagging Behind the Times," p. 910.

76.   Leighton Stamps, "Maternal Preference in Child Custody Decisions" *Journal of Divorce and Remarriage*, vol. 37, nos. 1-2 (2002).

77.   *Interim Report: Child Support Enforcement*, Joint Legislative Audit and Review Commission of the Virginia General Assembly, Senate Document #42 (2000), p. ii.

78.   William Dolan, "Empirical Study of Child Custody in Divorce Decrees in Arlington Country, Virginia, 7/1/89—12/31/90," in Seidenberg, *Fathers' Emergency Guide*, chap. 1, which cites further references. The assertion that fathers are awarded custody when they contest it and that courts are biased against mothers has been refuted in Ross Parke and Armin Brott, *Throwaway Dads* (New York: Houghton Mifflin, 1999), pp. 178f..

79.   Braver, *Divorced Dads*, chap. 5.

80.   Quoted in Daniel Amneus, *The Case for Father Custody* (Alhambra, California: Primrose, 1999), p. 4. "If we want to live like cattle," Amneus comments, "he has the right idea."

81.   Les Sillars, "Finally, Somebody Is Listening," *Alberta Report*, 11 May 1998. Little hard evidence indicates that children thrive better with mothers than with fathers following divorce, and some to the contrary. "Across a variety of assessments of psychological well-being (self-esteem, anxiety, depression, problem behaviors), children (especially boys) did significantly better in the custody of their fathers." K. Alison Clarke-Steward, "Advantages of Father Custody and Contact for the Psychological Well-Being of School-Age Children," *Journal of Applied Developmental Psychology* 17 (1996), p. 239. I will argue that this is not the important issue, however, and this finding does not justify removing children from mothers (even in their "best interest") who have done nothing wrong.

82.   Peter Jensen, "New Laws on Child Custody Should Help Fathers," *Vancouver Sun*, 18 December 2002.

83.   Phillips, *Sex-Change Society*, pp. 275, xvii.

84.   "Judge Slammed for Joking Email," Reuters, in *CNET News.com*, 7 July 1998. Nothing in the e-mail indicates it was intended facetiously.

85.   "The Fathers Also Rise," *New York* magazine, 18 November 1985.

86.   Fathers' and women's groups seem to agree that a father is likely to be awarded custody less because of his merits as a parent, or any failings in the mother, than because he has political connections. If old-fashioned gender bias were responsible for the treatment of

fathers, we would expect mothers who lose custody to be obviously unfit. Yet there is little evidence that non-custodial mothers are unfit any more than non-custodial fathers. Fathers and Children's Equality reports that "of the non-custodial mothers who come to FACE, 50 percent have ex-husbands who are in some way connected with the justice system—lawyers, owner of a court reporting service, court employees, etc." (correspondence with Jeff Golden, president of FACE, 31 August 2000).

87. Braver, *Divorced Dads*, chap. 7 and *passim*. See also figures quoted from the National Center for Health Statistics in Farrell, *Father and Child Reunion*, pp. 169, 278 note 1.

88. Ilene Wolcott and Jody Hughes, *Towards Understanding the Reasons for Divorce* (Melbourne: Australian Institute of Family Studies, Working Paper No. 20, June 1999).

89. Margaret Brinig and Douglas Allen, "These Boots Are Made for Walking: Why Most Divorce Filers are Women," *American Economics and Law Review*, vol. 2, issue 1 (Spring 2000), pp. 126-127, 129, 158 (original emphasis). Judith Wallerstein and Sandra Blakeslee found roughly two-thirds of divorces were sought by women "in the face of opposition" from the husband. *Second Chances* (New York: Ticknor and Fields, 1989), p. 39. These proportions may be higher when children are involved.

90. Elizabeth Enright, "A House Divided," *AARP The Magazine*, July-August 2004, pp. 54, 57, based on Xenia Montenegro, *The Divorce Experience* (Washington: AAUP, 2004), pp. 14-18; "*AARP The Magazine* Study on Divorce Finds that Women are Doing the Walking," AARP press release, 27 May 2004.

91. Shere Hite, *Women and Love* (New York: Knopf, 1987), p. 459; David Chambers, *Making Fathers Pay* (Chicago: University of Chicago Press, 1979), p. 29. These sources are far from biased toward fathers. Chambers appears to have no scruples about physically mutilating fathers who cannot keep up with child-support payments. See chapter 6.

92. Seidenberg, *Father's Emergency Guide*, 35 (original emphasis); see also p. 42, note 2.

93. Braver, *Divorced Dads*, p. 125.

94. Heather Bird, "Fathers Face Uphill Battle in Our Courts," *Toronto Sun*, 1 November 2001.

95. Dana Mack admits to an epiphany on this point: "I have to admit I listened with a less than wholly sympathetic ear," she writes, reflecting the views of many conservatives about parents who complain of the injustices of divorce courts. "If divorces make parents so miserable, I thought to myself, why do they insist on getting them? Don't they have a choice? . . . I've realized that in many cases they don't." *The Assault on Parenthood* (New York: Simon and Schuster, 1997), p. 86. Mack evidently feels she can only write sympathetically about "parents." A few pages later, when these parents become fathers, she seems to feel they should nonetheless be cut off from their children completely.

96. *Congressional Record*, 5 June 1998, p. S5734.

97. Maggie Gallagher, *The Abolition of Marriage* (Washington: Regnery, 1996), p. 5; Teresa Martin and Larry Bumpass, "Recent Trends in Marital Disruption," *Demography*, vol. 26, no. 1 (February 1989).

98. *Births: Preliminary Data for 2005*, National Center for Health Statistics Web site (http://www.cdc.gov/nchs/products/pubs/pubd/hestats/prelimbirths05/prelimbirths05.htm, 21 November 2006).

99. Gallagher, *Abolition of Marriage*, p. 9; Frank Furstenberg and Andrew Cherlin, *Divided Families* (Cambridge, Mass.: Harvard University Press, 1991), p. 22.

100. Wade Horn, *Father Facts 2* (Lancaster, Pennsylvania: National Fatherhood Initiative, n.d.), p. iii, 8. Larry Bumpass, "What's Happening to the Family: Interactions Between Demographics and Institutional Change," *Demography*, vol. 27, no. 4 (1990).

Notes

101. Recent research suggests that, if anyone is abandoning their children, it appears to be mothers under feminist influence. Jonathan Leake, "Dumped Dads Left Holding the Baby," *Sunday Times*, 8 August 2004, citing an unpublished report by John Haskey from the British Office of National Statistics.

102. Suzanne Speak, *et al.*, *Young Single Fathers: Participation in Fatherhood* (London: Family Policy Studies Centre, 1997).

103. M. Achatz and C. MacAllum, *Young Unwed Fathers* (Philadelphia: Public/Private Ventures, 1994), cited in Pamela Wilson, "Helping Young Dads Succeed," *Family Life Educator*, Spring 1997, p. 11.

104. Sara McLanahan and Irwin Garfinkel, "Unwed Parents: Myths, Realities, and Policy-making," Center for Research on Child Wellbeing Working Paper #02-15-FF, July 2002, n.p.

105. See chapter 6.

106. Quoted in Judy Parejko, *Stolen Vows* (Collierville, Tennessee: InstantPublisher, 2002), p. 98.

107. Quoted in Seidenberg, *Father's Emergency Guide*, p. 22. Some mothers take the logic of the system to its conclusion: "A woman accused of trying to swap her 19-month-old son to his father for $2,000 and a sport utility vehicle was jailed on kidnapping and extortion charges." "Mom Tried to Sell Kid to Dad, Police Say," Associated Press, 25 August 2003.

108. Sally Quinn, "Does Germany Condone Kidnapping?" *Washington Post*, 31 January 2002, p. A25.

109. Bryce Christensen, "The Strange Politics of Child Support," *Society*, vol. 39, no. 1 (November-December 2001), p. 65.

110. See Ira Daniel Turkat, "Divorce Related Malicious Mother Syndrome," *Journal of Family Violence*, vol. 10, no. 3, (1995).

111. Seidenberg, *Father's Emergency Guide*, p. 92 (original emphasis).

112. See chapter 4.

113. Robert Whelan (ed.), *Just a Piece of Paper?* (London: Institute of Economic Affairs, 1995), introduction, p. 3.

114. Gallagher, *Abolition of Marriage*, pp. 144, 149; similar conclusions are in Bridget Maher, "Divorce Reform: Forming Ties That Bind," *Insight*, no. 212 (Washington: Family Research Council, 16 February 2000).

115. Melanie Phillips, "Death Blow to Marriage," in Whelan, *Just a Piece of Paper?* p. 15.

116. Steven L. Varnis, "Broken Vows, Therapeutic Sentiments, Legal Sanctions," *Society*, vol. 35, no. 1 (November-December 1997), p. 35.

117. Quoted in Parejko, *Stolen Vows*, p. 98.

118. Gallagher, *Abolition of Marriage*, p. 147.

119. Phillips, *Sex-Change Society*, p. 261 (original emphasis). See a similar appraisal by Bryce Christensen, "Taking Stock: Assessing Twenty Years of 'No Fault' Divorce," in Whelan, *Just a Piece of Paper?*, pp. 58-59.

120. Online: http://www.no-one-is-married.com (accessed 24 October 2004). Truncellito's law license was suspended for filing the suit. See also Allen Parkman, *Good Intentions Gone Awry: No-Fault Divorce and the American Family* (Lanham: Rowman and Littlefield, 2000), chap. 1, and Parejko, *Stolen Vows*, for similar assessments.

121. See chapter 5.

122. A George Washington University law professor writes: "The *modus operandi* of lawyers" is to "delay as much as they can and frequently lay the groundwork for future

conflict (which ensures future business for themselves)." Quoted in Susan Tolchin and Martin Tolchin, *Dismantling America* (Boston: Houghton Mifflin, 1983), p. 20.

123. Helen M. Alvare, "Types and Styles of Family Proceedings," Report of the United States to the XII World Congress, International Association of Procedural Law, 2003, p. 26.

124. National Center for State Courts (http://www.ncsconline.org), using salaries from 2004.

125. Tim Tippins, "Are Family Courts Prejudiced Against Fathers?" *Insight*, 18 June 2001.

126. Robert Page, "'Family Courts': An Effective Judicial Approach to the Resolution of Family Disputes," *Juvenile and Family Court Journal*, vol. 44, no. 1 (1993), pp. 19, 20.

127. Herbert Jacob, "The Effects of Institutional Differences in the Recruitment Process," *Journal of Public Law* 13 (1964). Jacob concludes, "The bar has now a veto power over prospective judges." *Justice in America: Courts, Lawyers, and the Judicial Process* (Boston: Little Brown, 1984), p. 112. More recently described: G. Alan Tarr, Judicial Process and Judicial Policymaking (Belmont: West/Wadsworth, 1999), pp. 61, 67, 69-70. For the "cronyistic" politics of judicial appointments, see Richard Watson and Rondal Downing, *The Politics of the Bench and the Bar* (New York: John Wiley and Sons, 1969), pp. 98, 336. The bar exercises "the leading role in influencing judicial selection, be it by appointment or election." Harry Stumpf and John Culver, *The Politics of State Courts* (New York: Longman, 1992), p. 49.

128. Interview on WTTG television, Fox Channel 5 in Washington, broadcast 20 February 1999.

129. Ashton Applewhite, *Cutting Loose* (New York: HarperCollins, 1997), p. xii.

130. *Graves v. Graves*, 4 Va. App. 326, 333, 357 S.E.2d 554, 558 (1987). *Wilson v. Wilson*, 18 Va. App. 193 acknowledged the "wife's fault in leaving husband" but said it was irrelevant in demanding child support and attorneys' fees from the legally unimpeachable husband, who was also forced to pay extra child support for horseback riding lessons.

131. Yvonne Abraham, "Federal Suit Questions Probate Judge's Impartiality," *Boston Globe*, 12 June 1999, p. B1. Rotman has served as the Vice President of the Association of Family and Conciliation Courts according to the pamphlet advertising their 1998 conference.

132. Interview with Bill Lind on New Nation radio broadcast, 3 May 2000; Stephen Baskerville, "The Fix Is In," in Auriana Ojeda (ed.), *The Family: Opposing Viewpoints* (San Diego: Greenhaven Press, 2003).

133. Paul Vitello, "When the Divorce Court Leads to a Jail Cell," *New York Times*, 15 February 2007.

134. Michael Roskin, *et al.*, *Political Science* (Upper Saddle River, New Jersey: 8th edn., 2003), p. 90.

135. Robert Verkaik, "Loans 'Will Help Poor Wives Fund Divorces,'" *Independent*, 17 October 2001.

136. Al Knight, "Another Blow to Marriage," *Denver Post*, 20 June 2001. Feminist groups confirm this; see chapter 5.

137. Judith Regan, "An Open Letter to Mr. Clark," *Newsweek*, 13 March 1995, pp. 57-58.

138. Quoted in Braver, *et al.*, "Experiences of Family Law Attorneys."

139. Varnis, "Broken Vows," p. 37.

140. "Making It Easy to Steal a Man's Child," *St. Petersburg Times*, 11 April 1999. In op-ed columns, both conservative Maggie Gallagher (*Atlanta Constitution*, 14 January 2000) and liberal Richard Cohen (*Washington Post*, 11 April 2000) have urged that the concept be abandoned. See also Edward Kruk, "Shared Parental Responsibility: A Harm

Notes

Reduction-Based Approach to Divorce Law Reform," *Journal of Divorce and Remarriage*, vol. 43, no. 3-4 (2005), p. 122. The American Bar Association favors the term, despite admitting that it is "subjective" and allows courts to separate parents and children at will. (ABA Division for Public Education, "Protecting the Best Interests of Children," http://www.abanet.org, accessed 9 December 2006).

141. Quoted in Leving, *Fathers' Rights*, p. 196. See also Robert Mnookin, "Foster Care: In Whose Best Interest?" *Harvard Education Review* 43 (1973), p. 599.

142. "One of the factors used to determine 'best interests' is the length of time the child has been separated from the parent who is seeking custody." "Custody Decision-Making in Maryland: Practice, Principles, and Process," proceedings of a discussion held at the University of Maryland School of Law, 9 December 2003, Woodrow Wilson International Center for Scholars (n.p., n.d.), p. 14. No participant in this conference represented the views of non-custodial parents.

143. Stephen Barr "Refereeing the Ugliest Game in Town," *New Jersey Monthly*, May 1998, pp. 52-55, 71-74.

144. Walter Olson, "Suing Ourselves to Death: America's Litigation Boom Is Bad for Law and Society, *Washington Post*, 28 April 1991.

145. "The judge occupies a vital position not only because of his role in the judicial process but also because of his control over lucrative patronage positions." Such appointments "are generally passed out to the judge's political cronies or to persons who can help his private practice." Jacob, *Justice in America*, p. 112.

146. Page, "Family Courts," p. 21. Thus a widely criticized June 1999 article in *American Psychologist* by Louise Silverstein and Carl Auerbach, "Deconstructing the Essential Father," arguing that fathers (and mothers) are unnecessary to child-rearing, might itself be accepted as forensic evidence to justify removing a child altogether from a father (or mother) who is guilty of nothing.

147. "Goodbye Lords, Hello the Dictatorship of the Judges," *Sunday Times*, 14 November 1999.

148. Margaret Hagan explains the "recent explosion in our courts of cases . . . requiring the expert testimony of the psychological witness":

    Our common desperation seems to have produced the common delusion that experts actually exist who really can determine with the unerring instincts of a homing pigeon exactly where the best interests of the child lie, where the child should live, whether and how a child has been hurt, and who is unfit to be a parent at all, who should have the right and the duty to care for a child, who should see the child only under restricted conditions, and who should be kept away from the child altogether.

    Acceptance of their expertise has led us to trust professionals to make these decisions for the family court system. That means ultimately that we also grant them the power to make these decisions for our own families. The abstract need for society to protect its children becomes inevitably the rape of the rights of the real parents of individual children. Once again, the institutionalization of society's desire to "do good" results in terrible harm for those in the path of the "do gooders."

    The marriage of law and psychology has reached the heights of disproportionate power for the psychologists not just in the family courts but in all legal disputes in which a psychological matter is at issue. Judges buy the validity of the expertise of the confident psychological practitioner and no doubt welcome the opportunity to make their own decisions on some foundation other than personal opinion and bias.

    Whores of the Court: The Fraud of Psychiatric Testimony and the Rape of American Justice (New York: HarperCollins, 1997), p. 234.

149. New York: Millan, 1973, p. 38.

150. Braver, *Divorced Dads*, pp. 221-22 (original emphasis).

Notes

151. Quoted in Barbara Dafoe Whitehead, *The Divorce Culture* (New York: Vintage, 1998), p. 78.

152. Alvare, "Types and Styles of Family Proceedings," p. 11.

153. "A Child's-Eye View" *Washington Post*, 16 January 2002, p. C01.

154. Dave Brown, "Psychologists Make a Bundle While Family Courts Fiddle," *Ottawa Citizen*, 21 September 2001.

155. "Families in Crisis," report by the 1991-92 San Diego County Grand Jury (http://www.co.san-diego.ca.us/cnty/cntydepts/safety/grand/reports/report2.html).

156. Donna Laframboise, "Custody Assessors Decide Children's Fates, But Who Has Control over Them?" *National Post*, 30 January 1999, and correspondence with Donna Laframboise.

157. Richard Pienciak and Linda Yglesias, "Who Gets the Kids?" *New York Daily News*, 25 September 1998.

158. Ralph Underwager and Hollida Wakefield, *The Real World of Child Interrogations* (Springfield, Illinois: Charles C. Thomas, 1990), p. xi.

159. Kelly Patricia O'Meara, "Is Justice for Sale in L.A.?" *Insight*, vol. 15, no. 16 (3 May 1999), and interview with Kelly O'Meara.

160. Scott Winokur, "Judging Family-Law Jurists," *San Francisco Examiner*, 7 May 2000, and "New Allegations Raised Against Marin Judge," *San Francisco Examiner*, 2 August 2000; Peter Blumberg, "Three Strikes For Law-Breaking Judges Proposed," *Los Angeles Daily Journal*, 13 August 1999.

161. U.S. Department of Justice, United States Attorney, Eastern District of Arkansas, press release and indictment, 27 April 1999.

162. Alvare, "Types and Styles of Family Proceedings," p. 25.

163. Daniel Wise, "'Cronyism' Abounds in Court Appointments," *New York Law Journal*, 4 December 2001. New York judges are effectively chosen by "political connections": "Voters are instructed to 'select three of the following' and are presented with only three candidates," says the *Daily News*, which calls the system "hammer-and-sickle Kremlin elections" and notes that "in reality, these judges are selected by the Democratic Party county bosses . . . who violate integrity rules [and] who distribute millions of dollars in legal work to politically connected law firms." "Disorder in the Courts," *New York Daily News* editorial, 26 November 2001. Others describe "a culture of corruption in the matrimonial section of State Supreme Court." Andy Newman, "Investigation of Judge Touched Off Wider Inquiry, *New York Times*, 25 April 2003. See also Clifford Levy, *et al.*, "A Bronx Judiciary Awash in Patronage, All Legal," *New York Times*, 3 January 2004.

164. "Big Money Behind Custody Battles," WFAA News 8, Dallas, 4 May 2000. In 2001, parents in South Carolina protested before the state supreme court against attorneys *ad litem* for the "bias in their decision-making" and "outrageous fees." Josh Gelinas, "Parents Dispute Courts' Handling of Custody Cases," *Augusta Chronicle*, 11 January 2002.

165. John Brummett, "The Confession in Nick's Denial," *Arkansas Democrat-Gazette*, 28 April 1999; David Lieb in the Associated Press, 28 April 1999.

166. They seem to occupy positions of power reminiscent of "Dixiecrats" in perpetuating segregation. Tony Perkins, who sponsored Louisiana's celebrated "covenant marriage" law, reports that similar measures have failed in "seemingly sympathetic legislatures" because of "opposition from key committee chairmen who were divorce lawyers." Quoted by David McCrary, "States Ponder Legislating Antidotes to High Divorce Rate," *Salt Lake Tribune*, 28 January 2001.

167. John Brummett, "The Confession in Nick's Denial," *Arkansas Democrat-Gazette*, 29 April 1999, and correspondence.

Notes

168. Linda Satter, "Wilson Pleads Guilty to Racketeering Count," *Arkansas Democrat-Gazette*, 3 March 2000.

169. Quoted in the *New York Daily News*, 25 September, 1998. That lawyers intentionally inflame emotions is testified by lawyers themselves; see Braver, *et al.*, "Experiences of Family Law Attorneys."

170. C. Jesse Green, interview with Michael E. Tindall, *Michigan Lawyers Weekly* (http://www.michiganlawyersweekly.com/loty2000/tindall.htm; n.d., accessed 1 May 2002).

171. Heather Bird, "Fathers Face Uphill Battle in Our Courts," *Toronto Sun*, 1 November 2001.

172. "A Call to Dismantle the Divorce Industry," *Orlando Sentinel*, 10 February 1999.

173. Alvare, "Types and Styles of Family Proceedings," p. 14.

174. Parejko, *Stolen Vows*, p. 122.

175. R. H. Mnookin and L. Kornhauser, "Bargaining in the Shadow of the Law: The Case of Divorce," *Yale Law Journal* 88 (1979).

176. Bruce Young, "The Mediation Myth," paper delivered at the Forum on Men and Family Relationships, Canberra, Australia, 9-11 June 1998, published in *Everyman* 42 (March-April 2000), p. 47.

177. Seidenberg, *Father's Emergency Guide*, p. 76.

178. Alvare, "Types and Styles of Family Proceedings," pp. 19, 22.

179. Parejko, *Stolen Vows*, p. 10.

180. Alvare, "Types and Styles of Family Proceedings," p. 21 (emphasis added).

181. Art Moore, "The High Cost of Divorce," *WorldNetDaily*, 15 March 2002.

182. Richard Pienciak and Linda Yglesias, "N.Y. Divorce Court Hurts Kids Most They're Forgotten in Outdated System," *New York Daily News*, 25 September 1998, p. 41.

183. Braver, *Divorced Dads*, pp. 233-234.

184. Parejko, *Stolen Vows*, p. 11 (original emphasis).

185. Cristin Schmitz, "Force Divorcing Parents to Take Courses: Lawyers," *National Post*, 9 July 2001 (emphasis added).

186. Alvare, "Types and Styles of Family Proceedings," p. 12.

187. Jeff Baron, "Learning to Quell Custody Quarrels," *Washington Post*, 30 July 2001, p. B01 (emphasis added).

188. Clare Dyer, "What About the Kids?" *The Guardian*, 12 February 2002.

189. Sanford L. Braver, *et al.*, "The Content of Divorce Education Programs: Results of a Survey," *Family and Conciliation Courts Review*, vol. 34, no. 1 (January 1996).

190. Parejko, *Stolen Vows*, p. 19.

191. Kathy Coleman, "Custody Decision-Making in Maryland," pp. 133-134.

192. Patricia Morgan, "Conflict and Divorce: Like a Horse and Carriage?" in Robert Whelan (ed.), *Just a Piece of Paper?* (London: Institute of Economic Affairs, 1995), p. 32.

193. Quoted in Paul Rubin, "Judge Not," *Phoenix New Times*, 31 August 2000.

194. Nevada Legislature, Minutes of the Meeting of the Legislative Commission's Subcommittee on Family Courts (Assembly Concurrent Resolution No. 32), 21 January 1998 (http://www.leg.state.nv.us/69th/Interim/Studies/Courts/Minutes/1-21-98-min.html, accessed 9 March 2007).

195. The Australian Law Reform Commission, *Managing Justice: A Review of the Federal Civil Justice System*, Report No. 89 (2000), chapter 8 (esp. note 19); Gervase Greene, "Report Slams Family Court," *The Age*, 20 August 1999.

Notes

196. The Advisory Board on Family Law, Children Act Sub-Committee, *Making Contact Work*, "Letter to the Lord Chancellor," paragraph 1.16, and recommendation 16 (February 2002).

197. Quoted in Frances Gibb, "Head of Children's Courts Is Suspended," *The Times*, 17 November 2001.

198. Andrew Alderson, "Three Months' Jail for Mother Who Kept Child from His Father," *Daily Telegraph*, 2 February 2004.

199. Jannell McGrew, "Bill Would Outlaw Blocking Visitation," *Montgomery Advertiser*, 26 April 2005.

200. Nevada Legislature, Minutes of the Meeting of the Legislative Commission's Subcommittee on Family Courts (Assembly Concurrent Resolution No. 32), 14 November 1997, 16 April 1998, and 3 June 1998 (http://www.leg.state.nv.us/69th/Interim/Studies/Courts/Minutes, accessed 10 March 2007).

201. Michael A. Fox, *A Culture of Secrecy, Fear, and Judicial Abuse: A Report on the Butler County Juvenile and Domestic Relations Courts* (http://www.pacegroup.org/fox_report_without_doc.pdf, accessed 12 November 2004), pp. 2-3.

202. Mary Lolli, "Fox Takes GOP Heat," *Middletown Journal*, 24 July 2003.

203. Rachael Levy, *et al.*, "A Week-Long Examination of Family Court," *Las Vegas Sun*, 19-26 January 1997.

204. "Courts Leave Children Confused and Parents Feeling Like Criminals," *The Observer*, 9 July 2000; "Our Verdict: End Court Lottery," *The Observer*, 16 July 2000.

205. See the Conclusion. Also Jonathan Gruber, "Is Making Divorce Easier Bad for Children?" (Cambridge, Mass.: National Bureau of Economic Research, Working Paper 7968, October 2000).

Chapter 2 / Divorce and the Constitution

206. *And Justice for None* (Westlake, Ohio: Mary's Advocates, 2004), p. 34.

207. Glenda Riley, *Divorce: An American Tradition* (New York: Oxford University Press, 1991), p. 6.

208. Barbara Dafoe Whitehead, *The Divorce Culture* (New York: Vintage, 1998), pp. 70-71.

209. Judy Parejko, "No Fair Process in Divorce Laws," *Middletown Journal*, 27 January 2004.

210. *May v. Anderson*, 345 U.S. 528, 533 (1953); *Meyer v. Nebraska*, 262 U.S. 390, 399 (1923); *Stanley v. Illinois*, 405 U.S. 645 (1971). See Donald Hubin "Parental Rights and Due Process," *Journal of Law and Family Studies*, vol. 1, no. 2 (1999), 123 and *passim*.

211. Quoted in Bruce Hafen, "Children's Liberation and the New Egalitarianism: Some Reservations about Abandoning Youth to Their 'Rights.'" *Brigham Young University Law Review* (1976), pp. 615-616.

212. *Langton v. Maloney*, 527 F Supp 538, D.C. Conn. (1981); *Bell v. City of Milwaukee*, 746 F 2d 1205: U.S. Ct. App. 7th Cir. WI. (1984); *May v. Anderson*, 345 U.S. 528, 533 (1953); *Quilloin v. Walcott*, 98 S.Ct. 549; 434 U.S. 246, 255-56 (1978); *Troxel v. Granville*, 530 U.S. 57 (2000).

213. *Prince v. Massachusetts*, 321 U.S. 158, 166 (1944).

214. *Parham v. J. R. a Minor*, 422 U.S. 584, 602 (1979).

215. Robert Williams, "An Overview of Child Support Guidelines in the United States," in Margaret Campbell Haynes (ed.), *Child Support Guidelines: The Next Generation* (Washington: Office of Child Support Enforcement, April 1994), p. 2.

216. "It's Never Father's Day," *The Observer*, 21 October 2001.

Notes

217. Walter Olson, *The Litigation Explosion* (New York: Talley/Dutton, 1991).

218. The secrecy is acknowledged in *The Janiculum Project Recommendations*, National Council of Juvenile and Family Court Judges (n.p., 1998), p. 8.

219. Robert Page, "'Family Courts': An Effective Judicial Approach to the Resolution of Family Disputes," *Juvenile and Family Court Journal*, vol. 44, no. 1 (1993), pp. 9, 11. Page has also served as a director of the Association of Family and Conciliation Courts.

220. David Heleniak, "The New Star Chamber," *Rutgers Law Review*, vol. 57, no. 3 (Spring 2005), p. 1009.

221. C. Jesse Green, interview with Michael E. Tindall, *Michigan Lawyers Weekly* (http://www.michiganlawyersweekly.com/loty2000/tindall.htm; no date, accessed 1 May 2002).

222. Malcolm X and Alex Haley, *The Autobiography of Malcolm X* (New York: Grove Press, 1965), 21; *In Re Gault*, 387 U.S. 1, 27-28 (1967).

223. Yet according to standard legal authorities this distinction no longer exists. *Black's Law Dictionary*, 6th ed. (St. Paul, Minn., 1990), s.v. "Equity, courts of."

224. One family court judge apparently responded to a suit by summarily jailing the plaintiff. "Six days after being named a defendant in a $36 million lawsuit, State District Judge Thomas L. Kennedy had the plaintiff, father's rights advocate Michael Sandifer, jailed." Equal Justice Foundation of Colorado press release, 17 August 2001.

225. 60 U.S.L.W. 4532 (15 June 1992).

226. See chapter 1. Charles Ashman comments that the system "provides for a combination of secrecy and private-group influence which should not be tolerated in a free society, particularly when one considers the nearly limitless power judges gain by donning a robe." *The Finest Judges Money Can Buy* (Los Angeles: Nash Publishing, 1973), p. 243.

227. "Divorces are Public Acts," *Denver Post*, 3 February 2002. The bill was promoted by the family law committee of the Colorado Bar Association.

228. Reported in the *Boston Globe* and other newspapers, 10 December 1997.

229. American Fathers Coalition press release, 22 April 1997.

230. *John v. Johns*; Ark CtApp (en banc); No. 95-92, 4/3/96, cited in *Speak Out For Children* (newsletter of the Children's Rights Council), vol. 12, no. 1 (Fall 1996/Winter 1997), p. 11.

231. Eugene Volokh, "Parent-Child Speech and Child Custody Speech Restrictions," *New York Law Review* 81 (May 2006), p. 643. See also pp. 634-637.

232. *Ibid.*, pp. 637-639, 640-641, 654, 642-643, 673, 707-708.

233. New Jersey Council for Children's Rights press release, 1 April 2000. The press release claims that NJ-AFCC held a public seminar in which "one of the four discussion topics on the agenda relates to Alice's case. The NJ-AFCC is free to discuss the intimate details of Alice's case while Alice is forced to remain mute."

234. The article is quoted in chapter 4.

235. Documents from the law offices of David Sibley of Corpus Christi, Texas (http://www.davidsibley.com/FamilyLawFilings, accessed 8 December 2001).

236. Court documents.

237. "Disorder in the Courts," *Sunday Telegraph*, 9 July 2000.

238. From press releases issued in Canada (18 January 2001) and the Netherlands (n.d.).

239. "A User's Guide to Family Court," *The Age*, 10 September 1999.

240. "Disorder in the Courts."

241. David Wroe, "Judge Claims Intimidation in Row over Child Custody," *The Age*, 2 December 2003.

Notes

242. Letter from Angela Filippello, Principal Registrar of the Australia Family Court to the director of the Men's Network Web site, 18 February 1999.

243. Robert Verkaik, "Irvine Closes Down 'Anti-Judge' Website," *The Independent*, 7 November 1999.

244. "Pursued," *The Age*, 5 October 1999.

245. "Street Protester Beats Judges at Own Game," *The Australian*, 8 March 2000.

246. Bruce Bartlett, "Man Faces Libel Charges After Criticising Family Court Judge," *Saint John Telegraph Journal*, 9 January 2002, A4; Richard Foot, "Man Fights For Right to Picket Judge," *National Post*, 7 March 2002.

247. Louis McHardy and Meredith Hofford, *Final Report of the Child Custody and Visitation Focus Group, March 1-3, 1999* (http://www.vaw.umn.edu/FinalDocuments/custodyfin.htm, "File Last Modified on: 12/21/99.").

248. "Judd's Ex-Husband Jailed," Associated Press, 18 December 1999.

249. Alliance for Non-Custodial Parents Rights press release, 20 June 1998.

250. "Damages Sought Against Officials Who Denied Gadfly's Rights," Associated Press, 25 March 2006.

251. James Drew, "Judge Takes Bite Out of Ex-Maumee Man's Judicial Watchdog Site," *Toledo Blade*, 2 November 2001.

252. "Expanding Definition of Terrorism Challenged," *Empire Journal*, 8 August 2005.

253. Mike Linn, "Radio Comments Lead to 'Lookout' Fliers," *Montgomery Advertiser*, 7 July 2006.

254. "Message Proves Unsettling," *Times Union* (Albany, New York), 26 June 2006.

255. Court documents.

256. "Children Taken from Father after He Testifies Before Congress," *Speak Out For Children*, vol. 7, no. 4 (Fall 1992), p. 9.

257. See the chilling list of private matters into which family courts regularly delve in Jed H. Abraham, *From Courtship to Courtroom* (New York: Bloch, 1999), pp. 49-52.

258. Interview with Joseph Neufeld, who filed a petition on Dougherty's behalf for a writ of *habeas corpus*, 22 May 2000.

259. Abraham, *From Courtship to Courtroom*, p. 58.

260. John Caher, "New York State Law Review Commission Ponders Parent-Child Privilege," *New York Law Journal*, 9 November 2000.

261. Paul Singer, "Judge Orders Parents Not to Smoke," Associated Press, 13 September 2002.

262. "Smoke and Lose Your Son," *WorldNetDaily*, 26 March 2002.

263. Letter from attorney Lee Ann Pafford of Rikard and Dobson, PLLC to attorney Stephen Leffler, 12 July 2000. According to court documents, the father is also prohibited from taking his son to the doctor. He was also ordered to pay $3,500 to an attorney he did not hire for no specified reason other than the haircut.

264. Michael A. Cox, *A Culture of Secrecy, Fear, and Judicial Abuse: A Report on the Butler County Juvenile and Domestic Relations Courts* (n.d., n.p.; http://www.pacegroup.org/fox_report_without_doc.pdf, accessed 12 November 2004), 2-3 (emphasis original).

265. Correspondence from Liz Richards to various parties, 5 and 6 August 2001.

266. "ACLU Applauds Montgomery County Judge for Agreeing to Appoint Lawyers For Poor People Facing Jail Time," ACLU of Pennsylvania press release, 10 December 2003; Jan Ackerman, "Lawrence County Judges Free 37 Child-Support Offenders," *Pittsburgh*

Post-Gazette, 12 Septembeer 2002; interview with Jay Todd, who filed a Freedom of Information Act petition.

267. Carl Friedrich and Zbigniew Brzezinski, *Totalitarian Dictatorship and Autocracy* (Cambridge, Mass.: Harvard, 1965), p. 200.

268. Joe Mozingo, "Shackled Children in Legal Dilemma," *Los Angeles Times*, 18 April 1998, p. 1.

269. *The Liberator*, vol. 25, nos. 3-4 (March-April 1998). Police in Abingdon Township, Pennsylvania, did not return repeated telephone calls and e-mail inquiries.

270. "Enforcement of Protective Orders," U.S. Department of Justice, Office for Victims of Crime, Legal Series, Bulletin #4, January 2002, p. 2.

271. See chapter 4.

272. Wayne Anderson, *The Custody Hoax* (Goodland, Kansas: Vindicator, 1992), pp. 4-5.

273. Teresa Myers, "Case in Brief: Courts Uphold Criminal Penalties for the Failure to Pay Child Support," NCSL Web site (http://www.ncsl.org/programs/cyf/Criminalnon.htm, accessed 28 August 2001).

274. Citing *International Union, United Mine Workers of America v. Bagwell*, 512 U.S. 821 (1994); *U.S. v. Ballek*, 1999 WL 125955, 9th Cir. (Alaska), 11 March 1999 (emphasis added).

275. Citing *Black v. Division of Child Support Enforcement*, 686 A.2d 164 (Del. 1996).

276. See chapter 4.

277. Miriam Altman, "Litigating Domestic Abuse Cases under Ch. 209A," *Massachusetts Lawyers Weekly*, 23 October 1995, p. B6.

278. Judy Parejko, *Stolen Vows* (Collierville, Tennessee: InstantPublisher, 2002), p. 101.

279. E-mail communication from Eugene Wrona, Attorney at Law, Allentown, Pennsylvania, 28 February 2002, and telephone interview, 16 March 2002.

280. Ed Oliver, "Father Proves that Court Tapes Were Altered," *Massachusetts News*, December 2000.

281. Press release, Law Office of Gregory Hession, JD, 16 November 2000, and correspondence and interviews with Zed McLarnon and Gregory Hession.

282. John Ellement, "Court OK's Extradition in Child Support Case," *Boston Globe*, 10 February 1999.

283. *2004 Green Book*, House of Representatives, Ways and Means Committee Print WMCP:108-6, U.S. Government Printing Office Online via GPO Access, section 8 (http://frwebgate.access.gpo.gov/cgi-bin/getdoc.cgi?dbname=108_green_book& docid=f:wm006_08.wais).

284. Kevin Landrigan, "Lacking Support, Judicial Nominee Abandons Bid," *Telegraph* (Hudson, New Hampshire), 26 July 2001. See also Helen M. Alvare, "Types and Styles of Family Proceedings," Report of the United States to the XII World Congress, International Association of Procedural Law, 2003, pp. 1, 10.

285. "Virginia Shames Deadbeat Parents with Car Boots," Associated Press, 24 January 2000.

286. Associated Press, "A County Will Put Pressure on Debtors," *Detroit Free Press*, 21 January 2001.

287. Angela Rozas, "Web Site Doesn't Shame Deadbeats," *Times-Picayune*, 3 July 2000.

288. See *Brzonkala v. Morrison* 529 U.S. 598 (2000). *U.S. v. Faasse*, No. 98-2337 (6th Cir., 14 September 2001) has held that child-support enforcement, a police function, is "interstate commerce." See also, *U.S. v. King*, No. 01-1141 (2nd Cir., 3 January 2002).

289. *Congressional Record*, 7 September 2000, p. H7315.

290. *Moss v. Superior Court*, 17 Cal. 4th 396, 950 P.2d 59 (Cal. 1998).

291. *Pollock v. Williams*, 1944. 322 U.S. 4, 18.

292. Reuters News Service, 13 April 1998.

293. *The Recorder*, 12 March 1999; *U.S. v. Ballek*, 99 C.D.O.S. 1805.

294. John Locke, *Second Treatise on Civil Government* (various edns.), chap. 11, "Of the Extent of the Legislative Power," section 139.

295. Yahoo.com hosts a discussion group "for divorced or legally separated women to discuss how they have used divorce, child support, alimony, and the courts to make their ex-husbands their financial slaves." See chapter 5.

296. Yet the courts have upheld the law: *U.S. v. Rose*, 153 F.3d 208 (5th Cir. 1998); *U.S. v. Black*, 125 F.3d 454 (7th Cir. 1997); *U.S. v. Crawford*, 115 F.3d 1397 (8th Cir. 1997); *U.S. v. Hampshire*, 95 F.3d 999 (10th Cir. 1996); *U.S. v. Muench*, 153 F.3d 1298 (11th Cir. 1998). *U.S. v. Mussari*, 152 F.3d 1156 (9th Cir. 1998) held otherwise.

297. Janet Kerlin, "Judge Orders Release of Woman Held 2? Years Without Charges," Associated Press, 17 August 1998; "ACLU Seeks to Free RI Woman Jailed for Two Years without Trial, Lawyer," ACLU press release, 14 August 1998.

298. *Foretich v. District of Columbia*, Office of the Mayer, No. 02-5224 (D.C. Cir., 16 December 2003).

299. *Butler v. Commonwealth*, 132.Va.609, 110 S.E. 868 (1922).

300. Leslie Harris, *et al.*, "Making and Breaking Connections Between Parents' Duty to Support and Right to Control their Children," *Oregon Law Review* 69 (1990), p. 711. "Under the parental autonomy principle, parents generally may decide, free from government supervision, at what level and by what means they will support their children." *Ibid.*, p. 689.

301. Federalist #58, *The Federalist Papers* (Mentor paperback ed., 1961), p. 359.

302. Most states profit from their child-support program. See the next chapter.

303. Bryce Christensen, "The Strange Politics of Child Support," *Society*, vol. 39, no. 1 (November-December 2001), pp. 63-64.

304. Abraham, *From Courtship to Courtroom*, pp. 154-155.

305. Richard Wolf, "Deadbeat Parents Face Federal Time," *USA Today*, 15 April 1999.

306. NCSL Web site (http://www.ncsl.org/programs/cyf/cs.htm; accessed 19 July 2001).

307. *1998 Green Book*, House of Representatives, Ways and Means Committee Print WMCP:105-7, U.S. Government Printing Office Online via GPO Access, section 8 (http://frwebgate.access.gpo.gov/cgi-bin/useftp.cgi?IPaddress=162.140.64.21& filename=wm007_08.105&directory=/disk2/wais/data/105_green_book).

308. Welfare Information Network (WIN), "Innovations in Child Support Enforcement," *Resources for Welfare Decisions* (http://www.welfareinfo.org/sachsmarch.htm; accessed 28 September 2001).

309. Robert O'Harrow, "Uncle Sam Has All Your Numbers," *Washington Post*, 27 June 1999, p. A1.

310. Libertarian Party press release, 11 February 1998.

311. John Schneider, "Child Support Cuts GM Bonuses," *Lansing State Journal*, 17 October 2003.

312. Brigid McMenamin, "Payroll Paternalism," *Forbes*, 16 April 2001.

313. Robert Boczkiewicz, "State Fighting Feds in Appeals Court," *Topeka Capital-Journal*, 22 January 2000. Confirmed in an interview with Assistant Attorney General M. J.

Willoughby, 3 October 2001. The suit failed in both district and appeals court: 24 F. Supp. 2d 1192 and 214 F.3d 1196.

314. Christensen, "Strange Politics of Child Support," p. 69.

315. Michelle Ganow, "New Challenges for States in Financing Child Support," Welfare Information Network, *Issue Notes*, vol. 5, no. 7 (May 2001).

316. O'Harrow, "Uncle Sam."

317. "Banks in Bed with California Tax Board," *Privacy Times*, 22 March 1999.

318. WIN, "Innovations in Child Support Enforcement."

319. Charlie Cain, "ID Theft Fears Raised," *Detroit News*, 26 December 2003.

320. Associated Press, "Social Security Number Requirement Angers Hunters, Fishermen," *Anchorage Daily News*, 22 March 1999.

321. Welfare Information Network, "Innovations in Child Support Enforcement," *Resources for Welfare Decisions* (n.d.), (http://www.financeprojectinfo.org/Publications/ sachsmarch.htm (accessed 30 September 2004); see also their "Collaborations with Community-Based Organizations to Promote Responsible Fatherhood," *Resources For Welfare Decisions*, vol. 3, no. 8 (October 1999).

322. Stephen Baskerville, "The Federal Bureau of Marriage?" *Liberty*, July 2003.

323. Online: http://www.volunteersolutions.org/unitedwaysatx/org/opp/247311.html, accessed 21 November 2004.

324. O'Harrow, "Uncle Sam."

325. Quoted in Christensen, "Strange Politics of Child Support," p. 68.

326. Top 5 Questions Regarding Social Security Number Collection for Child Support Enforcement, NCSL Web site (http://www.ncsl.org/programs/cyf/ssnumb.htm, accessed 20 December 2003).

327. *The Haunted Land* (New York: Vintage, 1995), pp. 299-304, 328.

328. Private correspondence.

329. Quoted in John Tierney, "An Imbalance in the Battle over Custody," *New York Times*, 29 April 2000.

Chapter 3 / Deadbeat Dads or Plundered Pops?

330. Robyn Moormeister, "Dads on the Run," *Paradise Post*, 16 June 2001. "There's got to be a better way to do this," a New Jersey officer is quoted. "We have cops crashing through doors for civil debts." Eileen Markey, "Speziale Says Deadbeat Dad Hunt Draining His Resources," *North Jersey Herald and News*, 31 May 2002. Agents in Alaska were issued bulletproof vests, though "none has ever been shot at or assaulted," according to officials. Mike Chambers, "House Nixes Bid to Arm Child-Support Workers," Associated Press, 30 March 2004.

331. Bryce Christensen, "The Strange Politics of Child Support," *Society*, vol. 39, no. 1 (November-December 2001), p. 63.

332. Ronald Henry, "Child Support at a Crossroads: When the Real World Intrudes upon Academics and Advocates," *Family Law Quarterly*, vol. 33, no.1 (1999), p. 254.

333. Jed H. Abraham, *From Courtship to Courtroom* (New York: Bloch, 1999), p. 151.

334. "End Welfare Reform as We Know It," *American Spectator*, June 1995.

335. Department of Health and Human Services (HHS) press release, 28 September 1998.

336. "Child Support Collections Reach New Records," HHS press release, 31 December 1998. The omitted euphemism is "cases."

Notes

337. "Chronic Child Support Defaulters Arrested in Nationwide Sweep," HHS, Office of the Inspector General, press release, 31 July 2002; Ken Little, "10 Charged with Non-Support," *Observer-Dispatch* (http://www.uticaod.com/news/daily/local2.htm, no date, accessed 31 July 2002); Marilyn Gardner, "Making 'Deadbeat' Parents a Thing of the Past," *Christian Science Monitor*, 27 August 2002; Robert Pear, "U.S. Agents Arrest Dozens of Fathers in Support Cases," *New York Times*, 19 August 2002.

338. Hamil Harris and Sylvia Moreno, "Officials in Area Team Up to Arrest Deadbeat Parents," *Washington Post*, 8 November 1997, p. B01; Andy Soltis, "Hall of Shame," *New York Post*, 16 October 2006.

339. For DEA: http://www.usdoj.gov/dea/agency/staffing.htm.

340. The General Accounting Office (GAO), which warns that "states have underestimated the magnitude, complexity, and costs of the projects and operations," found at the beginning of the Clinton crackdowns that 66 percent of fathers who owe support "cannot afford to pay the amount ordered." *Interstate Child Support: Mothers Report Receiving Less Support from Out-of-State Fathers* (Washington: General Accounting Office, GAO/HRD-92-39FS, 9 January 1992).

341. "Chronic Child Support Defaulters."

342. Susannah Figura, "Where's Dad?" *Government Executive*, December 1998, p. 16. The article quotes numerous federal officials but no fathers.

343. William S. Comanor, "Child Support Payments: A Review of Current Policies," p. 3, and Ronald Henry, "Child Support Policy and the Unintended Consequences of Good Intentions," p. 135, both in Comanor (ed.), *The Law and Economics of Child Support Payments* (Cheltenham: Edward Elgar, 2004).

344. C. Jesse Green, interview with Michael E. Tindall, *Michigan Lawyers Weekly* (http://www.michiganlawyersweekly.com/loty2000/tindall.htm, no date, accessed 1 May 2002).

345. See chapter 1.

346. "By interviewing a random sample of single-parent families, the Census Bureau is able to generate a host of numbers that can be used to assess the performance of non-custodial parents in paying child support." *1998 Green Book*, U.S. House of Representatives, Ways and Means Committee Print 105-7 (Washington: U.S. Government Printing Office, 1998), p. 604.

347. Sanford L. Braver with Diane O'Connell, *Divorced Dads: Shattering the Myths* (New York: Tarcher/Putnam, 1998), pp. 21-22 and chap. 2, *passim* (emphasis original).

348. The GAO cites $89 billion, giving its source as HHS. But since no database supplies these figures, it is not clear where they come from. *Child Support Enforcement: Clear Guidance Would Help Ensure Proper Access to Information and Use of Wage Withholding by Private Firms* (Washington: General Accounting Office, GAO-02-349, March 2002), p. 2. Even were such a database to exist, it would prove only that parents had not paid debts imposed on them by the government, not debts they themselves had done anything to incur. Though the GAO found "inappropriate" collection measures, including that "non-custodial parents' wages have been improperly withheld," its list of sources consulted for the study does not include any non-custodial parents who pay the support.

349. Braver, *Divorced Dads*, p. 33 (note 22 cites previous studies with similar findings on unemployment) and chap. 4.

350. Kimberly Folse and Hugo Varela-Alvarez, "Long-Run Economic Consequences of Child Support Enforcement for the Middle Class," *Journal of Socio-Economics*, vol. 31, no. 3 (2002), pp. 273, 285. The authors are refuting Lenore Weitzman's highly influential but wildly inaccurate book, *The Divorce Revolution* (New York: Free Press, 1987). Weitzman, who has acknowledged her report was wrong, is also refuted

by Cynthia A. McNeely, "Lagging Behind The Times: Parenthood, Custody, and Gender Bias in the Family Court," *Florida State University Law Review*, vol. 25, no. 4 (Summer 1998).

351. Judi Bartfeld and Daniel Meyer, "Are There Really Deadbeat Dads?" *Social Service Review*, vol. 68 (1994), pp. 219-235.

352. Kathleen Parker, "The Deadbeat Dad Is Less a Scoundrel than an Object of Pity," *Orlando Sentinel*, 17 October 1999; Deborah Simmons, "Divorced Dads Taking It on the Chin, Then Some," *Washington Times*, 9 November 1999, p. E6.

353. Braver, *Divorced Dads*, p. 34.

354. K. C. Wilson, *The Multiple Scandals of Child Support* (Richmond, Virginia: Harbinger Press, 2002), p. 18.

355. As measured by either expenditures or total collections. *1998 Green Book*, section 8, table 8-1, p. 549.

356. Robert Seidenberg, *The Father's Emergency Guide to Divorce-Custody Battle* (Takoma Park, Maryland: JES, 1997), pp. 107-108, to whose account I am indebted; Irwin Garfinkel and Sara McLanahan, *Single Mothers and their Children, A New American Dilemma* (Washington: Urban Institute Press, 1986), pp. 24-25.

357. Comanor, "Child Support Payments," p. 8.

358. Department of Health and Human Services, *Child Support Enforcement (CSE) FY 2002 Preliminary Data Report*, 29 April 2003, figures 1 and 2.

359. Comanor, "Child Support Payments," p. 5.

360. Sanford L. Braver, *et al.*, "Adaption of the Non-Custodial Parents: Patterns over Time," paper presented at the conference of the American Psychological Association, Atlanta, Georgia, 1988; F. L. Sonenstein and C. A. Calhoun, "Determinants of Child Support: A Pilot Survey of Absent Parents," *Contemporary Policy Issues* 8 (1990); Carmen Solomon, *The Child Support Enforcement Program: Policy and Practice*, Congressional Research Service, 8 December 1989, pp. 1-3.

361. *2003 Green Book* (Washington: U.S. House of Representatives, Ways and Means Committee Print 108-6, 2004), p. 8-69 and table 8-5. Earlier versions are similar.

362. *1998 Green Book* , p. 596. See also *Child Support Enforcement: Effects of Declining Welfare Caseloads Are Beginning to Emerge* (Washington: General Accounting Office, GAO/HEHS-99-105, 1999), pp. 5ff.

363. *Report to the House of Representatives Committee on Ways and Means and the Senate Committee on Finance: Child Support Enforcement Incentive Funding* (Washington: Department of Health and Human Services, February 1997). The subsidy apparently fueled the corruption in Arkansas (described in chapter 1).

364. *2003 Green Book*, table 8-4. State enforcement agencies are among the most aggressive lobbyists to increase their federal payments. See "Statement of Nathaniel L. Young Jr., director, Virginia . . . division of child-support enforcement . . . before the . . . House Committee on Ways and Means Hearing on Child Support and Fatherhood, June 28, 2001."

365. Green, interview with Tindall.

366. HHS press release, 27 January 2000. Researchers of different sympathies agree that the enforcement crackdowns have had virtually no effect. "Children living with single mothers are no more likely to receive child support today than they were two decades ago," wrote Elaine Sorensen of the Urban Institute in 1999. "The figure was around 31 percent then, and it is around 31 percent today." "Dead-Broke Dads," *Washington Post*, 1 June 1999.

367. *Child Support Enforcement: Clear Guidance*, p. 7.

368. All states now have mandatory wage withholding for all child-support orders from the time the order is issued. Previously, this had been only a remedial measure against fathers who failed to pay. This "declares divorced fathers 'guilty' of being probable deadbeats simply by reason of being divorced." Braver, *Divorced Dads*, p. 103.

369. Department of Health and Human Services, *Child Support Enforcement FY 1998 Preliminary Data Report*, May 1999, figure 2, p. 35; *Child Support Enforcement: Effects of Declining Welfare Caseloads*, pp. 7-8. Wilson, *Multiple Scandals*, pp. 27ff.

370. As the Clinton administration was touting its success, the Ways and Means Committee was arriving at a very different conclusion. "In 1978, less than one-fourth of child-support payments were collected through the IV-D [welfare] program. This percentage, however, has increased every year since 1978. By 1993, more than two-thirds (67 percent) of all child-support payments were made through the IV-D program. The implication of this trend is that the IV-D program may be recruiting more and more cases from the private sector, bringing them into the public sector, providing them with subsidized services (or substituting Federal spending for State spending), but not greatly improving child-support collections." *1998 Green Book*, p. 610.

371. Jane Ross, *Child Support Enforcement: Opportunity to Reduce Federal and State Costs* (Washington: General Accounting Office, Report # GAO/T-HEHS-95-181), 13 June 1995, pp. 5-6.

372. Molly Olson, "Title IV-D: Child Support Collection and Enforcement, Welfare Service Program" (Roseville, Minnesota: Center for Parental Responsibility, March 2006).

373. "Statement of Leslie L. Frye, Chief, Office of Child Support California Department of Social Services Testimony Before the Subcommittee on Human Resources of the House Committee on Ways and Means . . . March 20, 1997," pp. 1-2.

374. William Akins, "Why Georgia's Child Support Guidelines Are Unconstitutional," *Georgia Bar Journal*, vol. 6, no. 2 (October 2000), pp. 9-10.

375. *Handbook on Child Support Enforcement*, Administration for Children and Families, Office of Child Support Enforcement, Washington, cover.

376. Braver relates a similar anecdote from a professional conference. *Divorced Dads*, p. 35.

377. Seidenberg, *Father's Emergency Guide*, p. 108. Christensen also found "windfalls to the custodial parents." "Strange Politics of Child Support," p. 66.

378. Robert J. Willis, "Child Support and the Problem of Economic Incentives," p. 42, and Robert A. McNeely and Cynthia A. McNeely, "Hopelessly Defective: An Examination of the Assumptions Underlying Current Child Support Guidelines," p. 170, both in William S. Comanor (ed.), *The Law and Economics of Child Support Payments* (Cheltenham: Edward Elgar, 2004).

379. Saul Hoffman and Greg Duncan, "The Effects of Incomes, Wages, and AFDC Benefits on Marital Disruption," *Journal of Human Resources* 30 (1995), pp. 19-41; Lowell Gallaway and Richard Vedder, *Poverty, Income Distribution, the Family and Public Policy* (Washington: Government Printing Office, 1986), pp. 84-89.

380. Folse and Varela-Alvarez, "Long-Run Economic Consequences," pp. 274, 283, 284.

381. "Strange Politics of Child Support," pp. 67, 63.

382. Christensen, "Strange Politics of Child Support," p. 65 (original emphasis).

383. Robert Page, "'Family Courts': An Effective Judicial Approach to the Resolution of Family Disputes," *Juvenile and Family Court Journal*, vol. 44, no. 1 (1993), pp. 9, 11 (original emphasis).

384. Helen Alvare, "Types and Styles of Family Proceedings," Report of the United States to the XII World Congress, International Association of Procedural Law, 2003, p. 5.

385. Online: http://www.acf.dhhs.gov/programs/cse/davidros.htm, accessed 15 October 2001.

Notes

386. Online: http://www.ncsea.org/about/, accessed 28 September 2001.

387. National Conference of State Legislatures Web site (http://www.ncsl.org/programs/cyf/BRANCH.HTM, accessed August 7, 2000.

388. See chapter 2.

389. Barry Koplen, *Minority Report: Virginia's Quadrennial Child Support Guideline Review Commission*, 20 July 1999.

390. Daniel Drummond, "Professor Ousted from Child-Support Panel," *Washington Times*, 4 August 2001; letter from Louis Rossiter, 28 August 2001. The panelist was dismissed expressly for his "opinions": "Upon reviewing your opinions published in the June 17, 2001, *Washington Times*, we question whether you would be able to work effectively with other Panel members," the secretary wrote. "I find it difficult to see how you could effectively participate along with representatives of other groups that very likely have different perspectives than yours." The purpose of such panels, as mandated by state and federal law, is to have a variety of viewpoints represented.

391. Akins, "Why Georgia's Child Support Guidelines Are Unconstitutional," p. 12. Most panels do not include an economist, despite a federal requirement that the cost of raising children be considered in creating guidelines.

392. "Revisiting the 'Politics of Fatherhood': Administrative Agencies, Family Life, and Public Policy," *PS: Political Science and Politics*, vol. 36, no. 4 (October 2003). "Some research findings suggest that unrealistically high child-support orders, in combination with other child-support enforcement policies, have a negative effect on contact between non-custodial parents and their children."

393. *In Re Marriage of Sandra Lee Holmberg v. Ronald Gerald Holmberg, et al.* State of Minnesota In Supreme Court, C7-97-926, C8-97-1132, C9-98-33, C7-97-1512 (Office of Appellate Courts, filed 28 January 1999).

394. *Ibid.* In most states enforcement agents themselves have the power to "adjust" child-support orders by administrative fiat, by-passing the courts and due process of law altogether, according to NCSL. Attempts have been made to legitimate this process and extend it to private contractors, again contrary to the separation of powers and granting administrative agencies and private companies virtually dictatorial powers over the personal finances of private citizens. "Child Support Distribution Act of 2000, HR 4678," House of Representatives Committee on Ways and Means press release, 20 July 2000.

395. Georgia Department of Human Resources *ex. rel. Charles R. Reddick Special Assistant Attorney General o/b/o Robin Kayla Sweat Samuel E. Sweat, Jr. Cynthia M. Sweat V. Michelle L. Sweat and Samuel Sweat, Sr.*, Civil Action No. 2000 C 127, decided 25 February 2002, Judge Dane Perkins, Superior Court, Atkinson County,Ga.

396. *Parrett v. Parrett*, 146 Wis. 2d 830 at 842, 432 NW 2d 664 (6) (1988, the Court of Appeals of Wisconsin).

397. *Gallaher v. Elam*, No. E2000-02719-COA-R3-CV (Tenn. App. 01/29/2002); Shirley Downing, "DHS Keeps Child Support Rules Intact," GoMemphis.com, 13 August 2002 (http://www.gomemphis.com/mca/local_news/article/0,1426,MCA_437_1322102,00.html, accessed 13 August 2002).

398. See chapter 1.

399. Akins, "Why Georgia's Child Support Guidelines Are Unconstitutional," p. 12.

400. James Johnston, "The Father of Today's Child Support Public Policy," *Fathering Magazine*, August 1999 (http://www.fathermag.com/907/child-support/, accessed 1 October 2001).

401. Bob Mook, "Reforms Might Benefit Child-Support Company," *Denver Business Journal*, vol. 48, no. 42 (27 June 1997), p. 18A(1).

Notes

402. Ginger Thompson, "Testimony before the Domestic Relations Subcommittee of the Joint Standing Committee on the Judiciary, September 12, 1999."

403. Koplen, *Minority Report*.

404. McNeely and McNeely, "Hopelessly Defective," p. 161.

405. R. Mark Rogers and Donald J. Bieniewicz, "Child Support Guidelines: Underlying Methodologies, Assumptions, and the Impact on Standards of Living," in William S. Comanor (ed.), *The Law and Economics of Child Support Payments* (Cheltenham: Edward Elgar, 2004), p. 87. This article, along with others by both Rogers and Bieniewicz (cited below) and Akins, "Why Georgia's Child Support Guidelines Are Unconstitutional," provide among the best economic analyses of why guidelines in current use throughout the U.S. and other countries result in awards that are wildly inflated, approximately twice the costs of raising children. Another cogent analysis is Roger Gay, "A Further Look at Child Support Guidelines," *PS: Political Science and Politics*, vol. 37, no. 4 (October 2004), pp. 729-730.

406. R. Mark Rogers, "Wisconsin-Style and Income Shares Child Support Guidelines: Excessive Burdens and Flawed Economic Foundation," *Family Law Quarterly*, vol. 33, no. 1 (Spring 1999).

407. Robert Williams, "Implementation of the Child Support Provisions of the Family Support Act: Child Support Guidelines, Updating of Awards, and Routine Income Withholding," in Irwin Garfinkel, *et al.*, (eds.), *Child Support and Child Well Being* (Washington: Urban Institute Press, 1994), pp. 104-105.

408. Donald J. Bieniewicz, "Improving State Child Support Guidelines," testimony to the Virginia Child Support Quadrennial Review Panel, 22 June 1999, p. 2, note 4.

409. Elaine Sorensen, *et al.*, *Examining Child Support Arrears in California* (Urban Institute, March 2003), Executive Summary, p. 16.

410. R. Mark Rogers, "Testimony on Hyde-Woolsey Child Support Bill, HR 1488, presented to the Human Resources Subcommittee of the House Ways and Means Committee, March 16, 2000."

411. U.S. Department of Health and Human Services, Office of Child Support Enforcement, *The Story Behind the Numbers: Who Owes the Child Support Debt?* (July 2004).

412. "Supportkids, Inc., Announces Major Funding," company press release, PRNewswire, 13 March 2000.

413. Wilson, *Multiple Scandals*, p. 50.

414. Kathleen Parker, "Deadbeat Dads More Myth than Reality," *Orlando Sentinel*, 24 January 1999, p. G3; Parke and Brott, *Throwaway Dads*, p. 68.

415. "Eye on Privateers: Maximus Inc.," Web site of the American Federation of State, County, and Municipal Employees, November 1999 (http://www.afscme.org/publications/leader/1999/99110108.htm).

416. *Child Support Enforcement*, pp. 3, 9.

417. The series ran 12 April - 3 May 1998.

418. David Fallis, "Ex-Aides to Curry Awaded Contracts," *Washington Post*, 23 July 2000, p. C01. The *Post* seems reluctant to reveal what the contracts were for.

419. Michael Dresser, "Audit Sought of Maximus Company," *Baltimore Sun*, 21 March 2002, and "Maximus Allegations to be Probed; Child Support Enforcer Accused of Misconduct," *Baltimore Sun*, 30 March 2002.

420. Ron Brown, "Officials Complained of R.A.I.D. 'Assault,'" *News and Advance*, 6 January 2002.

421. "Court Cuts Off Checks to MidAmerica," *Wichita Eagle*, 16 December 1998.

Notes

422. Greg Krikorian and Nicholas Ricarrdi, "For Parents Seeking Relief, Courts Don't Always Help," *Los Angeles Times*, 12 October 1998.

423. Greg Krikorian and Nicholas Ricarrdi, "In 9 of 10 Child Support Cases, D.A. Comes Up Empty-Handed," *Los Angeles Times*, 11 October 1998.

424. Greg Krikorian, "D.A.'s Sweep of Deliquent Parents Also Nets Criticism," *Los Angeles Times*, 7 August 1999.

425. "Corruption: New Scandals in L.A. Court," *Insight*, vol. 15, no. 45 (6 December 1999).

426. Nicholas Riccardi, "Special Report," *Los Angeles Times*, 15 August 1999, p. 1.

427. Greg Krikorian and Nicholas Riccardi, "Probe of Alleged Child Support Fraud Faulted," *Los Angeles Times*, 19 August 1999, Record edition, p. 1. All the GAO officials insisted on speaking anonymously, and the GAO report is not posted or listed on its Web site. A GAO public affairs officer (Susan Becker, 26 September 2001) told me such anonymity is very unusual.

428. "Father Figures: Darling Seeks a More Effective Child Support Agency," *The Times*, 2 July 1999; Andy McSmith, "Minister Says CSA Is 'Not Fit For Purpose' after Rise in Complaints," *The Independent*, 28 June 2006; "Minister: Reform of Child Support Agency to Take Years, *The Scotsman*, 4 July 2006.

429. Quoted in John Stapleton, "'Problem' Parents Doing Time," *The Australian*, 8-9 April 2000, p. 26.

430. *Child Support: The Financial Cost to the Taxpayer* (Melbourne, Australia: PIR Independent Research Group, September 2004), pp. 3, 7, 9, 20.

431. Jim Tharpe, "State May Be on Verge of Child Support Clash," *Atlanta Journal-Constitution*, 14 March 2002.

432. Donna Laframboise, "Having Her Wedding Cake and Eating It, Too," *National Post*, 22 February 2000, p. A21.

433. "Read All About Deadbeat Parents as Search Moves to N. Virginia," *Washington Times*, 31 October 2005, p. 1.

434. Henry, "Child Support at a Crossroads," pp. 236-237.

435. *Foster's Daily Democrat* (Dover, New Hampshire), 24 February 1998, letters. I am indebted to Paul Clements for documents and analysis of the figures.

436. Robert O'Harrow, "Uncle Sam Has All Your Numbers," *Washington Post*, 27 June 1999, p. A1.

437. Letter to Louis Rossiter, Virginia secretary of health and human resources, 4 August 2001.

438. Bruce Walker, "Deadbeat Dads? Look Closer," *Christian Science Monitor*, 16 August 1996, p. 18.

439. *Fearon v. Fearon*, 207 Va. at 931, 154 S.E.2d at 168.

440. Braver, *Divorced Dads*, p. 33, esp. note 22.

441. Ned Hunter, "Half Not Making Child Support Payments," *Rocky Mount Telegram* (n.d.; http://www.rockymounttelegram.com/news/newsfd/auto/feed/news/2003/10/26/1067228243.19830.7780.9188.html, accessed 27 October 2003).

442. *FY 2002 Preliminary Data Report*, 29 April 2003.

443. Kathryn Edin, *et al.*, *Low-Income, Non-Residential Fathers: Off-Balance in a Competitive Economy* (28 September 1998), HHS Web site (http://fatherhood.hhs.gov/ELN/eln98.htm); Polly Hughes, "Many Dads Who Don't Pay Child Support Are Destitute," *Houston Chronicle*, 18 December 1998.

444. Green, interview with Tindall; "A Little Help for Some 'Deadbeat' Dads."

Notes

445. "A Little Help for Some 'Deadbeat' Dads," *Washington Post*, 15 November 1995, p. A25.

446. Parke and Brott, *Throwaway Dads*, pp. 64-65.

447. Dave Brown, "The Booming Return of Debtors' Prisons," *Ottawa Citizen*, 16 March 2002.

448. Brook Masters, "Child Custody's Moving Problem," *Washington Post*, 20 September 1998, and court documents.

449. See chapter 1.

450. *1998 Green Book*, p. 598 and *passim*; David Rovella, "Bad for Debtors, Worse for Mothers," *National Law Journal*, 2 April 2001. The *Journal* quotes the American Academy of Matrimonial Lawyers saying that 500,000 child-support obligors have been through bankruptcy in the previous six years.

451. *Federal Register*, 17 December 1999 (64 FR 70919).

452. Walker, "Deadbeat Dads?"

453. Michael Sadowski, "Temperatures Lead to Record Numbers at Homeless Shelter," *Scranton Times Tribune*, 16 January 2004.

454. Peter Kilborn, "An All-American Town, a Sky-High Divorce Rate," *New York Times* 2 May 2004. See also Bryce Christensen, "Homeless America," in *Divided We Fall* (New Brunswick, N.J., 2006).

455. Eric Eckholm, "Plight Deepens for Black Men, Studies Warn," *New York Times*, 20 March 2006.

456. "Deadbeat Parents Targeted," *Gadsden Times*, 14 December 2002.

457. Ray Delgado, "Air Traffic Controller Held as 'Robust Robber,'" *San Francisco Chronicle*, 10 August 2001.

458. Steve Timko, "Lawyer Says Man Robbed Bank for Child Support," *Reno Gazette-Journal*, 17 May 2004.

459. Andy Newman, "Brooklyn Judges Faces Charges of Corruption, *New York Times*, 23 April 2004.

460. *Child Support: The Financial Cost*, p. 3.

461. Donald Hubin surveys the scholarship on the emotional and physical toll exacted on fathers by the confiscation of their children. "Parental Rights and Due Process," *Journal of Law and Family Studies*, vol. 1, no. 2 (1999), p. 142.

462. Christian Bottorff, "Court Refuses to Bump Judge for Comment in Custody Case," *The Tennessean*, 13 December 2002.

463. *Morning Star*, 11 March 1999.

464. Candis McLean, "Accepting Evidence Out of Court" *The Report*, 1 April 2002, pp. 22-23.

465. Donna Laframboise, "This Is About Punishing Dad," *National Post*, 28 March 2000.

466. Akins, "Why Georgia's Child Support Guidelines Are Unconstitutional," p. 10.

467. "Fathers Get the Shaft in Family Law Proceedings," *Law and Politics*, December 1995.

468. Green, interview with Tindall.

469. Chris Cobb, "Father Battles Paying Support to Student," *National Post*, 3 September 2001, and interview with Edward Kruk.

470. Sharon Coolidge, "Parents Pay Up to Avoid Prison," *Cincinnati Enquirer*, 9 November 2003.

471. "Child Support Amendment Comes to Attention of Hill," *Washington Times*, 27 April 1999. As of April 2002, the state was still prosecuting Brandley. "The obligation for

child support does not go away," said Janece Keetch, spokeswoman for the attorney general's office. Harvey Rice, "'It's Like a Double Insult,' Free From Prison, Brandley Baffled by Order to Pay Back Child Support," *Houston Chronicle*, 27 April 2002.

472. Kathleen Ostrander, "40-cent Child Support Bill Lands Father in Court," *Milwaukee Journal Sentinel*, 10 April 1998.

473. Steven Morelli, "New Child Support Program Disputed," *Times Leader* (Wilkes Barre, Pa.), 11 June 2001.

474. Cory J. Jensen (Legislative Assistant, Men's Health Network), "Statement Submitted for Consideration by the Committee on Ways and Means, Subcommittee on Human Resources, Hearing on Fatherhood, April 27, 1999," pp. 4-5.

475. Department of Justice press release, 22 December 1994.

476. *Baltimore City Office of Child Support Enforcement v. John S. Jr.*, cited in Seidenberg, *Father's Emergency Guide*, pp. 16-17; *Quintela v. Quintela*; Neb CtApp, 4 Neb. App. 396, 2/27/96, cited in *Speak Out For Children*, vol. 12, no. 1 (Fall 1996/Winter 1997), p. 11; Ronald Henry, "The Innocent Third Party: Victims of Paternity Fraud," *Family Law Quarterly*, vol. 40, no. 1 (Spring 2006), pp. 51-52.

477. Krikorian and Ricarrdi, "For Parents Seeking Relief"; Henry, "Innocent Third Party," p. 56.

478. Henry, "Innocent Third Party," pp. 54, 58, 63, 60-62, 66, 76.

479. Marie Woolf, "Government Will Clamp Down on the DIY Paternity Test 'Cowboys,'" *The Independent*, 29 December 2000.

480. James Hickey, "DNA Testing is Not a Crime," *Kitten News*, 5 September 2004.

481. Sarah Crichton, "Stepfather Ruled Liable for Adult Child," *The Age*, 4 January 2002.

482. "Court Says Father Must Support Stepchild," Canadian Press, 13 November 1998.

483. Jake Rupert, "'Double Dipping' Child Support to be Appealed," *National Post*, 18 July 2000; Cristin Schmitz, "Man Cut Off from Son at Birth Must Pay Support," *National Post*, 6 April 2002.

484. *Department of Revenue v. Ryan R.*, 62 Mass. App. Ct. 380 (2004)

485. KOB-TV Web site: "Governor Orders Investigation into Trevino Case," 12 December 2004 (http://www.kobtv.com/index.cfm?viewer=storyviewer&id=15631&cat=NMTOPSTORIES); "Woman May Have Already Conned Several Agencies about Child" 9 December 2004 (http://www.kobtv.com/index.cfm?viewer=storyviewer&id=15576&cat=SEARCH).

486. Dave Brown, "Avoiding Court Is Best Defence," *Ottawa Citizen*, 12 January 2002.

487. "Wife Guilty of Harboring Deadbeat Dad," *Oregonian*, 21 August 1999; Alliance for Non-Custodial Parents' Rights press release, 4 December 1999. The conviction was upheld by a federal appeals court in *United States v. Hill*, No. 00-30023 (9th Cir. 07/27/2001).

488. Quoted in Henry, "Child Support at a Crossroads," p. 240.

489. Greg Stone, "Son Who Owed Child Support Had Name on Accounts," *Charleston Gazette*, 21 July 2000.

490. "State Takes Money from Child to Pay his Support," Associated Press, 26 February 2003.

491. Jan Warner and Jan Collins, "Visitation That Isn't Spelled Out Can Often Lead to Disputes," Knight Ridder Newspapers (http://www.fortwayne.com/mld/newssentinel/living/10506825.htm, posted 27 December 2004).

492. Paula Beauchamp, "Divorced Dads Pay to See Kids," *Herald Sun*, 20 December 2003.

493. Gaby Hinsliff, "Brown Set for Male Tax Revolt," *The Observer*, 30 March 2003.

Notes

494. Erin McCormick, "'Bizarre' Ruling on Teenage Father," *San Francisco Examiner*, 1 December 1996; Supreme Court of Kansas, 252 Kan. 646; 847 P.2d 1273; 1993 Kan.; Associated Press, 30 October 1998; Dawson Bell, "Child Support Just, Court Says," *Detroit Free Press*, 21 February 2004. See also *Stringer v. Baker*, 104 P.3d 1132 (Okla.Civ. App. 1988).

495. Susan Hiller, "Elderly Man Who Said He Was Sexually Assaulted by Maid Awarded Damages," *National Post*, 3 October 2000.

496. Heidi Jeursivich, "Program's First Year a Success," *Richmond Times-Dispatch*, 12 July 1998.

497. Kim Bates, "Ex-Wife's Belated Bid for Support Jolts Man, 77," *Toledo Blade*, 28 February 2001.

498. Ann Givens, "Daughter Sues for Child Support," *Newsday*, 12 October 2005.

499. Leslie Parrilla, "Judge Orders Parents to Support 50-Year-Old Son," Scripps Howard News Service, reported in the *Ventura County Star*, 3 August 2001.

500. Joanna Weiss, "Trip to Aid Ailing Sister Leads to Court Battle," *Boston Globe*, 2 December 1999, p. B1.

501. Marjorie Rosen and Michael Haederle, "Felled by the Aftershocks," *People*, 27 May 1996, p. 121.

502. *Wilson v. Wilson*, 18 Va. App. 193 acknowledged the "wife's fault in leaving husband" but ruled it irrelevant in a support award from the involuntarily divorced husband, who was also ordered to pay the fees of an attorney he had not hired. On the other hand, "horseback riding for the child" was ruled relevant.

503. Account compiled from interviews with White's daughter and Todd Eckert, President of the Parent and Child Advocacy Coalition, who were assisting White before his death, and from reports in the *National Post*, 23, 25, and 27 March 2000, the *Vancouver Sun*, 24 March 2000, and the *Ottawa Citizen*, 27 March 2000.

504. Michelle Landsberg, "There's More Behind Father's 'Martyrdom,'" *Toronto Star*, 9 April 2000; Angela MacIsaac, "Ex-Girlfriend Miffed at How Custody Battle Is Portrayed," *Kamloops Daily News*,10 February 2003, p. A3

505. Jeff Lee, "Family Blames Justice System For Pushing Man to Suicide," *Vancouver Sun*, 23 March 2000.

506. John Maguire, "Crushed, and in Despair over Probate Court Treatment, Two Massachusetts Fathers Take Their Own Lives" (unpublished article written for the *Massachusetts News*, and interviews with the London family, August 1999.

507. Online: http://www.nacsa.org, accessed 1 October 2001. It was featured in *The Times*, 3 August 2000.

508. Alexandra Frean "CSA Demands 'Drove Father to Kill Himself,'" *The Times*, 3 August 2000.

509. John Stapleton, "'Problem' Parents Doin' Time," *The Australian*, 8-9 April 2000.

510. Bettina Arndt, "When Love Fails," *The Age*, 4 August 2001.

511. Augustine Kposowa., "Marital Status and Suicide in the National Longitudinal Mortality Study," *Journal of Epidemiology and Community Health* 54 (April 2000), pp. 254-261; University of California at Riverside press release (n.d.); reports by Reuters, CBS, and CNN, all on 15 March 2000; and correspondence with Augustine Kposowa.

512. Nancy West, "Family Waiting For Answers in Ex-Inmate's Death," *New Hampshire Sunday News*, 19 February 2000, p. 1A, and "Inmate Says Man Who Died Was Beaten at Jail," *New Hampshire Sunday News*, 5 March 2000, p. 16A; and interviews with the Armstrong family. The U.S. attorney's office in Concord, New Hampshire repeatedly refused to discuss the case.

513. WXIA-TV Web site (http://www.11alive.com/local/local_top_story.asp?storyid=14843; posted 23 February 2002).

514. Associated Press, "Georgia Inmate Said Killed Over Secret," *Savannah Morning News*, 1 August 2001.

515. *Speak Out For Children*, vol. 14, no. 1 (Spring 1999).

516. Ronald Mincy and Hillard Pouncy, "Paternalism, Child Support Enforcement, and Fragile Families," in Lawrence Mead (ed.), *The New Paternalism: Supervisory Approaches to Poverty* (Washington: Brookings, 1997), p. 144.

517. Web site of the Administration for Children and Families (http://www.acf.hhs.gov/programs/region2/marriages.doc, accessed 4 December 2003.

518. "HHS Awards Grants for Child Support Development Projects," HHS press release 2 January 2003.

519. "ACF Approves Child Support Demonstrations in Michigan and Idaho," HHS press release, 9 May 2003.

520. These advertisements were on the Ad Council Web site (http://www.adcouncil.org/fr_camp_current.html) in the summer of 1999 but appear to have been removed.

521. Katharine Biele, "Government's Fatherhood Campaign Takes to the TV," *Christian Science Monitor*, 16 April 1999.

522. Cathy Young, "Absent Dads Aren't Always to Blame for the Problems," *Detroit News*, 7 April 1999.

523. "HHS Fatherhood Initiative," *HHS Fact Sheet*, 21 June 1999.

524. "Child Support Debtors Get 5-Day Amnesty," *Washington Post*, 10 September 2000, p. C01.

525. Associated Press, "Domino's Pizza Blasts Attorney General for Role in Billboard Contest," *Detroit Free Press*, 8 October 2004.

526. Stuart Miller, "The Myth of Deadbeat Dads," *Wall Street Journal*, 2 March 1995, p. A14.

527. Online (http://www.ojp.usdoj.gov/bjs/jails.htm).

528. Tony Bartelme, "Prisoners Incarcerated for Child Support Debts Add to Charleston County Jail's Overcrowding," *Post and Courier*, 19 October 2003.

529. Richard Raeke, "County Eyes Work-Release Facility for 'Deadbeat Dads,'" *Walton County Tribune*, 14 March 1999.

530. Brian Nearing, "Facility Proposed for Deadbeat Dads," *Pittsburgh News*, 26 June 2001.

531. See chapter 2.

532. Letter from Lawrence Crow, Sheriff, Polk County, to Frances Griner, 25 July 2003. I am grateful to Ms. Griner for a copy of this letter. She reports that it took requests over three years to receive it.

Chapter 4 / Batterers or Protectors?

533. Eric Zorn, "A Seminar in Divorce, Down-And-Dirty Style," *Chicago Tribune*, 4 November 1988, p. 1.

534. "Oh Dad, Poor Dad," *Toronto Globe and Mail*, 12 April 1997, pp. D1-2.

535. Kara Morrison, "Yes, This Marriage Can Be Saved," *Detroit News*, 4 May 2000.

536. "Obtaining and Defending Against an Order of Protection," *Illinois Bar Journal*, vol. 93, no. 6 (June 2005).

537. "Speaking the Unspeakable," *Massachusetts Bar Association Newsletter*, vol. 33, no. 7 (June-July 1993), p. 1.

Notes

538. Lisa Scott, "Scream Queens Fuel Nightmarish VAWA System," The Price of Liberty Web site (http://www.thepriceofliberty.org/05/07/05/guest_scott.htm), 5 July 2005.

539. "Criminal Law Comes Home," *Yale Law Review*, vol. 116, no. 2 (2006), p. 10.

540. Dave Brown, "Gender-Bias Issue Raises 'Optics' Problem in Domestic Court," *Ottawa Citizen*, 21 February 2002.

541. *New Jersey Law Journal*, 21 April 1988, letters to the editor section, p. 6, quoted in Warren Farrell, *Women Can't Hear What Men Don't Say* (New York: Tarcher/Putnam, 1999), p. 153.

542. "The New Star Chamber," *Rutgers Law Review*, vol. 57, no. 3 (Spring 2005), p. 1009.

543. "Criminal Law Comes Home."

544. "Transforming A Flawed Policy: A Call To Revive Psychology and Science in Domestic Violence Research and Practice," *Aggression and Violent Behavior* 11 (2006), p. 478. "In examining research on battery, one sees that respected medical periodicals uncritically indulge the feminists in their inflammatory tendencies. . . . Medical journals have dropped their usual standards when reporting findings of the battery studies." Christina Hoff Sommers, *Who Stole Feminism?* (New York: Simon and Schuster, 1995), pp. 202-203.

545. Speech at Becker College, February 2000, quoted in press release from Law Office of Attorney Gregory A. Hession, JD, 30 July 2001 (http://www.massoutrage.com/rodirtytricks.htm).

546. "Criminal Law Comes Home," pp. 7-9.

547. Studies going back twenty-five years, many by feminist scholars, are listed in the appendix to Farrell, *Women Can't Hear*. See also his chap. 6, as well as Cathy Young, *Ceasefire: Why Women and Men Must Join Forces to Achieve True Equality* (New York: Free Press, 1999), chap. 4; Martin S. Fiebert, "References Examining Assaults by Women on their Spouses or Male Partners: An Annotated Bibliography," *Sexuality and Culture*, vol. 8, no. 3-4 (2004); Donald G. Dutton, *Rethinking Domestic Violence* (Vancouver: University of British Columbia Press, 2006); John Archer, "Sex Differences in Aggression Between Heterosexual Partners: A Meta-Analytic Review," *Psychological Bulletin*, vol. 126, no. 5 (September 2000); Murray A. Straus, "The Controversy over Domestic Violence by Women: A Methodological, Theoretical, and Sociology of Science Analysis," in X. B. Arriaga, and S. Oskamp, *Violence in Intimate Relationships* (Thousand Oaks: Sage, 1999).

548. Studies going back twenty-five years, many by feminist scholars, are listed in the appendix to Farrell, *Women Can't Hear*. See also his chap. 6, as well as Cathy Young, *Ceasefire: Why Women and Men Must Join Forces to Achieve True Equality* (New York: Free Press, 1999), chap. 4; Martin S. Fiebert, "References Examining Assaults by Women on their Spouses or Male Partners: An Annotated Bibliography," *Sexuality and Culture*, vol. 8, no. 3-4 (2004); Donald G. Dutton, *Rethinking Domestic Violence* (Vancouver: University of British Columbia Press, 2006); John Archer, "Sex Differences in Aggression Between Heterosexual Partners: A Meta-Analytic Review," *Psychological Bulletin*, vol. 126, no. 5 (September 2000); Murray A. Straus, "The Controversy over Domestic Violence by Women: A Methodological, Theoretical, and Sociology of Science Analysis," in X. B. Arriaga, and S. Oskamp, *Violence in Intimate Relationships* (Thousand Oaks: Sage, 1999).

549. Nancy Updike, "Hitting the Wall: After 20 Years of Domestic Violence Research, Scientists Can't Avoid Hard Facts," *Mother Jones*, May-June 1999.

550. Betty Friedan, *It Changed My Life: Writings on the Women's Movement* (Cambridge, Mass.: Harvard, 1998), p. 126.

551. Patricia Tjaden and Nancy Thoennes, *Extent, Nature, and Consequences of Intimate Partner Violence* (Washington: National Institute of Justice and the Centers for Disease Control and Prevention, July 2000, NCJ 181867).

552. Web site of Eric Smith, Macomb County, Michigan, prosecuting attorney (http://www.macombcountymi.gov/PROSECUTORSOFFICE/domestic_violence.htm). Why a public prosecutor keeps a personal Internet page to disseminate political opinions is not clear.

553. Valerie Schremp, "Domestic Violence Is Society's Menace," *St. Louis Post-Dispatch*, 4 February 2001.

554. John Waters, "Both Sexes Equally Offended by Bishops," *Irish Times*, 4 September 2000.

555. Young, *Ceasefire*, p. 97.

556. Online: http://www.usdoj.gov/ovw/domviolence.htm, accessed 24 August 2006.

557. Ann Tacket, Tackling Domestic Violence: The Role of Health Professionals (London: Home Office, 2004), p. 1.

558. Lenore Walker, *The Battered Woman* (New York: Harper and Row, 1979), p. 98.

559. "Psychological Abuse Found Harmful to Women's Health," Reuters in the *Washington Post*, 15 May 2000, p. A12.

560. "Who Will Speak for the Battered Men?" *The Sunday Times*, 15 November 1998.

561. Sarah Buel, "Suggestions for a Model Community Coordinated Response to Domestic Violence," presentation at American Probation and Parole Association Annual Institute, Phoenix, Arizona, 1994, in Grace Coleman, *et al.* (eds.), *1999 National Victim Assistance Academy*, chap. 8 (http://www.ojp.usdoj.gov/ovc/assist/nvaa99/chap8.htm; "last updated on Sunday, January 16, 2000.").

562. "When Violence Becomes Something to Fight Over," *Sunday Tribune*, 2 April 2000.

563. Callie Marie Rennison and Sarah Welchans, *Intimate Partner Violence* (Washington: U.S. Department of Justice, Bureau of Justice Statistics, May 2000, NCJ 178247), p. 5.

564. Testimony to the Child and Family Law Committee for HB351, 2003, quoted in *The Status of Men in New Hampshire: First Biennial Report of the New Hampshire Commission on the Status of Men*, 1 November 2005, p. 15 (http://www.nh.gov/csm/downloads/nh_status_of_men_2005.pdf).

565. "Leave No-Fault Divorce Alone," *Daily Herald*, 26 December 2004.

566. Sara Catania, "Taking Away Battered Women's Kids," *Mother Jones*, 1 July 2005.

567. Michael Getler, "A Little About Me, A Lot About "Breaking the Silence'" 2 December 2005; Carey Roberts, "PBS' 'Breaking the Silence' Not Ready for Prime Time," *ifeminists.com*, 19 October 2005 (http://www.ifeminists.net/introduction/editorials/2005/1019roberts.html).

568. See chapter 1.

569. Geraldine Stahly, "Battered Women's Problems with Child Custody," in *New Directions in Domestic Violence Research*, symposium at the annual meeting of the Western Psychological Association, Los Angeles, April 1990. See also Marsha Liss and Geraldine Stahly, "Domestic Violence and Child Custody," in Marsali Hansen and Michele Harway (eds.), *Battering and Family Therapy: A Feminist Perspective* (Thousand Oaks: Sage, 1993), pp. 175-187.

570. *Congressional Record*, 31 July 1997 (105th Congress, 1st session), p. S1129.

571. *Report of the American Psychological Association Presidential Task Force on Violence and the Family*, "Issues and Dilemmas in Family Violence," Issue #4 (Washington: n.d.; http://www.apa.org/pi/pii/familyvio/issue4.html; accessed 2 November 2001).

572. Louis McHardy and Meredith Hofford, *Final Report of the Child Custody and Visitation Focus Group, March 1-3, 1999* (http://www.vaw.umn.edu/FinalDocuments/custodyfin.htm, "File Last Modified on: 12/21/99," emphasis added).

Notes

573. Suk, "Criminal Law Comes Home," pp. 49-50.

574. Cathy Young, *Domestic Violence: An In-Depth Analysis* (Washington: Independent Women's Forum, September 2005), p. 22.

575. "Criminal Law Comes Home," pp. 17, 21.

576. Warren Farrell, *Father and Child Reunion* (New York: Tarcher/Putnam, 2001), p. 198

577. "Criminal Law Comes Home," pp. 21, 54.

578. Epstein, "Speaking the Unspeakable," p. 1.

579. "Retiring Judge Reveals that Restraining Orders Are Huge Problem," *Massachusetts News*, May 2001.

580. Cathy Young, "The Abuse of Restraining Orders," *Boston Globe*, 30 August 1999, p. A19.

581. Milton H. Raphaelson, "Time to Revisit Abuse Statute," *Western Massachusetts Law Tribune*, vol. 2, no. 16 (18-24 April 2001), p. 4.

582. "From the Editor," *Family Advocate*, vol. 18 (Winter 1996), p. 1020.

583. "Fathers Get the Shaft in Family Law Proceedings," *Law and Politics*, December 1995.

584. David Dunlap, "The Adult Abuse Act: Theory vs. Practice." *UMKC Law Review*, vol. 64 (1996), p. 686, quoted in Young, *Domestic Violence*, p. 23.

585. *Ibid.*

586. Young, *Ceasefire*, pp. 125-126.

587. "Enforcement of Protective Orders," U.S. Department of Justice, Office of Justice Programs, Office for Victims of Crime, Legal Series, Bulletin #4, January 2002, p. 3, citing Donald Cochran, *Project History of the Massachusetts Statewide Automated Restraining Order Registry* (Boston, Mass.: Office of the Commissioner of Probation, Massachusetts Trial Court, July 1994).

588. Patricia Tjaden and Nancy Thoennes, *Stalking in America: Findings From the National Violence Against Women Survey* (Washington: U.S. Department of Justice, National Institute of Justice, Centers for Disease Control and Prevention, 1998).

589. Kate Zernike, "Divorced Dads Emerge as a Political Force," *Boston Globe*, 19 May 1998.

590. National Public Radio, "Morning Edition" program, 29 December 1997.

591. Young, *Ceasefire*, p. 127.

592. Massachusetts Fatherhood Coalition press release, 25 May 1999, and interviews with members. None of these facts has been disputed by the state. Spokespersons for the Massachusetts Department of Social Services and David Douglas, a social worker who designed the program under which Stewart was jailed, refused to comment.

593. John Maguire, "The Booming Domestic Violence Industry," *Massachusetts News*, 2 August 1999.

594. "Pennsylvania Man Carpools to Court and Faces Contempt," Associated Press; posted on CNN.com, 14 August 2000 (http://www.cnn.com/2000/LAW/08/14/restraining.ap/index.html). I am grateful to Stanley Green for discussions on this case.

595. Leanne Robicheau, "Man Acquitted on Sex Charges," *Bangor Daily News*, 19 February 1999.

596. Gerard Noonan, "Call for Tougher Checks on AVOs," *Sydney Morning Herald*, 30 August 1999.

597. Louise Malenfant, "Men Don't Matter: A New Study Finds the *Ex Parte* Order Is a Woman's Best Weapon Prior to Divorce," *The Report*, 16 April 2001, p. 35.

598. Hession press release, 30 July 2001.

599. Heleniak, "New Star Chamber," pp. 1036-1037.

600. *Ibid.* pp. 1036-1037, 1042.

601. "Judicial Training: 'Your Job Is to Be a Wall,'" *New Jersey Law Journal*, 24 April 1995, p. 14.

602. Quotations are from Bleemer, "N.J. Judges."

603. Tim O'Brien, "Restraining-Order Violators Jailed Without Hearings in Essex County," *New Jersey Law Journal*, 25 November 2002.

604. Eric Collins, "Group Monitors Domestic Violence Court," *News-Record* of Greensboro, North Carolina, 18 January 2006.

605. Young, *Ceasefire*, pp. 131, 126.

606. Raphaelson, "Time to Revisit Abuse Statute."

607. "Father's Rights Forgotten by Laws," *Worcester Telegram and Gazette*, 6 April 1999.

608. Maguire, "Booming Domestic Violence Industry."

609. Hession press release, 30 July 2001.

610. Stephen Schroeder and David Sharp, "Fathers Also Deserve Legal Protection Against Abuse," *St. Petersburg Times*, 2 March 1992, p. 2. Attorneys Schroeder and Sharp continue: "Issued without notice, no chance to defend, this paper says he must immediately vacate his home, that he may not contact his wife, and that she has sole custody of the kids." He was also ordered continue to pay the mortgage, all utilities, and other "living expenses," in addition to child support.

611. Paul Carpenter, "PFA Blizzard Doesn't Stop the Brutes," *Morning Call*, 10 October 1999, p. B01.

612. "A Child's Unheeded Cry for Help," *Washington Post*, 8 June 2001, p. A1.

613. John Maguire, "Twenty Dollars an Hour to Visit Your Child," *Massachusetts News*, 2 August 1999, and correspondence with Joseph Rizoli (25 June 1999).

614. Stan Rains, "Visitation Center Dracula," *Fathering Magazine* (http://www.fathermag.com/007/visitation-center/; accessed 8 December 2001). Rains was placed under a gag order following the publication of this article, according to his attorney, David Sibley of Corpus Christi, Texas.

615. Jordana Hart, "On Neutral Ground," *Boston Globe*, 4 September 1999.

616. SVN Web site: http://www.svnetwork.net/301Guidelines.html, accessed 3 October 2001, emphasis added.

617. Maguire, "Twenty Dollars an Hour," and interview with Michael Ewing.

618. Robert Peterson, *The Impact of Manhatten's Specialized Domestic Violence Court*, (New York: New York City Criminal Justice Agency, 2004), p. 2.

619. Frank Donnelly, "Domestic Violence Court to Debut," *Staten Island Advance*, 14 December 2003.

620. Angela Gover, *et al.*, "Combating Domestic Violence: Findings from an Evaluation of a Local Domestic Violence Court," *Criminology and Public Policy*, vol. 3, no. 1 (2003), pp. 109-132, table 11.

621. Terje Langeland, "Railroaded for Domestic Violence Defendants, El Paso County's 'Fast Track' May Not Always Lead to Justice," *Colorado Springs Independent*, 15-21 August 2002.

622. Elizabeth Gettelman, "A New Order in the Court," *Mother Jones*, 1 July 2005.

623. Michael Rips and Amy Lester, "When Words Bear Witness," *New York Times*, 20 March 2006.

624. Peterson, *Manhatten's Domestic Violence Court*, p. 63.

Notes

625. "Official Ontario Government Press Release: Fact Sheet—Domestic Violence Protection Act—An Act to Better Protect Victims of Domestic Violence," 19 December 2000.

626. "Train AGs in Rudimentary Law," *Law Times*, 13 November 2001, p. 8.

627. Quoted in Dave Brown, "Skirmish Fails to Scratch the Formidable Feminist War Machine," *Ottawa Citizen*, 9 April 2002.

628. Robert Verkaik, "Crackdown Unveiled on Domestic Violence," *The Independent*, 19 November 2001.

629. Carl Friedrich and Zbigniew Brzezinski, *Totalitarian Dictatorship and Autocracy* (Cambridge, Mass.: Harvard, 1965), p. 216.

630. Rosemary H. T. O'Kane, *The Revolutionary Reign of Terror: The Role of Violence in Political Change* (Aldershot: Edward Elgar, 1991), pp. 22, 39, 253.

631. Documents from Warren County, Pennsylvania, in the author's possession.

632. Friedrich and Brzezinski, *Totalitarian Dictatorship*, p. 195.

633. Erin Pizzey, "How Feminists Tried to Destroy the Family," *Daily Mail*, 22 January 2007.

634. Donna Laframboise, "One-Stop Divorce Shops," *National Post*, 21 November 1998, and correspondence with Louise Malenfant.

635. *Ibid.*

636. Donna Laframboise, "Battered Shelters," *National Post*, 14 November 1998.

637. Philip Cook, *Abused Men: The Hidden Side of Domestic Violence* (Westport, Connecticut: Praeger, 1997).

638. Patricia Pearson, *When She Was Bad: Violent Women and the Myth of Innocence* (New York: Viking, 1997), pp. 142.

639. Interview on American Morning with Paula Zahn (CNN), "Actress and Model Tawny Kitaen Getting Some Very Unwanted Attention," aired 5 April 2002 (http://www.cnn.com/TRANSCRIPTS/0204/05/ltm.09.html). On October 26, 1999, an e-mail circular signed by Eileen King, said, "NOW in Washington needs summaries of cases in which a known batterer and/or child abuser has been granted custody (full or joint) or unsupervised access to a child or children. If you know that "Fathers' Rights" individuals/groups were involved, please include that information." More than seven years later, NOW has not published a single instance of any such *male* batterer or child abuser getting custody.

640. Farrell, *Women Can't Hear*, p. 137.

641. *Second Chances: Men, Women, and Children a Decade After Divorce* (New York: Ticknor & Fields, 1989), pp. 10-15.

642. *Surviving the Breakup: How Children and Parents Cope with Divorce* (New York: Basic Books, 1980), pp. 65-66, 68-69, 81, 86.

643. "We Should Work to Save Kids from Divorce," *Minneapolis Star Tribune*, 26 July 2000. See also Patrick Fagan and Robert Rector, *The Effects of Divorce on America* (Washington: Heritage Foundation, 2000).

644. Stephen Baskerville, *Family Violence in America: The Truth about Domestic Violence and Child Abuse* (Washington: American Coalition for Fathers and Children, 2006), chap. 6.

645. *Child Sexual Abuse, Assault, and Molest Issues*, Report No. 8, A Report by the 1991-92 San Diego County Grand Jury, 29 June 1992 (http://www.co.san-diego.ca.us/cnty/cnty depts/safety/grand/reports/report8.html).

646. The National Incidence Studies (NIS) of the Department of Health and Human Services are regarded as authoritative. Nevertheless, though it is not stated explicitly in the studies, an official at the National Clearinghouse on Child Abuse and Neglect Information,

342

which conducts the NIS, explained to me that, unlike the annual HHS reports on child maltreatment, the NIS studies are not limited to reports from state agencies (themselves not necessarily judicially substantiated) but also include cases based on proactive interviews with "sentinels" about abuse that is not reported but which, she said, they nevertheless somehow know is happening. Some might call this a "fishing expedition." Even these figures indicate that a miniscule percentage of child sex abuse accusations against fathers—the principal accusations used in custody battles—are substantiated. See below, note 142.

647. *When Child Protection Investigations Harm Children*, American Civil Liberties Union of Washington, October 1997. See also Dorothy Rabinowitz, *No Crueler Tyrannies: Accusation, False Witness, and other Terrors of our Times* (New York: Wall Street Journal Books, 2003).

648. Douglas Besharov, "Unfounded Allegations—A New Child Abuse Problem," *Public Interest* (Spring 1986), p. 22.

649. "Testimony of Jane Knitzer, Children's Defense Fund, Amendments to Social Services, Foster Care, and Child Welfare Programs, Hearing, Subcommittee on Public Assistance and Unemployment Compensation of the Committee on Ways and Means, U.S. House of Representatives," 22 and 27 March 1979.

650. Little Hoover Commission, *For the Sake of the Children: Restructuring Foster Care in California*, Report #115, 9 April 1992, conclusion.

651. Riya Bhattacharjee, "David Beauvais: Defender of the First Amendment," *Berkeley Daily Planet*, 28 April 2006.

652. Ross D. Parke and Armin A. Brott, *Throwaway Dads* (Boston: Houghton Mifflin, 1999), p. 44.

653. *Families in Crisis*, report by the 1991-92 San Diego County Grand Jury (http://www.co.san-diego.ca.us/cnty/cntydepts/safety/grand/reports/report2.html).

654. Susan Orr, *Child Protection at the Crossroads: Child Abuse, Child Protection, and Recommendations for Reform* (Los Angeles: Reason Public Policy Institute, October 1999), pp. 10-12 and *passim*. Orr recommends criminalizing child abuse, to concentrate investigations on truly serious cases and to ensure that parents receive due process protections.

655. *Families in Crisis*.

656. *Elusive Innocence* (Lafayette, Louisiana: Huntington House, 2002), p. 107.

657. Sylvia Ann Hewlett and Cornel West, *The War Against Parents* (New York: Houghton Mifflin, 1998), p. 109.

658. Quoted in Parke and Brott, *Throwaway Dads*, pp. 42-43.

659. *Families in Crisis*.

660. Georgia ACLU: http://www.acluga.org/docket.html and http://www.acluga.org/briefs/dfacs/injunction.pdf, accessed 7 May 2006.

661. Quoted in "Testimony of Christopher J. Klicka, Senior Counsel of the Home School Legal Defense Association, Hearing on Reauthorization of the Child Abuse Prevention and Treatment Act . . . House Committee on Education and the Workforce," 16 October 2001.

662. Richard Wexler, *Wounded Innocents: The Real Victims of the War Against Child Abuse* (Buffalo: Prometheus Books, 1990), p. 15 (emphasis added).

663. *Families in Crisis*, which also uses the term "child abuse industry."

664. *Child Sexual Abuse, Assault, and Molest Issues*.

665. Parke and Brott, *Throwaway Dads*, pp. 44, 46-48.

666. *Child Sexual Abuse, Assault, and Molest Issues*.

667. Dana Mack, *The Assault on Parenthood* (New York: Simon and Schuster, 1997), p. 67.

668. Richard Wexler, "Take the Child and Run: Tales From the Age of ASFA," *New England Law Review*, vol. 36, no. 1 (2002), pp. 130, 136-138.

669. Andrea Sedlak and Diane Broadhurst, *Executive Summary of the Third National Incidence Study of Child Abuse and Neglect* (Washington: U.S. Department of Health and Human Services, National Center on Child Abuse and Neglect, September 1996), pp. v, 3-4.

670. Family Violence Prevention Fund press release, 23 July 1999.

671. When an Australian study concluded that "children are most likely to be neglected or abused in single-parent families headed by women," feminists attempted to put a politically correct spin on it by blaming "domestic violence" by men. "These women have left the home," said the head of the Council for Single Mothers and Their Children, Elspeth McInnes. "Both they and their child are traumatised and face a long stretch of homelessness and poverty." Quoted in Vanessa Walker, "Single Mothers' Children at Risk," *The Australian*, 10 May 2001. The report is *Child Protection Australia 1999-00*, Australian Institute of Health and Welfare, Child Welfare Series #27 (Canberra: AIHW Cat. No. CWS-13, 2001).

672. "The specificity of acknowledged child abuse with respect to maternal domestic violence was extremely high." Gregory Parkinson, *et al.*, "Maternal Domestic Violence Screening in an Office-Based Pediatric Practice," *Pediatrics*, vol. 108, no. 3 (September 2001), p. e43.

673. Donald Dutton, "Domestic Abuse Assessment in Child Custody Disputes: Beware the Domestic Violence Research Paradigm," *Journal of Child Custody*, vol. 2, no. 4 (2005), p. 27.

674. Sedlak and Broadhurst, *Executive Summary* of NIS-3, pp. v, 3-4.

675. Orr, *Child Protection at the Crossroads*, p. 1, and references cited there.

676. *Child Sexual Abuse, Assault, and Molest Issues.*

677. Parke and Brott, *Throwaway Dads*, p. 39; Holida Wakefield and Ralph Underwager, "Sexual Abuse Allegations in Divorce and Custody Disputes," *Behavioral Sciences and the Law* 9 (1991); Holida Wakefield and Ralph Underwager, "Personality Characteristics of Parents Making False Accusations of Sexual Abuse in Custody Cases," *Issues in Child Abuse Accusations*, vol. 2, no. 3 (Summer 1990).

678. *Elusive Innocence*, p. 107.

679. Ralph Underwager and Hollida Wakefield, *The Real World of Child Interrogations* (Springfield, Illinois: Charles C. Thomas, 1990), p. 127.

680. U.S. Department of Health and Human Services, Children's Bureau, *Child Maltreatment 1996* (Washington: U.S. Government Printing Office, 1998), pp. xi-xii. See also *Child Maltreatment 2004* (2006).

681. Stepfathers seem to be lumped together with fathers in HHS child abuse studies.

682. *Child Maltreatment in the United Kingdom: A Study of the Prevalence of Child Abuse and Neglect* (London, 2000). Yet two zealous investigators of "crimes against children" acknowledge that "More attention has been focused on child sexual abuse during the past two decades than on any other form of child maltreatment." David Finkelhor and Lisa Jones, "Explanations for the Decline in Child Sexual Abuse Cases," *Juvenile Justice Bulletin*, January 2004, p. 10.

683. Leslie Margolin and John Craft, "Child Sexual Abuse by Caretakers," *Family Relations* 38 (1989); Martin Daly and Margo Wilson, "Child Abuse and Other Risks of Not Living with Both Parents," *Journal of Ethnology and Sociobiology* 6 (1985). Both cited in Maggie Gallagher, *The Abolition of Marriage* (Washington: Regnery, 1996), p. 36, notes 25 and 26.

684. Quoted in Sanford L. Braver with Diane O'Connell, *Divorced Dads: Shattering the Myths* (New York: Tarcher/Putnam, 1998), p. 210.

685. As calculated by Farrell, *Father and Child Reunion*, p. 203 (emphasis original), using NIS-3 data (see above, note 105).

686. Sedlak and Broadhurst, *Executive Summary* of NIS-3, pp. vi, 8.

687. *Ibid.*, tables 5-2, 5-3, 5-4, 6-3, 6-4.

688. Patrick Fagan and Dorothy Hanks, *The Child Abuse Crisis: The Disintegration of Marriage, Family, and the American Community* (Washington: Heritage Foundation "Backgrounder," 3 June 1997), pp. 8-12.

689. Robert Whelan, *Broken Homes and Battered Children: A Study of the Relationship between Child Abuse and Family Type* (London: Family Education Trust, 1993), p. 29. Whelan based his study on figures from the NSPCC, whose most recent report (cited above) reached similar conclusions that "violent acts towards children are more likely to be meted out by mothers than fathers." Following Whelan's study the British government stopped compiling figures. "It's impossible now to find out about the relative risks of biological and non-biological parents because Whitehall no longer wants them to be collected." Melanie Phillips, "The Darkest Secret of Child Sex Abuse," *Sunday Times*, 26 November 2000.

690. Fagan and Hanks, *Child Abuse Crisis*, p. 16.

691. Quoted in Linda Frum, "Anne Cools' Absence of Malice," *National Post*, 19 December 1998.

692. Gallagher, *Abolition of Marriage*, pp. 36-37.

693. Jean Bethke Elshtain, "The Lost Children," in Cynthia Daniels (ed.), *Lost Fathers* (New York: St. Martin's, 1998), p. 129.

694. Adrienne Burgess, *Fatherhood Reclaimed: The Making of the Modern Father* (London: Vermilion, 1997), p. 54.

695. David Rowland, *et al.*, "Household Risk and Child Sexual Abuse in a Low Income, Urban Sample of Women," *Adolescent and Family Health*, vol. 1, no. 1 (Winter 2000, http://www.afhjournal.org/docs/010110.asp).

696. Nancy Coney and Wade Mackey, "The Feminization of Domestic Violence in America," *Journal of Men's Studies*, vol. 8, no. 1 (October 1999), p. 45.

697. Andrea Sedlak and Diane Broadhurst, *Third National Incidence Study of Child Abuse and Neglect* (Washington: U.S. Department of Health and Human Services, National Center on Child Abuse and Neglect, September 1996), p. 6-11, table 6-4; *Murder in Families* (Washington: U.S. Department of Justice, Bureau of Justice Statistics, July 1994; Bureau of Justice Statistics Publications Catalog 1994-95, NCJ 143498), pp. 1,3, 5-6. The remaining 45 percent lumps fathers and stepfathers together and so almost certainly is comprised mostly of the latter.

698. Sedlak and Broadhurst, *Third National Incidence Study*.

699. Ruth Brenner, *et al.*, "Deaths Attributable to Injuries in Infants, United States, 1983-1991," *Pediatrics*, vol. 103, no. 5 (May 1999), pp. 968-974.

700. M. A. Green, "Time to Put 'Cot Death' to Bed?" *British Medical Journal* 319 (11 September 1999), pp. 697-700.

701. Jeremy Laurence, "'Cot Deaths' May Have Been Murders," *The Independent*, 6 January 1999.

702. U.S. Advisory Board on Child Abuse and Neglect, *A Nation's Shame: Fatal Child Abuse and Neglect in the United States* (Washington: U.S. Department of Health and Human Services, 1995).

703. Pearson, *When She Was Bad*, p. 110.

704. Marcia Herman-Giddens, *et al.*, "Underascertainment of Child Abuse Mortality in the United States," *Journal of the American Medical Association*, vol. 282, no. 5 (4 August 1999), pp. 463-467.

705. Young, *Ceasefire*, pp. 102, 104.

706. Patricia Pearson, "Nice Girls Who Kill Their Babies," *Women's Quarterly* 14 (Winter 1998).

707. "Killer Mom," *Washington Post* editorial, 2 July 1999, p. A26.

708. Rita J. Simon, "Not Serving the Child's Best Interests," *Women's Freedom Network Newsletter*, vol. 5, no. 3-4 (May/June and July/August 1998).

709. A September 26, 1999, article in the *Tribune* describes how the divorce court proceeded matter-of-factly to divide the family property without regard to "marital misconduct." Local mothers formed a "support group" for Lemak. One, who "hasn't forgotten the pain of her own failed first marriage," says her experience tells her Lemak "deserves pity, not prison." Stacy St. Clair, "Lemak Finds Sympathy from Naperville Women," *Daily Herald*, 14 February 2000.

710. Mitchell Zukoff, "Mother Charged in Killings 6 Children Found Strangled," *Boston Globe*, 9 September 1998.

711. Amy Klein, "Father Gets 8 Years in Montgomery Abuse Case," *Washington Post*, 28 February 1998.

712. Daniel Wise, "Mayor's Panel Rejects Brooklyn Family Court Judge for Second Term," *New York Law Journal*, 14 March 2001, p. 1.

713. Gordon Kent, *et al.*, "Judge Apologizes For Saying He Finds It's 'Abhorrent' When Parents Split," *Edmonton Journal*, 9 January 2003.

714. *Child Sexual Abuse, Assault, and Molest Issues.*

715. "4-Year Old Sexually Abused by BC Child Ministry," *LifeSite News* Special Report, 31 May 1999 (http://www.lifesite.net/ldn/1999/may/990531a.html, accessed 7 November 2001).

716. "Expert and Her Methods on Trial," *Detroit Free Press*, 3 November 1997.

717. "My Lie Sent My Father to Jail," *Redbook*, November 1999.

718. Ed Oliver, "Why Was Mother Shackled for Not Giving Baby to Strangers?" *Massachusetts News*, 20 February 2001, and interviews with Heidi Howard (16 April, 25 May, 27 June, and 18 July 2001), Neil Howard (5 July 2001), reporter Nev Moore (13 April 2001), attorney Gregory Hession (30 May 2001), and attorney David Grossack (17 June 2001). Officials with the Massachusetts Department of Social Services repeatedly declined comment.

719. "The Seventh Child to Die," *Washington Post* editorial, 27 October 2001, p. A26.

720. Online: http://www.inbar.org/content/posters/showposter.asp?img=8, accessed 30 April 2002.

721. Jane Hansen, "Georgia's Forgotten Children," *Atlanta Journal-Constitution*, 5 December 1999.

722. Cathy Young, "Do 'Protection Orders' Actually Violate Civil Rights?" *Jewish World Review*, n.d..

723. *War Against Parents*, p. 109: "If children are the clients, parents can quite easily become the adversaries—the people who threaten to take business away."

724. Quoted in Braver, *Divorced Dads*, p. 240.

725. Anne McMurray, "Violence Against Ex-Wives: Anger and Advocacy," *Health Care for Women International*, vol. 18, no. 6 (November-December 1997), pp. 543, 547 (emphasis added).

726. Claire Cooper, "Appeals Court Revisits Wife's Sentence," *Sacramento Bee*, 18 April 2002.

727. "Pilot's Crash into His Home Is Called Deliberate," *Washington Post*, 29 August 2001.

728. Alex Branch, "Couple Found Dead Were Divorcing," *Wichita Eagle*, 23 July 2001.

729. Sharon Price and Patrick McKenry, *Divorce* (London: Sage, 1988), pp. 59-60.

730. Alex Hall and Kevin Kelly, "Noncustodial Fathers in Groups: Maintaining the Parenting Bond," in Michael Andronico (ed.), *Men In Groups* (Washington: American Psychological Association, 1996).

731. Melody Fortunato, Fortunato and Associates, P.A. of Fort Lauderdale, Florida, private e-mail correspondence, 21 August 2001.

732. "Texas Doctor Kills Ex-Wife, Self," 6 July 1999, (http://wire.ap.org/?SLUG=DOCTORS %2dSHOT; Jason Blevins, "Dad Blames Killer's Wife in Slayings," *Denver Post*, 6 July 1999.

733. Mack, *Assault on Parenthood*, p. 79. On p. 86, she obliquely admits most of these parents are fathers.

734. Mike Mckee, "The Deadly Side of Family Law," *California Law Week*, 22 June 1999.

735. Nevada Legislature, Minutes of the Meeting of the Legislative Commission's Subcommittee on Family Courts (Assembly Concurrent Resolution No. 32), 21 January 1998, Las Vegas, Nevada (http://www.leg.state.nv.us/69th/Interim/Studies/Courts/Minutes/ 1-21-98-min.html, accessed 9 March 2007).

736. Joan Cheever, "The Year of Litigating Dangerously," *National Law Journal*, 12 October 1992, p. 29.

737. Brian McGrory, "Fear Invades the Courts," *Boston Globe*, 16 October 1994, p. 33.

738. Amy Worden, "Killing of a Prosecutor Chills Brethren," *Yahoo News*, 12 June 2000 (http://dailynews.yahoo.com/h/ao/20000612/cr/killing_of_a_prosecutor_chills_brethren _1.html; accessed 21 June 2000).

739. Mike Linn, "Radio Comments Lead to 'Lookout' Fliers," *Montgomery Advertiser*, 7 July 2006.

740. ABC News, 20/20, 30 December 1998.

741. *And Justice for None* (Westlake, Ohio: Mary's Advocates, 2004), p. 34.

742. "How the Church Betrayed Fatherhood," *Church of England Newspaper*, 14 June 2004.

Chapter 5 / Fathers and Feminism

743. New York: Vintage, 1965, p. 181.

744. Aldershot: Edward Elgar, 1991, pp. 22, 39, 253.

745. "The personal is political" slogan is described as "the core idea of most contemporary feminism" by political theorist Susan Moller Okin, *Justice, Gender, and the Family* (New York: Basic Books, 1989), p. 124. Historian Eugene Genovese has characterized it as "a fascist and a Stalinist slogan." *National Review*, 24 February 1997, pp. 55(3).

746. Melanie Phillips, *The Sex-Change Society* (London: Social Market Foundation, 1999), p. 266.

747. Daphne Patai, *Heterophobia: Sexual Harassment and the Future of Feminism* (Lanham: Rowman and Littlefield, 1998), p. 199. Patai is not referring to family law: "To conflate much of what today is labeled 'sexual harassment' with serious forms of sexual assault and abuse is to invite authoritarianism into our lives—the hand of the state everywhere in the private sphere, until there is virtually no private sphere left." *Ibid.*, p. 212.

748. Michael Weiss and Cathy Young, *Feminist Jurisprudence: Equal Rights or Neo-Paternalism?* (Washington: Cato Policy Analysis No. 256, 1996), note 33. Young has since become a critic of family courts.

749. Lawrence Hall, "Men Give Plan Low Marks," *Star-Ledger*, 16 August 1999.

750. "Law Will Require Men to Do Housework," *WorldNetDaily*, 9 April 2005 (http://www.worldnetdaily.com/news/article.asp?ARTICLE_ID=43714).

751. Ann Crittenden seems surprised by this: "Before the arrival of the first child, couples tend to share the housework fairly equally. But something about a baby encourages the resurgence of traditional gender roles." *The Price of Motherhood* (New York: Metropolitan Books, 2001), p. 25.

752. As long ago as 1948 mothers received sole custody in divorces they had instigated unilaterally and without legally recognized grounds. *Mullen v. Mullen*, 188 Va. 259, 269, 49 S.E.2d 349, 354 (1948).

753. NOW at one point created a "Clearinghouse Against Fathers' Rights" and solicited for dirt on fathers and fathers' groups to "educate" members of Congress.

754. "Share and Share Alike," *New Times*, 5 January 1994.

755. Quoted from a talk to the American Psychological Association by B. Murray, "Friedan Calls for More Research on Fathers and Parenting," *APA Monitor Online*, vol. 30, no. 5 (May 1999, http://www.apa.org/monitor/may99/friedan.html; accessed 28 November 2001).

756. "Must Women's Gain Be Men's Loss?" *The Independent*, 18 December 2000.

757. John Waters, "Feminism No Longer an Agent for True Change," *Irish Times*, 4 May 1999.

758. Cathy Young, *Ceasefire* (New York: Free Press, 1999), p. 7.

759. Michael Walzer, "The Revolutionary Uses of Repression," in Melvin Richter (ed.), *Essays in Theory and History* (Cambridge, Mass.: Harvard, 1970).

760. Chris Cobb, "Feminists Might Be Granted Own Hearing on Divorce Law," *National Post*, 5 July 2001; Ontario Women's Network on Custody and Access press release, 19 June 2001; Donna Laframboise, "When Dad Becomes a Dirty Word," *National Post*, 14 June 2001.

761. Quoted in Chris Cobb, "Women's Groups Balk at Sitting with Fathers' Rights Advocates," *Ottawa Citizen*, 7 June 2001.

762. Massachusetts Department of Social Services Web site (http://www.state.ma.us/dss/DViolence/DV_Overview.htm; accessed 1 October 2001).

763. Chris Cobb, "Dads Bash Divorce Survey," *Times-Colonist*, 20 May 2001.

764. Letter from Louis Rossiter, 28 August 2001.

765. "Families in Crisis," report by the 1991-92 San Diego County Grand Jury, p. 7.

766. Kathy Ferguson, "Male-Ordered Politics: Feminism and Political Science," in Terrence Ball (ed.), *Idioms of Inquiry* (Albany: SUNY, 1987), p. 222.

767. 17 May 1998.

768. Sylvia Ann Hewlett and Cornel West, *The War Against Parents* (Boston: Houghton Mifflin, 1998), p. 109.

769. Quoted in Rebecca Hagelin, "Getting Rid of Gramma," *WorldNetDaily*, 5 March 2002.

770. "There Must Be Fifty Ways to Start a Family," in Wade Horn, *et al.* (eds.), *The Fatherhood Movement* (Lanham: Lexington, 1999), p. 87.

771. Letter to Louis Rossiter, Virginia secretary of health and human resources, 4 August 2001.

Notes

772. "Where Were the Law Guardians?" *Village Voice*, 21 April 1998.

773. Barbara Olson, *Hell to Pay* (Washington: Regnery, 1999), p. 100.

774. "Truth Be Told," *Washington Post*, 10 August 2000, p. A29.

775. Eugene Narrett, "Hillary Really Means: It Takes a Government," *Insight*, 19 February 1996.

776. Quoted in Eugene Narrett, "We Must Protect the Bonds Between Husband, Wife and Family," *Middlesex News*, 11 April 1996.

777. Olson, *Hell to Pay*, pp. 105-106, 100, 114.

778. Quoted in Allan Carlson, "Creative Destruction, Family Style," *Intercollegiate Review*, vol. 37, no. 2 (Spring 2002), p. 53 (emphasis added).

779. Jean Bethke Elshtain, "The Family, Democratic Politics, and the Question of Authority," in Geoffrey Scarre (ed.), *Children, Parents, and Politics* (Cambridge: Cambridge University Press, 1989), p. 65.

780. James Dwyer, "Parents' Religion and Children's Welfare: Debunking the Doctrine of Parents' Rights," *California Law Review*, vol. 82, no. 6 (December 1994), p. 1447. The *Yoder* and *Pierce* precedents are among the strongest establishing parental rights; see Donald Hubin "Parental Rights and Due Process," *Journal of Law and Family Studies*, vol. 1, no. 2 (1999).

781. Quoted in Kay S. Hymowitz, *Ready or Not* (New York: Free Press, 1999), p. 43.

782. Frances Olsen, "The Politics of Family Law," in Martha Minow (ed.), *Family Matters* (New York: New Press, 1993), p. 336; originally published in *Journal of Law and Inequality* 2 (1984). Olsen adds: "Family law tends to pacify family members by concealing from their scrutiny how damaging and restrictive family relationships often are." This highly influential article was reprinted in at least one other anthology, a fact that itself testifies against her argument, since articles defending the rights of fathers are seldom published in law journals and almost never reprinted in academic books.

783. Chris Tinkler, "Teen May Never See Mum Again," *Herald Sun*, 20 June 2004.

784. Bryan Robinson, "Boy Gets Split From Father Who Killed His Mom, Embarks on Mission to End Abuse," ABC News Web site (http://www.abcnews.go.com/sections/US/GoodMorningAmerica/divorcing_parents_040726-1.html), 26 July 2004.

785. Esther Ngan-ling Chow and Catherine White Berheide (eds.), *Women, the Family, and Policy* (Albany: SUNY, 1994), introduction, p. 15.

786. Colin MacLeod, "Conceptions of Parental Autonomy," *Politics and Society*, vol. 25, no. 1 (March 1997), p. 118. MacLeod provides no documentation for these assertions in an ostensibly scientific journal.

787. Amy Gutman, *Democratic Education* (Princeton: Princeton University Press, 1987), p. 34.

788. Quoted in Allan Carlson, "Standing for Liberty: Marriage, Virtue, and the Political State," public lecture at the Family Research Council, 16 June 2004, subsequently published in *Conjugal America: On the Public Purposes of Marriage* (New Brunswick: Transaction, 2006). See Donald Bolas, "No-Fault Divorce: Born in the Soviet Union?" *Journal of Family Law*, vol. 14, no. 1 (1975).

789. Chow and Berheide, *Women, the Family, and Policy*, p. 18; Carol Pateman, "Feminist Critiques of the Public/Private Dichotomy," in Stanley Benn and Gerald Gaus (eds.), *Private and Public in Social Life* (London: Croom Helm, 1983); Okin, *Justice, Gender, and the Family*, pp. 23, 172-74, 179, and chap. 6 *passim*. Okin argues against any distinction between public and private and denies the legitimacy of any private sphere of life (though she makes an exception when her argument threatens to undermine abortion case law).

790. *Ibid.*, pp. 151-152 (emphasis added). A popular version of a similar message is Crittenden, *Price of Motherhood*.

791. Online: http://shop.barnesandnoble.com/booksearch/isbnInquiry.asp?userid=6ANFSCNRGS&mscssid=HXUJXUXP8S1F9KKVKWWJC53V5SGEF1C7&isbn=0465037038; accessed 31 October 2001.

792. John Lott and Larry Kenny, "How Dramatically Did Women's Suffrage Change the Size and Scope of Government?" University of Chicago Law School, John M. Olin Law and Economics Working Paper No. 60, pp. 5-6 (emphasis added).

793. Warren Farrell, *The Myth of Male Power* (New York: Berkley Books, 1993), p. 238.

794. Barbara Dafoe Whitehead, *The Divorce Culture* (New York: Vintage, 1998), pp. 15-16, 26.

795. National Association of Women Lawyers Web site (http://www.abanet.org/nawl/about/history.html, accessed 6 November 2004). I am grateful to Judy Parejko.

796. Matthus Kalmijn, *et al.*, "Interactions Between Cultural and Economic Determinations of Divorce in the Netherlands," *Journal of Marriage and Family* 66 (2004).

797. Amanda Banks, "Greer Cheers Divorcing Women," *The Australian*, 8 September 2004.

798. "Hope for Democracy in Iran," *Washington Post* op-ed column, 25 October 2004, A19.

799. Quoted in Sanford Braver, *Divorced Dads* (New York: Tarcher/Putnam, 1998), p. 114.

800. Interview with John Tierney, "The Big City: A New Look at Realities of Divorce," *New York Times*, 11 July 2000, B1.

801. Margaret Brinig and Douglas Allen, "These Boots Are Made for Walking," *American Economics and Law Review*, vol. 2, no. 1 (Spring 2000), pp. 156, 133.

802. Thomas Maugh, "Study's Advice to Husbands: Accept Wife's Influence," *Los Angeles Times*, 21 February 1998, citing J. M. Gottman, *et al.*, "Predicting Marital Happiness and Stability from Newlywed Interactions," *Journal of Marriage and the Family*, vol. 60, no. 1 (February 1998).

803. Dianna Thompson and Glenn Sacks, "Can Abolishing Sole Custody Curb Divorce?" *New York Sun*, 2 October 2002.

804. Judith Seltzer, "Consequences of Marriage Dissolution for Children," *Annual Review of Sociology*, vol. 20 (1994), pp. 258-259.

805. Quoted in Braver, *Divorced Dads*, p. 176.

806. "Ethics in Family Law: Is Family Law Advocacy a Contradiction in Terms?" paper presented to the Advocates' Society Conference in Nassau, Bahamas, 2 December 1995.

807. *The Abolition of Marriage* (Washington: Regnery, 1996), p. 145 (original emphasis).

808. Rosalind Miles, *Love, Sex, Death, and the Making of the Male* (New York: Summit Books, 1991), p. 23.

809. Quoted in Diana Bagnall, "Divorce: Split Ends," *The Bulletin*, 7 August 2002.

810. Linda Waite and Maggie Gallagher, *The Case for Marriage* (New York: Doubleday, 2000), p. 177.

811. Whitehead, *Divorce Culture*, pp. 54-61.

812. Glenn Sacks and Dianna Thompson, "Have Anti-Father Family Court Policies Led to a Men's Marriage Strike?" *Philadelphia Inquirer*, 5 July 2002; Gerard McManus, "Nowadays the Vow Is Not to Tie the Knot," *Sunday Tasmanian*, 26 May 2002, p. 11; Fathers-4-Equality press release, 7 June 2004; Cheltenham Group Web site (http://www.c-g.org.uk/); Jed Abraham, *From Courtship to Courtroom* (New York: Bloch, 1999), p. i.

813. Online: http://groups.yahoo.com/group/Ex-husband_is_now_my_slave/; accessed 24 January 2002.

814. Susannah Herbert, "Get Rich Girls, Get Divorced," *Sunday Telegraph*, 14 April 2002.

815. Judith Wallerstein and Joan Kelly, *Surviving the Breakup* (New York: Basic Books, 1980), p. 154.

816. Cited in Braver, *Divorced Dads*, p. 121.

817. David Chambers, "Justifying the Continued Use of Jail," in Minow, *Family Matters*, p. 354.

818. Online: http://messages.women.com/messages/MCat7/MBoard78/MSub257//showpost.pl?Board=Sub257&Number=25241&page=0&view=collapsed&sb=5; accessed 9 September 2000.

819. Michelle Gunn, "Easier for Women to Make the Break," *The Australian*, 5 July 1999.

820. Anne Wilson Schaef, *Women's Reality* (Minneapolis: Winston Press, 1985), p. 81.

821. Leotine Young, *Out of Wedlock* (New York: McGraw-Hill, 1954), p. 155. Contrary to feminist and government propaganda, it appears to be mothers, not fathers, who are now abandoning their children. Jonathan Leake, "Dumped Dads Left Holding the Baby," *Sunday Times*, 8 August 2004, citing an unpublished report by John Haskey from the British Office of National Statistics.

822. Schaef, *Women's Reality*, p. 80.

823. Paul Duggan, "NOW Rallies to Mother's Defense: Group Says Woman Needs Help, Not Prison, in Drowning of 5 Children," *Washington Post*, 3 September 2001, p. A03. The *Post* quotes a University of Houston law professor saying the district attorney must seek the death penalty because not doing so for a middle-class white defendant "would just fuel the criticism that racial and class biases influence which defendants get the death penalty." Apparently officials fear no criticism for gender bias.

824. Quoted by Phil Brennan, "NOW Throwing Lifebelt to Mom who Drowned Five Kids," *NewsMax.com*, 30 August 2001.

825. "Bigotry of Low Expectations: Double Standards for Parent Murderers," *National Review*, 28 August 2001.

826. Both quoted by David Limbaugh, "Remembering the Real Victims," *Townhall.com*, 1 September 2001 (http://www.townhall.com/columnists/davidlimbaugh/dl20010901.shtml).

827. Andrea Dworkin, *Woman Hating* (New York: E. P. Dutton, 1974), p. 189.

828. Though feminists decry the "feminization of poverty" and pose as the champions of children when it comes to perpetuating welfare dependency or collecting child support, it is clear that, given the choice, the exhilarating power accruing to single mothers is more than adequate compensation for pulling their children into poverty. "Independence, even in straitened and penurious forms," write middle-class feminists Barbara Ehrenreich, *et al.*, "still offers more sexual freedom than affluence gained through marriage and dependence on one man." *Re-Making Love* (New York: Anchor Press/Doubleday, 1986), p. 197. It is well known that an intact two-parent family is not only the safest but the most financially secure home for a child. William Galston and Elaine C. Kamarck, "Five Realities that Will Shape 21st Century Politics," *Blueprint: Ideas for a New Century*, Democratic Leadership Council (Fall 1998).

829. Melinda Blau, *Families Apart* (New York: Putnam, 1993), p. 89.

830. Karen Winner, *Divorced From Justice* (New York: HarperCollins, 1996); Braver, *Divorced Dads*, chap. 5.

831. "Are Family Courts Prejudiced Against Fathers?" *Insight*, 18 June 2001.

832. Ronald Henry, "'Primary Caretaker': Is It a Ruse?" *Family Advocate*, Summer 1994, p. 53.

833. Warren Farrell, *Women Can't Hear What Men Don't Say* (New York: Tarcher/Putnam, 1999), chap. 5.

834. Phillips, *Sex-Change Society*, pp. 101-103.

835. "Time For Mums to Welcome Dads to the Family," *The Independent*, 31 May 1999.

836. Andrea Gordon, "Dad Can't Carry a Load that Mom Won't Relinquish," *Toronto Star*, 5 June 2006.

837. Quoted in Cathy Young, *Ceasefire*, p. 56.

838. Wallerstein and Kelly, *Surviving the Breakup*, p. 125.

839. Edward Kruk, "The Disengaged Non-Custodial Father: Implications for Social Work Practice with the Divorced Family," *Social Work*, vol. 39, no. 1 (January 1994), p. 21.

840. Matt Born, "Custody Ruling Deals a Blow to House Husbands," *The Telegraph*, 19 April 2002.

841. Quoted in Young, *Ceasefire.*, pp. 59-61; Phyllis Chesler, *Mothers on Trial* (New York: McGraw-Hill, 1986), pp. 35-36, 153-55.

842. Tippins, "Are Family Courts Prejudiced Against Fathers?"

843. R. Mark Rogers and Donald J. Bieniewicz, "Child Cost Economics and Litigation Issues: An Introduction to Applying Cost Shares Child Support Guidelines," paper presented at the Southern Economic Association Annual Meeting, Section for National Association of Forensic Economics, Alexandria, Virginia (12 November 2000; revised, 20 November 2000), pp. 22-23.

844. Most recently: Park and Brott, *Throwaway Dads*; Young, *Ceasefire*; Farrell, *Women Can't Hear*. Paul Nathanson and Katherine Young, *Spreading Misandry* (Montreal: McGill-Queen's University Press, 2001) is less concerned specifically with fathers.

845. American Coalition for Fathers and Children press release, 20 August 1999.

846. Louise Silverstein and Carl Auerbach, "Deconstructing the Essential Father," *American Psychologist*, June 1999.

847. John Leo, "Mars to Venus: Back Off," *U.S. News and World Report*, 11 May 1998.

848. Patricia Pearson, *When She Was Bad: Violent Women and the Myth of Innocence* (New York: Viking, 1997), pp. 142f (original emphasis).

849. Norman Podhoretz, "Our Endangered Species: Fathers," *New York Post*, 17 June 1986, 51, quoted in Young, *Ceasefire*, 51.

850. *Good Weekend* magazine, 26 August 2000, p. 18.

851. Kate Zernike, "Men on the Verge, Divorced Dads Emerge as a Political Force," *Boston Globe*, 19 May 1998.

852. Young, *Ceasefire*, p. 129.

853. James Madison, Federalist #51, *The Federalist Papers*, ed. Clinton Rossiter (New York: Mentor paperback edn., 1961), p. 322.

854. David Blankenhorn, *Fatherless America* (New York: Basic Books, 1995); David Popenoe, *Life Without Father* (New York: Free Press, 1996).

855. Horn, "Did You Say 'Movement'?" p. 12; Coats, "Beyond Government," pp. 118-119; Pearlstein, "Fatherhood and Language," p.128, all.in Wade Horn, *et al.* (eds.), *The Fatherhood Movement* (Lanham: Lexington, 1999).

856. *The Assault on Parenthood* (New York: Simon and Schuster, 1997), pp. 65, 91.

857. NOW "Legislative Update," 3 December 1999.

858. "National Fatherhood Initiative Awarded Grant to Build Texas Fatherhood Initiative," NFI press release, 17 December 1999.

859. See chapter 3.

Notes

860. Louis McHardy and Meredith Hofford, *Final Report of the Child Custody and Visitation Focus Group, March 1-3, 1999* (http://www.vaw.umn.edu/FinalDocuments/custodyfin.htm. "File Last Modified on: 12/21/99").

861. HHS gives about $10 million yearly to states to create these centers. HHS Fact Sheet, 16 March 2001.

862. Michael Crowley, "Next Goal of Welfare Is to Help Fathers, *Boston Globe*, 19 December 1999.

863. Abraham, *From Courtship to Courtroom*, p. 155.

864. Cristin Schmitz, "Force Divorcing Parents to Take Courses: Lawyers," *National Post*, 9 July 2001.

865. Paul Bloomberg, "County Needs Stricter Child-Support Laws," letter to the *Los Angeles Daily Journal*, 21 August 2001.

866. "Judge Offers 'Deadbeat Dads' Jail or Vasectomy," *NewsMax.com*, 6 May 2004 (http://www.newsmax.com/archives/articles/2004/5/6/160620.shtml); "Deadbeat Dads Offered Surgical Alternative," *WCPO.com*, 6 May 2004 (http://www.wcpo.com/news/2004/local/05/06/dad.html).

Chapter 6 / The Politics of Fatherhood

867. *The Family on Trial* (London: Pennsylvania State University Press, 1981), pp. 4, 8-9, 201.

868. Quoted in Glenn Sacks and Dianna Thompson, "Fathers and Gender Bias," *Minneapolis Star Tribune*, 21 June 2002.

869. *Second Treatise on Civil Government*, sections 74, 105-6, in *Two Treatises of Government*, ed. Peter Laslett (New York: Cambridge, 1960), pp. 360, 380-382.

870. J. G. A. Pocock, *Three British Revolutions: 1641, 1688, 1776* (Princeton: Princeton University Press, 1980).

871. John Demos, *A Little Commonwealth* (New York: Oxford, 1970).

872. Gordon Wood, *The Creation of the American Republic, 1776-1787* (Williamsburg: Institute of Early American History and Culture, 1969), p. 418.

873. Michael Walzer, *Regicide and Revolution: Speeches at the Trial of Louis XVI* (New York: Cambridge University Press, 1974), introduction.

874. Carol Pateman, *The Sexual Contract* (Stanford: Stanford University Press, 1988).

875. *Leviathan*, part II, chap. 20 (Harmondsworth: Penguin, 1982), p. 254. "The transformation of reproduction from biological processes into morally and legally based institutions of kinship and marriage probably marks the point at which social organisation emerged in evolutionary history," writes Patricia Morgan. "Fatherhood, that 'creation of society,' exemplifies the rule-making and rule-following without which no cultural is possible." *Farewell to the Family* (London: Institute of Economic Affairs, 1999), p. 190.

876. This is brilliantly argued in Michael Walzer, *The Revolution of the Saints* (Cambridge, Mass.: Harvard University Press, 1965).

877. Wood emphasizes the repressive and puritanical features of republicanism in *Creation of the American Republic*.

878. For the affinity between the puritanical features in modern feminism and the puritans' descendents among the "religious right," see Peter Beinart, "Private Matters," *New Republic*, 15 February 1999.

879. Mary Wollstonecraft, *A Vindication of the Rights of Woman* (various eds.), introduction (para. 6, 15), chap. 4 (para. 9, 10, 23).

Notes

880. Compare both Nancy Reagan and Hillary Clinton as lightening rods for opposition to their husbands' administrations.

881. Carole Vance, *Pleasure and Danger: Exploring Female Sexuality* (Boston: Routledge and Kegan Paul, 1984), 23f.

882. *The Nature and Evolution of Female Sexuality* (New York: Random House, 1972), p. 52 (original emphasis).

883. See the Introduction, above.

884. Daniel Amneus, *The Case for Father Custody* (Alhambra, California: Primrose, 1999), p. iii.

885. Amneus himself addresses some of the following problems in *The Garbage Generation* (Alhambra, California: Primrose, 1990).

886. "Not Just Another Pair of Hands," in Wade Horn, *et al.* (eds.), *The Fatherhood Movement* (Lanham: Lexington, 1999), p. 41.

887. Barbara Dafoe Whitehead, *The Divorce Culture* (New York: Vintage, 1998), pp. 120, 125.

888. "Compared to children from homes disrupted by death, children from divorced homes have more psychological problems." Robert Emery, *Marriage, Divorce, and Children's Adjustment* (Newbury Park: Sage, 1988), p. 94. "Death is usually involuntary, while divorce is voluntary on the part of at least one parent, a distinction that is not lost on children." Whitehead, *Divorce Culture*, p. 98. Blankenhorn makes a similar point, though he distorts it with his insistence that all fatherlessness results from "abandonment": "Death puts an end to fathers. Abandonment puts an end to fatherhood." Blankenhorn makes no attempt to prove such abandonment. *Fatherless America*, pp. 23-24.

889. *And Justice for None* (Westlake, Ohio: Mary's Advocates, 2004), p. 35.

890. *Leviathan*, part I, chap. 13 (Penguin edn.), p. 183.

891. Quoted in Melanie Phillips, *The Sex-Change Society* (London: Social Market Foundation, 1999), p. 271.

892. Private e-mail correspondence, 18 December 1999.

893. Again, the genders may be reversed (and when they are the reasons are likely to be political), as we have seen.

894. Susan Moller Okin, *Justice, Gender, and the Family* (New York: Basic Books, 1989), p. 135: "Without just families, how can we expect to have a just society? . . . If the relationship between a child's parents does not conform to basic standards of justice, how can we expect that child to grow up with a sense of justice?" Okin's question, which follows that of John Stuart Mill in *The Subjection of Women*, is legitimate. But her justice is ideological, gender justice, and her definition of injustice is political. Her sisterhood's newfound power to have family members taken away in handcuffs and jailed without trial receives no similar scrutiny.

895. Anne-Marie Cusac, "Arrest My Kid: He Needs Mental Health Care," *The Progressive*, July 2001.

896. Ed Oliver, "Middlesex County Court Charged with Corruption" *Massachusetts News*, December 2000, and interviews with Zed McLarnon, 25 May 2001, and his attorney, Gregory A. Hession, 30 May 2001. The social worker/husband, David Douglas, and other DSS officials have declined to comment.

897. S. Mira and G. E. Finley, "Harms to Children and Parents Inherent to Abuse Investigations," *Children of Divorced, Separated, and Never-Married Families*, vol. 19, no. 1, pp. 22-23.

898. Whitehead, *Divorce Culture*, pp. 125-126, 164.

Notes

899. Jeffery Leving, *Fathers' Rights* (New York: Basic Books, 1997), p. 43.

900. "The Affluent Young of Generation Y," *New York Times*, 10 September 2000. I am grateful to Mark Lindamood.

901. Heather Antecol and Kelly Bedard, "Teenage Delinquency: The Role of Child Support Payments and Father's Visitation," in William S. Comanor (ed.), *The Law and Economics of Child Support Payments* (Cheltenham: Edward Elgar, 2004), p. 265.

902. John Thomas (ed.), *Slavery Attacked* (Englewood Cliffs: Prentice-Hall, 1965), p. 124. G. K. Chesterton, *The Superstition of Divorce*, chap. 6: "If my association of divorce with slavery seems only a far-fetched and theoretical paradox . . . let them merely remember the time when they read "Uncle Tom's Cabin," and ask themselves whether the oldest and simplest of the charges against slavery has not always been the breaking up of families."

903. James Washington (ed.), *A Testament of Hope* (San Francisco: Harper and Row, 1986), p. 292.

904. Don Eberly, "No Democracy Without Dads," in Horn, *et al.*, *Fatherhood Movement*.

905. Michael Walzer, *The Company of Critics: Social Criticism and Political Commitment in the Twentieth Century* (New York: Basic Books, 1988).

906. Quoted in Amneus, *Case for Father Custody*, p. 405.

907. "The End of Courtship," *The Public Interest*, n.d.

908. Bob Just, "Son of Divorce," *WorldNetDaily*, 12 March 2005 (http://worldnetdaily.com/news/article.asp?ARTICLE_ID=43269).

909. Ray A. Seutter and Martin Rovers, "Emotionally Absent Fathers: Furthering the Understanding of Homosexuality" *Journal of Psychology and Theology* 32 (2004).

910. Aviezer Tucker, *et al.*, "From Republican Virtue to Technology of Political Power: Three Episodes of Czech Nonpolitical Politics," *Political Science Quarterly*, vol. 115, no. 3 (Fall 2000).

911. "The Power of the Powerless," trans. Paul Wilson, in Jan Vladislav (ed.), *Living in Truth* (London: Faber and Faber, 1986), 54; "Politics and Conscience," in Paul Wilson (ed.), *Open Letters* (New York: Vintage: 1992), 260.

Conclusion: Ending the War

912. "A Day in the Life of a Socialist Citizen," in *Radical Principles* (New York: Basic Books, 1980), p. 135.

913. "Why Are We Here," *The Family in America*, vol. 18, no. 6 (June 2004), p. 2.

914. *Superstition of Divorce* (1920, various editions), chap. 5, "The Story of the Family," and *Divorce Versus Democracy* (1916, various editions).

915. Frederick Douglass, "Speech on the Dred Scott Decision," in Howard Brotz (ed.), *Negro Social and Political Thought, 1850-1920* (New York: Basic Books, 1966), pp. 251-252.

916. Barbara Dafoe Whitehead, *The Divorce Culture* (New York: Vintage, 1998), p. 104.

917. *Ibid.*, pp. 91-92.

918. Philip Abbott, *The Family on Trial* (London: Pennsylvania State University Press, 1981), p. 174.

919. "Defining Daddy Down," *The American Enterprise*, vol. 10, no. 5 (September-October 1999), p. 33.

920. Quoted by Rabbi Daniel Lapin in *The American Enterprise*, vol. 10, no. 6 (November-December 1999), p. 65.

921. Speech at the CPAC Conference, Arlington, Virginia, February 2002.

Notes

922. Ronald Steel, forward to *Public Opinion* (Free Press, 1997), xv.

923. Jennifer Roback Morse, *Love and Economics* (Dallas: Spence, 2001), pp. 130-136.

924. *Ibid.*, p. 144.

925. Suzanne Fields, "Tracing 100 Years of Parenting Tips, Finding Parents Know Best" (review of Ann Hulbert, *Raising America: Experts, Parents, and a Century of Advice about Children*), *Washington Times*, 18 May 2003.

926. Allan C. Carlson, "Toward a Theory of the Autonomous Family," *The Family in America*, vol. 16, no. 4 (April 2002).

927. Roback Morse, *Love and Economics*, 154; Dana Mack, *The Assault on Parenthood* (New York: Simon and Schuster, 1997), p. 21.

928. Kay S. Hymowitz, *Ready or Not: Why Treating Children As Small Adults Endangers Their Future—And Ours* (New York: Free Press, 1999).

929. Mack, *Assault on Parenthood*, pp. 21-22.

930. Paul Craig Roberts and Lawrence M. Stratton, *The Tyranny of Good Intentions* (Roseville, California: Prima Publishing, 2000).

931. See the revised paperback edition of Phyllis Schlafly, *The Supremacists* (Dallas: Spence, 2006).

932. Quoted in Joe Woodard, "Instant Divorce Can Mean Long-Term Woes," *Calgary Herald*, 31 December 2001.

933. Steven L. Varnis, "Broken Vows, Therapeutic Sentiments, Legal Sanctions," *Society*, vol. 35, no. 1 (November-December 1997), p. 35.

934. "Microsoft and Campaign Finance Reform," *Washington Times*, 29 November 1999, p. A16.

935. Paul James Birch, *et al.*, "Assessing the Impact of Community Marriage Policies on County Divorce Rates," *Family Relations*, vol. 53, no. 5 (October 2004). For Marriage Savers, see http://www.marriagesavers.org/MS%20Report%20Card%202006.htm.

936. See chapter 3.

937. Allen Parkman, *Good Intentions Gone Awry: No-Fault Divorce and the American Family* (Lanham: Rowman and Littlefield, 2000), pp. 9–10, to which I am indebted throughout this section.

938. "Reforming No-Fault Divorce," syndicated column, 17 January 2007.

939. Robert Whelan (ed.), *Just a Piece of Paper?* (London: Institute of Economic Affairs, 1995), introduction, p. 3.

940. Quoted in Bridget Maher, "Divorce Reform: Forming Ties That Bind," *Insight*, no. 212 (Washington: Family Research Council, 16 February 2000), p. 11, note 46.

941. Quoted in Judy Parejko, *Stolen Vows: The Illusion of No-Fault Divorce and the Rise of the American Divorce Industry* (Collierville, Tennessee: InstantPublisher, 2002), p. 52.

942. Candis McLean, "Look Who Doesn't Want a Divorce," *Alberta Report*, 11 January 1999.

943. Patricia Morgan, "Conflict and Divorce: Like a Horse and Carriage?" in Whelan, *Just a Piece of Paper?*, 22, 29 (emphasis original).

944. Judith Wallerstein and Sandra Blakeslee, *Second Chances: Men, Women, and Children a Decade After Divorce* (New York: Houghton Mifflin, 1996), p. 11.

945. Quoted in Megan Rosenfeld, "Study Tracks the Children of Divorce Into Adulthood," *Los Angeles Times*, 12 November 1987.

946. Ann Mitchell, *Children in the Middle* (London: Tavistock, 1985); Judson Landis, "The Trauma of Children When Parents Divorce," *Marriage and Family Living*, vol. 22, no. 1 (February 1960).

Notes

947. "Joint Physical Custody Lowers the Divorce Rate," *Speak Out for Children,* vol. 12, no. 4 (Fall 1997 / Winter 1998), p. 8.

948. Brinig and Allen, "These Boots Are Made for Walking," pp. 138–139.

949. Richard Kuhn and John Guidubaldi, "Child Custody Policies and Divorce Rates in the US," paper presented at the 11th Annual Conference of the Children's Rights Council, Washington, DC, 23–26 October 1997 (http://www.vix.com/crc/sp/spcrc97.htm). See also Alexander Hillery, "The Case for Joint Custody," in David Levy (ed.), *The Best Parent Is Both Parents* (Norfolk: Hampton Roads, 1993).

950. Robert Bauserman, "Child Adjustment in Joint-Custody Versus Sole-Custody Arrangements: A Meta-Analytic Review," *Journal of Family Psychology,* vol. 16, no. 1 (March 2002), p. 91.

951. Isabel A. Lerman, "Adjustment of Latency Age Children in Joint and Single Custody Arrangements," California School of Professional Psychology PhD dissertation, 1989.

952. Kim Evonne Rockwell-Evans, "Parental and Children's Experiences and Adjustment in Maternal Versus Joint Custody Families " North Texas State University PhD dissertation, 1991.

953. Rebecca J. Glover and Connie Steele, "Comparing the Effects on the Child of Post-Divorce Parenting Arrangements," *Journal of Divorce,* vol. 12, no. 2–3 (1989), p. 194.

954. William Bender, "Joint Custody: The Option of Choice," *Journal of Divorce and Remarriage,* vol. 21, no. 3–4 (1994), p. 119.

955. Quoted in Ross D. Parke and Armin A. Brott, *Throwaway Dads: The Myths and Barriers that Keep Men from Being the Fathers They Want to Be* (Boston and New York: Houghton Mifflin, 1999), p. 172.

956. "Joint Custody of Children Act, District of Columbia, May 10, 1995 Hearing, Testimony of Ronald K. Henry," pp. 6–7.

957. Gloria Woods, "'Father's Rights' Groups: Beware Their Real Agenda" (NOW Internet site: http://www.now.org/nnt/03–97/father.html; accessed 1 October 2001).

958. Mark R. Chellgren, "Lawmaker Uses Own Law to Seek Kids," Associated Press, 1 August 2001.

959. "Congress Explores Marriage Incentives for Welfare Recipients," VFPF Internet site (http://endabuse.org/newsflash/index.php3?Search=Article&NewsFlashID=256; accessed 31 October 2001), 1 June 2001.

960. NOW Internet site (http://www.now.org/organiza/conferen/1996/resoluti.html#alert, accessed 1 October 2001).

961. House Concurrent Resolution 182, 105th Congress, 1st session, 30 October 1997.

962. Woods, "'Father's Rights' Groups."

963. Michael Friedman, "The So-Called High Conflict Couple: A Closer Look," *American Journal of Family Therapy,* vol. 32 (2004), pp. 105, 115–116.

964. J. B. Kelly, quoted in Friedman, "So-Called High Conflict Couple," p. 102.

965. Judith Seltzer, "Father By Law: Effects of Joint Legal Custody on Nonresident Fathers' Involvement with Children," *Demography,* vol. 35, no. 2 (May 1998).

966. S. A. Wolchik, *et al.,* "Maternal versus Joint Custody: Children's Postseparation Experiences and Adjustment," *Journal of Clinical Child Psychiatry, vol. 14, no. 1 (1985),* pp. 5–10.

967. What constitutes legitimate "grounds" for divorce is not in serious contention. Some jurisdictions still recognize legal grounds for divorce, even if they are no longer required for a divorce to be granted. These grounds have antecedents going back centuries. (So claims that fault divorce would trap women in marriages with philandering or violent husbands are dishonest. See below.)

Notes

968. "Death Blow to Marriage," in Whelan, *Just a Piece of Paper?*, p. 15.

969. Tim O'Brien, "Help Child Support By Altering Divorce Law," *Detroit News*, 22 May 2001.

970. Linda J. Waite, *et al., Does Divorce Make People Happy?* (New York: Institute for American Values, 2002), p. 4.

971. *Love and Economics,* p. 104.

972. Susan Orr, *Child Protection at the Crossroads* (Los Angeles: Reason Public Policy Institute, October 1999). Orr currently directs the Children's Bureau at the Department of Health and Human Services.

973. Edward Kruk, "Shared Parental Responsibility: A Harm Reduction-Based Approach to Divorce Law Reform," *Journal of Divorce and Remarriage,* vol. 43, no. 3–4 (2005), p. 136.

974. Patrick F. Fagan and Wade F. Horn, "How Congress Can Protect the Rights of Parents to Raise their Children," Issue Bulletin, no. 227 (Washington: Heritage Foundation, 23 July 1996), pp. 1–2.

INDEX

Index

Bell, Deborah, 241

Bendheim-Thoman Center for Research on Child Wellbeing, 27

Benotto, Mary Lou, 237

Berheide, Catherine White, 231

Besharov, Douglas, 196

best interest of the child, 22, 33, 50-53, 57, 78, 81-83, 88, 136, 145, 149-150, 153, 225, 229, 273, 300, 305, 306, 315, 319

Best of Life's Little Instruction Calendar, The, 274

Beyond the Best Interests of the Child, 53

Bieniewicz, Donald J., 130, 248

Bill of Rights, 23, 33, 80-81, 95, 98, 111, 149, 158, 183, 189, 250, 263, 294, 308

Bird, Heather, 39, 63

Black, Lisa, 206

Blakeslee, Sandra, 194, 300

Blankenhorn, David, 12, 251, 267

Blau, Melinda, 243

Bleak House, 29

Bloomberg, Paul, 255

Blumner, Robyn, 51

Boston Globe, 179, 187, 207, 218, 250

Bradley, Bill, 15, 113

Brandley, Clarence, 147

Braver, Sanford, 17-18, 36-37, 39, 53-54, 116-117, 119, 139, 243

Breaking the Silence: Children's Stories, 200

Brett, Terry, 157

bribery, 59, 273

Briffault, Robert, 267

Brinig, Margaret, 38, 235, 299

Brink, Malia, 91

Brinton, Crane, 221

Brita, Rick, 186

British Child Support Agency (CSA), 136, 157

British Columbia Supreme Court, 156

British Columbia, University of, 146

British Home Office, 170-171

British House of Lords, 50

British Medical Journal, 204

Brott, Armin, 197, 249, 268

Brown, Dave, 54

Brummett, John, 61-62

Brzezinski, Zbigniew, 91, 190

bureaucracies, social services, 19, 21, 23, 33, 103, 105, 108, 113, 114, 115, 117, 125-126, 131, 136, 138-9, 141, 148, 159-160, 162, 168, 183, 186, 191, 196-200, 209-210, 212-214, 221, 225-227, 229, 233, 279, 284-287, 291, 309, 310

Burgess, Adrienne, 203

Burke and Herbert Bank and Trust Company, 106

Burke, Taylor, 106

Burmeister, Sonny, 88

Bush, George W., 12, 14, 107, 113-114, 160, 252-253, 267

Buster, Steven K., 135

Butler, Daniel, 179

Butler, David, 145

C

California Dept. of Social Services, 226

California, University of, Riverside, 157

Cameron, David, 15

Campion, John, 26

Canadian Bar Assn., 66, 255

Canadian Charter of Rights, 86

Canadian Supreme Court, 86, 150

Cardani, Christopher, 151

Carlson, Allan, 282, 291

Carpenter, Paul, 185

Carr-Gregg, Michael, 152

CBS-TV, 157

Ceausescu, Nicolae, 109

Center on the American Experiment, 194

Central Queensland University, 136

Chacon, Emma, 105

Chambers, David, 38, 240

Champney, Larry, 210

Charalambous, Mark, 180, 184

Chesler, Phyllis, 248

Chesterton, G. K., 282, 300

Chicago Tribune, 206

Chicago, University of, 87

child abuse, 12, 34-35, 58, 79, 93, 100, 165, 167, 181, 186-188, 193-214, 228, 298, 303-304, 307-308, 310, 342, 343, 344, 345; *see also "false accusations of abuse"*

Child Care Resources, 227

child protective services (*see also "social workers"*), 17, 22, 196-197, 214, 284

child support, 15, 17, 18, 22, 28, 30, 32, 36, 41, 43, 47, 60, 61, 62, 64, 87, 91, 93, 96-100, 101-108, 111-164, 172, 179, 183, 219, 225-226, 227, 235, 237, 239, 243, 247, 248-249, 253, 254, 255, 256, 267, 270, 274, 285, 298, 305, 306-307, 309, 314, 316, 318, 326, 328, 329-330, 331, 332, 334-335, 341, 351

Child Support Enforcement, Office of, 96, 106, 115, 118, 123, 160

Child Support Guidelines Project, 128

child-support guidelines, 118-119, 122, 125-131, 133, 137, 143-144, 145, 156, 249, 331, 332

Child Support Recovery Act, 97, 99

Child Tax Credit, 152

children, criminalization of, 292

children, politicization of, 227-230, 291-292

Children of Divorce Protection Act, 65

Children's Defense Fund, 196, 228

Chinnock, William, 89

Chow, Esther Ngan-ling, 231

Christensen, Bryce, 15, 43, 103, 112, 124

Christian Science Monitor, 113, 161

Church of England, 220

Cincinnati Enquirer, 146

civilization, 12, 14-15, 259-266, 277, 279, 281

Clinton, Bill, 12-13, 15, 113, 121, 160, 164, 228, 267

Clinton, Hillary, 228-229

Close Wealth Management, 239

CNN, 157, 181

Coats, Dan, 251

Cohen, Richard, 228

Coles, Robert, 53

Index

Index

Index

Index

Index

Index